Nelson's English Series
General Editor—ERNEST BERNBAUM

ANTHOLOGY OF ROMANTICISM AND GUIDE THROUGH THE ROMANTIC MOVEMENT

VOLUME TWO

ANTHOLOGY OF ROMANTICISM AND GUIDE THROUGH THE ROMANTIC MOVEMENT

IN FIVE VOLUMES

By

ERNEST BERNBAUM
Professor of English
University of Illinois

ANTHOLOGY OF ROMANTICISM

VOLUME TWO

SELECTIONS FROM THE PRE-ROMANTIC MOVEMENT

Selected and Edited by

ERNEST BERNBAUM

Professor of English
University of Illinois

THOMAS NELSON AND SONS

NEW YORK

1931

COPYRIGHT, 1929,
THOMAS NELSON AND SONS
Published, October, 1929
Second Printing, June, 1931

PRINTED IN THE UNITED STATES OF AMERICA

CONTENTS

LORD SHAFTESBURY
The Moral Sense............................ 13
The Harmony of the Moral World and the Na-
tural..................................... 15

COLLEY CIBBER
Loveless Reforms............................ 20
Lady Easy's Forbearance.................... 22

RICHARD STEELE
The Poets and Virtue....................... 23
The Principle of Domestic Tragedy........... 24
In Defense of Sentimental Comedy........... 25
Jenny Distaff Reforms a Rake............... 26
The Calamities of the Virtuous.............. 27

JOHN HUGHES
Virtue in Distress.......................... 31
FROM Remarks on the Fairie Queen........... 35

THE ARABIAN NIGHTS....................... 36

LADY WINCHILSEA
A Nocturnal Reverie........................ 42

SAMUEL CROXALL
FROM The Vision............................ 44

GEORGE HICKES
Translation of the Incantation of Hervor...... 44

LADY ELIZABETH WARDLAW
FROM Hardyknute........................... 45

WILLIAM HAMILTON
The Braes of Yarrow........................ 48

5

ALLAN RAMSAY
Preface to the Evergreen.................... 52
Sweet William's Ghost...................... 55

DAVID MALLET
William and Margaret....................... 57

JAMES THOMSON
FROM The Seasons.......................... 59
FROM The Castle of Indolence............... 74

JOHN DYER
Grongar Hill............................... 79

GEORGE BERKELEY
Prospect of Planting Arts and Learning in
America.................................. 84

GEORGE LILLO
The Theory of Domestic Tragedy............ 85
The Good Character of George Barnwell....... 85

SOAME JENYNS
FROM An Essay on Virtue.................... 86

HENRY BROOKE (earlier period)
FROM Universal Beauty...................... 88
Prologue to 'Gustavus Vasa'................. 91

WILLIAM SHENSTONE
FROM The Schoolmistress.................... 92

EDWARD YOUNG
FROM The Complaint, or Night Thoughts...... 94
FROM Conjectures on Original Composition..... 97

ROBERT BLAIR
FROM The Grave............................ 100

WILLIAM WHITEHEAD
FROM On Ridicule.......................... 103
The Enthusiast............................. 105

MARK AKENSIDE
FROM The Pleasures of Imagination........... 108

CONTENTS

JOSEPH WARTON
    FROM The Enthusiast...................... III
    FROM An Essay on the Genius and Writings of
        Pope.................................. 115

WILLIAM COLLINS
    A Song from Shakspere's Cymbeline.......... 121
    Ode Written in the Beginning of 1746......... 122
    Ode to Evening............................. 123
    Ode on the Poetical Character............... 125
    The Passions............................... 127
    Ode on the Popular Superstitions of the High-
        lands of Scotland........................ 131

JOHN GILBERT COOPER
    FROM The Power of Harmony............... 139

THOMAS WARTON
    FROM The Pleasures of Melancholy............ 141
    FROM Observations on the Fairy Queen........ 143
    FROM The Grave of King Arthur.............. 148
    Sonnet on Dugdale's 'Monasticon'............ 149
    Sonnet Written at Stonehenge................ 150
    Sonnet to the River Lodon................... 150

THOMAS GRAY (earlier period)
    Hymn to Adversity.......................... 151
    Elegy Written in a Country Churchyard....... 152
    The Progress of Poesy....................... 157
    The Bard 162

SAMUEL RICHARDSON
    The Power of Innocence..................... 167
    The Death of Clarissa Harlowe............... 170
    The Death of Lovelace...................... 174

DAVID HARTLEY
    The Laws of Association.................... 175

RICHARD JAGO
    FROM The Goldfinches...................... 178

JOHN DALTON
    FROM A Descriptive Poem.................. 179

CONTENTS

JANE ELLIOT
    The Flowers of the Forest.................... 181

THOMAS AMORY
    FROM The Life and Opinions of John Buncle ... 182

LAURENCE STERNE
    The Lesson of Universal Good-Will........... 184
    The Death of Le Fever....................... 186
    Nannette.................................. 188
    Maria.................................... 189
    Dear Sensibility!.......................... 190

JAMES MACPHERSON
    FROM Ossian............................... 191

RICHARD HURD
    FROM Letters on Chivalry and Romance....... 196

THOMAS LELAND
    FROM Longsword, an Historical Romance...... 203

CHRISTOPHER SMART
    FROM A Song to David...................... 205

EVAN EVANS
    A Panegyric Upon Owain Gwynedd........... 207

THOMAS GRAY (later period)
    Letters Concerning Ossian................... 208
    The Descent of Odin........................ 213
    The Triumphs of Owen...................... 216
    Caràdoc.................................. 217
    Conan.................................... 218
    The Death of Hoël......................... 218
    The Fatal Sisters.......................... 219

HORACE WALPOLE
    FROM The Castle of Otranto................. 221

THOMAS PERCY
    The Ancient Ballad of Chevy-Chase.......... 227
    Sir Patrick Spence......................... 237
    Robin Hood and Guy of Gisborne........... 239

CONTENTS

OLIVER GOLDSMITH
The Vicar of Wakefield Describes His Family.. 247
The Deserted Village......................... 249

HENRY BROOKE (later period)
FROM The Fool of Quality.................. 262
FROM Conrade, a Fragment................. 267

HENRY MACKENZIE
FROM The Man of Feeling.................. 268
FROM Julia de Roubigné.................... 271
On Robert Burns........................... 272

JEAN ADAMS
There's Nae Luck About the House........... 273

LADY ANNE LINDSAY
Auld Robin Gray........................... 275

JAMES BEATTIE
FROM The Minstrel......................... 277

ROBERT FERGUSON
FROM Leith Races.......................... 280

JOHN LANGHORNE
FROM The Country Justice.................. 282

THOMAS DAY
FROM The Desolation of America............. 283

THOMAS CHATTERTON
The Boddynge Flourettes Bloshes............. 286
An Excelente Balade of Charitie............. 288

MAURICE MORGANN
On Shakspere.............................. 292

JOHN MAYNE
Logan Braes............................... 297

THOMAS JAMES MATHIAS
Dialogue at the Tomb of Argantyr........... 298
The Twilight of the Gods.................... 299
An Incantation............................. 299

The Renovation of the World............... 300
Tudor...................................... 301

HUGH DOWNMAN
Death Song of Ragnar Lodbrach.............. 302

JAMES JOHNSTONE
Lodbrokar-Quitha........................... 303

WILLIAM COWPER
To a Young Lady............................ 304
√FROM The Task............................. 304
On the Receipt of My Mother's Picture....... 312
To Mary.................................... 316
The Castaway............................... 318

HUGH BLAIR
On Pastoral Poetry......................... 320

EDWARD JERNINGHAM
The Weaving of the Raven Banner........... 321
A New Poetic World........................ 321

ROBERT BURNS
Mary Morison.............................. 322
The Holy Fair............................. 323
Epistle to J. Lapraik...................... 329
The Cotter's Saturday Night................ 330
To a Mouse................................ 337
To a Mountain Daisy....................... 338
Epistle to a Young Friend.................. 340
A Bard's Epitaph.......................... 343
Address to the Unco Guid.................. 344
John Anderson, My Jo...................... 346
The Lovely Lass of Inverness............... 347
A Red, Red Rose........................... 347
Auld Lang Syne............................ 348
Sweet Afton............................... 349
To Mary in Heaven......................... 350

WILLIAM BECKFORD
FROM The History of the Caliph Vathek....... 351

ANONYMOUS: REVIEW OF THE POETIC EDDA.... 358

WILLIAM LISLE BOWLES
  Evening...................................... 361
  Dover Cliffs................................. 362

GILBERT WHITE
  The Tortoise................................. 362

ERASMUS DARWIN
  FROM The Botanic Garden...................... 364

JOSEPH STERLING
  Scalder: An Ode.............................. 366
  FROM The Twilight of the Gods............... 367

RICHARD HOLE
  FROM Arthur, or the Northern Enchantment... 367
  FROM The Tomb of Gunnar.................. 369
  Fragment.................................... 369

FRANK SAYERS
  Frea's Plea to Hela......................... 370
  The Dying Rhapsody of Oswald.............. 371

WILLIAM GILPIN
  Picturesque Beauty.......................... 371

JAMES BRUCE
  FROM Travels to Discover the Source of the Nile 373

WILLIAM BARTRAM
  Incidents and Scenes in Florida.............. 378

MARY WOLLSTONECRAFT
  FROM The Rights of Woman................. 385

WILLIAM GODWIN
  FROM Political Justice....................... 388

RICHARD POLWHELE
  Regner Lodbrog.............................. 396
  FROM Gram and Gro........................ 397
  FROM Hother................................ 398
  FROM The Incantation of Herva 399

ANN RADCLIFFE
FROM The Mysteries of Udolpho.............. 400

MATTHEW GREGORY LEWIS
FROM The Monk........................... 405

WILLIAM TAYLOR
Lenora (from Bürger)...................... 409
FROM Wortigerne, a Playe.................. 418

AMOS SIMON COTTLE
FROM The Descent of Odin.................. 420

JOSEPH COTTLE
FROM Alfred.............................. 422

JAMES LAWRENCE
FROM The Empire of the Nairs.............. 423

NOTES AND COMMENTS...................... 427

INDEX TO AUTHORS AND TITLES 465

ANTHONY ASHLEY COOPER
EARL OF SHAFTESBURY

[THE MORAL SENSE]

(FROM AN INQUIRY CONCERNING VIRTUE OR MERIT)

THE mind, which is spectator or auditor of other minds, cannot be without its eye and ear, so as to discern proportion, distinguish sound, and scan each sentiment or thought which comes before it. It can let nothing escape its censure. It feels the soft and 5 harsh, the agreeable and disagreeable, in the affections; and finds a foul and fair, a harmonious and a dissonant, as really and truly here, as in any musical numbers or in the outward forms or representations of sensible things. Nor can it withhold its admira- 10 tion and ecstasy, its aversion and scorn, any more in what relates to one than to the other of these subjects. So that to deny the common and natural sense of a sublime and beautiful in things will appear affectation merely, to anyone who considers duly of this 15 affair.

Now as in the sensible kind of objects the species or images of bodies, colors, and sounds are perpetually moving before our eyes, and acting on our senses, even when we sleep; so in the moral and 20 intellectual kind, the forms and images of things are no less active and incumbent on the mind, at all seasons, and even when the real objects themselves are absent.

13

In these vagrant characters or pictures of manners 25
which the mind of necessity figures to itself, and
carries still about it, the heart cannot possibly remain
neutral, but constantly takes part one way or other.
However false or corrupt it be within itself, it finds
the difference, as to beauty and comeliness, between 30
one heart and another, one turn of affection, one
behavior, one sentiment, and another; and accordingly, in all disinterested cases, must approve in some
measure of what is natural and honest, and disap-
prove what is dishonest and corrupt. . . . 35

The corruption of moral sense, . . . the wrong
sense or false imagination of right and wrong, . . .
can proceed only from the force of custom and education in opposition to Nature, as may be noted in
those countries where, according to custom or politic 40
institution, certain actions naturally foul and odious
are repeatedly viewed with applause and honor ascribed to them. For thus 'tis possible that a man,
forcing himself, may eat the flesh of his enemies,
not only against his stomach but against his nature, 45
and think it nevertheless both right and honorable,
as supposing it to be of considerable service to his
community and capable of advancing the name and
spreading the terror of his nation. . . .

That it is possible for a creature capable of using 50
reflection to have a liking or dislike of moral actions,
and consequently a sense of right and wrong, before
such time as he may have any settled notion of
a God, is what will hardly be questioned, it being a
thing not expected, or any way possible, that a crea- 55
ture such as man, arising from his childhood slowly
and gradually to several degrees of reason and reflection, should at the very first be taken up with
those speculations, or more refined sort of reflections, about the subject of God's existence. 60

Let us suppose that a creature who, wanting

reason and being unable to reflect, has notwithstanding many good qualities and affections,—as love to his kind, courage, gratitude, or pity. 'Tis certain that if you give to this creature a reflecting faculty 65 it will at the same instant approve of gratitude, kindness, and pity, be taken with any show or representation of the social passion, and think nothing more amiable than this or more odious than the contrary. And this is to be capable of virtue, and to have 70 a sense of right and wrong.

1699(?)   1709

[THE HARMONY OF THE MORAL WORLD, AND THE NATURAL]

(FROM THE MORALISTS: A RHAPSODY)

THE balance of Europe, of trade, of power, is strictly sought after; while few have heard of the balance of their passions, or thought of holding these scales even. Few are acquainted with this province, or knowing in these affairs. But were we more so, 5 as this inquiry would make us, we should then see beauty and decorum here as well as elsewhere in Nature, and the order of the moral world would then equal that of the natural. By this the beauty of virtue would appear, and hence, as has been shown, 10 the supreme and sovereign beauty, the original of all which is good or amiable. . . .

Ye fields and woods, my refuge from the toilsome world of business, receive me in your quiet sanctuaries, and favor my retreat and thoughtful soli- 15 tude.—Ye verdant plains, how gladly I salute ye!— Hail all ye blissful mansions! known seats! delightful prospects! majestic beauties of this earth, and all ye rural powers and graces!—Blessed be ye chaste abodes of happiest mortals, who here in peaceful 20 innocence enjoy a life unenvied, though divine; whilst with its blessed tranquillity it affords a happy leisure and retreat for man, who, made for contemplation, and to search his own and other natures, may here best meditate the cause of things and, placed 25 amidst the various scenes of nature, may nearer view her works.

O glorious Nature! supremely fair, and sovereignly good! All-loving and all-lovely, all-divine! Whose looks are so becoming, and of such infinite 30 grace; whose study brings such wisdom, and whose contemplation such delight; whose every single work affords an ampler scene, and is a nobler spectacle, than all which ever Art presented!—O mighty Nature! wise substitute of Providence! impowered 35 creatress! or thou impowering deity, supreme creator! Thee I invoke, and thee alone adore. To thee this solitude, this place, these rural meditations are sacred; whilst thus inspired with harmony of thought, though unconfined by words, and in loose 40 numbers, I sing of Nature's order in created beings, and celebrate the beauties which resolve in thee, the source and principle of all beauty and perfection. . . .

"The appearances of ill, you say, are not neces- 45 sarily that ill they represent to you?"

"I own it."

"Therefore what they represent may possibly be good?"

"It may." 50

"And therefore there may possibly be no real ill in things, but all may be perfectly concurrent to one interest—the interest of that universal One?"

"It may be so."

"Why, then, if it *may* be so (be not surprised), 55 it follows that it *must* be so, on the account of that

great unit and simple self-principle which you have
granted in the 'Whole.' For whatever is possible in
the whole, the nature or mind of the whole will put
in execution for the whole's good; and if it be pos-   60
sible to exclude ill, it will exclude it. Therefore,
since, notwithstanding the appearances, 'tis possible
that ill may actually be excluded, count upon it that
actually it is excluded. . . ."

Our element of earth . . . yonder we see culti-   65
vated with such care by the early swains now work-
ing in the plain below. Unhappy restless men, who
first disdained these peaceful labors, gentle rural
tasks, performed with such delight! What pride
or what ambition bred this scorn? Hence all those   70
fatal evils of your race! Enormous luxury, despis-
ing homely fare, ranges through seas and lands,
rifles the globe; and men ingenious to their misery
work out for themselves the means of heavier labor,
anxious cares, and sorrow. Not satisfied to turn   75
and manure for their use the wholesome and beneficial mould of this their earth, they dig yet deeper,
and seeking out imaginary wealth, they search its
very entrails. . . .

The wildness pleases. We seem to live alone with   80
Nature. We view her in her inmost recesses, and
contemplate her with more delight in these original
wilds than in the artificial labyrinths and feigned
wildernesses of the palace. The objects of the place,
the scaly serpents, the savage beasts, and poisonous   85
insects, how terrible soever, or how contrary to
human nature, are beauteous in themselves, and fit
to raise our thoughts in admiration of that divine
wisdom, so far superior to our short views. Unable
to declare the use or service of all things in this   90
universe, we are yet assured of the perfection of all,

and of the justice of that economy to which all
things are subservient, and in respect of which things
seemingly deformed are amiable: disorder becomes
regular, corruption wholesome, and poisons . . . 95
prove healing and beneficial.

But behold! through a vast tract of sky before
us the mighty Atlas rears his lofty head, covered
with snow above the clouds. Beneath the mountain's foot the rocky country rises into hills, a proper 100
basis of the ponderous mass above, where huge em-
bodied rocks lie piled on one another and seem to
prop the high arch of heaven.—See with what
trembling steps poor mankind tread the narrow brink
of the deep precipices! From whence with giddy 105
horror they look down, mistrusting even the ground
which bears them, whilst they hear the hollow sound
of torrents underneath and see the ruin of the impending rock, with falling trees which hang with
their roots upwards and seem to draw more ruin 110
after them. Here thoughtless men, seized with the
newness of such objects, become thoughtful and
willingly contemplate the incessant changes of this
earth's surface. They see, as in one instant, the
revolutions of past ages, the fleeting forms of things, 115
and the decay even of this our globe, whose youth
and first formation they consider, whilst the apparent
spoil and irreparable breaches of the wasted mountain show them the world itself only as a noble ruin,
and make them think of its approaching period.—   120

But here, midway the mountain, a spacious border
of thick wood harbors our wearied travelers, who
now are come among the ever-green and lofty pines,
the firs, and noble cedars, whose towering heads
seem endless in the sky, the rest of trees appearing 125
only as shrubs beside them. And here a different
horror seizes our sheltered travelers, when they
see the day diminished by the deep shapes of the

vast wood which, closing thick above, spreads darkness and eternal night below. The faint and gloomy 130
light looks horrid as the shade itself; and the profound stillness of these places imposes silence upon
men, struck with the hoarse echoings of every sound
within the spacious caverns of the wood. Here space
astonishes. Silence itself seems pregnant, whilst an 135
unknown force works on the mind and dubious objects move the wakeful sense. Mysterious voices
are either heard or fancied; and various forms of
deity seem to present themselves and appear more
manifest in these sacred sylvan scenes, such as of 140
old gave rise to temples and favored the religion of
the ancient world. Even we ourselves, who in plain
characters may read divinity from so many bright
parts of earth, choose rather these obscurer places to
spell out that mysterious Being, which to our weak 145
eyes appears at best under a veil of cloud. . . .

"Your Genius, the Genius of the place, and the
Great Genius, have at last prevailed. I shall no
longer resist the passion growing in me for things
of a natural kind; where neither art, nor the conceit 150
or caprice of man, has spoiled their genuine order
by breaking in upon that primitive state. Even the
rude rocks, the mossy caverns, the irregular un-
wrought grottoes and broken falls of waters, with
all the horrid graces of the wilderness itself, as rep- 155
resenting Nature more, will be the more engaging
and appear with a magnificence beyond the formal
mockery of princely gardens.—But tell me, I entreat
you, how comes it that, excepting a few philosophers
of your sort, the only people who are enamored in 160
this way, and seek the woods, the rivers, or sea-
shores, are your poor vulgar lovers?"

"Say not this," replied he, "of lovers only. For

is it not the same with poets, and all those other students in Nature, and the arts which copy after her? In short, is not this the real case of all who are lovers either of the Muses or the Graces?"

"However," said I, "all those who are deep in this romantic way are looked upon, you know, as a people either plainly out of their wits or overrun with melancholy and enthusiasm. We always endeavor to recall them from these solitary places. And I must own that often when I have found my fancy run this way I have checked myself, not knowing what it was possessed me when I was passionately struck with objects of this kind."

"No wonder," replied he, "if we are at a loss when we pursue the shadow for the substance. . . ."

1711

COLLEY CIBBER

[LOVELESS REFORMS]

(Love's Last Shift; V, ii)

[Loveless deserted his wife Amanda eight years ago. On meeting her again, he does not recognize her. He courts her as a mistress, and she reluctantly resorts to "love's last shift" to win him back. The next morning she discloses herself to him as follows.]

Amanda: Arm your mind with gentle pity first, or I am lost forever.

Loveless: I am all pity, all faith, expectation, and confused amazement; be kind, be quick, and ease my wonder.

Amanda: Look on me well; revive your dead remembrance; and oh, for pity's sake (*kneels*) hate

me not for loving long and faithfully! Forgive this
innocent attempt of a despairing passion, and I shall
die in quiet.   10

Loveless (*amazed*): Ha! speak on!

Amanda: It will not be—the word's too weighty
for my faltering tongue, and my soul sinks beneath
the fatal burden. Oh! (*falls to the ground*).

Loveless: Ha! she faints! Look up, fair creature;   15
behold a heart that bleeds for your distress, and
fain would share the weight of your oppressive
sorrows. Oh, thou hast raised a thought within
me that shocks my soul.

Amanda (*rising*): 'Tis done—the conflict's past   20
and Heaven bids me speak undaunted. Know then,
even all the boasted raptures of your last night's
love you found in your Amanda's arms!—I am your
wife . . . forever blessed or miserable as your next
breath shall sentence me. . . .   25

Loveless: Oh! I am confounded with my guilt,
and tremble to behold thee. . . . I have wronged
you . . . basely wronged you. . . .

Amanda: One kind, one pitying look, cancels
those wrongs forever. . . .   30

Loveless: Oh! seal my pardon with thy trembling
lips while with this tender grasp of fond reviving
love I seize my bliss and stifle all thy wrongs
forever (*embraces her*).

Amanda: No more; I'll wash away their mem-   35
ory in tears of flowing joy.

Loveless: Oh, thou hast roused me from my deepest lethargy of vice. Thus let me kneel and pay
my thanks to her whose conquering virtue has at
last subdued me. Here will I fix, thus prostrate,   40
sigh my shame, and wash my crimes in never ceasing tears of penitence.

Acted, 1696

[LADY EASY'S FORBEARANCE]

(THE CARELESS HUSBAND; V, iv)

[Lady Easy wins back her unfaithful husband by patient love, as shown in the following scene. She has caught Sir Charles and her maid asleep together, "Sir Charles without his periwig." She speaks:]

PROTECT me, Virtue, Patience, Reason!
Teach me to bear this killing sight, or let
Me think my dreaming senses are deceived!
For sure a sight like this might raise the arm
Of duty, even to the breast of love! At least   5
I'll throw this vizor of my patience off,
Now wake him in his guilt,
And barefaced front him with my wrongs;
I'll talk to him till he blushes, nay till he—
Frowns on me perhaps—and then   10
I'm lost again.—The ease of a few tears
Is all that's left to me;
And duty too forbids me to insult
When I have vowed obedience. Perhaps
The fault's in me, and nature has not formed   15
Me with the thousand little requisites
That warm the heart to love.
Somewhere there is a fault,
But Heaven best knows what both of us deserve.—
    Ha! bare-headed, and in so sound a sleep!   20
Who knows while thus exposed to the unwholesome air
But Heaven offended may overtake his crime,
And in some languishing distemper leave him
A severe example of its violated laws,—
Forbid it, mercy, and forbid it, love: 25
This may prevent it.
    (*Takes a steenkirk off her neck and lays it gently on his head.*)

Acted, 1704

RICHARD STEELE

[THE POETS AND VIRTUE]

I HAVE always been of the opinion . . . that virtue sinks deepest into the heart of man when it comes
recommended by the powerful charms of poetry.
The most active principle in our mind is the imagination; to it a good poet makes his court perpet-   5
ually and by this faculty takes care to gain it first.
Our passions and inclinations come over next, and
our reason surrenders itself with pleasure in the
end.   Thus the whole soul is insensibly betrayed
into morality by bribing the fancy with beautiful   10
and agreeable images of those very things, that in
the books of the philosophers appear austere and
have at the best but a kind of forbidden aspect.   In
a word, the poets do, as it were, strew the rough
paths of virtue so full of flowers that we are not   15
sensible of the uneasiness of them and imagine
ourselves in the midst of pleasures and the most
bewitching allurements at the time we are making
a progress in the severest duties of life.

All then agree that licentious poems do, of all   20
writings, soonest corrupt the heart; and why should
we not be as universally persuaded that the grave
and serious performances of such as write in the
most engaging manner, by a kind of divine impulse, must be the most effectual persuasives to   25
goodness?   If therefore I were blessed with a son
in order to the forming of his manners (which is
making him truly my son) I should be continually
putting into his hand some fine poet.   The graceful

sentences and the manly sentiments so frequently 3
to be met with in every great and sublime writer, are,
in my judgment, the most ornamental and valuable
furniture that can be for a young gentleman's head;
methinks they show like so much rich embroidery
upon the brain. Let me add to this that humanity 35
and tenderness (without which there can be no true
greatness in the mind) are inspired by the Muses
in such pathetical language, that all we find in prose
authors towards the raising and improving of these
passions, is in comparison but cold, or lukewarm 40
at the best.

Nov. 24, 1709

[THE PRINCIPLE OF DOMESTIC TRAGEDY]

WHEN unhappy catastrophes make up part of
the history of princes, and persons who act in high
spheres, or are represented in the moving language
and well-wrought scenes of tragedians, they do not
fail of striking us with terror; but then they affect 5
us only in a transient manner, and pass through our
imaginations as incidents in which our fortunes are
too humble to be concerned, or which writers form
for the ostentation of their own force; or, at most,
as things fit rather to exercise the powers of our 10
minds than to create new habits in them. Instead
of such high passages, I was thinking it would be
of great use (if anybody could hit it) to lay before
the world such adventures as befall persons not
exalted above the common level. This, methought, 15
would better prevail upon the ordinary race of men,
who are so prepossessed with outward appearances
that they mistake fortune for nature, and believe
nothing can relate to them that does not happen to
such as live and look like themselves. 20

May 16, 1710

[IN DEFENSE OF THE SENTIMENTAL COMEDY, THE CONSCIOUS LOVERS]

THE chief design of this was to be an innocent performance, and the audience have abundantly shown how ready they are to support what is visibly intended that way. Nor do I make any difficulty to acknowledge that the whole was writ for the sake of the scene of the Fourth Act, wherein Mr. Bevil evades the quarrel with his friend, and hope it may have some effect upon the Goths and Vandals that frequent the theatres, or a more polite audience may supply their absence.

But this incident and the case of the father and daughter are esteemed by some people no subjects of comedy; but I cannot be of their mind, for anything that has its foundation in happiness and success must be allowed to be the object of comedy; and sure it must be an improvement of it to introduce a joy too exquisite for laughter, that can have no spring but in delight, which is the case of this young lady. I must, therefore, contend that the tears which were shed on that occasion flowed from reason and good sense, and that men ought not to be laughed at for weeping till we are come to a more clear notion of what is to be imputed to the hardness of the head and the softness of the heart; and I think it was very politely said of Mr. Wilks, to one who told him there was a General weeping for Indiana, "I'll warrant he'll fight ne'er the worse for that." To be apt to give way to the impressions of humanity, is the excellence of a right disposition and the natural working of a well-turned spirit.

Dec. 1, 1722

[JENNY DISTAFF REFORMS A RAKE]

THERE was at the further end of her garden a
kind of wilderness, in the middle of which ran a soft
rivulet by an arbor of jessamine. In this place I
usually passed my retired hours and read some romantic or poetical tale till the close of the evening. 5
It was near that time in the heat of summer, when
gentle winds, soft murmurs of water, and notes of
nightingales had given my mind an indolence which
added to that repose of soul, twilight and the end of
a warm day naturally throw upon the spirits. It 10
was at such an hour and in such a state of tranquillity I sat, when, to my unexpressible amazement
I saw my lord walking towards me, whom I knew
not till that moment to have been in the country.
I could observe in his approach the perplexity which 15
attends a man big with design; and I had, while he
was coming forward, time to reflect that I was betrayed, the sense of which gave me a resentment suitable to such a baseness. But, when he entered into
the bower where I was, my heart flew towards him, 20
and I confess, a certain joy came into my mind with
an hope that he might then make a declaration of
honor and passion. This threw my eye upon him
with such tenderness as gave him power with a
broken accent to begin.   25

"Madam—you will wonder for it is certain you
must have observed—though I fear you will mis-
interpret the motives—but by Heaven and all that is
sacred! if you could ——"

Here he made a full stand and I recovered power 30
to say, "The consternation I am in you will not,
I hope, believe—an helpless innocent maid—besides
that, the place."

He saw me in as great confusion as himself, which

attributing to the same causes, he had the audacious- 35
ness to throw himself at my feet, talk of the stillness
of the evening, and then ran into deifications of my
person, pure flames, constant love, eternal raptures
and a thousand other phrases drawn from the images
we have of Heaven, which ill men use for the serv- 40
ice of Hell were run over with uncommon vehe-
mence. After which he seized me in his arms: his
design was too evident.

In my utmost distress I fell upon my knees—"My
lord, pity me! On my knees—on my knees in the 45
cause of virtue as you were lately in that of wickedness. Can you think of destroying the labor of a
whole life, the purpose of a long education for the
base service of a sudden appetite? To throw one
that loves you, that dotes on you out of the company 50
and the road of all that is virtuous and praise-
worthy? Have I taken in all the instructions of
piety, religion and reason for no other end but to
be the sacrifice of lust, and abandoned to scorn?
Assume yourself, my lord, and do not attempt to 55
vitiate a temple sacred to innocence, honor and
religion. If I have injured you stab this bosom and
let me die, but not be ruined by the hand I love."

The ardency of my passion made me incapable of
uttering more; and I saw my lover astonished and 60
reformed by my behavior.

June 25, 1709

[THE CALAMITIES OF THE VIRTUOUS]

I HAVE been looking at the fire and in a pensive
manner reflecting upon the great misfortunes and
calamities incident to human life, among which
there are none that touch so sensibly as those which
befall persons who eminently love and meet with 5
fatal interruptions of their happiness when they least

expect it. The piety of children to parents, and the
affection of parents to their children, are the effects
of instinct; but the affection between lovers and
friends is founded on reason and choice, which has   10
always made me think the sorrows of the latter
much more to be pitied than those of the former.
The contemplation of distresses of this sort softens
the mind of man and makes the heart better. It
extinguishes the seeds of envy and ill-will towards   15
mankind, corrects the pride of prosperity and beats
down all that fierceness and insolence which are
apt to get into the minds of the daring and fortunate.
For this reason the wise Athenians, in their theatrical
performances laid before the eyes of the people the   20
greatest afflictions which could befall human life, and
insensibly polished their tempers by such representations. Among the modern, indeed, there has arisen
a chimerical method of disposing the fortune of the
persons represented, according to what they call   25
poetical justice, and letting none be unhappy but
those who deserve it. In such cases an intelligent
spectator, if he is concerned, knows he ought not
to be so, and can learn nothing from such a tenderness but that he is a weak creature whose passions   30
cannot follow the dictates of his understanding. It
is very natural when one is got into such a way of
thinking to recollect those examples of sorrow which
have made the strongest impression upon our imaginations. An instance or two of such you will give   35
me leave to communicate.

A young gentleman and lady of ancient and honorable houses in Cornwall had from their childhood
entertained for each other a generous and noble
passion which had been long opposed by their   40
friends, by reason of the inequality of their fortunes;
but their constancy to each other, and obedience
to those on whom they depended wrought so much

upon their relations, that these celebrated lovers were at length joined in marriage. Soon after their 45 nuptials, the bridegroom was obliged to go into a foreign country, to take care of a considerable fortune which was left him by a relation and came very opportunely to improve their moderate circumstances. They received the congratulations of all 50 the country on this occasion, and I remember it was a common sentence in every one's mouth, "You see how faithful love is rewarded."

He took this agreeable voyage and sent home every post fresh accounts of his success in his af- 55 fairs abroad, but at last (though he designed to return with the next ship) he lamented in his letters that business would detain him some time longer from home, because he would give himself the pleasure of an unexpected arrival. 60

The young lady, after the heat of the day, walked every evening on the seashore near which she lived, with a familiar friend, her husband's kinswoman, and diverted herself with what objects they met there, or upon discourses of the future methods of 65 life in the happy change of their circumstances. They stood one evening on the shore together in a perfect tranquillity, observing the setting of the sun, the calm face of the deep and the silent heaving of the waves which gently rolled towards them and 70 broke at their feet; when at a distance her kinswoman saw something afloat on the waters, which she fancied was a chest, and with a smile told her she saw it first and if it came ashore full of jewels she had a right to it. 75

They both fixed their eyes upon it and entertained themselves with the subject of the wreck, the cousin still asserting her right but promising if it was a prize, to give her a very rich coral for the child of which she was then big, provided she 80 might be god-mother. Their mirth soon abated when they observed upon the nearer approach that it was a human body. The young lady who had a heart naturally filled with pity and compassion made many melancholy reflections on the occasion. 85

"Who knows," said she, "but this man may be the only hope and heir of a wealthy house, the darling of indulgent parents who are now in impertinent mirth and pleasing themselves with the thoughts of offering him a bride they have got ready for him? 90 Or may he not be the master of a family that wholly depended upon his life? There may, for aught we know, be half a dozen fatherless children and a tender wife now exposed to poverty by his death. What pleasure might he have promised himself in 95 the different welcome he was to have from her and them? But let us go away; it is a dreadful sight! The best office we can do, is to take care that the poor man, whoever he is, may be decently buried." 100

She turned away when a wave threw the carcass on the shore. The kinswoman immediately shrieked out, "Oh, my cousin!" and fell upon the ground. The unhappy wife went to help her friend when she saw her own husband at her feet and dropped in a 105 swoon upon the body. An old woman who had been the gentleman's nurse came out about this time to call the ladies in to supper, and found her child (as she always called him) dead on the shore, her mistress and kinswoman both lying dead by him. 110 Her loud lamentations and calling her young master to life soon awakened the friend from her trance; but the wife was gone forever.

When the family and neighborhood got together round the bodies no one asked any question, but the 115 objects before them told the story.

Oct. 15, 1709

JOHN HUGHES

[VIRTUE IN DISTRESS]

I HAVE more than once had occasion to mention a noble saying of Seneca, the philosopher, that a virtuous person struggling with misfortunes and rising above them, is an object on which the Gods themselves may look down with delight. I shall 5 therefore set before my reader a scene of this kind of distress in private life for the speculation of this day.

An eminent citizen, who had lived in good fashion and credit, was by a train of accidents and by an 10 unavoidable perplexity in his affairs reduced to a low condition. There is a modesty usually attending faultless poverty, which made him rather choose to reduce his manner of living to his present circumstances, than solicit his friends in order to support 15 the show of an estate when the substance was gone. His wife, who was a woman of sense and virtue, behaved herself on this occasion with uncommon decency, and never appeared so amiable in his eyes as now. Instead of upbraiding him with the ample 20 fortune she had brought, or the many great offers she had refused for his sake, she redoubled all the instances of her affection, while her husband was continually pouring out his heart to her in complaints that he had ruined the best woman in the 25 world. He sometimes came home at a time when she did not expect him, and surprised her in tears, which she endeavored to conceal, and always put on an air of cheerfulness to receive him. To lessen their expense, their eldest daughter (whom I shall 30 call Amanda) was sent into the country, to the house

of an honest farmer who had married a servant of
the family. This young woman was apprehensive
of the ruin which was approaching, and had privately engaged a friend in the neighborhood to give   35
her an account of what passed from time to time
in her father's affairs. Amanda was in the bloom
of her youth and beauty, when the lord of the manor,
who often called in at the farmer's house as he
followed his country sports, fell passionately in love   40
with her. He was a man of great generosity but
from a loose education had contracted a hearty aversion to marriage. He therefore entertained a design
upon Amanda's virtue which at present he thought
fit to keep private. The innocent creature, who never   45
suspected his intentions, was pleased with his person,
and having observed his growing passion for her,
hoped by so advantageous a match she might quickly
be in a capacity of supporting her impoverished
relations. One day as he called to see her, he   50
found her in tears over a letter she had just received from her friend, which gave an account that
her father had lately been stripped of every thing
by an execution. The lover, who with some difficulty found out the cause of her grief, took this oc-   55
casion to make her a proposal. It is impossible to
express Amanda's confusion when she found his
pretensions were not honorable. She was now deserted of all her hopes and had no power to speak;
but rushing from him in the utmost disturbance,   60
locked herself up in her chamber. He immediately
dispatched a messenger to her father with the following letter:

"Sir,
I have heard of your misfortune, and have offered your   65
daughter, if she will live with me, to settle on her four
hundred pounds a year, and to lay down the sum for which
you are now distressed. I will be so ingenuous as to tell

you that I do not intend marriage: but if you are wise, you will use your authority with her not to be too nice, when she has an opportunity of saving you and your family and of making herself happy.

I am, Etc."

This letter came to the hands of Amanda's mother; she opened and read it with great surprise and concern. She did not think it proper to explain herself to the messenger but desiring him to call again the next morning, she wrote to her daughter as follows:

"Dearest Child,

Your father and I have just now received a letter from a gentleman who pretends love to you, with a proposal that insults our misfortunes and would throw us to a lower degree of misery than anything which is come upon us. How could this barbarous man think that the tenderest of parents would be tempted to supply their want by giving up the best of children to infamy and ruin? It is a mean and cruel artifice to make this proposal at a time when he thinks our necessities must compel us to anything; but we will not eat the bread of shame; and therefore we charge thee not to think of us but to avoid the snare which is laid for thy virtue. Beware of pitying us: it is not so bad as you have perhaps been told. All things will yet be well, and I shall write my child better news.

I have been interrupted. I know not how I was moved to say things would mend. As I was going on I was startled by a noise of one that knocked at the door, and hath brought us an unexpected supply of a debt which had long been owing. Oh, I will now tell thee all. It is some days I have lived almost without support having conveyed what little money I could raise to your poor father—thou wilt weep to think where he is, yet be assured he will be soon at liberty. That cruel letter would have broke his heart but I have concealed it from him. I have no companion at present besides little Fanny, who stands watching my looks as I write and is crying for her sister. She says she is sure you are not well, having discovered that my present trouble is about you. But do not think I would thus repeat my sorrows to grieve thee; no, it is to entreat thee not to make them insupportable by adding what would be worse than all. Let us bear cheerfully an affliction, which we have not brought on ourselves, and remember there is a power who can better deliver us out of it than by the loss of thy innocence. Heaven preserve my dear child.

Thy affectionate mother ——"   115

The messenger, notwithstanding he promised to deliver this letter to Amanda, carried it first to his master, who he imagined would be glad to have an opportunity of giving it into her hands himself. His master was impatient to know the success of 120 his proposal and therefore broke open the letter privately to see the contents. He was not a little moved at so true a picture of virtue in distress: but at the same time was infinitely surprised to find his offers rejected. However, he resolved not to sup- 125 press the letter, but carefully sealed it up again and carried it to Amanda. All his endeavors to see her were in vain till she was assured he brought a letter from her mother. He would not part with it, but upon condition that she should read it without leav- 130 ing the room. While she was perusing it he fixed his eyes on her face with the deepest attention: her concern gave a new softness to her beauty, and when she burst into tears he could no longer refrain from bearing a part in her sorrow, and telling her that 135 he too had read the letter, and was resolved to make reparation for having been the occasion of it. My reader will not be displeased to see the second epistle which he now wrote to Amanda's mother.

"Madam,   140
I am full of shame and will never forgive myself if I have not your pardon for what I lately wrote. It was far from my intention to add trouble to the afflicted; nor could anything but my being a stranger to you, have betrayed me into a fault for which, if I live, I shall endeavor to make you 145 amends as a son. You cannot be unhappy while Amanda is your daughter; nor shall be, if anything can prevent it which is in the power of,

Madam,
Your most obedient   150
Humble Servant ——"

This letter he sent by his steward and soon after went up to town himself to complete the generous act he had now resolved on. By his friendship and assistance Amanda's father was quickly in a condi- 155 tion of retrieving his perplexed affairs. To conclude, he married Amanda and enjoyed the double satis-faction of having restored a worthy family to their former prosperity, and of making himself happy by an alliance to their virtues.   16A

                                                    May 10, 1712

FROM REMARKS ON THE FAIRIE QUEEN

THAT which seems the most liable to exception in this work is the model of it, and the choice the author has made of so romantic a story. . . . The whole frame of it (*The Fairie Queen*) would appear monstrous, if it were to be examined by the rules 5 of epic poetry, as they have been drawn from the practice of Homer and Virgil; but as it is plain the author never designed it by those rules, I think it ought rather to be considered as a poem of a par-ticular kind, describing, in a series of allegorical 10 adventures or episodes, the most noted virtues and vices. To compare it, therefore, with the models of antiquity, would be like drawing a parallel be-tween the Roman and the Gothic architecture. . . . It ought to be considered, too, at the time when our 15 author wrote, the remains of the old Gothic chivalry were not quite abolished; it was not many years be-fore that the famous Earl of Surrey, remarkable for his wit and poetry in the reign of King Henry VIII, took a romantic journey to Florence, the place 20 of his mistress's birth, and published there a chal-lenge against all nations in defense of her beauty.

As to the stanza in which the Fairie Queen is written, though the author cannot be commended in

the choice of it, yet it is much more harmonious in ²⁵
its kind than the heroic verse of that age. . . . The
defect of it in long or narrative poems is apparent;
the same measure, closed always by a full stop, in the
same place, by which every stanza is made as it were
a distinct paragraph, grows tiresome by continual ³⁰
repetition, and frequently breaks the sense, when it
ought to be carried on without interruption. With
this exception the reader will, however, find it
harmonious, full of well-sounding epithets, and of
such elegant turns on the thought and words, that ³⁵
Dryden himself owned he learned these graces of
verse chiefly from our author, and does not scruple
to say that "in this particular, only Virgil surpassed
him among the Romans, and only Mr. Waller among
the English." ⁴⁰

1715

FROM THE ARABIAN NIGHTS

[THE MERCHANT AND THE GENIE]

THERE was formerly a merchant who had a great
estate in lands, goods, and money. He had abundance of deputies, factors, and slaves. He was
obliged from time to time to take journeys and talk
with his correspondents; and one day being under a ⁵
necessity of going a long journey about an affair
of importance, he took horse and put a portmanteau
behind him with some biscuit and dates, because he
had a great desert to pass over where he could have
no manner of provisions. He arrived without any ¹⁰
accident at the end of his journey, and having dispatched his affairs took horse again in order to return
home.

The fourth day of his journey he was so much
incommoded by the heat of the sun and the reflec- ¹⁵

tion of that heat from the earth that he turned out of the road to refresh himself under some trees that he saw in the country. There he found at the root of a great walnut tree a fountain of very clear running water, and alighting, tied his horse to a branch of a tree and sitting down by the fountain took some biscuit and dates out of his portmanteau, and as he ate his dates threw the shells about on both sides of him. When he had done eating, being a good Mussulman, he washed his hands, his face, and his feet and said his prayers.

He had not made an end, but was still on his knees, when he saw a genie appear, all white with age and of a monstrous bulk, who advancing towards him with a scimitar in his hand spoke to him in a terrible voice, thus: "Rise up, that I may kill thee with this scimitar as you have killed my son," and accompanied those words with a frightful cry. The merchant, being as much frightened at the hideous shape of the monster as at those threatening words, answered him trembling, "Alas! my good lord, of what crime can I be guilty towards you that you should take my life?" "I will," replies the genie, "kill thee as thou hast killed my son." "Oh heaven!" says the merchant, "how should I kill your son? I did not know him nor never saw him." "Did not you sit down when you came hither?" replies the genie, "did not you take dates out of your portmanteau and as you ate them, did not you throw the shells about on both sides?" "I did all that you say," answers the merchant. "I cannot deny it." "If it be so," replies the genie, "I tell thee that thou hast killed my son, and the way was thus. When you threw your nut shells about, my son was passing by, and you threw one of 'em into his eye, which killed him; therefore I must kill thee." "Ah! my lord, pardon me!" cried the merchant. "No pardon," an-

swers the genie, "no mercy; is it not just to kill him
that has killed another?" "I agree to it," says the
merchant, "but certainly I never killed your son; 55
and if I have it was unknown to me, and I did it
innocently; therefore I beg you to pardon me and to
suffer me to live." "No, no," says the genie, per-
sisting in his resolution. "I must kill thee since thou
hast killed my son"; and then taking the merchant by 60
the arm, threw him with his face upon the ground
and lifted up his scimitar to cut off his head.

The merchant, all in tears, protested he was innocent, bewailed his wife and children, and spoke to
the genie in the most moving expressions that could 65
be uttered. The genie with his scimitar still lifted
up had so much patience as to hear the wretch make
an end of his lamentations, but would not relent.
"All this whining," says the monster, "is to no purpose, though you should shed tears of blood that 70
shall not hinder me to kill thee as thou kill'dst my
son." "Why!" replied the merchant, "can nothing
prevail with you? Will you absolutely take away
the life of a poor innocent?" "Yes," replied the
genie, "I am resolved upon it." . . . 75

.   .   .   .

When the merchant saw that the genie was going
to cut off his head he cried out aloud, and said to
him, "For heaven's sake, hold out your hand! Allow
me one word, be so good as to grant me some respite, allow me but time to bid my wife and children 80
adieu, and to divide my estate among them by will
that they may not go to law with one another after
my death; and when I have done so, I will come
back to this same place and submit to whatever
you shall please to order concerning me." "But," 85
says the genie, "if I grant you the time you demand,
I doubt you'll never return." "If you will believe
my oath," answers the merchant, "I swear by all

that's sacred that I will come and meet you here
without fail." "What time do you demand then?" 90
replies the genie. "I ask a year," says the merchant, "I can not have less to order my affairs and
to prepare myself to die without regret. But I promise you that this day twelve months I will return
under these trees to put myself into your hands." 95
"Do you take heaven to be witness to this promise?"
says the genie. "I do," answers the merchant, "and
repeat it, and you may rely upon my oath." Upon
this the genie left him near the fountain and dis-
appeared.   100

The merchant, being recovered from his fright,
mounted his horse and set forward on his journey;
and as he was glad on the one hand that he had
escaped so great a danger, he was mortally sorry on
the other when he thought on his fatal oath. When 105
he came home, his wife and children received him
with all the demonstrations of a perfect joy. But he,
instead of making them answerable returns, fell a
weeping bitterly, from whence they readily conjec-
tured that something extraordinary had befallen him. 110
His wife asked the reason of his excessive grief and
tears. "We are all overjoyed," says she, "at your
return, but you frighten us to see you in this condition; pray tell us the cause of your sorrow." "Alas!"
replies the husband, "the cause of it is that I have 115
but a year to live," and then told what had passed
betwixt him and the genie, and that he had given
him his oath to return at the end of the year to
receive death from his hands.

When they heard this sad news, they all began 120
to lament heartily; his wife made a pitiful outcry,
beat her face and tore her hair. The children, being
all in tears, made the house resound with their
groans; and the father, not being able to overcome

nature, mixed his tears with theirs; so that, in a word, it was the most affecting spectacle that any man could behold.

Next morning the merchant applied himself to put his affairs in order, and first of all to pay his debts. He made presents to his friends, gave great alms to the poor, set his slaves of both sexes at liberty, divided his estate among his children, appointed guardians for such of them as were not come of age; and restoring to his wife all that was due to her by contract of marriage, he gave her over and above all that he could do by law.

At last the year expired, and go he must. He put his burial clothes in his portmantle; but never was there such grief seen as when he came to bid his wife and children adieu. They could not think of parting, but resolved to go along and to die with him; but finding that he must be forced to part with those dear objects he spoke to 'em thus, "My dear wife and children," says he, "I obey the order of heaven in quitting you, follow my example, submit courageously to this necessity and consider that it's the destiny of man to die." Having said those words, he went out of the hearing of the cries of his family, and taking his journey arrived at the place where he promised to meet the genie on the day appointed. He alighted, and setting himself down by the fountain waited the coming of the genie with all the sorrow imaginable. While he languished in this cruel expectation, a good old man leading a bitch appeared and drew near him. They saluted one another, after which the old man says to him, "Brother, may I ask you why you are come into this desert place, where there is nothing but evil spirits and by consequence you can not be safe? To look upon these fine trees indeed, one would think the place inhabited; but it is a true wilderness, where it is not safe to stay long."

The merchant satisfied his curiosity and told him the adventure which obliged him to be there. The old man listened to him with astonishment, and when he had done cried out, "This is the most surprising thing in the world, and you are bound by the most inviolable oath; however, I will be witness of your interview with the genie," and sitting down by the merchant, they talked together. . . .

. . . While the merchant and the old man that led the bitch were talking, they saw another old man coming to them, followed by two black dogs. After they had saluted one another, he asked them what they did in that place. The old man with the bitch told him the adventure of the merchant and genie with all that had past betwixt them, particularly the merchant's oath. He added that this was the day agreed on, and that he was resolved to stay and see the issue.

The second old man, thinking it also worth his curiosity, resolved to do the like; he likewise sat down by them, and they had scarce begun to talk together, but there came a third old man who, addressing himself to the two former, asked why the merchant that sat with them looked so melancholy. They told him the reason of it, which appeared so extraordinary to him that he resolved to be witness to the result, and for that end sat down with 'em.

In a little time they perceived in the field a thick vapor, like a cloud of dust raised by a whirlwind, advancing towards them, which vanished all of a sudden; and then the genie appeared, who without saluting them, came up to the merchant with his drawn scimitar, and taking him by the arm says, "Get thee up that I may kill thee as thou didst kill my son." The merchant and the three old men, being frightened, began to lament and to fill the air with their cries. . . .

. . . When the old man that led the bitch saw the 200 genie lay hold of the merchant and about to kill him without pity, he threw himself at the feet of the monster and, kissing them, says to him, "Prince of genii, I most humbly request you to suspend your anger and do me the favor to hear me; I will tell you 205 the history of my life and of the bitch you see, and if you think it more wonderful and surprising than the adventure of the merchant you are going to kill, I hope you will pardon the poor unfortunate man the third of his crime." The genie took some time 210 to consult upon it, but answered at last, "Well, then, I agree to it."

transl. 1706

LADY WINCHILSEA

A NOCTURNAL REVERIE

In such a night, when every louder wind
Is to its distant cavern safe confined,
And only gentle Zepyhr fans his wings,
And lonely Philomel, still waking, sings;
Or from some tree, famed for the owl's delight,   5
She hollowing clear, directs the wanderer right;
In such a night, when passing clouds give place,
Or thinly veil the heaven's mysterious face;
When in some river, overhung with green,
The waving moon and trembling leaves are seen;   10
When freshened grass now bears itself upright,
And makes cool banks to pleasing rest invite,
Whence springs the woodbine and the bramble-rose,
And where the sleepy cowslip sheltered grows;

Whilst now a paler hue the foxglove takes,   15
Yet chequers still with red the dusky brakes;
When scattered glow-worms, but in twilight fine,
Show trivial beauties watch their hour to shine,
Whilst Salisbury stands the test of every light
In perfect charms and perfect virtue bright;   20
When odors which declined repelling day
Through temperate air uninterrupted stray:
When darkened groves their softest shadows wear,
And falling waters we distinctly hear;
When through the gloom more venerable shows   25
Some ancient fabric, awful in repose,
While sunburnt hills their swarthy looks conceal
And swelling haycocks thicken up the vale;
When the loosed horse now, as his pasture leads,
Comes slowly grazing through th' adjoining meads,   30
Whose stealing pace, and lengthened shade we fear,
Till torn up forage in his teeth we hear;
When nibbling sheep at large pursue their food,
And unmolested kine re-chew the cud;
When curlews cry beneath the village-walls,   35
And to her straggling brood the partridge calls;
Their shortlived jubilee the creatures keep,
Which but endures whilst tyrant-man does sleep;
When a sedate content the spirit feels,
And no fierce light disturb, whilst it reveals;   40
But silent musings urge the mind to seek
Something too high for syllables to speak;
Till the free soul to a composedness charmed,
Finding the elements of rage disarmed,
O'er all below a solemn quiet grown,   45
Joys in th' inferior world and thinks it like her own:
In such a night let me abroad remain
Till morning breaks and all's confused again;
Our cares, our toils, our clamors are renewed,
Or pleasures, seldom reached, again pursued.   50

1713

GEORGE HICKES

SAMUEL CROXALL

from THE VISION

Pᴇɴsɪᴠᴇ beneath a spreading oak I stood
That veiled the hollow channel of the flood:
Along whose shelving bank the violet blue
And primrose pale in lovely mixture grew.
High overarched the bloomy woodbine hung,   5
The gaudy goldfinch from the maple sung;
The little warbling minstrel of the shade
To the gay morn her due devotion paid.
Next, the soft linnet echoing to the thrush
With carols filled the smelling briar-bush;   10
While Philomel attuned her artless throat,
And from the hawthorn breathed a trilling
    note.
Indulgent Nature smiled in every part,
And filled with joy unknown my ravished
    heart:
Attent I listened while the feathered throng   15
Alternate finished and renewed their song.

1715

GEORGE HICKES

TRANSLATION OF THE OLD NORSE INCANTATION OF HERVOR

[Hervor, the daughter of the dead hero Angantyr, owner of the magical sword Tirfing, goes to Angantyr's tomb, and summons him up from the dead in order to secure the sword. He is reluctant, because there is a curse upon the weapon.]

Hervor: Awake, Angantyr! Hervor, the only daughter of thee and Suafu, doth awaken thee. Give

me out of the tomb the hardened sword which the
dwarfs made for Suafurlama. Hervardur, Hiorvardur, Hrani, and Angantyr, with helmet and coat 5
of mail, and a sharp sword with shield and accoutrements, and bloody spear, I woke you all
under the roots of trees. Are the sons of Andgrym
who delighted in mischief now become dust and
ashes? Can none of Eynor's sons now speak with 10
me out of the habitations of the dead! Harvardur!
Hiorvardur! So may you all be within your ribs
as a thing that is hanged up to putrify among insects, unless you deliver me the sword which the
dwarfs made . . . and the glorious belt. 15

Angantyr: Daughter Hervor, full of spells to
raise the dead, why dost thou call so? Wilt thou
run on to thy own mischief? Thou art mad and
out of thy senses who art desperately resolved to
waken dead men. I was not buried either by father 20
or other friends. Two which lived after me got
Tirfing, one of whom is now possessor thereof.

Hervor: Thou dost not tell the truth! So let Odin
hide thee in the tomb as thou hast Tirfing by thee.
Art thou unwilling, Angantyr, to give an inheritance 25
to thy only child?

1703

LADY ELIZABETH WARDLAW

FROM HARDYKNUTE

STATELY stepped he east the wa',
    And stately stepped he west,
Full seventy years he now had seen,
    With scarce seven years of rest.
He lived when Britons' breach of faith 5
    Wrought Scotland mickle wae;

And aye his sword tauld to their cost,
  He was their deadly fae.

High on a hill his castle stood,
  With ha's and towers a height,   10
And goodly chambers fair to see,
  Where he lodged mony a knight.
His dame sae peerless ance and fair,
  For chaste and beauty deemed,
Nae marrow had in all the land,   15
  Save Eleanor the Queen.

Full thirteen sons to him she bare,
  All men of valor stout;
In bloody fight with sword in hand
  Nine lost their lives bot doubt: 20
Four yet remain, lang may they live
  To stand by liege and land;
High was their fame, high was their might,
  And high was their command.

Great love they bare to Fairly fair,   25
  Their sister saft and dear,
Her girdle shaw'd her middle gimp,
  And gowden glist her hair.
What waefu' wae her beauty bred?
  Waefu' to young and auld,   30
Waefu' I trow to kyth and kin,
  As story ever tauld.

The king of Norse in summer tyde,
  Puffed up with pow'r and might,
Landed in fair Scotland the isle   35
  With mony a hardy knight.
The tydings to our good Scots king
  Came, as he sat at dine,

With noble chiefs in brave array,
   Drinking the blood-red wine.   40

"To horse, to horse, my royal liege,
   Your faes stand on the strand,
Full twenty thousand glittering spears
   The king of Norse commands."
Bring me my steed Mage dapple gray,   45
   Our good king rose and cried,
A trustier beast in a' the land
   A Scots king nevir tried.

Go little page, tell Hardyknute,
   That lives on hill sae hie,   50
To draw his sword, the dread of faes,
   And haste and follow me.
The little page flew swift as dart
   Flung by his master's arm.
"Come down, come down, lord Hardyknute,   55
   And rid your king frae harm."

Then red red grew his dark-brown cheeks,
   Sae did his dark-brown brow;
His looks grew keen, as they were wont
   In dangers great to do;   60
He's ta'en a horn as green as grass,
   And gi'en five sounds sae shill,
That trees in green wood shook thereat,
   Sae loud rang ilka hill.

                           1719

WILLIAM HAMILTON OF BANGOUR

THE BRAES OF YARROW

IN IMITATION OF THE ANCIENT SCOTS MANNER

A. Busk ye, busk ye, my bonny bonny bride,
    Busk ye, busk ye, my winsome marrow,
  Busk ye, busk ye, my bonny bonny bride,
    And think nae mair on the Braes of Yarrow.

B. Where gat ye that bonny bonny bride?   5
    Where gat ye that winsome marrow?
A. I gat her where I dare na weil be seen,
    Puing the birks on the Braes of Yarrow.

Weep not, weep not, my bonny bonny bride,
    Weep not, weep not, my winsome marrow;   10
  Nor let thy heart lament to leive
    Puing the birks on the Braes of Yarrow.

B. Why does she weep, thy bonny bonny bride?
    Why does she weep, thy winsome marrow?
  And why dare ye nae mair weil be seen   15
    Puing the birks on the Braes of Yarrow?

A. Lang maun she weep, lang maun she, maun she
    weep,
    Lang maun she weep with dule and sorrow;
  And lang maun I naer mair weil be seen
    Puing the birks on the Braes of Yarrow.   20

For she has tint her luver, luver dear,
    Her luver dear, the cause of sorrow;
  And I hae slain the comliest swain
    That eir pu'd birks on the Braes of Yarrow.

Why rins thy stream, O Yarrow, Yarrow, reid?   25
    Why on thy braes heard the voice of sorrow?
And why yon melancholious weids
    Hung on the bonny birks of Yarrow?

What's yonder floats on the rueful rueful flude?
    What's yonder floats?   O dule and sorrow!   30
O 'tis he the comely swain I slew
    Upon the duleful Braes of Yarrow.

Wash, O wash his wounds, his wounds in tears,
    His wounds in tears with dule and sorrow;
And wrap his limbs in mourning weids,   35
    And lay him on the Braes of Yarrow.

Then build, then build, ye sisters, sisters sad,
    Ye sisters sad, his tomb with sorrow;
And weep around in waeful wise
    His hapless fate on the Braes of Yarrow.   40

Curse ye, curse ye, his useless, useless shield,
    My arm that wrought the deed of sorrow,
The fatal spear that pierced his breast,
    His comely breast on the Braes of Yarrow.

Did I not warn thee, not to, not to luve?   45
    And warn from fight? but to my sorrow
Too rashly bauld a stronger arm
    Thou mett'st, and fell'st on the Braes of Yar-
       row.

C. Sweet smells the birk, green grows, green grows
       the grass,
    Yellow on Yarrow's bank the gowan,   50
Fair hangs the apple frae the rock,
    Sweet the wave of Yarrow flowan.

A. Flows Yarrow sweet? as sweet, as sweet flows
    Tweed,
  As green its grass, its gowan as yellow,
As sweet smells on its braes the birk,   55
  The apple frae its rock as mellow.

Fair was thy luve, fair, fair indeed thy luve,
  In flow'ry bands thou didst him fetter;
Tho' he was fair, and weil beluved again
  Than me he never luved thee better.   60

Busk ye, then busk, my bonny bonny bride,
  Busk ye, busk ye, my winsome marrow,
Busk ye, and luve me on the banks of Tweed,
  And think nae mair on the Braes of Yarrow.

C. How can I busk, a bonny bonny bride?   65
  How can I busk, a winsome marrow?
How luve him upon the banks of Tweed,
  That slew my luve on the Braes of Yarrow?

O Yarrow fields, may never, never rain
  Nor dew thy tender blossoms cover,   70
For there was basely slain my luve,
  My luve, as he had not been a lover.

The boy put on his robes, his robes of green,
  His purple vest, 'twas my awn sewing:
Ah! wretched me! I little, little kenned   75
  He was in these to meet his ruin.

The boy took out his milk-white, milk-white
    steed,
  Unheedful of my dule and sorrow:
But ere the to-fall of the night
  He lay a corps on the Braes of Yarrow.

Much I rejoyced that waeful, waeful day;
   I sang, my voice the woods returning:
But lang ere night the spear was flown,
   That slew my luve, and left me mourning.

What can my barbarous, barbarous father do,   85
   But with his cruel rage pursue me?
My luver's blood is on thy spear,
   How canst thou, barbarous man, then wooe
     me?

My happy sisters may be, may be proud
   With cruel and ungentle scoffin',   90
May bid me seek on Yarrow's Braes
   My luver nailed in his coffin.

My brother Douglas may upbraid, upbraid,
   And strive with threatning words to muve me:
My luver's blood is on thy spear,   95
   How canst thou ever bid me luve thee?

Yes, yes, prepare the bed, the bed of luve,
   With bridal sheets my body cover,
Unbar, ye bridal maids, the door,
   Let in the expected husband lover.   100

But who the expected husband, husband is?
   His hands, methinks, are bathed in slaughter:
Ah me! what ghastly spectre's yon
   Comes in his pale shroud, bleeding after?

Pale as he is, here lay him, lay him down,   105
   O lay his cold head on my pillow;
Take aff, take aff, these bridal weids,
   And crown my careful head with willow.

Pale tho' thou art, yet best, yet best beluved,
  O could my warmth to life restore thee! 110
Yet lye all night between my breists,
  No youth lay ever there before thee.

Pale, pale indeed, O luvely, luvely youth!
  Forgive, forgive so foul a slaughter:
And lye all night between my breists; 115
  No youth shall ever lye there after.

A. Return, return, O mournful, mournful bride,
  Return, and dry thy useless sorrow:
Thy luver heeds none of thy sighs,
  He lyes a corps on the Braes of Yarrow. 120

1724

ALLAN RAMSAY

PREFACE TO THE EVERGREEN

I HAVE observed that readers of the best and most
exquisite discernment frequently complain of our
modern writings as filled with affected delicacies and
studied refinements, which they would gladly exchange for that natural strength of thought and sim- 5
plicity of style our forefathers practiced. To such,
I hope, the following collection of poems will not be
displeasing.

When these good old bards wrote, we had not yet
made use of imported trimming upon our clothes, 10
nor of foreign embroidery in our writings. Their
poetry is the product of their own country, not pil-
fered and spoiled in the transportation from abroad.
Their images are native, and their landscapes domestic; copied from those fields and meadows we every 15
day behold.

The morning rises (in the poet's description) as she does in the Scottish horizon. We are not carried to Greece or Italy for a shade, a stream, or a breeze. The groves rise in our own valleys; the rivers flow 20 from our own fountains; and the winds blow upon our own hills. I find not fault with those things as they are in Greece or Italy; but with a Northern poet for fetching his materials from these places in a poem of which his own country is the scene, as our 25 hymners to the spring and makers of pastorals frequently do.

This miscellany will likewise recommend itself by the diversity of subjects and humor it contains. The grave description and the wanton story, the moral 30 saying and the mirthful jest, will illustrate and alternately relieve each other.

The reader whose temper is spleened with the vices and follies now in fashion, may gratify his humor with the satires he will here find upon the 35 follies and vices that were uppermost two or three hundred years ago. The man whose inclinations are turned to mirth will be pleased to know how the good fellow of a former age told his jovial tale; and the lover may divert himself with the old fashioned 40 sonnet of an amorous poet in Queen Margaret and Queen Mary's days. In a word, the following collection will be such another prospect to the eye of the mind as to the outward eye is the various meadow, where flowers of different hue and smell are mingled 45 together in a beautiful irregularity.

I hope also the reader, when he dips into these poems, will not be displeased with this reflection, that he is stepping back into the times that are past and that exist no more. Thus, the manners and cus- 50 toms then in vogue, as he will find them here described, will have all the air and charm of novelty; and that seldom fails of exciting attention and pleasing the mind. Besides, the numbers in which these images are conveyed, as they are not now commonly practiced, will appear new and amusing. 55

The different stanza and varied cadence will likewise much soothe and engage the ear, which in poetry especially must be always flattered. However, I do not expect that these poems should please everybody; nay, the critical reader must needs find several faults, for I own that there will be found in these volumes two or three pieces whose antiquity is their greatest value. Yet still I am persuaded there are many more that shall merit approbation and applause than censure and blame. The best works are but a kind of miscellany, and the cleanest corn is not without some chaff; no, not after often winnowing. Besides, dispraise is the easiest part of learning, and but at best the offspring of uncharitable wit. Every clown can see that the furrow is crooked; but where is the man that will plow me one straight? 60 65 70

There is nothing can be heard more silly than one's expressing his ignorance of his native language; yet, such there are who can vaunt of acquiring a tolerable perfection in the French or Italian tongues if they have been a fortnight in Paris, or a month in Rome. But show them the most elegant thoughts in a Scots dress, they as disdainfully as stupidly condemn it as barbarous. But the true reason is obvious: every one that is born never so little superior to the vulgar would fain distinguish themselves from them by some manner or other, and such, it would appear, cannot arrive at a better method. But this affected class of fops give no uneasiness, not being numerous; for the most part of our gentlemen, who are generally masters of the most useful and politest languages, can take pleasure (for a change) to speak and read their own. 75 80 85

SWEET WILLIAM'S GHOST

THERE came a ghost to Margret's door,
    With many a grievous grone,
And ay he tirled at the pin,
    But answer made she none.

Is this my father, Philip?   5
    Or is't my brother John?
Or is't my true love Willie,
    From Scotland new come home?

'Tis not thy father Philip,
    Nor yet thy brother John: 10
But 'tis thy true love Willie
    From Scotland new come home.

O sweet Margret! O dear Margret!
    I pray thee speak to mee:
Give me my faith and troth, Margret,   15
    As I gave it to thee.

Thy faith and troth thou'se nevir get,
    Of me shalt nevir win,
Till that thou come within my bower,
    And kiss my cheek and chin.   20

If I should come within thy bower,
    I am no earthly man:
And should I kiss thy rosy lipp,
    Thy days will not be lang.

O sweet Margret! O dear Margret!   25
    I pray thee speak to mee:
Give me my faith and troth, Margret,
    As I gave it to thee.

Thy faith and troth thou'se nevir get,
 Of me shalt nevir win,   30
Till thou take me to yon kirk yard,
 And wed me with a ring.

My bones are buried in a kirk yard
 Afar beyond the sea,
And it is but my sprite, Margret, 35
 That's speaking now to thee.

She stretched out her lily-white hand,
 As for to do her best:
Hae there your faith and troth, Willie,
 God send your soul good rest. 40

Now she has kilted her robes of green,
 A piece below her knee:
And a' the live-lang winter night
 The dead corps followed shee.

Is there any room at your head, Willie? 45
 Or any room at your feet?
Or any room at your side, Willie?
 Wherein that I may creep?

There's nae room at my head, Margret,
 There's nae room at my feet, 50
There's nae room at my side, Margret,
 My coffin is made so meet.

Then up and crew the red red cock,
 And up then crew the gray:
'Tis time, 'tis time, my dear Margret, 55
 That I were gane away.

No more the ghost to Margret said,
 But, with a grievous grone,

Evanished in a cloud of mist,
  And left her all alone.   60

O stay, my only true love, stay,
  The constant Margret cried:
Wan grew her cheeks, she closed her een,
  Stretched her saft limbs, and died.

                                                   1740

DAVID MALLET
(EDITOR)

WILLIAM AND MARGARET

'Twas at the silent solemn hour,
  When night and morning meet;
In glided Margaret's grimly ghost,
  And stood at William's feet.

Her face was like an April morn   5
  Clad in a wintry cloud;
And clay-cold was her lily hand
  That held her sable shroud.

So shall the fairest face appear,
  When youth and years are flown: 10
Such is the robe that kings must wear,
  When death has reft their crown.

Her bloom was like the springing flower,
  That sips the silver dew;
The rose was budded in her cheek,   15
  Just opening to the view.

But love had, like the canker-worm,
  Consumed her early prime;

The rose grew pale, and left her cheek,
   She died before her time.   20

"Awake!" she cried, "thy true love calls,
   Come from her midnight grave:
Now let thy pity hear the maid
   Thy love refused to save.

"This is the dark and dreary hour   25
   When injured ghosts complain;
When yawning graves give up their dead,
   To haunt the faithless swain.

"Bethink thee, William, of thy fault,
   Thy pledge and broken oath!   30
And give me back my maiden vow,
   And give me back my troth.

"Why did you promise love to me,
   And not that promise keep?
Why did you swear my eyes were bright,   35
   Yet leave those eyes to weep?

"How could you say my face was fair,
   And yet that face forsake?
How could you win my virgin heart,
   Yet leave that heart to break?   40

"Why did you say my lip was sweet,
   And make the scarlet pale?
And why did I, young, witless maid!
   Believe the flattering tale?

"That face, alas! no more is fair,   45
   Those lips no longer red:
Dark are my eyes, now closed in death,
   And every charm is fled.

"The hungry worm my sister is;
  This winding-sheet I wear: 50
And cold and weary lasts our night,
  Till that last morn appear.

"But hark! the cock has warned me hence;
  A long and last adieu!
Come see, false man, how low she lies,   55
  Who died for love of you."

The lark sung loud; the morning smiled
  With beams of rosy red:
Pale William quaked in every limb,
  And raving left his bed.   60

He hied him to the fatal place
  Where Margaret's body lay;
And stretched him on the green-grass turf
  That wrapt her breathless clay.

And thrice he called on Margaret's name,   65
  And thrice he wept full sore;
Then laid his cheek to her cold grave,
  And word spake never more!

1724

JAMES THOMSON

FROM THE SEASONS

FROM PREFACE

Nothing can have a better influence towards the revival
of poetry than the choosing of great and serious subjects,
such as at once amuse the fancy, enlighten the head, and
warm the heart. These give a weight and dignity to the
poem; nor is the pleasure—I should say rapture—both the   5
writer and the reader feels unwarranted by reason or fol-

lowed by repentant disgust. To be able to write on a dry,
barren theme is looked upon by some as the sign of a
happy, fruitful genius:—fruitful indeed! like one of the
pendant gardens in Cheapside, watered every morning by the   10
hand of the Alderman himself. And what are we commonly
entertained with on these occasions save forced unaffecting
fancies, little glittering prettinesses, mixed turns of wit and
expression, which are as widely different from native poetry
as buffoonery is from the perfection of human thinking? A   15
genius fired with the charms of truth and nature is tuned to
a sublimer pitch, and scorns to associate with such subjects.

I know no subject more elevating, more amusing; more
ready to awake the poetical enthusiasm, the philosophical
reflection, and the moral sentiment, than the works of na-   20
ture. Where can we meet with such variety, such beauty,
such magnificence? All that enlarges and transports the
soul! What more inspiring than a calm, wide survey of
them? In every dress nature is greatly charming—whether
she puts on the crimson robes of the morning, the strong   25
effulgence of noon, the sober suit of the evening, or the deep
sables of blackness and tempest! How gay looks the spring!
how glorious the summer! how pleasing the autumn! and
how venerable the winter!—But there is no thinking of these
things without breaking out into poetry; which is, by-the-by,   30
a plain and undeniable argument of their superior excellence.

For this reason the best, both ancient, and modern, poets
have been passionately fond of retirement, and solitude. The
wild romantic country was their delight. And they seem
never to have been more happy, than when, lost in unfre-   35
quented fields, far from the little busy world, they were at
leisure, to meditate, and sing the works of nature.

FROM WINTER

[HARDSHIPS AND BENEVOLENCE]

THE keener tempests come; and, fuming dun
From all the livid east or piercing north,
Thick clouds ascend, in whose capacious womb
A vapory deluge lies, to snow congealed.
Heavy they roll their fleecy world along,   5
And the sky saddens with the gathered storm.

Through the hushed air the whitening shower de-
    scends,
At first thin wavering, till at last the flakes
Fall broad and wide and fast, dimming the day
With a continual flow. The cherished fields   10
Put on their winter robe of purest white;
'Tis brightness all, save where the new snow melts
Along the mazy current; low the woods
Bow their hoar head; and ere the languid sun
Faint from the west emits his evening ray,   15
Earth's universal face, deep-hid and chill,
Is one wild dazzling waste, that buries wide
The works of man. Drooping, the laborer-ox
Stands covered o'er with snow, and then demands
The fruit of all his toil. The fowls of heaven,   20
Tamed by the cruel season, crowd around
The winnowing store, and claim the little boon
Which Providence assigns them. One alone,
The redbreast, sacred to the household gods,
Wisely regardful of th' embroiling sky,   25
In joyless fields and thorny thickets leaves
His shivering mates, and pays to trusted man
His annual visit: half-afraid, he first
Against the window beats; then brisk alights
On the warm hearth; then, hopping o'er the floor,   30
Eyes all the smiling family askance,
And pecks, and starts, and wonders where he is,
Till, more familiar grown, the table-crumbs
Attract his slender feet. The foodless wilds
Pour forth their brown inhabitants. The hare,   35
Though timorous of heart and hard beset
By death in various forms—dark snares, and dogs,
And more unpitying men,—the garden seeks,
Urged on by fearless want. The bleating kind
Eye the black heaven, and next the glistening earth,   40
With looks of dumb despair; then, sad dispersed,
Dig for the withered herb through heaps of snow.

Now, shepherds, to your helpess charge be kind:
Baffle the raging year, and fill their pens
With food at will; lodge them below the storm,   45
And watch them strict, for from the bellowing east,
In this dire season, oft the whirlwind's wing
Sweeps up the burthen of whole wintry plains
At one wide waft, and o'er the hapless flocks,
Hid in the hollow of two neighboring hills,   50
The billowy tempest whelms, till, upward urged,
The valley to a shining mountain swells,
Tipped with a wreath high-curling in the sky.
    As thus the snows arise, and foul and fierce
All Winter drives along the darkened air,   55
In his own loose-revolving fields the swain
Disastered stands; sees other hills ascend,
Of unknown, joyless brow, and other scenes,
Of horrid prospect, shag the trackless plain;
Nor finds the river nor the forest, hid   60
Beneath the formless wild, but wanders on
From hill to dale, still more and more astray,
Impatient flouncing through the drifted heaps,
Stung with the thoughts of home. The thoughts of
            home
Rush on his nerves, and call their vigor forth   65
In many a vain attempt. How sinks his soul,
What black despair, what horror fills his heart,
When, for the dusky spot which fancy feigned
His tufted cottage rising through the snow,
He meets the roughness of the middle waste,   70
Far from the track and blest abode of man,
While round him night resistless closes fast,
And every tempest, howling o'er his head,
Renders the savage wilderness more wild!
Then throng the busy shapes into his mind   75
Of covered pits unfathomably deep
(A dire descent!), beyond the power of frost;
Of faithless bogs; of precipices huge,

Smoothed up with snow; and—what is land un-
    known,
What water—of the still unfrozen spring,   80
In the loose marsh or solitary lake,
Where the fresh fountain from the bottom boils.
These check his fearful steps; and down he sinks
Beneath the shelter of the shapeless drift,
Thinking o'er all the bitterness of death,   85
Mixed with the tender anguish nature shoots
Through the wrung bosom of the dying man—
His wife, his children, and his friends unseen.
In vain for him th' officious wife prepares
The fire fair-blazing and the vestment warm;   90
In vain his little children, peeping out
Into the mingling storm, demand their sire,
With tears of artless innocence. Alas!
Nor wife nor children more shall he behold,
Nor friends nor sacred home: on every nerve   95
The deadly Winter seizes, shuts up sense,
And, o'er his inmost vitals creeping cold,
Lays him along the snows a stiffened corse,
Stretched out and bleaching in the northern blast.
    Ah, little think the gay licentious proud   100
Whom pleasure, power, and affluence surround;
They who their thoughtless hours in giddy mirth,
And wanton, often cruel, riot waste;
Ah, little think they, while they dance along,
How many feel, this very moment, death   105
And all the sad variety of pain:
How many sink in the devouring flood,
Or more devouring flame; how many bleed,
By shameful variance betwixt man and man;
How many pine in want, and dungeon glooms,   110
Shut from the common air, and common use
Of their own limbs; how many drink the cup
Of baleful grief, or eat the bitter bread
Of misery; sore pierced by wintry winds,

How many shrink into the sordid hut   115
Of cheerless poverty; how many shake
With all the fiercer tortures of the mind,
Unbounded passion, madness, guilt, remorse:
Whence tumbled headlong from the height of life,
They furnish matter for the tragic Muse;   120
Even in the vale, where wisdom loves to dwell,
With friendship, peace, and contemplation joined,
How many, racked with honest passions, droop
In deep retired distress; how many stand
Around the deathbed of their dearest friends,   125
And point the parting anguish. Thought fond man
Of these, and all the thousand nameless ills,
That one incessant struggle render life,
One scene of toil, of suffering, and of fate,
Vice in his high career would stand appalled,   130
And heedless rambling impulse learn to think;
The conscious heart of charity would warm,
And her wide wish benevolence dilate;
The social tear would rise, the social sigh;
And into clear perfection, gradual bliss,   135
Refining still, the social passions work.

                                        1726

FROM SUMMER

[LIFE'S MEANING TO THE GENEROUS MIND]

FOREVER running an enchanted round,
Passes the day, deceitful vain and void,
As fleets the vision o'er the formful brain,
This moment hurrying wild th' impassioned soul,
The next in nothing lost. 'Tis so to him,   5
The dreamer of this earth, an idle blank;
A sight of horror to the cruel wretch,
Who all day long in sordid pleasure rolled,

Himself an useless load, has squandered vile,
Upon his scoundrel train, what might have cheered   10
A drooping family of modest worth.
But to the generous still-improving mind,
That gives the hopeless heart to sing for joy,
Diffusing kind beneficence around,
Boastless,—as now descends the silent dew,—   15
To him the long review of ordered life
Is inward rapture, only to be felt.

1727

FROM SPRING

[THE DIVINE FORCE IN SPRING]

COME, gentle Spring, ethereal mildness, come!
And from the bosom of yon dropping cloud,
While music wakes around, veiled in a shower
Of shadowing roses, on our plains descend!
    O Hertford, fitted or to shine in courts   5
With unaffected grace, or walk the plain
With Innocence and Meditation joined
In soft assemblage, listen to my song,
Which thy own season paints, when nature all
Is blooming and benevolent, like thee.   10
    And see where surly Winter passes off,
Far to the north, and calls his ruffian blasts:
His blasts obey, and quit the howling hill,
The shattered forest, and the ravaged vale;
While softer gales succeed, at whose kind touch—   15
Dissolving snows in livid torrents lost—
The mountains lift their green heads to the sky.
As yet the trembling year is unconfirmed,
And Winter oft at eve resumes the breeze,
Chills the pale morn, and bids his driving sleets   20
Deform the day delightless; so that scarce
The bittern knows his time, with bill engulfed,

To shake the sounding marsh, or from the shore
The plovers when to scatter o'er the heath
And sing their wild notes to the listening waste.   25
At last from Aries rolls the bounteous sun,
And the bright Bull receives him.   Then no more
Th' expansive atmosphere is cramped with cold,
But, full of life and vivifying soul,
Lifts the light clouds sublime and spreads them
        thin,   30
Fleecy and white, o'er all-surrounding heaven;
Forth fly the tepid airs, and, unconfined,
Unbinding earth, the moving softness strays.
Joyous, th' impatient husbandman perceives
Relenting nature, and his lusty steers   35
Drives from their stalls, to where the well-used
        plough
Lies in the furrow, loosened from the frost;
There, unrefusing, to the harnessed yoke
They lend their shoulder, and begin their toil,
Cheered by the simple song and soaring lark;   40
Meanwhile incumbent o'er the shining share
The master leans, removes th' obstructing clay,
Winds the whole work, and sidelong lays the
        glebe.
White through the neighboring fields the sower
        stalks,
With measured step, and liberal throws the grain   45
Into the faithful bosom of the ground;
The harrow follows harsh, and shuts the scene.
    Be gracious, Heaven! for now laborious man
Has done his part.   Ye fostering breezes, blow!
Ye softening dews, ye tender showers, descend!   50
And temper all, thou world-reviving sun,
Into the perfect year!   Nor ye who live
In luxury and ease, in pomp and pride,
Think these lost themes unworthy of your ear.
Such themes as these the rural Maro sung   55

To wide-imperial Rome, in the full height
Of elegance and taste, by Greece refined.
In ancient times, the sacred plough employed
The kings and awful fathers of mankind;
And some, with whom compared your insect
      tribes   60
Are but the beings of a summer's day,
Have held the scale of empire, ruled the storm
Of mighty war, then with victorious hand,
Disdaining little delicacies, seized
The plough, and, greatly independent, scorned   65
All the vile stores corruption can bestow.
Ye generous Britons, venerate the plough;
And o'er your hills and long-withdrawing vales
Let Autumn spread his treasures to the sun,
Luxuriant and unbounded! As the sea,   70
Far through his azure, turbulent domain,
Your empire owns, and from a thousand shores
Wafts all the pomp of life into your ports,
So with superior boon may your rich soil,
Exuberant, Nature's better blessings pour   75
O'er every land, the naked nations clothe,
And be th' exhaustless granary of a world.
    Nor only through the lenient air this change,
Delicious, breathes: the penetrative sun,
His force deep-darting to the dark retreat   80
Of vegetation, sets the steaming power
At large, to wander o'er the verdant earth,
In various hues—but chiefly thee, gay green!
Thou smiling Nature's universal robe,
United light and shade, where the sight dwells   85
With growing strength and ever new delight.
From the moist meadow to the withered hill,
Led by the breeze, the vivid verdure runs,
And swells and deepens to the cherished eye.
The hawthorn whitens; and the juicy groves   90
Put forth their buds, unfolding by degrees,

Till the whole leafy forest stands displayed
In full luxuriance to the sighing gales,
Where the deer rustle through the twining brake,
And the birds sing concealed. At once, arrayed   95
In all the colors of the flushing year
By Nature's swift and secret-working hand,
The garden glows, and fills the liberal air
With lavished fragrance, while the promised fruit
Lies yet a little embryo, unperceived,   100
Within its crimson folds.   Now from the town,
Buried in smoke and sleep and noisome damps,
Oft let me wander o'er the dewy fields,
Where freshness breathes, and dash the trembling
          drops
From the bent bush, as through the verdant maze 105
Of sweet-briar hedges I pursue my walk;
Or taste the smell of dairy; or ascend
Some eminence, Augusta, in thy plains,
And see the country, far diffused around,
One boundless blush, one white-empurpled shower 110
Of mingled blossoms, where the raptured eye
Hurries from joy to joy, and, hid beneath
The fair profusion, yellow Autumn spies.

.   .   .   .

What is this mighty breath, ye sages, say,
That in a powerful language, felt not heard,   115
Instructs the fowl of heaven, and through their
          breast
These arts of love diffuses?   What but God?
Inspiring God! who boundless spirit all,
And unremitting energy, pervades,
Adjusts, sustains, and agitates the whole.   120
He ceaseless works alone, and yet alone
Seems not to work; with such perfection framed
Is this complex, stupendous scheme of things.
But, though concealed, to every purer eye

Th' informing author in his works appears: 125
Chief, lovely Spring, in thee, and thy soft scenes,
The smiling God is seen; while water, earth,
And air attest his bounty; which exalts
The brute creation to this finer thought,
And annual melts their undesigning hearts   130
Profusely thus in tenderness and joy.
　　Still let my song a nobler note assume,
And sing th' infusive force of Spring on man,
When heaven and earth, as if contending, vie
To raise his being, and serene his soul.   135
Can he forbear to join the general smile
Of nature? Can fierce passions vex his breast,
While every gale is peace, and every grove
Is melody? Hence from the bounteous walks
Of flowing Spring, ye sordid sons of earth,   140
Hard, and unfeeling of another's woe;
Or only lavish to yourselves; away!
But come, ye generous minds, in whose wide
　　thought,
Of all his works, creative bounty burns
With warmest beam!   145

                                       1728

FROM AUTUMN

[THE PLEASING SADNESS OF THE
DECLINING YEAR]

BUT see! the fading many-colored woods,
Shade deepening over shade, the country round
Imbrown, a crowded umbrage, dusk and dun,
Of every hue from wan declining green
To sooty dark. These now the lonesome Muse,   5
Low-whispering, lead into their leaf-strown walks,
And give the season in its latest view.
Meantime, light-shadowing all, a sober calm

Fleeces unbounded ether, whose least wave
Stands tremulous, uncertain where to turn   10
The gentle current, while, illumined wide,
The dewy-skirted clouds imbibe the sun,
And through their lucid veil his softened force
Shed o'er the peaceful world. Then is the time,
For those whom wisdom and whom nature charm,   15
To steal themselves from the degenerate crowd,
And soar above this little scene of things,
To tread low-thoughted Vice beneath their feet,
To soothe the throbbing passions into peace,
And woo lone Quiet in her silent walks.   20
Thus solitary, and in pensive guise,
Oft let me wander o'er the russet mead
And through the saddened grove, where scarce is
    heard
One dying strain to cheer the woodman's toil.
Haply some widowed songster pours his plaint,   25
Far, in faint warblings, through the tawny copse;
While congregated thrushes, linnets, larks,
And each wild throat whose artless strains so late
Swelled all the music of the swarming shades,
Robbed of their tuneful souls, now shivering sit   30
On the dead tree, a dull despondent flock;
With not a brightness waving o'er their plumes,
And naught save chattering discord in their note.
Oh, let not, aimed from some inhuman eye,
The gun the music of the coming year   35
Destroy, and harmless, unsuspecting harm,
Lay the weak tribes a miserable prey,
In mingled murder fluttering on the ground!
The pale descending year, yet pleasing still,
A gentler mood inspires: for now the leaf   40
Incessant rustles from the mournful grove,
Oft startling such as, studious, walk below,
And slowly circles through the waving air;
But should a quicker breeze amid the boughs

Sob, o'er the sky the leafy deluge streams,   45
Till, choked and matted with the dreary shower,
The forest walks, at every rising gale,
Roll wide the withered waste and whistle bleak.
Fled is the blasted verdure of the fields,
And, shrunk into their beds, the flowery race   50
Their sunny robes resign; even what remained
Of stronger fruits fall from the naked tree;
And woods, fields, gardens, orchards, all around,
The desolated prospect thrills the soul.

                                                          1730

A HYMN

[CONCLUDING THE SEASONS]

THESE, as they change, Almighty Father, these,
Are but the varied God. The rolling year
Is full of Thee. Forth in the pleasing Spring
Thy beauty walks, thy tenderness and love.
Wide-flush the fields; the softening air is balm;   5
Echo the mountains round; the forest smiles;
And every sense, and every heart is joy.
Then comes thy glory in the summer-months,
With light and heat refulgent. Then thy sun
Shoots full perfection through the swelling year: 10
And oft thy voice in dreadful thunder speaks;
And oft at dawn, deep noon, or falling eve,
By brooks and groves, in hollow-whispering gales.
Thy bounty shines in autumn unconfined,
And spreads a common feast for all that lives.   15
In winter awful thou! with clouds and storms
Around thee thrown, tempest o'er tempest rolled
Majestic darkness! on the whirlwind's wing,
Riding sublime, thou bidst the world adore,
And humblest nature with thy northern blast.   20
      Mysterious round! what skill, what force Divine,

Deepfelt, in these appear! a simple train,
Yet so delightful mixed, with such kind art,
Such beauty and beneficence combined:
Shade, unperceived, so softening into shade;   25
And all so forming an harmonious whole;
That, as they still succeed, they ravish still.
But wandering oft, with brute unconscious gaze,
Man marks not Thee, marks not the mighty hand;
That, ever-busy, wheels the silent spheres;   30
Works in the secret deep; shoots, steaming, thence
The fair profusion that o'erspreads the spring:
Flings from the sun direct the flaming day;
Feeds every creature; hurls the tempest forth;
And, as on earth this grateful change revolves,   35
With transport touches all the springs of life.
    Nature, attend! join every living soul,
Beneath the spacious temple of the sky,
In adoration join; and ardent raise
One general song! To Him, ye vocal gales,   40
Breathe soft, whose spirit in your freshness breathes.
Oh, talk of Him in solitary glooms
Where o'er the rock the scarcely waving pine
Fills the brown shade with a religious awe;
And ye, whose bolder note is heard afar,   45
Who shake the astonished world, lift high to heaven
Th' impetuous song, and say from whom you rage.
His praise, ye brooks, attune, ye trembling rills;
And let me catch it as I muse along.
Ye headlong torrents, rapid and profound;   50
Ye softer floods, that lead the humid maze
Along the vale; and thou, majestic main,
A secret world of wonders in thyself,
Sound His stupendous praise, whose greater voice
Or bids you roar, or bids your roarings fall.   55
So roll your incense, herbs, and fruits, and flowers,
In mingled clouds to Him, whose sun exalts,

Whose breath perfumes you, and whose pencil
      paints.
Ye forests, bend, ye harvests, wave to Him;
Breathe your still song into the reaper's heart,   60
As home he goes beneath the joyous moon.
Ye that keep watch in Heaven, as earth asleep
Unconscious lies, effuse your mildest beams;
Ye constellations, while your angels strike,
Amid the spangled sky, the silver lyre.   65
Great source of day! blest image here below
Of thy Creator, ever pouring wide,
From world to world, the vital ocean round,
On nature write with every beam His praise.
The thunder rolls: be hushed the prostrate world,   70
While cloud to cloud returns the solemn hymn.
Bleat out afresh, ye hills; ye mossy rocks,
Retain the sound; the broad responsive low,
Ye valleys, raise; for the Great Shepherd reigns,
And his unsuffering kingdom yet will come.   75
Ye woodlands, all awake; a boundless song
Burst from the groves; and when the restless day,
Expiring, lays the warbling world asleep,
Sweetest of birds! sweet Philomela, charm
The listening shades, and teach the night His praise.   80
Ye chief, for whom the whole creation smiles;
At once the head, the heart, the tongue of all,
Crown the great hymn! in swarming cities vast,
Assembled men to the deep organ join
The long resounding voice, oft breaking clear,   85
At solemn pauses, through the swelling base;
And, as each mingling flame increases each,
In one united ardor rise to Heaven.
Or if you rather choose the rural shade,
And find a fane in every sacred grove,   90
There let the shepherd's lute, the virgin's lay,
The prompting seraph, and the poet's lyre,
Still sing the God of Seasons as they roll.

For me, when I forget the darling theme,
Whether the blossom blows, the Summer ray   95
Russets the plain, inspiring Autumn gleams,
Or Winter rises in the blackening east —
Be my tongue mute, my fancy paint no more,
And, dead to joy, forget my heart to beat.

Should Fate command me to the furthest verge   100
Of the green earth, to distant barbarous climes,
Rivers unknown to song; where first the sun
Gilds Indian mountains, or his setting beam
Flames on the Atlantic isles, 'tis nought to me;
Since God is ever present, ever felt,   105
In the void waste as in the city full;
And where He vital breathes, there must be joy.
When even at last the solemn hour shall come,
And wing my mystic flight to future worlds,
I cheerfully will obey; there with new powers,   110
Will rising wonders sing. I cannot go
Where Universal Love not smiles around,
Sustaining all yon orbs, and all their suns;
From seeming evil still educing good,
And better thence again, and better still,   115
In infinite progression. But I lose
Myself in Him, in light ineffable!
Come, then, expressive silence, muse His praise.

1730

FROM THE CASTLE OF INDOLENCE

O MORTAL man, who livest here by toil,
Do not complain of this thy hard estate:
That like an emmet thou must ever moil
Is a sad sentence of an ancient date;
And, certes, there is for it reason great,   5
For though sometimes it makes thee weep and
        wail,
And curse thy star, and early drudge and late,

Withouten that would come an heavier bale—
Loose life, unruly passions, and diseases pale.

In lowly dale, fast by a river's side,   10
With woody hill o'er hill encompassed round,
A most enchanting wizard did abide,
Than whom a fiend more fell is nowhere found.
It was, I ween, a lovely spot of ground;
And there a season atween June and May,   15
Half prankt with spring, with summer half im-
    browned,
A listless climate made, where, sooth to say,
No living wight could work, ne carèd even for play.

Was naught around but images of rest:
Sleep-soothing groves, and quiet lawns between;   20
And flowery beds that slumbrous influence kest,
From poppies breathed; and beds of pleasant
    green,
Where never yet was creeping creature seen.
Meantime unnumbered glittering streamlets
    played,
And hurlèd everywhere their waters sheen,   25
That, as they bickered through the sunny glade,
Though restless still themselves, a lulling murmur
    made.

Joined to the prattle of the purling rills,
Were heard the lowing herds along the vale,
And flocks loud-bleating from the distant hills, 30
And vacant shepherds piping in the dale;
And now and then sweet Philomel would wail,
Or stock doves 'plain amid the forest deep,
That drowsy rustled to the sighing gale;
And still a coil the grasshopper did keep: 35
Yet all these sounds, yblent, inclinèd all to sleep.

Full in the passage of the vale, above,
A sable, silent, solemn forest stood,
Where naught but shadowy forms was seen to
          move,
As Idless fancied in her dreaming mood;   40
And up the hills, on either side, a wood
Of blackening pines, aye waving to and fro,
Sent forth a sleepy horror through the blood;
And where this valley winded out, below,
The murmuring main was heard, and scarcely heard,
          to flow.   45

A pleasing land of drowsyhed it was:
Of dreams that wave before the half-shut eye;
And of gay castles in the clouds that pass,
Forever flushing round a summer sky.
There eke the soft delights, that witchingly   50
Instil a wanton sweetness through the breast,
And the calm pleasures, always hovered nigh;
But whate'er smacked of 'noyance or unrest
Was far, far off expelled from this delicious nest.

The landskip such, inspiring perfect ease,   55
Where Indolence (for so the wizard hight)
Close-hid his castle mid embowering trees,
That half shut out the beams of Phœbus bright,
And made a kind of checkered day and night.
Meanwhile, unceasing at the massy gate,   60
Beneath a spacious palm, the wicked wight
Was placed; and, to his lute, of cruel fate
And labor harsh complained, lamenting man's estate.

Thither continual pilgrims crowded still,
From all the roads of earth that pass there by;   65
For, as they chaunced to breathe on neighboring
          hill,
The freshness of this valley smote their eye,

And drew them ever and anon more nigh,
Till clustering round th' enchanter false they
    hung,
Ymolten with his syren melody,   70
While o'er th' enfeebling lute his hand he flung,
And to the trembling chords these tempting verses
    sung:

'Behold, ye pilgrims of this earth, behold!
See all but man with unearned pleasure gay!
See her bright robes the butterfly unfold,   75
Broke from her wintry tomb in prime of May.
What youthful bride can equal her array?
Who can with her for easy pleasure vie?
From mead to mead with gentle wing to stray,
From flower to flower on balmy gales to fly,   80
Is all she has to do beneath the radiant sky.

'Behold the merry minstrels of the morn,
The swarming songsters of the careless grove,
Ten thousand throats that, from the flowering
    thorn,
Hymn their good God and carol sweet of love,   85
Such grateful kindly raptures then emove!
They neither plough nor sow; ne, fit for flail,
E'er to the barn the nodding sheaves they drove;
Yet theirs each harvest dancing in the gale,
Whatever crowns the hill or smiles along the vale. 90

'Outcast of Nature, man! the wretched thrall
Of bitter-dropping sweat, of sweltry pain,
Of cares that eat away thy heart with gall,
And of the vices, an inhuman train,
That all proceed from savage thirst of gain: 95
For when hard-hearted Interest first began
To poison earth, Astræa left the plain;
Guile, violence, and murder seized on man,

And, for soft milky streams, with blood the rivers
     ran.'

    .   .   .   .

He ceased. But still their trembling ears retained 100
The deep vibrations of his 'witching song,
That, by a kind of magic power, constrained
To enter in, pell-mell, the listening throng:
Heaps poured on heaps, and yet they slipped along
In silent ease; as when beneath the beam   105
Of summer moons, the distant woods among,
Or by some flood all silvered with the gleam,
The soft-embodied fays through airy portal stream.

    .   .   .   .

Of all the gentle tenants of the place,
There was a man of special grave remark;   110
A certain tender gloom o'erspread his face,
Pensive, not sad; in thought involved, not dark;
As soote this man could sing as morning lark,
And teach the noblest morals of the heart;
But these his talents were yburied stark: 115
Of the fine stores he nothing would impart,
Which or boon Nature gave, or nature-painting
     Art.

To noontide shades incontinent he ran,
Where purls the brook with sleep-inviting sound,
Or when Dan Sol to slope his wheels began,   120
Amid the broom he basked him on the ground,
Where the wild thyme and camomil are found;
There would he linger, till the latest ray
Of light sate trembling on the welkin's bound,
Then homeward through the twilight shadows
     stray,   125

Sauntering and slow: so had he passèd many a
    day.

Yet not in thoughtless slumber were they passed;
For oft the heavenly fire, that lay concealed
Beneath the sleeping embers, mounted fast,
And all its native light anew revealed;   130
Oft as he traversed the cerulean field,
And marked the clouds that drove before the wind,
Ten thousand glorious systems would be build,
Ten thousand great ideas filled his mind:
But with the clouds they fled, and left no trace
    behind.   135

1748

JOHN DYER

GRONGAR HILL

Silent Nymph, with curious eye!
Who, the purple evening, lie
On the mountain's lonely van,
Beyond the noise of busy man;
Painting fair the form of things,   5
While the yellow linnet sings;
Or the tuneful nightingale
Charms the forest with her tale;
Come, with all thy various hues,
Come, and aid thy sister Muse;   10
Now while Phœbus riding high
Gives lustre to the land and sky!
Grongar Hill invites my song;
Draw the landscape bright and strong;
Grongar, in whose mossy cells   15
Sweetly musing Quiet dwells;
Grongar, in whose silent shade,
For the modest Muses made,

So oft I have, the evening still,
At the fountain of a rill,   20
Sate upon a flowery bed,
With my hand beneath my head;
While strayed my eyes o'er Towy's flood,
Over mead, and over wood,
From house to house, from hill to hill,   25
'Till Contemplation had her fill.

About his chequered sides I wind,
And leave his brooks and meads behind,
And groves, and grottoes where I lay,
And vistas shooting beams of day: 30
Wide and wider spreads the vale,
As circles on a smooth canal:
The mountains round—unhappy fate!
Sooner or later, of all height,
Withdraw their summits from the skies,   35
And lessen as the others rise:
Still the prospect wider spreads,
Adds a thousand woods and meads;
Still it widens, widens still,
And sinks the newly-risen hill.   40

Now I gain the mountain's brow,
What a landscape lies below!
No clouds, no vapors intervene,
But the gay, the open scene
Does the face of nature show,   45
In all the hues of heaven's bow!
And, swelling to embrace the light,
Spreads around beneath the sight.

Old castles on the cliffs arise,
Proudly towering in the skies!   50
Rushing from the woods, the spires
Seem from hence ascending fires!
Half his beams Apollo sheds
On the yellow mountain-heads!
Gilds the fleeces of the flocks,   55

And glitters on the broken rocks!
  Below me trees unnumbered rise,
Beautiful in various dyes:
The gloomy pine, the poplar blue,
The yellow beech, the sable yew,   60
The slender fir, that taper grows,
The sturdy oak with broad-spread boughs;
And beyond the purple grove,
Haunt of Phillis, queen of love!
Gaudy as the opening dawn,   65
Lies a long and level lawn
On which a dark hill, steep and high,
Holds and charms the wandering eye!
Deep are his feet in Towy's flood,
His sides are clothed with waving wood,   70
And ancient towers crown his brow,
That cast an awful look below;
Whose ragged walls the ivy creeps,
And with her arms from falling keeps;
So both a safety from the wind   75
On mutual dependence find.
  'Tis now the raven's bleak abode;
'Tis now th' apartment of the toad;
And there the fox securely feeds;
And there the poisonous adder breeds   80
Concealed in ruins, moss, and weeds;
While, ever and anon, there falls
Huge heaps of hoary moldered walls.
Yet time has seen, that lifts the low,
And level lays the lofty brow,   85
Has seen this broken pile complete,
Big with the vanity of state;
But transient is the smile of fate!
A little rule, a little sway,
A sunbeam in a winter's day,   90
Is all the proud and mighty have
Between the cradle and the grave.

And see the rivers how they run,
Through woods and meads, in shade and sun,
Sometimes swift, sometimes slow,   95
Wave succeeding wave, they go
A various journey to the deep,
Like human life to endless sleep!
Thus is nature's vesture wrought,
To instruct our wandering thought;   100
Thus she dresses green and gay,
To disperse our cares away.
   Ever charming, ever new,
When will the landscape tire the view!
The fountain's fall, the river's flow,   105
The woody valleys warm and low;
The windy summit, wild and high,
Roughly rushing on the sky;
The pleasant seat, the ruined tower,
The naked rock, the shady bower;   110
The town and village, dome and farm,
Each gives each a double charm,
As pearls upon an Æthiop's arm.
   See, on the mountain's southern side,
Where the prospect opens wide,   115
Where the evening gilds the tide;
How close and small the hedges lie!
What streaks of meadows cross the eye!
A step methinks may pass the stream,
So little distant dangers seem;   120
So we mistake the future's face,
Eyed through Hope's deluding glass;
As yon summits soft and fair
Clad in colors of the air,
Which to those who journey near,   125
Barren, brown, and rough appear;
Still we tread the same coarse way;
The present's still a cloudy day.
   O may I with myself agree,

And never covet what I see: 130
Content me with an humble shade,
My passions tamed, my wishes laid;
For while our wishes wildly roll,
We banish quiet from the soul:
'Tis thus the busy beat the air; 135
And misers gather wealth and care.

Now, even now, my joys run high,
As on the mountain-turf I lie;
While the wanton Zephyr sings,
And in the vale perfumes his wings; 140
While the waters murmur deep;
While the shepherd charms his sheep;
While the birds unbounded fly,
And with music fill the sky,
Now, even now, my joys run high. 145

Be full, ye courts, be great who will;
Search for Peace with all your skill:
Open wide the lofty door,
Seek her on the marble floor,
In vain ye search, she is not there; 150
In vain ye search the domes of Care!
Grass and flowers Quiet treads,
On the meads, and mountain-heads,
Along with Pleasure, close allied,
Ever by each other's side: 155
And often, by the murmuring rill,
Hears the thrush, while all is still,
Within the groves of Grongar Hill.

1726

GEORGE BERKELEY

VERSES ON THE PROSPECT OF PLANTING ARTS AND LEARNING IN AMERICA

THE Muse, disgusted at an age and clime
  Barren of every glorious theme,
In distant lands now waits a better time,
  Producing subjects worthy fame:

In happy climes where from the genial sun   5
  And virgin earth such scenes ensue,
The force of art in nature seems outdone,
  And fancied beauties by the true:

In happy climes, the seat of innocence,
  Where nature guides and virtue rules,   10
Where men shall not impose for truth and sense
  The pedantry of courts and schools.

There shall be sung another golden age,
  The rise of empire and of arts,
The good and great inspiring epic rage,   15
  The wisest heads and noblest hearts.

Not such as Europe breeds in her decay;
  Such as she bred when fresh and young,
When heavenly flame did animate her clay,
  By future poets shall be sung.   20

Westward the course of empire takes its way;
  The four first acts already past,
A fifth shall close the drama with the day;
  Time's noblest offspring is the last.

c.1726   1752

GEORGE LILLO

from GEORGE BARNWELL

[THE THEORY OF DOMESTIC TRAGEDY]

TRAGEDY is so far from losing its dignity, by
being accommodated to the circumstances of the
generality of mankind, that it is more truly august
in proportion to the extent of its influence, and the
numbers that are properly affected by it. As it is   5
more truly great to be the instrument of good to
many who stand in need of our assistance than to a
very small part of that number.

If princes, etc. were alone liable to misfortunes
arising from vice or weakness in themselves or   10
others, there would be good reason for confining the
characters in tragedy to those of superior rank; but
since the contrary is evident, nothing can be more
reasonable than to proportion the remedy to the
disease. . . .   15

Plays founded on moral tales in private life may
be of admirable use, by carrying conviction to the
mind with such irresistible force as to engage all
the faculties and powers of the soul in the cause of
virtue, by stifling vice in its first principles.   20

1731

[THE GOOD CHARACTER OF BARNWELL]

[George Barnwell is led astray, and becomes an embezzler
and a murderer; but his master Trueman and Trueman's
daughter still admire his virtues:]

Trueman: Never had youth a higher sense of
virtue: justly he thought, and as he thought he
practised; never was life more regular than his; an

understanding uncommon at his years—an open,
generous, manliness of temper—his manners easy, 5
unaffected and engaging.

   Maria: This and much more you might have said
with truth. He was the delight of every eye and
joy of every heart that knew him.

   .   .   .   .

   Maria: Trueman, do you think a soul so delicate 10
as his, so sensible of shame, can e'er submit to live
a slave to vice?

   Trueman: Never, never! So well I know him,
I'm sure this act of his, so contrary to his nature,
must have been caused by some unavoidable neces- 15
sity.

Acted, 1731

SOAME JENYNS

FROM AN ESSAY ON VIRTUE

WERE once these maxims fixed, that God's our
    friend,
Virtue our good, and happiness our end,
How soon must reason o'er the world prevail,
And error, fraud, and superstition fail!
None would hereafter then with groundless fear 5
Describe th' Almighty cruel and severe,
Predestinating some without pretence
To Heaven, and some to Hell for no offence;
Inflicting endless pains for transient crimes,
And favoring sects or nations, men or times. 10
To please him none would foolishly forbear
Or food, or rest, or itch in shirts of hair,
Or deem it merit to believe or teach
What reason contradicts, within its reach;
None would fierce zeal or piety mistake, 15
Or malice for whatever tenet's sake,

Or think salvation to one sect confined,
And Heaven too narrow to contain mankind.

.   .   .   .

No servile tenets would admittance find
Destructive of the rights of humankind;   20
Of power divine, hereditary right,
And non-resistance to a tyrant's might.
For sure that all should thus for one be cursed,
Is but great nature's edict just reversed.
No moralists then, righteous to excess,   25
Would show fair Virtue in so black a dress,
That they, like boys, who some feigned sprite array,
First from the spectre fly themselves away:
No preachers in the terrible delight,
But choose to win by reason, not affright;   30
Not, conjurors like, in fire and brimstone dwell,
And draw each moving argument from Hell.

.   .   .   .

No more applause would on ambition wait,
And laying waste the world be counted great,
But one good-natured act more praises gain,   35
Than armies overthrown, and thousands slain;
No more would brutal rage disturb our peace,
But envy, hatred, war, and discord cease;
Our own and others' good each hour employ,
And all things smile with universal joy;   40
Virtue with Happiness, her consort, joined,
Would regulate and bless each human mind,
And man be what his Maker first designed.

1734

HENRY BROOKE

HENRY BROOKE

FROM UNIVERSAL BEAUTY

[THE DEITY IN EVERY ATOM]

THUS beauty, mimicked in our humbler strains,
Illustrious through the world's great poem reigns!
The One grows sundry by creative power,
Th' eternal's found in each revolving hour;
Th' immense appears in every point of space,   5
Th' unchangeable in nature's varying face;
Th' invisible conspicuous to our mind,
And Deity in every atom shrined.

[NATURE SUPERIOR TO CIVILIZATION]

O NATURE, whom the song aspires to scan!
O Beauty, trod by proud insulting man,
This boasted tyrant of thy wondrous ball,
This mighty, haughty, little lord of all;
This king o'er reason, but this slave to sense,   5
Of wisdom careless, but of whim immense;
Towards thee incurious, ignorant, profane,
But of his own, dear, strange productions vain!
Then with this champion let the field be fought,
And nature's simplest arts 'gainst human wisdom
        brought.   10
Let elegance and bounty here unite—
There kings beneficent and courts polite;
Here   nature's   wealth—there   chemist's   golden
        dreams;
Her   texture   here—and   there   the   statesman's
        schemes;
Conspicuous here let sacred truth appear—   15
The courtier's word, and lordling's honor, there;

Here native sweets in boon profusion flow—
There smells that scented nothing of a beau;
Let justice here unequal combat wage—
Nor poise the judgment of the law-learned sage; 20
Though all-proportioned with exactest skill,
Yet gay as woman's wish, and various as her will.
  O say ye pitied, envied, wretched great,
Who veil pernicion with the mask of state!
Whence are those domes that reach the mocking
    skies, 25
And vainly emulous of nature rise?
Behold the swain projected o'er the vale!
See slumbering peace his rural eyelids seal;
Earth's flowery lap supports his vacant head,
Beneath his limbs her broidered garments spread; 30
Aloft her elegant pavilion bends,
And living shade of vegetation lends,
With ever propagated bounty blessed,
And hospitably spread for every guest:
No tinsel here adorns a tawdry woof, 35
Nor lying wash besmears a varnished roof;
With native mode the vivid colors shine,
And Heaven's own loom has wrought the weft
    divine,
Where art veils art, and beauties' beauties close,
While central grace diffused throughout the system
    flows. 40

[THE SPLENDOR OF INSECTS]

GEMMED o'er their heads the mines of India gleam,
And heaven's own wardrobe has arrayed their frame;
Each spangled back bright sprinkling specks adorn,
Each plume imbibes the rosy-tinctured morn;
Spread on each wing, the florid seasons glow, 5
Shaded and verged with the celestial bow,
Where colors blend an ever-varying dye,

And wanton in their gay exchanges vie.
Not all the glitter fops and fair ones prize,
The pride of fools, and pity of the wise;   10
Not all the show and mockery of state,
The little, low, fine follies of the great;
Not all the wealth which eastern pageants wore,
What still our idolizing worlds adore;
Can boast the least inimitable grace   15
Which decks profusive this illustrious race.

[MORAL LESSONS FROM ANIMAL LIFE]

YE SELF-SUFFICIENT sons of reasoning pride,
Too wise to take Omniscience for your guide,
Those rules from insects, birds, and brutes discern
Which from the Maker you disdain to learn!
The social friendship, and the firm ally,   5
The filial sanctitude, and nuptial tie,
Patience in want, and faith to persevere,
Th' endearing sentiment, and tender care,
Courage o'er private interest to prevail,
And die all Decii for the public weal.   10

[PROMPTINGS OF DIVINE INSTINCT]

DISPERSED through every copse or marshy plain,
Where hunts the woodcock or the annual crane,
Where else encamped the feathered legions spread
Or bathe incumbent on their oozy bed,
The brimming lake thy smiling presence fills,   5
And waves the banners of a thousand hills.
Thou speed'st the summons of thy warning voice:
Winged at thy word, the distant troops rejoice,
From every quarter scour the fields of air,
And to the general rendezvous repair;   10
Each from the mingled rout disporting turns,
And with the love of kindred plumage burns.

Thy potent will instinctive bosoms feel,
And here arranging semilunar, wheel;
Or marshalled here the painted rhomb display   15
Or point the wedge that cleaves th' aërial way:
Uplifted on thy wafting breath they rise;
Thou pav'st the regions of the pathless skies,
Through boundless tracts support'st the journeyed
       host
And point'st the voyage to the certain coast,—   20
Thou the sure compass and the sea they sail,
The chart, the port, the steerage, and the gale!

1735

PROLOGUE TO 'GUSTAVUS VASA'

BRITONS! this night presents a state distressed:
Though brave, yet vanquished; and though great,
       oppressed.
Vice, ravening vulture, on her vitals preyed;
Her peers, her prelates, fell corruption swayed:
Their rights, for power, the ambitious weakly sold: 5
The wealthy, poorly, for superfluous gold.
Hence wasting ills, hence severing factions rose,
And gave large entrance to invading foes:
Truth, justice, honor, fled th' infected shore;
For freedom, sacred freedom, was no more.   10
   Then, greatly rising in his country's right,
Her hero, her deliverer sprung to light:
A race of hardy northern sons he led,
Guiltless of courts, untainted, and unread;
Whose inborn spirit spurned th' ignoble fee,   15
Whose hands scorned bondage, for their hearts were
       free.
  Ask ye what law their conquering cause con-
       fessed?—
Great Nature's law, the law within the breast:
Formed by no art, and to no sect confined,

But stamped by Heaven upon th' unlettered mind.   20
    Such, such of old, the first born natives were
Who breathed the virtues of Britannia's air,
Their realm when mighty Cæsar vainly sought,
For mightier freedom against Cæsar fought,
And rudely drove the famed invader home,   25
To tyrannize o'er polished—venal Rome.
    Our bard, exalted in a freeborn flame,
To every nation would transfer this claim:
He to no state, no climate, bounds his page,
But bids the moral beam through every age.   30
Then be your judgment generous as his plan;
Ye sons of freedom! save the friend of man.

                                        1739

WILLIAM SHENSTONE

FROM THE SCHOOLMISTRESS

Her cap, far whiter than the driven snow,
Emblem right meet of decency does yield:
Her apron dyed in grain, as blue, I trow,
As is the harebell that adorns the field;
And in her hand, for sceptre, she does wield   5
Tway birchen sprays; with anxious fear entwined,
With dark distrust, and sad repentance filled;
And steadfast hate, and sharp affliction joined,
And fury uncontrolled, and chastisement unkind.

        .   .   .   .

A russet stole was o'er her shoulders thrown;   10
A russet kirtle fenced the nipping air;
'Twas simple russet, but it was her own;
'Twas her own country bred the flock so fair!
'Twas her own labor did the fleece prepare;
And, sooth to say, her pupils ranged around,   15
Through pious awe, did term it passing rare;
For they in gaping wonderment abound,

And think, no doubt, she been the greatest wight on
    ground.

. . . .

   Lo, now with state she utters the command!
   Eftsoons the urchins to their tasks repair;   20
   Their books of stature small they take in hand,
   Which with pellucid horn securèd are;
   To save from finger wet the letters fair:
   The work so gay, that on their back is seen,
   St. George's high achievements does declare;   25
   On which thilk wight that has y-gazing been
Kens the forth-coming rod, unpleasing sight, I ween!

   Ah, luckless he, and born beneath the beam
   Of evil star! it irks me whilst I write!
   As erst the bard by Mulla's silver stream,   30
   Oft, as he told of deadly dolorous plight,
   Sighed as he sung, and did in tears indite.
   For brandishing the rod, she doth begin
   To loose the brogues, the stripling's late delight!
   And down they drop; appears his dainty skin,   35
Fair as the furry coat of whitest ermilin.

   O ruthful scene! when from a nook obscure,
   His little sister doth his peril see:
   All playful as she sate, she grows demure;
   She finds full soon her wonted spirits flee;   40
   She meditates a prayer to set him free:
   Nor gentle pardon could this dame deny,
   (If gentle pardon could with dames agree)
   To her sad grief that swells in either eye,
And wrings her so that all for pity she could die.   45

. . . .

   The other tribe, aghast, with sore dismay,
   Attend, and conn their tasks with mickle care:
   By turns, astonied, every twig survey,
   And, from their fellow's hateful wounds, beware;

Knowing, I wist, how each the same may share; 50
Till fear has taught them a performance meet,
And to the well-known chest the dame repairs;
Whence oft with sugared cates she doth 'em greet,
And ginger-bread y-rare; now, certes, doubly sweet!

. . . .

Yet nursed with skill, what dazzling fruits appear! 55
Even now sagacious foresight points to show
A little bench of heedless bishops here,
And there a chancellor in embryo,
Or bard sublime. if bard may e'er be so,
As Milton, Shakspere, names that ne'er shall die! 60
Though now he crawl along the ground so low,
Nor weeting how the muse should soar on high.
Wisheth, poor starveling elf! his paper kite may fly.

1737

EDWARD YOUNG

from THE COMPLAINT, OR NIGHT THOUGHTS

[IN THE DARKNESS OF NIGHT]

Tired nature's sweet restorer, balmy Sleep!
He, like the world, his ready visit pays
Where Fortune's smiles; the wretched he forsakes,
Swift on his downy pinion flies from woe,
And lights on lids unsullied with a tear. 5
From short (as usual) and disturbed repose,
I wake: how happy they who wake no more!
Yet that were vain, if dreams infest the grave.
I wake, emerging from a sea of dreams
Tumultuous, where my wrecked, desponding thought 10

From wave to wave of fancied misery
At random drove, her helm of reason lost;
Though now restored, 'tis only change of pain,
A bitter change! severer for severe.
The day too short for my distress; and Night,   15
E'en in the zenith of her dark domain,
Is sunshine to the color of my fate.
   Night, sable goddess! from her ebon throne,
In rayless majesty, now stretches forth
Her leaden scepter o'er a slumbering world.   20
Silence how dead! and darkness how profound!
Nor eye nor listening ear an object finds:
Creation sleeps. 'Tis as the general pulse
Of life stood still, and Nature made a pause,
An awful pause, prophetic of her end.   25
And let her prophecy be soon fulfilled!
Fate, drop the curtain! I can lose no more.
   Silence and Darkness, solemn sisters, twins
From ancient Night, who nurse the tender thought
To reason, and on reason build resolve   30
(That column of true majesty in man),
Assist me! I will thank you in the grave,
The grave your kingdom; there this frame shall fall
A victim sacred to your dreary shrine.

1742

LIVE EVER HERE?

LIVE ever here, Lorenzo? Shocking thought!
So shocking, they who wish disown it, too;
Disown from shame what they from folly crave.
Live ever in the womb nor see the light?
For what live ever here? With laboring step   5
To tread our former footsteps? pace the round
Eternal? to climb life's worn, heavy wheel,
Which draws up nothing new? to beat, and beat
The beaten track? to bid each wretched day

The former mock? to surfeit on the same,   10
And yawn our joys? or thank a misery
For change, though sad? to see what we have seen;
Hear, till unheard, the same old slabbered tale?
To taste the tasted, and at each return
Less tasteful? o'er our palates to decant   15
Another vintage? strain a flatter year,
Through loaded vessels and a laxer tone?
Crazy machines, to grind earth's wasted fruits!

                                                        1743

WELCOME, DEATH!

THEN welcome, death! thy dreaded harbingers,
Age and disease; disease, though long my guest;
That plucks my nerves, those tender strings of life;
Which, plucked a little more, will toll the bell,
That calls my few friends to my funeral;   5
Where feeble nature drops, perhaps, a tear,
While reason and religion, better taught.
Congratulate the dead, and crown his tomb
With wreath triumphant. Death is victory;
It binds in chains the raging ills of life: 10
Lust and ambition, wrath and avarice,
Dragged at his chariot-wheel, applaud his power.
That ills corrosive, cares importunate,
Are not immortal too, O death! is thine.
Our day of dissolution!—name it right;   15
'Tis our great pay-day; 'tis our harvest, rich
And ripe: What though the sickle, sometimes keen,
Just scars us as we reap the golden grain?
More than thy balm, O Gilead! heals the wound.
Birth's feeble cry, and death's deep dismal groan,   20
Are slender tributes low-taxed nature pays
For mighty gain: the gain of each, a life!
But O! the last the former so transcends,
Life dies, compared: life lives beyond the grave.

And feel I, death! no joy from thought of thee,   25
Death, the great counsellor, who man inspires
With every nobler thought and fairer deed!
Death, the deliverer, who rescues man!
Death, the rewarder, who the rescued crowns!
Death, that absolves my birth; a curse without it!   30
Rich death, that realizes all my cares,
Toils, virtues, hopes; without it a chimera!
Death, of all pain the period, not of joy;
Joy's source, and subject, still subsist unhurt;
One, in my soul; and one, in her great sire;   35
Though the four winds were warring for my dust.
Yes, and from winds, and waves, and central night,
Though prisoned there, my dust too I reclaim,
(To dust when drop proud nature's proudest
    spheres,)
And live entire. Death is the crown of life: 40
Were death denied, poor man would live in vain;
Were death denied, to live would not be life;
Were death denied, e'en fools would wish to die.
Death wounds to cure: we fall; we rise; we reign!
Spring from our fetters; fasten in the skies;   45
Where blooming Eden withers in our sight:
Death gives us more than was in Eden lost.
This king of terrors is the prince of peace.
When shall I die to vanity, pain, death?
When shall I die?—When shall I live for ever?   50

1743

FROM CONJECTURES ON ORIGINAL COMPOSITION

BUT there are who write with vigor and success,
to the world's delight and their own renown. These
are the glorious fruits where genius prevails. The
mind of a man of genius is a fertile and pleasant
field, pleasant as Elysium, and fertile as Tempe; it   5

enjoys a perpetual spring. Of that spring, originals
are the fairest flowers; imitations are of quicker
growth, but fainter bloom. Imitations are of two
kinds; one of nature, one of authors: the first we
call Originals, and confine the term Imitation to the 10
second. I shall not enter into the curious inquiry
of what is, or is not, strictly speaking, original, content with what all must allow, that some compositions are more so than others; and the more they are
so, I say, the better. Originals are and ought to be 15
great favorites, for they are great benefactors; they
extend the republic of letters, and add a new province
to its dominion. Imitators only give us a sort of
duplicates of what we had, possibly much better,
before, increasing the mere drug of books, while all 20
that makes them valuable, knowledge and genius, are
at a stand. The pen of an original writer, like
Armida's wand, out of a barren waste calls a blooming spring. Out of that blooming spring, an imi-
tator is a transplanter of laurels, which sometimes 25
die on removal, [and] always languish in a foreign
soil. . . .

We read imitation with somewhat of his languor
who listens to a twice-told tale. Our spirits rouse at
an original that is a perfect stranger, and all throng 30
to learn what news from a foreign land. And though
it comes like an Indian prince, adorned with feathers
only, having little of weight, yet of our attention
it will rob the more solid, if not equally new. Thus
every telescope is lifted at a new-discovered star; 35
it makes a hundred astronomers in a moment, and
denies equal notice to the sun. But if an original,
by being as excellent as new, adds admiration to surprise, then are we at the writer's mercy; on the
strong wind of his imagination, we are snatched 40
from Britain to Italy, from climate to climate, from
pleasure to pleasure; we have no home, no thought,

of our own till the magician drops his pen. And then falling down into ourselves, we awake to flat realities, lamenting the change, like the beggar who dreamt himself a prince. . . .

But why are originals so few? Not because the writer's harvest is over, the great reapers of antiquity having left nothing to be gleaned after them; nor because the human mind's teeming time is past, or because it is incapable of putting forth unprecedented births; but because illustrious examples engross, prejudice, and intimidate. They engross our attention, and so prevent a due inspection of ourselves; they prejudice our judgment in favor of their abilities, and so lessen the sense of our own; and they intimidate us with the splendor of their renown, and thus under diffidence bury our strength. Nature's impossibilities and those of diffidence lie wide asunder. . . .

Had Milton never wrote, Pope had been less to blame. But when in Milton's genius, Homer, as it were, personally rose to forbid Britons doing him that ignoble wrong, it is less pardonable, by that effeminate decoration, to put Achilles in petticoats a second time. How much nobler had it been, if his numbers had rolled on in full flow, through the various modulations of masculine melody, into those grandeurs of solemn sound which are indispensably demanded by the native dignity of heroic song! How much nobler, if he had resisted the temptation of that Gothic demon, which modern poesy tasting, became mortal! O how unlike the deathless, divine harmony of three great names (how justly joined!) of Milton, Greece, and Rome! His verse, but for this little speck of mortality in its extreme parts, as his hero had in his heel, like him, had been invulnerable and immortal. But unfortunately, that was undipped in Helicon, as this in Styx. Harmony as

well as eloquence is essential to poesy; and a mur- 80
der of his music is putting half Homer to death.
Blank is a term of diminution; what we mean by
blank verse is verse unfallen, uncursed; verse re-
claimed, reënthroned in the true language of the
gods, who never thundered, nor suffered their Homer 85
to thunder, in rhyme. . . .

When such an ample area for renowned adventure in original attempts lies before us, shall we be
as mere leaden pipes, conveying to the present age
small streams of excellence from its grand reservoir 90
in antiquity, and those too, perhaps, mudded in the
pass? Originals shine like comets; have no peer
in their path; are rivaled by none, and the gaze of
all. All other compositions (if they shine at all)
shine in clusters, like the stars in the galaxy, where, 95
like bad neighbors, all suffer from all, each particular being diminished and almost lost in the
throng.

If thoughts of this nature prevailed, if ancients
and moderns were no longer considered as masters 100
and pupils, but as hard-matched rivals for renown,
then moderns, by the longevity of their labors, might
one day become ancients themselves. And old time,
that best weigher of merits, to keep his balance
even, might have the golden weight of an Augustan 105
age in both his scales; or rather our scale might descend, and that of antiquity (as a modern match for
it strongly speaks) might kick the beam.

1759   1759

ROBERT BLAIR

from THE GRAVE

SEE yonder hallowed fane;—the pious work
Of names once famed, now dubious or forgot,

And buried midst the wreck of things which were;
There lie interred the more illustrious dead.
The wind is up: hark! how it howls! Methinks 5
Till now I never heard a sound so dreary:
Doors creak, and windows clap, and night's foul
      bird,
Rooked in the spire, screams loud: the gloomy aisles,
Black-plastered, and hung round with shreds of
      'scutcheons
And tattered coats of arms, send back the sound 10
Laden with heavier airs, from the low vaults,
The mansions of the dead.—Roused from their
      slumbers,
In grim array the grisly spectres rise,
Grin horrible, and, obstinately sullen,
Pass and repass, hushed as the foot of night. 15
Again the screech-owl shrieks: ungracious sound!
I'll hear no more; it makes one's blood run chill.

     .   .   .   .   .

Oft in the lone churchyard at night I've seen,
By glimpse of moonshine chequering through the
      trees,
The school-boy, with his satchel in his hand, 20
Whistling aloud to bear his courage up,
And lightly tripping o'er the long flat stones,
(With nettles skirted, and with moss o'ergrown,)
That tell in homely phrase who lie below.
Sudden he starts, and hears, or thinks he hears, 25
The sound of something purring at his heels;
Full fast he flies, and dares not look behind him,
Till out of breath he overtakes his fellows;
Who gather round, and wonder at the tale
Of horrid apparition, tall and ghastly, 30
That walks at dead of night, or takes his stand
O'er some new-opened grave; and (strange to tell!)
Evanishes at crowing of the cock.

The new-made widow, too, I've sometimes spied,
Sad sight! slow moving o'er the prostrate dead: 35
Listless, she crawls along in doleful black,
Whilst bursts of sorrow gush from either eye,
Fast falling down her now untasted cheek:
Prone on the lowly grave of the dear man
She drops; whilst busy, meddling memory,   40
In barbarous succession musters up
The past endearments of their softer hours,
Tenacious of its theme.   Still, still she thinks
She sees him, and indulging the fond thought,
Clings yet more closely to the senseless turf,   45
Nor heeds the passenger who looks that way.

. . . .

When the dread trumpet sounds, the slumbering
        dust,
Not unattentive to the call, shall wake,
And every joint possess its proper place
With a new elegance of form unknown   50
To its first state.   Nor shall the conscious soul
Mistake its partner, but, amidst the crowd
Singling its other half, into its arms
Shall rush with all the impatience of a man
That's new come home, who having long been absent 55
With haste runs over every different room
In pain to see the whole.   Thrice happy meeting!
Nor time nor death shall part them ever more.
'Tis but a night, a long and moonless night,
We make the grave our bed, and then are gone.   60

Thus at the shut of even the weary bird
Leaves the wide air and, in some lonely brake,
Cowers down and dozes till the dawn of day,
Then claps his full-fledged wings and bears away.

1743

WILLIAM WHITEHEAD

from ON RIDICULE

Our mirthful age, to all extremes a prey,
Even courts the lash, and laughs her pains away,
Declining worth imperial wit supplies,
And Momus triumphs, while Astræa flies.
No truth so sacred, banter cannot hit,   5
No fool so stupid but he aims at wit.
Even those whose breasts ne'er planned one virtuous
          deed,
Nor raised a thought beyond the earth they tread:
Even those can censure, those can dare deride
A Bacon's avarice, or a Tully's pride   10
And sneer at human checks by Nature given.
To curb perfection e'er it rival Heaven:
Nay, chiefly such in these low arts prevail,
Whose want of talents leaves them time to rail.
Born for no end, they worse than useless grow,   15
(As waters poison, if they cease to flow;)
And pests become, whom kinder fate designed
But harmless expletives of human kind.
See with what zeal th' insidious task they ply!
Where shall the prudent, where the virtuous fly?   20
Lurk as ye can, if they direct the ray,
The veriest atoms in the sunbeams play.
No venial slip their quick attention 'scapes;
They trace each Proteus through his hundred
          shapes;
To Mirth's tribunal drag the caitiff train,   25
Where Mercy sleeps, and Nature pleads in vain.

          .   .   .   .

Here then we fix, and lash without control
These mental pests, and hydras of the soul

Acquired ill-nature, ever prompt debate,
A zeal for slander, and deliberate hate: 30
These court contempt, proclaim the public foe,
And each, Ulysses like, should aim the blow.
    Yet sure, even here, our motives should be known:
Rail we to check his spleen, or ease our own?

Does injured virtue every shaft supply,   35
Arm the keen tongue, and flush th' erected eye?
Or do we from ourselves ourselves disguise?
And act, perhaps, the villain we chastise?
Hope we to mend him? hopes, alas, how vain!
He feels the lash, not listens to the rein.   40
    'Tis dangerous too, in these licentious times,
Howe'er severe the smile, to sport with crimes.
Vices when ridiculed, experience says,
First lose that horror which they ought to raise,
Grow by degrees approved, and almost aim at   45
      praise.

   .   .   .   .

[The] fear of man, in his most mirthful mood,
May make us hypocrites, but seldom good.

   .   .   .   .

Besides, in men have varying passions made
Such nice confusions, blending light with shade,
That eager zeal to laugh the vice away   50
May hurt some virtue's intermingling ray.

   .   .   .   .

Then let good-nature every charm exert,
And while it mends it, win th' unfolding heart.
Let moral mirth a face of triumph wear,
Yet smile unconscious of th' extorted tear.   55
See with what grace instructive satire flows,
Politely keen, in Clio's numbered prose!
That great example should our zeal excite,
And censors learn from Addison to write.
So, in our age, too prone to sport with pain,   60

Might soft humanity resume her reign;
Pride without rancor feel th' objected fault,
And folly blush, as willing to be taught;
Critics grow mild, life's witty warfare cease,
And true good-nature breathe the balm of peace.   65

1743

THE ENTHUSIAST

ONCE—I remember well the day,
'Twas ere the blooming sweets of May
    Had lost their freshest hues,
When every flower on every hill,
In every vale, had drank its fill   5
    Of sunshine and of dews.

In short, 'twas that sweet season's prime
When Spring gives up the reins of time
    To Summer's glowing hand,
And doubting mortals hardly know   10
By whose command the breezes blow
    Which fan the smiling land.

'Twas then, beside a greenwood shade
Which clothed a lawn's aspiring head,
    I urged my devious way,   15
With loitering steps regardless where,
So soft, so genial was the air,
    So wondrous bright the day.

And now my eyes with transport rove
O'er all the blue expanse above,   20
    Unbroken by a cloud!
And now beneath delighted pass,
Where winding through the deep-green grass
    A full-brimmed river flowed.

I stop, I gaze; in accents rude,   25
To thee, serenest Solitude,
    Bursts forth th' unbidden lay;
'Begone vile world! the learned, the wise,
The great, the busy, I despise,
    And pity even the gay.   30

'These, these are joys alone, I cry,
'Tis here, divine Philosophy,
    Thou deign'st to fix thy throne!
Here contemplation points the road
Through nature's charms to nature's God!   35
    These, these are joys alone!

'Adieu, ye vain low-thoughted cares,
Ye human hopes, and human fears,
    Ye pleasures and ye pains!'
While thus I spake, o'er all my soul   40
A philosophic calmness stole,
    A stoic stillness reigns.

The tyrant passions all subside,
Fear, anger, pity, shame, and pride,
    No more my bosom move;   45
Yet still I felt, or seemed to feel
A kind of visionary zeal
    Of universal love.

When lo! a voice, a voice I hear!
'Twas Reason whispered in my ear   50
    These monitory strains:
'What mean'st thou, man? wouldst thou unbind
The ties which constitute thy kind,
    The pleasures and the pains?

'The same Almighty Power unseen,   55
Who spreads the gay or solemn scene

To contemplation's eye,
Fixed every movement of the soul,
Taught every wish its destined goal,
    And quickened every joy.   60

'He bids the tyrant passions rage,
He bids them war eternal wage,
    And combat each his foe:
Till from dissensions concords rise,
And beauties from deformities,   65
    And happiness from woe.

'Art thou not man, and dar'st thou find
A bliss which leans not to mankind?
    Presumptuous thought and vain
Each bliss unshared is unenjoyed,   70
Each power is weak unless employed
    Some social good to gain.

'Shall light and shade, and warmth and air,
With those exalted joys compare
    Which active virtue feels,   75
When on she drags, as lawful prize,
Contempt, and Indolence, and Vice,
    At her triumphant wheels?

'As rest to labor still succeeds,
To man, whilst virtue's glorious deeds   80
    Employ his toilsome day,
This fair variety of things
Are merely life's refreshing springs,
    To sooth him on his way.

'Enthusiast go, unstring thy lyre,   85
In vain thou sing'st if none admire,
    How sweet soe'er the strain.
And is not thy o'erflowing mind,

.Unless thou mixest with thy kind,
    Benevolent in vain?   90

  'Enthusiast go, try every sense,
If not thy bliss, thy excellence,
    Thou yet hast learned to scan;
At least thy wants, thy weakness know,
And see them all uniting show   95
    That man was made for man.'

                            1754

MARK AKENSIDE

FROM THE PLEASURES OF IMAGINATION

[THE ÆSTHETIC AND MORAL INFLUENCE OF NATURE]

          FRUITLESS is the attempt,
By dull obedience and by creeping toil
Obscure, to conquer the severe ascent
Of high Parnassus. Nature's kindling breath
Must fire the chosen genius; Nature's hand   5
Must string his nerves, and imp his eagle-wings,
Impatient of the painful steep, to soar
High as the summit, there to breathe at large
Ethereal air, with bards and sages old,
Immortal sons of praise.   10

  .   .   .   .
      Even so did Nature's hand
To certain species of external things
Attune the finer organs of the mind:
So the glad impulse of congenial powers,
Or of sweet sounds, or fair-proportioned form,   15
The grace of motion, or the bloom of light,
Thrills through imagination's tender frame,
From nerve to nerve; all naked and alive

They catch the spreading rays, till now the soul
At length discloses every tuneful spring,   20
To that harmonious movement from without
Responsive.

            .   .   .   .   .   .

What then is taste, but these internal powers
Active, and strong, and feelingly alive
To each fine impulse? a discerning sense   25
Of decent and sublime, with quick disgust
From things deformed, or disarranged, or gross
In species? This, nor gems, nor stores of gold,
Nor purple state, nor culture can bestow;
But God alone, when first his active hand   30
Imprints the secret bias of the soul.
He, mighty parent wise and just in all,
Free as the vital breeze or light of heaven,
Reveals the charms of nature. Ask the swain
Who journeys homeward from a summer day's   35
Long labor, why, forgetful of his toils
And due repose, he loiters to behold
The sunshine gleaming as through amber clouds
O'er all the western sky; full soon, I ween,
His rude expression and untutored airs,   40
Beyond the power of language, will unfold
The form of beauty smiling at his heart—
How lovely! how commanding!

            .   .   .   .

Oh! blest of Heaven, whom not the languid songs
Of Luxury, the siren! nor the bribes   45
Of sordid Wealth, nor all the gaudy spoils
Of pageant Honor, can seduce to leave
Those ever-blooming sweets which, from the store
Of Nature, fair Imagination culls
To charm th' enlivened soul! What though not all   50
Of mortal offspring can attain the heights
Of envied life, though only few possess
Patrician treasures or imperial state;

Yet Nature's care, to all her children just,
With richer treasure and an ampler state,   55
Endows at large whatever happy man
Will deign to use them. His the city's pomp;
The rural honors his. Whate'er adorns
The princely dome, the column and the arch,
The breathing marbles and the sculptured gold,   60
Beyond the proud possessor's narrow claim,
His tuneful breast enjoys. For him the Spring
Distils her dews, and from the silken gem
Its lucid leaves unfolds; for him the hand
Of Autumn tinges every fertile branch   65
With blooming gold, and blushes like the morn.
Each passing hour sheds tribute from her wings;
And still new beauties meet his lonely walk,
And loves unfelt attract him. Not a breeze
Flies o'er the meadow, not a cloud imbibes   70
The setting sun's effulgence, not a strain
From all the tenants of the warbling shade
Ascends, but whence his bosom can partake
Fresh pleasure unreproved. Nor thence partakes
Fresh pleasure only; for th' attentive mind,   75
By this harmonious action on her powers,
Becomes herself harmonious: wont so oft
In outward things to meditate the charm
Of sacred order, soon she seeks at home
To find a kindred order, to exert   80
Within herself this elegance of love,
This fair-inspired delight; her tempered powers
Refine at length, and every passion wears
A chaster, milder, more attractive mien.
   But if to ampler prospects, if to gaze   85
On Nature's form where, negligent of all
These lesser graces, she assumes the part
Of that Eternal Majesty that weighed
The world's foundations, if to these the mind
Exalts her daring eye; then mightier far   90

Will be the change, and nobler. Would the forms
Of servile custom cramp her generous powers?
Would sordid policies, the barbarous growth
Of ignorance and rapine, bow her down
To tame pursuits, to indolence and fear?   95
Lo! she appeals to Nature, to the winds
And rolling waves, the sun's unwearied course,
The elements and seasons: all declare
For what th' Eternal Maker has ordained
The powers of man: we feel within ourselves   100
His energy divine: he tells the heart
He meant, he made us, to behold and love
What he beholds and loves, the general orb
Of life and being; to be great like him,
Beneficent and active.   Thus the men   105
Whom nature's works can charm, with God himself
Hold converse; grow familiar, day by day,
With his conceptions; act upon his plan;
And form to his, the relish of their souls.

1744

JOSEPH WARTON

from THE ENTHUSIAST; OR, THE LOVER OF NATURE

Ye green-robed Dryads, oft at dusky eve
By wondering shepherds seen, to forests brown
To unfrequented meads, and pathless wilds,
Lead me from gardens decked with art's vain pomps.
Can gilt alcoves, can marble-mimic gods,   5
Parterres embroidered, obelisks, and urns
Of high relief; can the long, spreading lake,
Or vista lessening to the sight; can Stow,
With all her Attic fanes, such raptures raise,
As the thrush-haunted copse, where lightly leaps   10
The fearful fawn the rustling leaves along,

And the brisk squirrel sports from bough to bough,
While from an hollow oak, whose naked roots
O'erhang a pensive rill, the busy bees
Hum drowsy lullabies? The bards of old,   15
Fair Nature's friends, sought such retreats, to charm
Sweet Echo with their songs; oft too they met
In summer evenings, near sequestered bowers,
Or mountain nymph, or Muse, and eager learnt
The moral strains she taught to mend mankind.   20

. . . .

Rich in her weeping country's spoils, Versailles
May boast a thousand fountains, that can cast
The tortured waters to the distant heavens:
Yet let me choose some pine-topped precipice
Abrupt and shaggy, whence a foamy stream,   25
Like Anio, tumbling roars; or some bleak heath,
Where straggling stands the mournful juniper,
Or yew-tree scathed; while in clear prospect round
From the grove's bosom spires emerge, and smoke
In bluish wreaths ascends, ripe harvests wave,   30
Low, lonely cottages, and ruined tops
Of Gothic battlements appear, and streams
Beneath the sunbeams twinkle.

. . . .

Happy the first of men, ere yet confined
To smoky cities; who in sheltering groves,   35
Warm caves, and deep-sunk valleys lived and loved,
By cares unwounded; what the sun and showers,
And genial earth untillaged, could produce,
They gathered grateful, or the acorn brown
Or blushing berry; by the liquid lapse   40
Of murmuring waters called to slake their thirst,
Or with fair nymphs their sun-brown limbs to
        bathe;
With nymphs who fondly clasped their favorite
        youths,
Unawed by shame, beneath the beechen shade,

Nor wiles nor artificial coyness knew.   45
Then doors and walls were not; the melting maid
Nor frown of parents feared, nor husband's threats;
Nor had cursed gold their tender hearts allured:
Then beauty was not venal. Injured Love,
Oh! whither, god of raptures, art thou fled?   50

    .   .   .   .

What are the lays of artful Addison,
Coldly correct, to Shakspere's warblings wild?
Whom on the winding Avon's willowed banks
Fair Fancy found, and bore the smiling babe
To a close cavern (still the shepherds show   55
The sacred place, whence with religious awe
They hear, returning from the field at eve,
Strange whisperings of sweet music through the
          air).
Here, as with honey gathered from the rock,
She fed the little prattler, and with songs   60
Oft soothed his wondering ears; with deep delight
On her soft lap he sat, and caught the sounds.
    Oft near some crowded city would I walk,
Listening the far-off noises, rattling cars,
Loud shouts of joy, sad shrieks of sorrow, knells   65
Full slowly tolling, instruments of trade,
Striking mine ears with one deep-swelling hum.
Or wandering near the sea, attend the sounds
Of hollow winds and ever-beating waves.
Even when wild tempests swallow up the plains,   70
And Boreas' blasts, big hail, and rains combine
To shake the groves and mountains, would I sit,
Pensively musing on the outrageous crimes
That wake Heaven's vengeance: at such solemn
          hours,
Demons and goblins through the dark air shriek,   75
While Hecat, with her black-browed sisters nine,
Rides o'er the Earth, and scatters woes and death.
Then, too, they say, in drear Egyptian wilds

The lion and the tiger prowl for prey
With roarings loud! The listening traveller   80
Starts fear-struck, while the hollow echoing vaults
Of pyramids increase the deathful sounds.
    But let me never fail in cloudless nights,
When silent Cynthia in her silver car
Through the blue concave slides, when shine the
    hills,   85
Twinkle the streams, and woods look tipped with
    gold,
To seek some level mead, and there invoke
Old Midnight's sister, Contemplation sage,
(Queen of the rugged brow and stern-fixed eye,)
To lift my soul above this little earth,   90
This folly-fettered world: to purge my ears,
That I may hear the rolling planet's song,
And tuneful turning spheres: if this be barred
The little fays, that dance in neighboring dales,
Sipping the night-dew, while they laugh and love,   95
Shall charm me with aërial notes.—As thus
I wander musing, lo, what awful forms
Yonder appear! sharp-eyed Philosophy
Clad in dun robes, an eagle on his wrist,
First meets my eye; next, virgin Solitude   100
Serene, who blushes at each gazer's sight;
Then Wisdom's hoary head, with crutch in hand,
Trembling, and bent with age; last Virtue's self,
Smiling, in white arrayed, who with her leads
Sweet Innocence, that prattles by her side,   105
A naked boy!—Harassed with fear I stop,
I gaze, when Virtue thus—'Whoe'er thou art,
Mortal, by whom I deign to be beheld
In these my midnight walks; depart, and say,
That henceforth I and my immortal train   110
Forsake Britannia's isle; who fondly stoops
To vice, her favorite paramour.' She spoke,
And as she turned, her round and rosy neck,

Her flowing train, and long ambrosial hair,
Breathing rich odors, I enamored view.   115
   O who will bear me then to western climes,
Since virtue leaves our wretched land, to fields
Yet unpolluted with Iberian swords,
The isles of innocence, from mortal view
Deeply retired, beneath a plantain's shade,   120
Where happiness and quiet sit enthroned,
With simple Indian swains, that I may hunt
The boar and tiger through savannahs wild,
Through fragrant deserts and through citron groves?
There fed on dates and herbs, would I despise   125
The far-fetched cates of luxury, and hoards
Of narrow-hearted avarice; nor heed
The distant din of the tumultuous world.

                                                  1744

FROM AN ESSAY ON THE GENIUS AND
WRITINGS OF POPE

To the Rev. Dr. Young:
   . . . I revere the memory of Pope, I respect and
honor his abilities but I do not think him at the
head of his profession. In other words, in that
species of poetry wherein Pope excelled, he is superior to all mankind, and I only say that this species   5
of poetry is not the most excellent one of the art.
   We do not, it should seem, sufficiently attend to
the difference there is betwixt a *man of wit, a man of
sense,* and a *true poet.* Donne and Swift were undoubtedly men of wit and men of sense, but what   10
traces have they left of *pure poetry?* It is remarkable that Dryden says of Donne, "He was the greatest
wit though not the greatest poet of this nation."
Fontenelle and La Motte are entitled to the former
character but what can they urge to gain the lat-   15
ter? Which of these characters is the most valu-

able and useful is entirely out of the question; all I
plead for is to have their several provinces kept
distinct from each other and to impress on the reader
that a clear head and acute understanding are not 20
sufficient alone to make a *poet,* that the most solid
observations on human life expressed with the utmost elegance and brevity are *morality,* and not
poetry, that the *Epistles* of Boileau in *rhyme* are no
more poetical than the *Characters* of La Bruyère 25
in *prose,* and that it is a creative and glowing
Imagination, "acer spiritus ac vis," and that alone
that can stamp a writer with this exalted and very
uncommon character which so few possess and of
which so few can properly judge. 30

For one person who can adequately relish and
enjoy a work of imagination, twenty are to be found
who can taste and judge of observations on familiar life and the manners of the age. *The Satires*
of Ariosto are more read than the *Orlando Furioso* 35
or even Dante. Are there so many cordial admirers
of Spenser and Milton, as of Hudibras if we strike
out of the number of these supposed admirers those
who appear such out of fashion and not of feeling?
Swift's *Rhapsody on Poetry* is far more popular than 40
Akenside's noble *Ode to Lord Huntingdon.* The
Epistles on the Characters of Men and Women and
your sprightly Satires, my good friend, are more
frequently perused and quoted than *L'Allegro* and
Il Penseroso of Milton. Had you written only 45
these Satires, you would, indeed, have gained the
title of a man of wit, and a man of sense, but, I am
confident would not insist on being denominated a
poet merely on their account.

"Non satis est puris versum prescribere verbis." 50

It is amazing this matter should ever have been
mistaken when Horace has taken particular and

repeated pains to settle and adjust the opinion in question. He has more than once disclaimed all right and title to the name of *poet* on the score of his ethic and satiric pieces.

"—Neque enim concludere versum
   Dixeris esse satis ——"

are lines often repeated but whose meaning is not extended and weighed as it ought to be. Nothing can be more judicious than the method he prescribes, of trying whether any composition be essentially poetical or not; which is to drop entirely the measures and numbers and transpose and invert the order of the words; and in this unadorned manner to peruse the passage. If there be really in it a true poetical spirit all your inversions and transpositions will not disguise and extinguish it, but it will retain its luster like a diamond unset and thrown back into the rubbish of the mine. Let us make a little experiment on the following well-known lines, "Yes, you despise the man that is confined to books, who rails at humankind from his study, though what he learns, he speaks, and may perhaps advance some general maxims or may be right by chance. The coxcomb bird, so grave and so talkative that cries, "whore, knave, and cuckold," from his cage, though he rightly call many a passenger, you hold him no philosopher. And yet, such is the fate of all extremes, men may be read too much, as well as books. We grow more partial for the sake of the observer to observations which we ourselves make, less so to written wisdom because another's. Maxims are drawn from notions, and those from guess." What shall we say of this passage? Why, that it is most excellent sense, but just as poetical as the "qui fit Maecenas" of the author who recommends this method of trial. Take ten lines of the *Iliad, Paradise*

Lost or even of the *Georgics* of Virgil and see
whether by any process of critical chemistry you   90
can lower and reduce them to the tameness of prose.
You will find that they will appear like Ulysses in
his disguise of rags, still a hero, though lodged in the
cottage of the herdsman Eumaeus.

The sublime and the pathetic are the two chief   95
nerves of all genuine poesy. What is there trans-
cendently sublime or pathetic in Pope? In his works
there is, indeed, "nihil inane, nihil arcessitum; puro
tamen fonti quam magno flumini proprior," as the
excellent Quintilian remarks of Lysias. And because   100
I am, perhaps, unwilling to speak out in plain English, I will adopt the following passage of Voltaire,
which in my opinion, as exactly characterizes Pope
as it does his model Boileau, for whom it was
originally designed, "Incapable peut-être du sublime   105
qui élève l'ame, et du Sentiment qui l'attendrit,
mais fait pour éclairer ceux à qui la nature accorda
l'un et l'autre, laborieux, sévère, précis, pur, har-
mónieux, il devint, enfin, le poète de la Raison."

Our English poets may, I think, be disposed in   110
four different classes and degrees. In the first class
I would place our only three sublime and pathetic
poets, Spenser, Shakspere, Milton. In the second
class should be ranked such as possessed the true
poetical genius in a more moderate degree, but who   115
had noble talents for moral, ethical and panegyrical
poesy. At the head of these are Dryden, Prior,
Addison, Cowley, Waller, Garth, Fenton, Gay, Den-
ham, Parnell. In the third class may be placed men
of wit, of elegant taste and lively fancy in describ-   120
ing familiar life, though not the higher scenes of
poetry. Here may be numbered Butler, Swift,
Rochester, Donne, Dorset, Oldham. In the fourth
class the mere versifiers, however smooth and mellif-
luous some of them may be thought, should be   125

disposed. Such as Pitt, Sandys, Fairfax, Broome, Buckingham, Landsdown. This enumeration is not intended as a complete catalogue of writers and in their proper order but only to mark out briefly the different species of our celebrated authors. In which 130 of these classes Pope deserves to be placed the following work is intended to determine.

. . . .

Thus have I endeavored to give a critical account, with freedom, but it is hoped with impartiality, of each of Pope's works; by which review it will appear, 135 that the largest portion of them is of the didactic, moral, and satyric kind; and consequently, not of the most poetic species of poetry; whence it is manifest, that good sense and judgment were his characteristical excellencies, rather than fancy and inven- 140 tion: not that the author of *The Rape of the Lock,* and *Eloisa,* can be thought to want imagination; but because his imagination was not his predominant talent, because he indulged it not, and because he gave not so many proofs of this talent as of the 145 other. This turn of mind led him to admire French models; he studied Boileau attentively; formed himself upon him, as Milton formed himself upon the Grecian and Italian sons of Fancy. He stuck to describing modern manners; but those manners, be- 150 cause they are familiar, uniform, artificial, and polished, are, in their very nature, unfit for any lofty effort of the Muse. He gradually became one of the most correct, even, and exact poets that ever wrote; polishing his pieces with a care and assiduity, that 155 no business or avocation ever interrupted; so that if he does not frequently ravish and transport his reader, yet he does not disgust him with unexpected inequalities, and absurd improprieties. Whatever poetical enthusiasm he actually possessed, he with- 160 held and stifled. The perusal of him affects not our

minds with such strong emotions as we feel from
Homer and Milton; so that no man of a true poetical spirit, is master of himself while he reads them.
Hence, he is a writer fit for universal perusal; 165
adapted to all ages and stations; for the old and for
the young; the man of business and the scholar. He
who would think *The Fairy Queen, Palamon and
Arcite, The Tempest,* or *Comus,* childish and romantic, might relish Pope. Surely, it is no narrow 17?
and niggardly encomium, to say he is the great Poet
of Reason, the first of ethical authors in verse. And
this species of writing is, after all, the surest road
to an extensive reputation. It lies more level to the
general capacities of men, than the higher flights of 175
more genuine poetry. We all remember when even
a Churchill was more in vogue than a Gray. He that
treats of fashionable follies and the topics of the day,
that describes present persons and recent events, finds
many readers, whose understandings and whose pas- 180
sions he gratifies. The name of Chesterfield on one
hand, and of Walpole on the other, failed not to
make a poem bought up and talked of. And it
cannot be doubted that the *Odes* of Horace which
celebrated, and the *Satires* which ridiculed, well- 185
known and real characters at Rome, were more
eagerly read and more frequently cited, than the
Æneid and the *Georgics* of Virgil.

Where then, according to the question proposed
at the beginning of this Essay, shall we with justice 190
be authorized to place our admired Pope? Not, as-
suredly, in the same rank with Spenser, Shakspere,
and Milton; however justly we may applaud the
Eloisa and *Rape of the Lock;* but, considering the
correctness, elegance, and utility of his works, the 195
weight of sentiment, and the knowledge of man they
contain, we may venture to assign him a place, next

to Milton, and just above Dryden. Yet, to bring
our minds steadily to make this decision, we must
forget, for a moment, the divine *Music Ode* of Dry- 200
den; and may, perhaps, then be compelled to confess,
that though Dryden be the greater genius, yet Pope
is the better artist.

The preference here given to Pope above other
modern English poets, it must be remembered, is 205
founded on the excellencies of his works in general,
and taken all together; for there are parts and passages in other modern authors, in Young and in
Thomson, for instance, equal to any of Pope; and
he has written nothing in a strain so truly sublime, 210
as *The Bard* of Gray.

1756

WILLIAM COLLINS

A SONG FROM SHAKSPERE'S CYMBELINE

Sung by Guiderus and Arviragus over Fidele, supposed to
be dead.

To FAIR Fidele's grassy tomb
   Soft maids and village hinds shall bring
Each opening sweet, of earliest bloom,
   And rifle all the breathing spring.

No wailing ghost shall dare appear,   5
   To vex with shrieks this quiet grove:
But shepherd lads assemble here,
   And melting virgins own their love.

No withered witch shall here be seen,
   No goblins lead their nightly crew: 10

The female fays shall haunt the green,
   And dress thy grave with pearly dew.

The redbreast oft at evening hours
   Shall kindly lend his little aid,
With hoary moss, and gathered flowers,   15
   To deck the ground where thou art laid.

When howling winds, and beating rain,
   In tempests shake the sylvan cell,
Or midst the chace on every plain,
   The tender thought on thee shall dwell.   20

Each lonely scene shall thee restore,
   For thee the tear be duly shed:
Beloved, till life could charm no more;
   And mourned, till Pity's self be dead.

                       1744

ODE

WRITTEN IN THE BEGINNING OF THE YEAR 1746

How sleep the brave who sink to rest
By all their country's wishes blest!
When Spring, with dewy fingers cold,
Returns to deck their hallowed mould,
She there shall dress a sweeter sod   5
Than Fancy's feet have ever trod.

By fairy hands their knell is rung,
By forms unseen their dirge is sung;
There Honor comes, a pilgrim grey,
To bless the turf that wraps their clay;   10
And Freedom shall awhile repair,
To dwell a weeping hermit there!

                       1746

ODE TO EVENING

If AUGHT of oaten stop or pastoral song
May hope, chaste Eve, to soothe thy modest ear,
    Like thy own solemn springs,
    Thy springs and dying gales,

O nymph reserved, while now the bright-haired sun   5
Sits in yon western tent, whose cloudy skirts,
    With brede ethereal wove,
    O'erhang his wavy bed:

Now air is hushed, save where the weak-eyed bat,
With short, shrill shriek, flits by on leathern wing;   10
    Or where the beetle winds
    His small but sullen horn,

As oft he rises 'midst the twilight path,
Against the pilgrim borne in heedless hum:
    Now teach me, maid composed,   15
    To breathe some softened strain,

Whose numbers, stealing through thy darkening vale,
May not unseemly with its stillness suit,
    As, musing slow, I hail
    Thy genial loved return!   20

For when thy folding-star, arising, shows
His paly circlet, at his warning lamp
    The fragrant Hours, and elves
    Who slept in flowers the day,

And many a nymph who wreathes her brows with
      sedge,   25

And sheds the freshening dew, and, lovelier still,
   The pensive Pleasures sweet,
   Prepare thy shadowy car.

Then lead, calm votaress, where some sheety lake
Cheers the lone heath, or some time-hallowed pile   30
   Or upland fallows grey
   Reflect its last cool gleam.

But when chill blustering winds or driving rain
Forbid my willing feet, be mine the hut
   That from the mountain's side   35
   Views wilds, and swelling floods,

And hamlets brown, and dim-discovered spires,
And hears their simple bell, and marks o'er all
   Thy dewy fingers draw
   The gradual dusky veil.   40

While Spring shall pour his showers, as oft he wont,
And bathe thy breathing tresses, meekest Eve;
   While Summer loves to sport
   Beneath thy lingering light;

While sallow Autumn fills thy lap with leaves;   45
Or winter, yelling through the troublous air,
   Affrights thy shrinking train,
   And rudely rends thy robes;

So long, sure-found beneath the sylvan shed,
Shall Fancy, Friendship, Science, rose-lipped Health,   50
   Thy gentlest influence own,
   And hymn thy favorite name!

                                   1747

ODE ON THE POETICAL CHARACTER

STROPHE

As ONCE—if not with light regard
I read aright that gifted bard
(Him whose school above the rest
His loveliest Elfin Queen has blest)—
One, only one, unrivalled fair   5
Might hope the magic girdle wear,
At solemn tourney hung on high,
The wish of each love-darting eye;
Lo! to each other nymph in turn applied,
  As if, in air unseen, some hovering hand,   10
Some chaste and angel friend to virgin fame,
    With whispered spell had burst the starting
      band,
It left unblest her loathed, dishonored side;
  Happier, hopeless fair, if never
  Her baffled hand, with vain endeavor,   15
Had touched that fatal zone to her denied!
Young Fancy thus, to me divinest name,
  To whom, prepared and bathed in heaven,
  The cest of amplest power is given,
  To few the godlike gift assigns   20
  To gird their blest, prophetic loins,
And gaze her visions wild, and feel unmixed her
    flame!

EPODE

The band, as fairy legends say,
Was wove on that creating day
When He who called with thought to birth   25
Yon tented sky, this laughing earth,

And dressed with springs and forests tall,
And poured the main engirting all,
Long by the loved enthusiast wooed,
Himself in some diviner mood,   30
Retiring, sate with her alone,
And placed her on his sapphire throne,
The whiles, the vaulted shrine around,
Seraphic wires were heard to sound,
Now sublimest triumph swelling,   35
Now on love and mercy dwelling;
And she, from out the veiling cloud,
Breathed her magic notes aloud,
And thou, thou rich-haired Youth of Morn,
And all thy subject-life, was born!   40
The dangerous passions kept aloof,
Far from the sainted growing woof:
But near it sate ecstatic Wonder,
Listening the deep applauding thunder;
And Truth, in sunny vest arrayed,   45
By whose the tarsel's eyes were made;
All the shadowy tribes of mind,
In braided dance, their murmurs joined,
And all the bright uncounted powers
Who feed on heaven's ambrosial flowers.   50
Where is the bard whose soul can now
Its high presuming hopes avow?
Where he who thinks, with rapture blind,
This hallowed work for him designed?

ANTISTROPHE

High on some cliff, to heaven up-piled,   55
Of rude access, of prospect wild,
Where, tangled round the jealous steep,
Strange shades o'erbrow the valleys deep,
And holy genii guard the rock,

Its glooms embrown, its springs unlock,   60
While on its rich ambitious head
An Eden, like his own, lies spread,
I view that oak, the fancied glades among,
  By which as Milton lay, his evening ear,
From many a cloud that dropped ethereal dew,   65
  Nigh sphered in heaven, its native strains
        could hear,
On which that ancient trump he reached was
        hung:
  Thither oft, his glory greeting,
  From Waller's myrtle shades retreating,
With many a vow from Hope's aspiring tongue,   70
My trembling feet his guiding steps pursue;
  In vain—such bliss to one alone
  Of all the sons of soul was known,
  And Heaven and Fancy, kindred powers,
  Have now o'erturned th' inspiring bowers,   75
Or curtained close such scene from every future
        view.

                    1746

THE PASSIONS

An Ode for Music

When Music, heavenly maid, was young,
While yet in early Greece she sung,
The Passions oft, to hear her shell,
Thronged around her magic cell,
Exulting, trembling, raging, fainting,   5
Possessed beyond the Muse's painting;
By turns they felt the glowing mind
Disturbed, delighted, raised, refined:

Till once, 'tis said, when all were fired,
Filled with fury, rapt, inspired,   10

From the supporting myrtles round
They snatched her instruments of sound;
And, as they oft had heard apart
Sweet lessons of her forceful art,
Each (for madness ruled the hour)   15
Would prove his own expressive power.

First Fear in hand, its skill to try,
    Amid the chords bewildered laid,
And back recoiled, he knew not why,
    Even at the sound himself had made.   20

Next Anger rushed: his eyes, on fire,
In lightnings owned his secret stings;
In one rude clash he struck the lyre,
    And swept with hurried hand the strings.

With woeful measures wan Despair   25
    Low, sullen sounds his grief beguiled;
A solemn, strange, and mingled air—
    'Twas sad by fits, by starts 'twas wild.

But thou, O Hope, with eyes so fair,
    What was thy delightful measure?   30
    Still it whispered promised pleasure,
And bade the lovely scenes at distance hail!

Still would her touch the strain prolong;
    And from the rocks, the woods, the vale,
She called on Echo still, through all the song; 35
    And where her sweetest theme she chose,
A soft responsive voice was heard at every close,
And Hope, enchanted, smiled, and waved her golden
            hair.

And longer had she sung—but with a frown
                    Revenge impatient rose; 40
He threw his blood-stained sword in thunder
        down.
                    And with a withering look
    The war-denouncing trumpet took,
    And blew a blast so loud and dread,
Were ne'er prophetic sounds so full of woe. 45

        And ever and anon he beat
        The doubling drum with furious heat;
And though sometimes, each dreary pause be-
        tween,
        Dejected Pity, at his side,
        Her soul-subduing voice applied, 50
Yet still he kept his wild unaltered mien,
While each strained ball of sight seemed bursting
        from his head.
Thy numbers, Jealousy, to naught were fixed,
        Sad proof of thy distressful state;
Of differing themes the veering song was mixed, 55
And now it courted Love, now raving called on Hate.

        With eyes upraised, as one inspired,
        Pale Melancholy sate retired,
        And from her wild sequestered seat,
        In notes by distance made more sweet, 60
Poured through the mellow horn her pensive soul;
        And, dashing soft from rocks around,
        Bubbling runnels joined the sound:
Through glades and glooms the mingled measure
        stole,
Or o'er some haunted stream, with fond delay, 65
        Round an holy calm diffusing,
        Love of peace and lonely musing,
    In hollow murmurs died away.

But O how altered was its sprightlier tone,
When Cheerfulness, a nymph of healthiest hue,   70
   Her bow across her shoulder flung,
  Her buskins gemmed with morning dew;
Blew an inspiring air, that dale and thicket rung,
 The hunter's call, to faun and dryad known!
The oak-crowned sisters, and their chaste-eyed
   queen,   75
  Satyrs, and sylvan boys, were seen,
  Peeping from forth their alleys green;
  Brown Exercise rejoiced to hear;
And Sport leaped up, and seized his beechen
   spear.

  Last came Joy's ecstatic trial: 80
   He, with viny crown advancing,
  First to the lively pipe his hand addressed;
But soon he saw the brisk awakening viol,
  Whose sweet entrancing voice he loved the
   best.

They would have thought, who heard the strain, 85
They saw in Tempe's vale her native maids,
  Amidst the festal-sounding shades,
   To some unwearied minstrel dancing,
While, as his flying fingers kissed the strings,
  Love framed with Mirth a gay fantastic
   round;   90
  Loose with her tresses seen, her zone un-
   bound,
   And he, amidst his frolic play,
  As if he would the charming air repay,
Shook thousand odors from his dewy wings.

  O Music! sphere-descended maid!   95
  Friend of Pleasure, Wisdom's aid!
  Why, goddess, why, to us denied,
  Lay'st thou thy ancient lyre aside?

As in that loved Athenian bower
You learned an all-commanding power,   100
Thy mimic soul, O nymph endeared,
Can well recall what then it heard.
Where is thy native simple heart,
Devote to Virtue, Fancy, Art?
Arise as in that elder time,   105

Warm, energic, chaste, sublime!
Thy wonders, in that godlike age,
Fill thy recording sister's page:
'Tis said, and I believe the tale,
Thy humblest reed could more prevail,   110
Had more of strength, diviner rage,
Than all which charms this laggard age,
E'en all at once together found,
Cecilia's mingled world of sound.
O bid our vain endeavors cease: 115
Revive the just designs of Greece;
Return in all thy simple state;
Confirm the tales her sons relate!

1746

ODE ON THE POPULAR SUPERSTITIONS OF THE HIGHLANDS OF SCOTLAND

Considered as the Subject of Poetry

I

H——, thou return'st from Thames, whose naiads
    long
  Have seen thee lingering, with a fond delay,
  'Mid those soft friends, whose hearts, some future
    day,
Shall melt, perhaps, to hear thy tragic song.
Go, not unmindful of that cordial youth   5

Whom, long-endeared, thou leav'st by Levant's
    side;
Together let us wish him lasting truth,
    And joy untainted, with his destined bride.
Go! nor regardless, while these numbers boast
    My short-lived bliss, forget my social name;   10
But think, far off, how on the Southern coast
    I met thy friendship with an equal flame!
Fresh to that soil thou turn'st, whose every vale
    Shall prompt the poet, and his song demand:
To thee thy copious subjects ne'er shall fail;   15
    Thou need'st but take the pencil to thy hand,
And paint what all believe who own thy genial land.

II

There must thou wake perforce thy Doric quill;
    'Tis Fancy's land to which thou sett'st thy feet,
    Where still, 'tis said, the fairy people meet   20
Beneath each birken shade on mead or hill.
There each trim lass that skims the milky store
    To the swart tribes their creamy bowl allots;
By night they sip it round the cottage door,
    While airy minstrels warble jocund notes.   25
There every herd, by sad experience, knows
    How, winged with fate, their elf-shot arrows fly;
When the sick ewe her summer food foregoes,
    Or, stretched on earth, the heart-smit heifers lie.
Such airy beings awe th' untutored swain: 30
    Nor thou, though learned, his homelier thoughts
        neglect;
Let thy sweet Muse the rural faith sustain:
    These are the themes of simple, sure effect,
That add new conquests to her boundless reign,
And fill, with double force, her heart-commanding
        strain.   35

III

Even yet preserved, how often may'st thou hear,
  Where to the pole the boreal mountains run,
  Taught by the father to his listening son,
Strange lays, whose power had charmed a Spenser's
    ear.
At every pause, before thy mind possessed,   40
  Old Runic bards shall seem to rise around,
With uncouth lyres, in many-colored vest,
  Their matted hair with boughs fantastic crowned:
Whether thou bid'st the well-taught hind repeat
  The choral dirge that mourns some chieftain
    brave,   45
When every shrieking maid her bosom beat,
  And strewed with choicest herbs his scented
    grave;
Or whether, sitting in the shepherd's shiel,
  Thou hear'st some sounding tale of war's alarms,
When, at the bugle's call, with fire and steel,   50
  The sturdy clans poured forth their bony swarms,
And hostile brothers met to prove each other's arms.

IV

'Tis thine to sing, how, framing hideous spells,
  In Skye's lone isle the gifted wizard seer,
  Lodged in the wintry cave with [Fate's fell
    spear;]   55
Or in the depth of Uist's dark forests dwells:
How they whose sight such dreary dreams engross,
  With their own visions oft astonished droop,
When o'er the watery strath or quaggy moss
  They see the gliding ghosts unbodied troop;   60
Or if in sports, or on the festive green,
  Their [destined] glance some fated youth descry,

Who, now perhaps in lusty vigor seen
    And rosy health, shall soon lamented die:
For them the viewless forms of air obey,   65
    Their bidding heed, and at their beck repair.
They know what spirit brews the stormful day,
    And, heartless, oft like moody madness stare
To see the phantom train their secret work prepare.

V

[To monarchs dear, some hundred miles astray,   70
    Oft have they seen Fate give the fatal blow!
    The seer, in Skye, shrieked as the blood did flow,
When headless Charles warm on the scaffold lay!
As Boreas threw his young Aurora forth,
    In the first year of the first George's reign,   75
And battles raged in welkin of the North,
    They mourned in air, fell, fell Rebellion slain!
And as, of late, they joyed in Preston's fight,
    Saw at sad Falkirk all their hopes near crowned,
They raved, divining, through their second sight,   80
    Pale, red Culloden, where these hopes were
        drowned!
Illustrious William! Britain's guardian name!
    One William saved us from a tyrant's stroke;
He, for a sceptre, gained heroic fame;
    But thou, more glorious, Slavery's chain hast
        broke,   85
To reign a private man, and bow to Freedom's yoke!

VI

These, too, thou'lt sing! for well thy magic Muse
    Can to the topmost heaven of grandeur soar!
    Or stoop to wail the swain that is no more!
Ah, homely swains! your homeward steps ne'er lose;   90

Let not dank Will mislead you to the heath:
    Dancing in mirky night, o'er fen and lake,
He glows, to draw you downward to your death,
    In his bewitched, low, marshy willow brake!]
What though far off, from some dark dell espied,   95
His glimmering mazes cheer th' excursive sight,
Yet turn, ye wanderers, turn your steps aside,
    Nor trust the guidance of that faithless light;
For, watchful, lurking 'mid th' unrustling reed,
    At those mirk hours the wily monster lies,   100
And listens oft to hear the passing steed,
    And frequent round him rolls his sullen eyes,
If chance his savage wrath may some weak wretch
        surprise.

VII

Ah, luckless swain, o'er all unblest indeed!
    Whom, late bewildered in the dank, dark fen,   105
    Far from his flocks and smoking hamlet then,
To that sad spot [where hums the sedgy weed:]
    On him, enraged, the fiend, in angry mood,
    Shall never look with Pity's kind concern,
But instant, furious, raise the whelming flood   110
    O'er its drowned bank, forbidding all return.
Or, if he meditate his wished escape
    To some dim hill that seems uprising near,
To his faint eye the grim and grisly shape,
    In all its terrors clad, shall wild appear.   115
Meantime, the watery surge shall round him rise,
    Poured sudden forth from every swelling source.
What now remains but tears and hopeless sighs?
    His fear-shook limbs have lost their youthly force,
And down the waves he floats, a pale and breathless 120
        corse.

VIII

For him, in vain, his anxious wife shall wait,
    Or wander forth to meet him on his way;
    For him, in vain, at to-fall of the day,
His babes shall linger at th' unclosing gate.
Ah, ne'er shall he return! Alone, if night   125
    Her travelled limbs in broken slumbers steep,
With dropping willows dressed, his mournful sprite
    Shall visit sad, perchance, her silent sleep:
Then he, perhaps, with moist and watery hand,
    Shall fondly seem to press her shuddering cheek,   130
And with his blue-swoln face before her stand,
    And, shivering cold, these piteous accents speak:
'Pursue, dear wife, thy daily toils pursue
    At dawn or dusk, industrious as before;
Nor e'er of me one hapless thought renew,   135
    While I lie weltering on the oziered shore,
Drowned by the kelpie's wrath, nor e'er shall aid
        thee more!'

IX

Unbounded is thy range; with varied style
    Thy Muse may, like those feathery tribes which
        spring
    From their rude rocks, extend her skirting wing   140
Round the moist marge of each cold Hebrid isle
To that hoar pile which still its ruin shows:
    In whose small vaults a pigmy-folk is found,
Whose bones the delver with his spade upthrows,
    And culls them, wondering, from the hallowed
        ground!   145
Or thither, where, beneath the showery West,
    The mighty kings of three fair realms are laid:

Once foes, perhaps, together now they rest;
   No slaves revere them, and no wars invade:
Yet frequent now, at midnight's solemn hour,   150
   The rifted mounds their yawning cells unfold,
And forth the monarchs stalk with sovereign power,
   In pageant robes, and wreathed with sheeny gold,
And on their twilight tombs aërial council hold.

X

But oh, o'er all, forget not Kilda's race,   155
   On whose bleak rocks, which brave the wasting tides,
   Fair Nature's daughter, Virtue, yet abides.
Go, just as they, their blameless manners trace!
Then to my ear transmit some gentle song
   Of those whose lives are yet sincere and plain,   160
Their bounded walks the rugged cliffs along,
   And all their prospect but the wintry main.
With sparing temperance, at the needful time,
   They drain the sainted spring, or, hunger-pressed,
Along th' Atlantic rock undreading climb,   165
   And of its eggs despoil the solan's nest.
Thus blest in primal innocence they live,
   Sufficed and happy with that frugal fare
Which tasteful toil and hourly danger give.
   Hard is their shallow soil, and bleak and bare;   170
Nor ever vernal bee was heard to murmur there!

XI

Nor need'st thou blush, that such false themes engage
   Thy gentle mind, of fairer stores possessed;
   For not alone they touch the village breast,
But filled in elder time th' historic page.   175

There Shakspere's self, with every garland
      crowned,—
    [Flew to those fairy climes his fancy sheen!]—
In musing hour, his wayward Sisters found,
    And with their terrors dressed the magic scene.
From them he sung, when, 'mid his bold design,   180
    Before the Scot afflicted and aghast,
The shadowy kings of Banquo's fated line
    Through the dark cave in gleamy pageant passed.
Proceed, nor quit the tales which, simply told,
    Could once so well my answering bosom pierce; 185
Proceed! in forceful sounds and colors bold,
    The native legends of thy land rehearse;
To such adapt thy lyre and suit thy powerful verse.

XII

In scenes like these, which, daring to depart
    From sober truth, are still to nature true,   190
    And call forth fresh delight to Fancy's view,
Th' heroic muse employed her Tasso's art!
How have I trembled, when, at Tancred's stroke,
    Its gushing blood the gaping cypress poured;
When each live plant with mortal accents spoke,   195
    And the wild blast upheaved the vanished sword!
How have I sat, when piped the pensive wind,
    To hear his harp, by British Fairfax strung,—
Prevailing poet, whose undoubting mind
    Believed the magic wonders which he sung!   200
Hence at each sound imagination glows;
    [*The MS. lacks a line here.*]
Hence his warm lay with softest sweetness flows;
    Melting it flows, pure, numerous, strong, and
        clear,
And fills th' impassioned heart, and wins th' har-
      monious ear.   205

XIII

All hail, ye scenes that o'er my soul prevail,
  Ye [splendid] friths and lakes which, far away,
  Are by smooth Annan filled, or pastoral Tay,
Or Don's romantic springs; at distance, hail!
The time shall come when I, perhaps, may tread   210
  Your lowly glens, o'erhung with spreading broom,
Or o'er your stretching heaths by fancy led
[Or o'er your mountains creep, in awful gloom:]
Then will I dress once more the faded bower.
  Where Jonson sat in Drummond's [classic] shade, 215
Or crop from Teviot's dale each [lyric flower]
  And mourn on Yarrow's banks [where Willy's
      laid!]
Meantime, ye Powers that on the plains which bore
  The cordial youth, on Lothian's plains, attend,
Where'er he dwell, on hill or lowly muir,   220
  To him I lose your kind protection lend,
And, touched with love like mine, preserve my ab-
      sent friend!

1749   1788

JOHN GILBERT COOPER

FROM THE POWER OF HARMONY

HAIL, thrice hail
Ye solitary seats, where Wisdom seeks
Beauty and Good, th' unseparable pair,
Sweet offspring of the sky, those emblems fair
Of the celestial cause, whose tuneful word   5
From discord and from chaos raised this globe
And all the wide effulgence of the day.
From him begins this beam of gay delight,

When aught harmonious strikes th' attentive mind;
In him shall end; for he attuned the frame   10
Of passive organs with internal sense,
To feel an instantaneous glow of joy,
When Beauty from her native seat of Heaven,
Clothed in ethereal wildness, on our plains
Descends, ere Reason with her tardy eye   15
Can view the form divine; and through the world
The heavenly boon to every being flows.

    .   .   .   .

Nor less admire those things, which viewed apart
Uncouth appear, or horrid; ridges black
Of shagged rocks, which hang tremendous o'er   20
Some barren heath; the congregated clouds
Which spread their sable skirts, and wait the wind
To burst th' embosomed storm; a leafless wood,
A moldering ruin, lightning-blasted fields;
Nay, e'en the seat where Desolation reigns   25
In brownest horror; by familiar thought
Connected to this universal frame,
With equal beauty charms the tasteful soul
As the gold landscapes of the happy isles
Crowned with Hesperian fruit: for Nature formed   30
One plan entire, and made each separate scene
Co-operate with the general of all
In that harmonious contrast.

    .   .   .   .

From these sweet meditations on the charms
Of things external, on the genuine forms   35
Which blossom in creation, on the scene
Where mimic art with emulative hue
Usurps the throne of Nature unreproved,

On the just concord of mellifluent sounds;
The soul, and all the intellectual train   40
Of fond desires, gay hopes, or threatening fears,
Through this habitual intercourse of sense
Is harmonized within, till all is fair
And perfect; till each moral power perceives
Its own resemblance, with fraternal joy,   45
In every form complete, and smiling feels
Beauty and Good the same.

1745

THOMAS WARTON

FROM THE PLEASURES OF MELANCHOLY

BENEATH yon ruined abbey's moss-grown piles
Oft let me sit, at twilight hour of eve,
Where through some western window the pale moon
Pours her long-levelled rule of streaming light,
While sullen, sacred silence reigns around,   5
Save the lone screech-owl's note, who builds his
       bower
Amid the moldering caverns dark and damp,
Or the calm breeze that rustles in the leaves
Of flaunting ivy, that with mantle green
Invests some wasted tower. Or let me tread   10
Its neighboring walk of pines, where mused of old
The cloistered brothers: through the gloomy void
That far extends beneath their ample arch
As on I pace, religious horror wraps
My soul in dread repose. But when the world   15
Is clad in midnight's raven-colored robe,
'Mid hollow charnel let me watch the flame
Of taper dim, shedding a livid glare
O'er the wan heaps, while airy voices talk
Along the glimmering walls, or ghostly shape,   20

At distance seen, invites with beckoning hand
My lonesome steps through the far-winding vaults.
Nor undelightful is the solemn noon
Of night, when, haply wakeful, from my couch
I start: lo, all is motionless around!   25
Roars not the rushing wind; the sons of men
And every beast in mute oblivion lie;
All nature's hushed in silence and in sleep:
O then how fearful is it to reflect
That through the still globe's awful solitude   30
No being wakes but me! till stealing sleep
My drooping temples bathes in opiate dews.
Nor then let dreams, of wanton folly born,
My senses lead through flowery paths of joy:
But let the sacred genius of the night   35
Such mystic visions send as Spenser saw
When through bewildering Fancy's magic maze,
To the fell house of Busyrane, he led
Th' unshaken Britomart; or Milton knew,
When in abstracted thought he first conceived   40
All Heaven in tumult, and the seraphim
Come towering, armed in adamant and gold.

    .   .   .   .   .   .

Through Pope's soft song though all the Graces
      breathe,
And happiest art adorn his Attic page,
Yet does my mind with sweeter transport glow,   45
As, at the root of mossy trunk reclined,
In magic Spenser's wildly-warbled song
I see deserted Una wander wide
Through wasteful solitudes and lurid heaths,
Weary, forlorn, than when the fated fair   50
Upon the bosom bright of silver Thames
Launches in all the lustre of brocade,
Amid the splendors of the laughing sun:

The gay description palls upon the sense,
And coldly strikes the mind with feeble bliss.   55

.   .   .   .

The tapered choir, at the late hour of prayer,
Oft let me tread, while to th' according voice
The many-sounding organ peals on high
The clear slow-dittied chant or varied hymn,
Till all my soul is bathed in ecstasies   60
And lapped in Paradise. Or let me sit
Far in sequestered aisles of the deep dome;
There lonesome listen to the sacred sounds,
Which, as they lengthen through the Gothic vaults,
In hollow murmurs reach my ravished ear.   65
Nor when the lamps, expiring, yield to night,
And solitude returns, would I forsake
The solemn mansion, but attentive mark
The due clock swinging slow with sweepy sway,
Measuring Time's flight with momentary sound.   70

1747

FROM OBSERVATIONS ON THE FAIRY QUEEN OF SPENSER

.   .   .   .

It is absurd to think of judging either Ariosto
or Spenser by precepts which they did not attend
to. We who live in the days of writing by rule are
apt to try every composition by those laws which
we have been taught to think the sole criterion of   5
excellence. Critical taste is universally diffused, and
we require the same order and design which every
modern performance is expected to have, in poems
where they never were regarded or intended. Spen-
ser, and the same may be said of Ariosto, did not live   10

in an age of planning. His poetry is the careless
exuberance of a warm imagination and a strong sensibility. It was his business to engage the fancy,
and to interest the attention by bold and striking
images, in the formation and the disposition of
which, little labor or art was applied. The various
and the marvellous were the chief sources of delight. Hence we find our author ransacking alike
the regions of reality and romance, of truth and
fiction, to find the proper decoration and furniture
for his fairy structure. Born in such an age, Spenser wrote rapidly from his own feelings, which at
the same time were naturally noble. Exactness in
his poem would have been like the cornice which a
painter introduced in the grotto of Calypso. Spenser's beauties are like the flowers in Paradise,

> Which not nice Art
> In beds and curious knots, but Nature boon
> Pour'd forth profuse, on hill, and dale, and plain;
> Both where the morning sun first warmly smote
> The open field, or where the unpierc'd shade
> Imbrown'd the noon-tide bowers.
> —*Paradise Lost,* iv, 241.

If *The Fairy Queen* be destitute of that arrange-
ment and economy which epic severity requires, yet
we scarcely regret the loss of these while their place
is so amply supplied by something which more pow-
erfully attracts us; something which engages the affections, the feelings of the heart, rather than the
cold approbation of the head. If there be any poem
whose graces please because they are situated beyond
the reach of art, and where the force and faculties
of creative imagination delight because they are un-
assisted and unrestrained by those of deliberate
judgment, it is this. In reading Spenser, if the critic
is not satisfied, yet the reader is transported.

·   ·   ·   ·   ·   ·   ·

I cannot dismiss this section without a wish that this neglected author [Chaucer], whom Spenser proposed as the pattern of his style, and to whom he is indebted for many noble inventions, should be more universally studied. This is at least what one might 50 expect in an age of research and curiosity. Chaucer is regarded rather as an old, than as a good, poet. We look upon his poems as venerable relics, not as beautiful compositions; as pieces better calculated to gratify the antiquarian than the critic. He abounds 55 not only in strokes of humor, which is commonly supposed to be his sole talent, but of pathos and sublimity not unworthy a more refined age. His old manners, his romantic arguments, his wildness of painting, his simplicity and antiquity of expression, 60 transport us into some fairy region, and are all highly pleasing to the imagination. It is true that his uncouth and unfamiliar language disgusts and deters many readers; but the principal reason of his being so little known and so seldom taken into hand, 65 is the convenient opportunity of reading him with pleasure and facility in modern imitations. For when translation, as such imitations from Chaucer may be justly called, at length becomes substituted as the means of attaining a knowledge of any 70 difficult and ancient author, the original not only begins to be neglected and excluded as less easy, but also despised as less ornamental and elegant. Thus the public taste becomes imperceptibly vitiated, while the genuine model is superseded, and gradually gives 75 way to the establishment of a more specious but false resemblance. Thus, to many readers, happy to find the readiest accommodation for their indolence and their illiteracy, think themselves sufficient masters of Homer from Pope's translation; and thus, by an in- 80 discreet comparison, Pope's translation is commonly preferred to the Grecian text, in proportion as the former is furnished with more frequent and shining metaphors, more lively descriptions, and in general appears to be more full and florid, more elaborate and various.

. . . .

In reading the works of a poet who lived in a remote age, it is necessary that we should look back upon the customs and manners which prevailed in that age. We should endeavor to place ourselves in the writer's situation and circumstances. Hence we shall become better enabled to discover how his turn of thinking, and manner of composing, were influenced by familiar appearances and established objects which are utterly different from those with which we are at present surrounded. For want of this caution, too many readers view the knights and damsels, the tournaments and enchantments, of Spenser with modern eyes; never considering that the encounters of chivalry subsisted in our author's age, that romances were then most eagerly and universally studied, and that consequently Spenser from the fashion of the times was induced to undertake a recital of chivalrous achievements, and to become, in short, a *romantic* poet.

Spenser, in this respect, copied real manners no less than Homer. A sensible historian observes that "Homer copied true natural manners, which, however rough and uncultivated, will always form an agreeable and interesting picture; but the pencil of the English poet (Spenser) was employed in drawing the affectations and conceits and fopperies of chivalry." This, however, was nothing more than an imitation of real life; as much, at least, as the plain descriptions in Homer, which corresponded to the simplicity of manners then subsisting in Greece.

Mechanical critics will perhaps be disgusted at the liberties I have taken in introducing so many anecdotes of ancient chivalry. But my subject re- 120 quired frequent proofs of this sort. Nor could I be persuaded that such enquiries were, in other respects, either useless or ridiculous; as they tended, at least, to illustrate an institution of no frivolous or indifferent nature. Chivalry is commonly looked 125 upon as a barbarous sport or extravagant amusement of the dark ages. It had, however, no small influence on the manners, policies, and constitutions of ancient times, and served many public and important purposes. It was the school of fortitude, honor, 130 and affability. Its exercises, like the Grecian games, habituated the youth to fatigue and enterprise, and inspired the noblest sentiments of heroism. It taught gallantry and civility to a savage and ignorant people, and humanized the native ferocity of the Nor- 135 thern nations. It conduced to refine the manners of the combatants by exciting an emulation in the devices and accoutrements, the splendor and parade, of their tilts and tournaments; while its magnificent festivals, thronged with noble dames and courteous 140 knights, produced the first efforts of wit and fancy.

I am still further to hope that, together with other specimens of obsolete literature in general hinted at before, the many references I have made in particular to romances, the necessary appendage of an- 145 cient chivalry, will also plead their pardon. For however monstrous and unnatural these compositions may appear to this age of reason and refinement, they merit more attention than the world is willing to bestow. They preserve many curious 150 historical facts, and throw considerable light on the nature of the feudal system. They are the pictures

of ancient usages and customs; and represent the
manners, genius, and character of our ancestors.
Above all, such are their terrible graces of magic 155
and enchantment, so magnificently marvellous are
their fictions and fablings, that they contribute, in a
wonderful degree, to rouse and invigorate all the
powers of imagination; to store the fancy with those
sublime and alarming images which poetry best de- 160
lights to display.

                                        1754

FROM THE GRAVE OF KING ARTHUR

[THE PASSING OF THE KING]

O'ER Cornwall's cliffs the tempest roared,
High the screaming sea-mew soared;
On Tintagel's topmost tower
Darksome fell the sleety shower;
Round the rough castle shrilly sung   5
The whirling blast, and wildly flung
On each tall rampart's thundering side
The surges of the tumbling tide:
When Arthur ranged his red-cross ranks
On conscious Camlan's crimsoned banks: 10
By Mordred's faithless guile decreed
Beneath a Saxon spear to bleed!
Yet in vain a paynim foe
Armed with fate the mighty blow;
For when he fell, an Elfin Queen   15
All in secret, and unseen,
O'er the fainting hero threw
Her mantle of ambrosial blue;
And bade her spirits bear him far,
In Merlin's agate-axled car,   20
To her green isle's enamelled steep
Far in the navel of the deep.

O'er his wounds she sprinkled dew
From flowers that in Arabia grew:
On a rich enchanted bed   25
She pillowed his majestic head;
O'er his brow, with whispers bland,
Thrice she waved an opiate wand;
And to soft music's airy sound,
Her magic curtains closed around.   30
There, renewed the vital spring,
Again he reigns a mighty king;
And many a fair and fragrant clime,
Blooming in immortal prime,
By gales of Eden ever fanned,   35
Owns the monarch's high command:
Thence to Britain shall return
(If right prophetic rolls I learn),
Born on Victory's spreading plume,
His ancient sceptre to resume;   40
Once more, in old heroic pride,
His barbèd courser to bestride;
His knightly table to restore,
And brave the tournaments of yore.

1777

SONNET WRITTEN IN A BLANK LEAF OF DUGDALE'S 'MONASTICON'

DEEM not devoid of elegance the sage,
By Fancy's genuine feelings unbeguiled,
Of painful pedantry the poring child,
Who turns, of these proud domes, th' historic page,
Now sunk by Time, and Henry's fiercer rage.   5
Think'st thou the warbling Muses never smiled
On his lone hours? Ingenuous views engage
His thoughts, on themes, unclassic falsely styled,
Intent. While cloistered Piety displays
Her moldering roll, the piercing eye explores   10

New manners, and the pomp of elder days,
Whence culls the pensive bard his pictured stores.
Nor rough nor barren are the winding ways
Of hoar antiquity, but strown with flowers.

1777

SONNET WRITTEN AT STONEHENGE

THOU noblest monument of Albion's isle!
Whether by Merlin's aid from Scythia's shore,
To Amber's fatal plain Pendragon bore,
Huge frame of giant-hands, the mighty pile,
T' entomb his Britons slain by Hengist's guile: 5
Or Druid priests, sprinkled with human gore,
Taught 'mid thy massy maze their mystic lore:
Or Danish chiefs, enriched with savage spoil,
To Victory's idol vast, an unhewn shrine,
Reared the rude heap: or, in thy hallowed round,   10
Repose the kings of Brutus' genuine line;
Or here those kings in solemn state were crowned:
Studious to trace thy wondrous origin,
We must on many an ancient tale renowned.

1777

SONNET TO THE RIVER LODON

AH! WHAT a weary race my feet have run,
Since first I trod thy banks with alders crowned,
And thought my way was all through fairy ground,
Beneath thy azure sky and golden sun,
Where first my Muse to lisp her notes begun!   5
While pensive Memory traces back the round,
Which fills the varied interval between;
Much pleasure, more of sorrow, marks the scene.
Sweet native stream! those skies and suns so pure
No more return, to cheer my evening road!   10
Yet still one joy remains: that not obscure

Nor useless, all my vacant days have flowed,
From youth's gray dawn to manhood's prime ma-
       ture;
Nor with the Muse's laurel unbestowed.

1777

THOMAS GRAY

HYMN TO ADVERSITY

DAUGHTER of Jove, relentless power,
   Thou tamer of the human breast,
Whose iron scourge and torturing hour
   The bad affright, afflict the best!
Bound in thy adamantine chain,   5
The proud are taught to taste of pain,
And purple tyrants vainly groan
With pangs unfelt before, unpitied and alone.

When first thy sire to send on earth
   Virtue, his darling child, designed,   10
To thee he gave the heavenly birth,
   And bade to form her infant mind.
Stern, rugged nurse! thy rigid lore
With patience many a year she bore;
What sorrow was thou bad'st her know,   15
And from her own she learned to melt at other's
     woe.

Scared at thy frown terrific, fly
   Self-pleasing Folly's idle brood,
Wild Laughter, Noise, and thoughtless Joy,
   And leave us leisure to be good: 20
Light they disperse, and with them go
The summer friend, the flattering foe;
By vain Prosperity received,
To her they vow their truth and are again believed.

Wisdom in sable garb arrayed,   25
    Immersed in rapturous thought profound,
And Melancholy, silent maid
    With leaden eye, that loves the ground,
Still on thy solemn steps attend;
Warm Charity, the genial friend,   30
With Justice, to herself severe,
And Pity, dropping soft the sadly-pleasing tear.

Oh, gently on thy suppliant's head,
    Dread goddess, lay thy chastening hand!
Not in thy Gorgon terrors clad,   35
    Nor circled with the vengeful band
(As by the impious thou art seen),
With thundering voice and threatening mien,
With screaming Horror's funeral cry,
Despair, and fell Disease, and ghastly Poverty: 40

Thy form benign, O goddess, wear,
    Thy milder influence impart;
Thy philosophic train be there
    To soften, not to wound, my heart;
The generous spark extinct revive,   45
Teach me to love and to forgive,
Exact my own defects to scan,
What others are to feel, and know myself a man.

                          1748

ELEGY

Written in a Country Churchyard

The curfew tolls the knell of parting day,
    The lowing herd winds slowly o'er the lea,
The ploughman homeward plods his weary way,
    And leaves the world to darkness and to me.

Now fades the glimmering landscape on the sight,   5
   And all the air a solemn stillness holds,
Save where the beetle wheels his droning flight,
   And drowsy tinklings lull the distant folds;

Save that from yonder ivy-mantled tower
   The moping owl does to the moon complain   10
Of such, as wandering near her secret bower,
   Molest her ancient solitary reign.

Beneath those rugged elms, that yew-tree's shade,
   Where heaves the turf in many a moldering heap,
Each in his narrow cell forever laid,   15
   The rude forefathers of the hamlet sleep.

The breezy call of incense-breathing morn,
   The swallow twittering from the straw-built shed,
The cock's shrill clarion, or the echoing horn,
   No more shall rouse them from their lowly bed.   20

For them no more the blazing hearth shall burn,
   Or busy housewife ply her evening care:
No children run to lisp their sire's return,
   Or climb his knees the envied kiss to share.

Oft did the harvest to their sickle yield,   25
   Their furrow oft the stubborn glebe has broke;
How jocund did they drive their team afield!
   How bowed the woods beneath their sturdy
      stroke!

Let not Ambition mock their useful toil,
   Their homely joys, and destiny obscure;   30
Nor Grandeur hear with a disdainful smile,
   The short and simple annals of the poor.

The boast of heraldry, the pomp of power,
  And all that beauty, all that wealth e'er gave,
Awaits alike th' inevitable hour.   35
  The paths of glory lead but to the grave.

Nor you, ye proud, impute to these the fault,
  If Memory o'er their tomb no trophies raise,
Where through the long-drawn aisle and fretted
      vault
  The pealing anthem swells the note of praise.   40

Can storied urn or animated bust
  Back to its mansion call the fleeting breath?
Can Honor's voice provoke the silent dust,
  Or Flattery soothe the dull cold ear of Death?

Perhaps in this neglected spot is laid   45
  Some heart once pregnant with celestial fire;
Hands that the rod of empire might have swayed,
  Or waked to ecstasy the living lyre.

But Knowledge to their eyes her ample page
  Rich with the spoils of time did ne'er unroll;   50
Chill Penury repressed their noble rage,
  And froze the genial current of the soul.

Full many a gem of purest ray serene,
  The dark unfathomed caves of ocean bear:
Full many a flower is born to blush unseen,   55
  And waste its sweetness on the desert air.

Some village Hampden, that, with dauntless breast
  The little tyrant of his fields withstood;
Some mute inglorious Milton here may rest,
  Some Cromwell guiltless of his country's blood.   60

Th' applause of listening senates to command,
    The threats of pain and ruin to despise,
To scatter plenty o'er a smiling land,
    And read their history in a nation's eyes,

Their lot forbade: nor circumscribed alone   65
    Their growing virtues, but their crimes confined;
Forbade to wade through slaughter to a throne,
    And shut the gates of mercy on mankind,

The struggling pangs of conscious truth to hide,
    To quench the blushes of ingenuous shame,   70
Or heap the shrine of Luxury and Pride
    With incense kindled at the Muse's flame.

Far from the madding crowd's ignoble strife,
    Their sober wishes never learned to stray;
Along the cool sequestered vale of life   75
    They kept the noiseless tenor of their way.

Yet even these bones from insult to protect,
    Some frail memorial still erected nigh,
With uncouth rhymes and shapeless sculpture
        decked,
    Implores the passing tribute of a sigh.   80

Their names, their years, spelt by th' unlettered
        Muse,
    The place of fame and elegy supply:
And many a holy text around she strews,
    That teach the rustic moralist to die.

For who, to dumb forgetfulness a prey,   85
    This pleasing anxious being e'er resigned,
Left the warm precincts of the cheerful day,
    Nor cast one longing lingering look behind?

On some fond breast the parting soul relies,
    Some pious drops the closing eye requires;   90
Even from the tomb the voice of Nature cries,
    Even in our ashes live their wonted fires.

For thee, who mindful of th' unhonored dead
    Dost in these lines their artless tale relate,
If chance, by lonely contemplation led,   95
    Some kindred spirit shall inquire thy fate.

Haply some hoary-headed swain may say,
    'Oft have we seen him at the peep of dawn
Brushing with hasty steps the dews away
    To meet the sun upon the upland lawn.   100

'There at the foot of yonder nodding beech
    That wreathes its old fantastic roots so high,
His listless length at noontide would he stretch,
    And pore upon the brook that babbles by.

'Hard by yon wood, now smiling as in scorn,   105
    Muttering his wayward fancies he would rove;
Now drooping, woeful-wan, like one forlorn,
    Or crazed with care, or crossed in hopeless love.

'One morn I missed him on the customed hill,
    Along the heath, and near his favorite tree;   110
Another came; nor yet beside the rill,
    Nor up the lawn, nor at the wood was he;

'The next with dirges due in sad array
    Slow through the church-way path we saw him
        borne,—
Approach and read (for thou canst read) the lay   115
    Graved on the stone beneath yon agèd thorn.'

THE EPITAPH

Here rests his head upon the lap of earth
  A youth to fortune and to fame unknown;
Fair Science frowned not on his humble birth,
  And Melancholy marked him for her own.

Large was his bounty, and his soul sincere;   120
  Heaven did a recompense as largely send:
He gave to Misery (all he had) a tear,
  He gained from Heaven ('twas all he wished) a
      friend.

No farther seek his merits to disclose,   125
  Or draw his frailties from their dread abode
(There they alike in trembling hope repose,)—
  The bosom of his Father and his God.

                                            1751

THE PROGRESS OF POESY

I. 1

  Awake, Æolian lyre, awake,
And give to rapture all thy trembling strings!
    From Helicon's harmonious springs
A thousand rills their mazy progress take;
    The laughing flowers that round them
        blow   5
    Drink life and fragrance as they flow.
Now the rich stream of music winds along
    Deep, majestic, smooth, and strong,
  Through verdant vales and Ceres' golden
        reign:
    Now rolling down the steep amain,   10
    Headlong, impetuous, see it pour;
The rocks and nodding groves rebellow to the roar.

I. 2

Oh sovereign of the willing soul,
Parent of sweet and solemn-breathing airs,
   Enchanting shell! the sullen Cares   15
And frantic Passions hear thy soft control.
On Thracia's hills the Lord of War
Has curbed the fury of his car
And dropped his thirsty lance at thy command.
   Perching on the sceptred hand   20
Of Jove, thy magic lulls the feathered king
   With ruffled plumes and flagging wing;
   Quenched in dark clouds of slumber lie
The terror of his beak and lightnings of his eye.

I. 3

   Thee the voice, the dance, obey,   25
   Tempered to thy warbled lay.
   O'er Idalia's velvet-green
The rosy-crownèd Loves are seen,
     On Cytherea's day,
With antic Sports and blue-eyed Pleas-
   ures   30
Frisking light in frolic measures:
Now pursuing, now retreating,
   Now in circling troops they meet;
To brisk notes in cadence beating
   Glance their many-twinkling feet.   35
Slow melting strains their Queen's approach de-
   clare:
   Where'er she turns the Graces homage
   pay;
With arms sublime, that float upon the air,
   In gliding state she wins her easy way;
O'er her warm cheek and rising bosom move   40
The bloom of young Desire and purple light of Love.

II. 1

Man's feeble race what ills await:
Labor, and Penury, the racks of Pain,
  Disease, and Sorrow's weeping train,
And Death, sad refuge from the storms of
    Fate!   45
    The fond complaint, my song, disprove,
    And justify the laws of Jove.
Say, has he given in vain the heavenly Muse?
    Night, and all her sickly dews,
Her spectres wan, and birds of boding cry, 50
    He gives to range the dreary sky;
    Till down the eastern cliffs afar
Hyperion's march they spy, and glittering shafts of
    war.

II. 2

In climes beyond the solar road,
Where shaggy forms o'er ice-built mountains
    roam,   55
  The Muse has broke the twilight-gloom
To cheer the shivering native's dull abode.
    And oft, beneath the odorous shade
    Of Chili's boundless forests laid,
She deigns to hear the savage youth repeat, 60
    In loose numbers wildly sweet,
Their feather-cinctured chiefs and dusky loves.
    Her track, where'er the goddess roves,
    Glory pursue, and generous Shame,
Th' unconquerable Mind, and Freedom's holy flame. 65

II. 3

Woods that wave o'er Delphi's steep,
Isles that crown th' Ægean deep,

Fields that cool Ilissus laves,
Or where Mæander's amber waves
    In lingering labyrinths creep,   70
How do your tuneful echoes languish,
Mute but to the voice of Anguish?
Where each old poetic mountain
    Inspiration breathed around,
Every shade and hallowed fountain   75
    Murmured deep a solemn sound;
Till the sad Nine in Greece's evil hour,
    Left their Parnassus for the Latian
    plains:
Alike they scorn the pomp of tyrant Power,
    And coward Vice that revels in her   80
    chains.
When Latium had her lofty spirit lost,
They sought, O Albion! next, thy sea-encircled coast.

III. 1

Far from the sun and summer-gale,
In thy green lap was Nature's darling laid,
    What time, where lucid Avon strayed,   85
To him the mighty mother did unveil
    Her awful face: the dauntless child
    Stretched forth his little arms, and smiled.
'This pencil take,' she said, 'whose colors clear
    Richly paint the vernal year.   90
Thine too these golden keys, immortal boy!
    This can unlock the gates of Joy;
    Of Horror that, and thrilling Fears,
Or ope the sacred source of sympathetic tears.'

III. 2

Nor second he that rode sublime   95
Upon the seraph-wings of Ecstasy,

    The secrets of th' abyss to spy.
He passed the flaming bounds of Place and
        Time:
    The living throne, the sapphire blaze,
    Where angels tremble while they gaze,   100
He saw; but, blasted with excess of light,
    Closed his eyes in endless night.
Behold where Dryden's less presumptuous car
    Wide o'er the fields of glory bear
    Two coursers of ethereal race,   105
With necks in thunder clothed, and long-resounding
        pace!

III. 3

Hark! his hands the lyre explore:
Bright-eyed Fancy, hovering o'er,
Scatters from her pictured urn
Thoughts that breathe and words that
    burn.   110
    But, ah, 'tis heard no more!
O lyre divine, what daring spirit
Wakes thee now?   Though he inherit
Nor the pride nor ample pinion
    That the Theban Eagle bear,   115
Sailing with supreme dominion
    Through the azure deep of air,
Yet oft before his infant eyes would run
    Such forms as glitter in the Muse's ray,
With orient hues unborrowed of the sun: 120
    Yet shall he mount, and keep his distant
        way
Beyond the limits of a vulgar fate,
Beneath the good how far—but far above the great.

1754   1757

THE BARD

I. 1

'RUIN seize thee, ruthless king!
Confusion on thy banners wait;
   Though fanned by conquest's crimson
      wing,
They mock the air with idle state.
   Helm, nor hauberk's twisted mail,   5
Nor even thy virtues, tyrant, shall avail
To save thy secret soul from nightly fears,
   From Cambria's curse, from Cambria's
      tears!'
Such were the sounds that o'er the crested pride
   Of the first Edward scattered wild dis-
     may,   10
As down the steep of Snowdon's shaggy side
   He wound with toilsome march his long
     array.
Stout Gloucester stood aghast in speechless
     trance;
'To arms!' cried Mortimer, and couched his quiver-
     ing lance.

I. 2

   On a rock, whose haughty brow   15
Frowns o'er old Conway's foaming flood,
   Robed in the sable garb of woe,
With haggard eyes the poet stood
   (Loose his beard and hoary hair
Streamed, like a meteor, to the troubled air),   20
And with a master's hand and prophet's fire
   Struck the deep sorrows of his lyre:
'Hark how each giant oak and desert cave
   Sighs to the torrent's awful voice beneath!

O'er thee, oh king! their hundred arms they
      wave,   25
    Revenge on thee in hoarser murmurs
      breathe,
Vocal no more, since Cambria's fatal day,
To high-born Hoel's harp or soft Llewellyn's lay.

I. 3

    'Cold is Cadwallo's tongue,
      That hushed the stormy main;   30
Brave Urien sleeps upon his craggy bed;
    Mountains, ye mourn in vain
     Modred, whose magic song
Made huge Plinlimmon bow his cloud-topped
    head:
     On dreary Arvon's shore they lie,   35
    Smeared with gore and ghastly pale;
Far, far aloof th' affrighted ravens sail;
    The famished eagle screams, and passes
    by.
Dear lost companions of my tuneful art,
    Dear as the light that visits these sad eyes,   40
Dear as the ruddy drops that warm my heart,
    Ye died amidst your dying country's
    cries—
    No more I weep: they do not sleep!
On yonder cliffs, a grisly band,
    I see them sit; they linger yet   45
Avengers of their native land:
With me in dreadful harmony they join,
And weave with bloody hands the tissue of thy line.

II. 1

    'Weave the warp and weave the woof,
    The winding-sheet of Edward's race;   50

Give ample room and verge enough
The characters of hell to trace:
Mark the year, and mark the night,
When Severn shall re-echo with affright
The shrieks of death through Berkley's roofs that
ring,   55
Shrieks of an agonizing king!
She-wolf of France, with unrelenting fangs,
That tear'st the bowels of thy mangled
mate,
From thee be born who o'er thy country hangs
The scourge of Heaven: what terrors
round him wait!   60
Amazement in his van, with Flight combined,
And Sorrow's faded form, and Solitude behind.

II. 2

'Mighty victor, mighty lord!
Low on his funeral couch he lies:
No pitying heart, no eye, afford   65
A tear to grace his obsequies.
Is the Sable Warrior fled?
Thy son is gone; he rests among the dead.
The swarm that in thy noontide beam were
born?
Gone to salute the rising morn.   70
Fair laughs the morn and soft the zephyr
blows,
While, proudly riding o'er the azure
realm,
In gallant trim the gilded vessel goes,
Youth on the prow, and Pleasure at the
helm,
Regardless of the sweeping Whirlwind's sway, 75
That, hushed in grim repose, expects his evening
prey.

II. 3

'Fill high the sparkling bowl,
　　The rich repast prepare;
Reft of a crown, he yet may share the feast:
　　Close by the regal chair   80
　　　　Fell Thirst and Famine scowl
A baleful smile upon their baffled guest.
　　　　Heard ye the din of battle bray,
　　Lance to lance, and horse to horse?
Long years of havoc urge their destined course, 85
　　And through the kindred squadrons mow
　　　　their way.
Ye towers of Julius, London's lasting shame,
　　With many a foul and midnight murther
　　　　fed,
Revere his consort's faith, his father's fame,
　　And spare the meek usurper's holy head!   90
　　　　Above, below, the rose of snow,
　　Twined with her blushing foe, we spread:
　　　　The bristled Boar in infant gore
　　Wallows beneath thy thorny shade.
Now, brothers, bending o'er th' accursed loom,   95
Stamp we our vengeance deep, and ratify his doom!

III. 1

　　'Edward, lo! to sudden fate
(Weave we the woof: the thread is spun)
　　Half of thy heart we consecrate.
(The web is wove. The work is done.)   100
　　Stay, oh stay! nor thus forlorn
Leave me unblessed, unpitied, here to mourn!
In yon bright track, that fires the western skies,
　　They melt, they vanish from my eyes.

But oh! what solemn scenes on Snowdon's
        height,   105
    Descending slow, their glittering skirts
        unroll?
Visions of glory, spare my aching sight!
    Ye unborn ages, crowd not on my soul!
No more our long-lost Arthur we bewail:
All hail, ye genuine kings, Britannia's issue, hail!   110

III. 2

'Girt with many a baron bold,
Sublime their starry fronts they rear;
    And gorgeous dames, and statesmen old
    In bearded majesty, appear.
    In the midst a form divine!   115
Her eye proclaims her of the Briton line;
Her lion-port, her awe-commanding face,
    Attempered sweet to virgin-grace.
What strings symphonious tremble in the air,
What strains of vocal transport round her play 120
Hear from the grave, great Taliessin, hear:
    They breathe a soul to animate thy clay.
Bright Rapture calls, and, soaring as she sings,
Waves in the eye of Heaven her many-colored
        wings.

III. 3

    'The verse adorn again   125
      Fierce War and faithful Love
And Truth severe, by fairy Fiction
    dressed.
      In buskined measures move
      Pale Grief and pleasing Pain,

With Horror, tyrant of the throbbing breast.   130
      A voice, as of the cherub-choir,
      Gales from blooming Eden bear;
And distant warblings lessen on my ear,
      That, lost in long futurity, expire.
Fond impious man, think'st thou yon sanguine
      cloud,   135
      Raised by thy breath, has quenched the
      orb of day?
To-morrow he repairs the golden flood,
      And warms the nations with redoubled
      ray.
      Enough for me; with joy I see
The different doom our Fates assign: 140
      Be thine Despair and sceptred Care;
To triumph and to die are mine.'
He spoke, and headlong from the mountain's
      height
Deep in the roaring tide he plunged to endless night.
                1757

[For selections from Gray's later works, see p. 208 below.]

SAMUEL RICHARDSON

from CLARISSA HARLOWE

[THE POWER OF INNOCENCE]

Mr. Lovelace to John Belford, Esq.

Now, Belford, see us all sitting in judgment, resolved to punish the fair briberess—I, and the
mother, the hitherto dreaded mother, the nieces
Sally, Polly, the traiteress Dorcas, and Mabell, a
guard as it were over Dorcas that she might not run   5

away and hide herself: all predetermined and of
necessity predetermined, from the journey I was going to take and my precarious situation with her—
and hear her [Clarissa] *unbolt, unlock, unbar* the
door; then as it proved afterwards, put the key into   10
the lock on the outside, lock the door and put it in
her pocket—Will, I knew below, who would give
me notice if, while we were all above she should
mistake her way and go downstairs instead of coming into the dining-room: the street doors also doubly   15
secured and every shutter to the windows round the
house fastened that no noise or screaming should be
heard (such was the brutal preparation!)—And then
hear her step towards us and instantly see her enter
among us confiding in her own innocence and with   20
a majesty in her person and manner that is natural
to her, but which then shone out in all its glory.—
Every tongue silent, every eye awed, every heart
quaking, mine in a particular manner, sunk throb-
less and twice below its usual region to once at my   25
throat—a shameful recreant!—She silent too, looking round her, first on me, then on the mother, as
no longer fearing her, then on Sally, Polly and the
culprit Dorcas—such the glorious power of innocence exerted at that awful moment.   30

She would have spoken but could not, looking
down my guilt into confusion. A mouse might have
been heard passing over the floor; her own light
feet and rustling silks could not have prevented it
for she seemed to tread air and to be all soul. She   35
passed backwards and forwards, now towards me,
now towards the door several times, before speech
could get the better of indignation; and at last after
twice or thrice hemming to recover her articulate
voice—"O thou contemptible and abandoned Love-   40
lace! thinkest thou that I see not through this poor

villainous plot of thine and of these thy wicked ac-
complices?"

"Thou, woman, (looking at the mother) once my
terror! always my dislike, but now my detestation, 45
shouldest once more (for thine perhaps was the
preparation) have provided for me intoxicating
potions to rob me of my senses.

"And then thou wretch! (turning to me) mightest
more securely have depended upon such a low con- 50
trivance as this!

"And ye vile women who perhaps have been the
ruin body and soul of hundreds of innocents, (you
show me how in full assembly) know that I am not
married—ruined as I am by your help, I bless God, 55
I am not married to this miscreant—and I have
friends that will demand my honor at your hands!—
And to whose authority I will apply, for none has
this man over me. Look to it then what further
insults you offer me or incite him to offer me. I 60
am a person, though thus vilely betrayed, of rank
and fortune. I never will be his and to your utter
ruin will find friends to pursue you, and now I have
this full proof of your detestable wickedness and
have heard your base incitements, will have no 65
mercy upon you!"

They could not laugh at the poor figure I made.
Lord! how every devil, conscience-shaken, trembled!

What a dejection must ever fall to the lot of guilt 70
were it given to innocence always thus to exert itself!

1748

[THE DEATH OF CLARISSA]

Mr. Belford to Robert Lovelace, Esq.:

THE colonel was the first that took my attention, kneeling on the side of the bed, the lady's right hand in both his with his face covered, bathing it with his tears although she had been comforting him, as the women since told me, in elevated strains 5 but broken accents.

On the other side of the bed sat the good widow, her face overwhelmed with tears, leaning her head against the bed's head in a most disconsolate manner and turning her face to me as soon as she saw me. 10 "O, Mr. Belford!" cried she with folded hands, "The dear lady,"—a heavy sob permitted her not to say more.

Mrs. Smith with clasped fingers and uplifted eyes as if imploring help from the only power which 15 could give it, was kneeling down by the bed's feet, tears in large drops trickling down her cheeks.

Her nurse was kneeling between the widow and Mrs. Smith, her arms extended. In one hand she held an ineffectual cordial which she had just been 20 offering to her dying mistress, her face was swollen with weeping (though used to such scenes as this) and she turned her eyes towards me as if she called upon me by them to join in the helpless sorrow, a fresh stream bursting from them as I approached the 25 bed.

The maid of the house, with her face upon her folded arms, as she stood leaning against the wainscot, more audibly expressed her grief than any of the others. 30

The lady had been silent a few minutes, and speechless as they thought, moving her lips without

uttering a word, one hand, as I said, in her cousin's.
But when Mrs. Lovick on my approach pronounced
my name, "O! Mr. Belford," said she with a faint
inward voice but very distinct nevertheless,—"Now!
—Now! (in broken periods she spoke)—I bless God
for his mercies to his poor creature—will all soon
be over—a few—a very few moments—will end
this strife—and I shall be happy."

"Comfort here, sir," turning her head to the colonel, "Comfort my cousin—see! the blame—able
kindness—he would not wish me to be happy—so
soon!"

Here she stopped for two or three minutes ear-
nestly looking upon him, then resuming, "My dearest cousin," said she, "Be comforted—what is dying
but the common lot?—The mortal frame may seem
to labor—but that is all. It is not so hard to die as
I believed it to be. The preparation is the difficulty
—I bless God I have had time for that, the rest is
worse to beholders than to me! I am all blessed hope
—hope itself." She looked what she said, a sweet
smile beaming over her countenance.

After a short silence, "Once more, my dear
cousin," said she, but still in broken accents, "Com-
mend me most dutifully to my father and mother,"
there she stopped. And then proceeding—"To my
sister, to my brother, to my uncles—and tell them I
bless them with my parting breath—for all their
goodness to me—even for their displeasure—I bless
them—most happy has been to me my punishment
here! Happy indeed!"

She was silent for a few moments lifting up her
eyes, and the hand her cousin held not between his.
Then, "O death!" said she, "Where is thy sting!"
(The words I remember to have heard in the burial
service read over my uncle and poor Belton.) And

after a pause—"It is good for me that I was afflicted!" Words of scripture I suppose.   70

Then turning towards us who were lost in speechless sorrow, "O dear, dear gentlemen," said she,
"You know not what foretastes, what assurances"—
and there she again stopped and looked up as if in a
thankful rapture, sweetly smiling. Then turning her   75
head towards me, "Do you, sir, tell your friend that
I forgive him! And I pray to God to forgive him!"
—Again pausing and lifting up her eyes as if praying that he would. "Let him know how happily I
die!—And that such as my own I wish to be his last   80
hour."

She was again silent for a few moments, and then
resuming—"My sight fails me!—Your voices only—
(for we both applauded her Christian, her divine
frame, though in accents as broken as her own) and   85
the voice of grief is alike in all. Is not this Mr.
Morden's hand?" pressing one of his with that he
had just let go. "Which is Mr. Belford's?" holding out the other. I gave her mine. "God Almighty
bless you both," said she. "And make you both—in   90
your last hour—for you must come to this—happy
as I am."

She paused again, her breath growing shorter,
and after a few minutes, "And now, my dearest
cousin, give me your hand—nearer—still nearer"—   95
drawing it towards her, and she pressed it with her
dying lips, "God protect you dear, dear sir, and
once more receive my best and most grateful thanks,
and tell my dear Miss Howe, and vouchsafe to see
and to tell my worthy Norton—she will be one day, 100
I fear not, though now lowly in her fortunes, a saint
in heaven—tell them both that I remember them
with thankful blessings in my last moments! And
pray God to give them happiness here for many,
many years, for the sake of their friends and lovers, 105

and an heavenly crown hereafter, and such assurances of it as I have through the all satisfying merits of my blessed Redeemer."

Her sweet voice and broken periods, methinks, still fill my ears and never will be out of my memory. 110

After a short silence in a more broken and faint accent, "And you, Mr. Belford," pressing my hand, "May God preserve you and make you sensible of all your errors—you see, in me, how all ends—may you be"—and down sunk her head upon her pillow 115 she fainting away and drawing from us her hands.

We thought she was then gone, and each gave way to a violent burst of grief.

But soon showing signs of returning life our attention was again engaged, and I besought her, 120 when a little recovered, to complete in my favor her half pronounced blessing. She waved her hand to us both and bowed her head six several times, as we have since recollected, as if distinguishing every person present, not forgetting the nurse and the 125 maid-servant, the latter having approached the bed, weeping as if crowding in for the divine lady's last blessing, and she spoke falteringly and inwardly, "Bless—bless—bless—you all—and—now—and now —(holding up her almost lifeless hands for the last 130 time) Come—O—come—blessed Lord—Jesus!"

And with these words, the last but half pronounced, expired; such a smile, such a charming serenity overspreading her sweet face at the instant as she seemed to manifest her eternal happiness al- 135 ready begun.

O Lovelace!—But I can write no more!

1748

[THE DEATH OF LOVELACE]

From F. J. de la Tour to John Belford, Esq.:

CONTRARY to all expectation he lived over the
night, but suffered much, as well from his impatience
and disappointment as from his wounds; for he
seemed very unwilling to die.

He was delirious at times in the two last hours, 5
and then several times cried out as if he had seen
some frightful specter, "Take her away! Take
her away!" but named nobody. And sometimes
praised some lady (that Clarissa, I suppose, whom
he had invoked when he received his death's wound) 10
calling her, "Sweet excellence! Divine creature!
Fair sufferer!—" And once he said "Look down,
blessed spirit, look down," and there stopped, his
lips, however, moving.

At nine in the morning, he was seized with con- 15
vulsions, and fainted away, and it was a quarter of
an hour before he came out of them. His few
last words I must not omit as they show an ultimate
composure which may administer some consolation
to his honorable friends. "Blessed," said he, ad- 20
dressing himself no doubt to heaven, for his dying
eyes were lifted up—a strong convulsion prevented
him for a few moments saying more—but recovering, he again with great fervor (lifting up his eyes,
and his spread hands) pronounced the word blessed. 25
Then in a seeming ejaculation he spoke inwardly so
as not to be understood; at last he distinctly pronounced these three words,

"Let this expiate!"

And then, his head sinking on his pillow, he expired 30
at about half an hour after ten.

1748

DAVID HARTLEY

[THE LAWS OF ASSOCIATION]

FROM OBSERVATIONS ON MAN

SENSATIONS are those internal feelings of the mind, which arise from the impressions made by external objects upon the several parts of our bodies.

All of our other internal feelings may be called ideas. Some of these appear to spring up in the mind of themselves, some are suggested by words, others arise in other ways. Many writers comprehend sensations under ideas; but I everywhere use these words in the senses here ascribed to them.

The ideas which resemble sensations are called ideas of sensation: all the rest may therefore be called intellectual ideas.

It will appear in the course of these observations, that the ideas of sensation are the elements of which all the rest are compounded. Hence ideas of sensation may be termed simple, intellectual ones complex.

The pleasures and pains are comprehended under the sensations and ideas, as these are explained above. For all our pleasures and pains are internal feelings, and, conversely, all our internal feelings seem to be attended with some degree either of pleasure or pain. However, I shall, for the most part, give the names of pleasure and pain only to such degrees as are considerable; referring all low, evanescent ones to the head of mere sensations and ideas.

The pleasures and pains may be ranged under seven general classes, viz:

1. Sensation;
2. Imagination;
3. Ambition;
4. Self-interest;
5. Sympathy;
6. Theopathy; and
7. The Moral Sense; according as they rise from:
    1. The impressions made on the external senses;
    2. Natural or artificial beauty or deformity;
    3. The opinions of others concerning us;
    4. Our possession or want of the means of happiness, and security from, or subjection to, the hazards of misery;
    5. The pleasures and pains of our fellow-creatures;
    6. The affections excited in us by the contemplation of the Deity; or
    7. Moral beauty and deformity.

. . . .

. . . All the intellectual pleasures and pains are deducible ultimately from the sensible ones, if one can show of each intellectual pleasure and pain in particular, that it takes its rise from other pleasures and pains, either sensible or intellectual. For thus none of the intellectual pleasures and pains can be original. But the sensible pleasures and pains are evidently originals. They are therefore the only ones, i. e., they are the common sources from whence all the intellectual pleasures and pains are ultimately derived.

. . . .

The sensible pleasures are the first pleasures of which we are capable, and are the foundation of the intellectual ones, which are formed from them in succession, according to the law of association, as before explained.   Now which way soever we may turn our view, that which is prior in the order of nature is always less perfect and principal, than that which is posterior, the last of two contiguous states being the end, the first the means subservient to that end, though itself be an end in respect of some foregoing state, the sensible pleasures therefore cannot be supposed of equal value and dignity with the intellectual, to the generation of which they are made subservient.

.   .   .   .

It is evident, that the pleasures of imagination were not intended for our primary pursuit, because they are, in general, the first of our intellectual pleasures, which are generated from the sensible ones by association, come to their height early in life, and decline in old age. . . . The pleasures of imagination are the next remove above the sensible ones, and have, in their proper place and degree, a great efficacy in improving and perfecting our natures. They are to men in the early part of their adult age, what playthings are to children; they teach them a love for regularity, exactness, truth, simplicity; they lead them to the knowledge of many important truths relating to themselves, the external world, and its author; they habituate to invent, and reason by analogy and induction; and when the social, moral and religious affections begin to be generated in us, we may make a much quicker progress towards the perfection of our natures by having a due stock of knowledge, in natural and artificial things, of a relish for natural and artificial beauty.   It deserves particular notice here, that the language used in

respect of the ideas, pleasures, and pains of imagination, is applicable to those of the moral sense, with
a peculiar fitness and significancy; as vice versa, the
proper language of the moral sense does, in many
cases, add great beauty to poetry, oratory, etc., when 100
used catachrestically.   And we may observe in general, that as the pleasures of imagination are manifestly intended to generate and augment the higher
orders, particularly those of sympathy, theopathy,
and the moral sense; so these last may be made to 105
improve and perfect those.

1749

RICHARD JAGO

from THE GOLDFINCHES

ALL in a garden, on a currant bush,
  With wondrous art they built their airy seat;
In the next orchard lived a friendly thrush
  Nor distant far a woodlark's soft retreat.

Here blessed with ease, and in each other blessed,   5
  With early songs they waked the neighboring
        groves,
Till time matured their joys, and crowned their nest
  With infant pledges of their faithful loves.

And now what transport glowed in either's eye!
  What equal fondness dealt th' allotted food!   10
What joy each other's likeness to descry;
  And future sonnets in the chirping brood!

But ah! what earthly happiness can last?
  How does the fairest purpose often fail?
A truant schoolboy's wantonness could blast   15

  Their flattering hopes, and leave them both to
    wail.

The most ungentle of his tribe was he,
    No generous precept ever touched his heart;
With concord false, and hideous prosody,
    He scrawled his task, and blundered o'er his part. 2)

On mischief bent, he marked, with ravenous eyes,
    Where wrapped in down the callow songsters lay;
Then rushing, rudely seized the glittering prize,
    And bore it in his impious hands away!

But how shall I describe, in numbers rude,   25
    The pangs for poor Chrysomitris decreed,
When from her secret stand aghast she viewed
    The cruel spoiler perpetrate the deed?

'O grief of griefs!' with shrieking voice she cried,
    'What sight is this that I have lived to see!   30
O! that I had in youth's fair season died,
    From love's false joys and bitter sorrows free.'
                                            1753

JOHN DALTON

FROM A DESCRIPTIVE POEM

        To NATURE's pride,
    Sweet Keswick's vale, the Muse will guide:
    The Muse who trod th' enchanted ground,
    Who sailed the wondrous lake around,
    With you will haste once more to hail   5
    The beauteous brook of Borrodale.

        .   .   .   .

Let other streams rejoice to roar
Down the rough rocks of dread Lodore,
Rush raving on with boisterous sweep,
And foaming rend the frighted deep;   10
Thy gentle genius shrinks away
From such a rude unequal fray;
Through thine own native dale where rise
Tremendous rocks amid the skies,
Thy waves with patience slowly wind,   15
Till they the smoothest channel find,
Soften the horrors of the scene,
And through confusion flow serene.

    Horrors like these at first alarm,
But soon with savage grandeur charm,   20
And raise to noblest thought the mind:
Thus by the fall, Lodore, reclined,
The craggy cliff, impendent wood,
Whose shadows mix o'er half the flood,
The gloomy clouds which solemn sail,   25
Scarce lifted by the languid gale.

.   .   .   .

Channels by rocky torrents torn,
Rocks to the lake in thunder borne,
Or such as o'er our heads appear,
Suspended in their mid-career,   30
To start again at his command
Who rules fire, water, air, and land,
I view with wonder and delight,
A pleasing, though an awful sight.

.   .   .   .

And last, to fix our wandering eyes,   35
Thy roots, O Keswick, brighter rise
The lake and lofty hills between,

Where Giant Skiddow shuts the scene.
　Supreme of mountains, Skiddow, hail!
To whom all Britain sinks a vale!　　　　　　40
Lo, his imperial brow I see
From foul usurping vapors free!
'Twere glorious now his side to climb,
Boldly to scale his top sublime,
And thence—My Muse, these flights forbear,　45
Nor with wild raptures tire the fair.

                                        1755

JANE ELLIOT

THE FLOWERS OF THE FOREST

I've heard them lilting, at our ewe-milking,
Lasses a-lilting, before the dawn of day;
But now they are moaning, on ilka green loaning;
The Flowers of the Forest are a' wede away.

At bughts in the morning nae blythe lads are scorn-
　　　　ing;　　　　　　　　　　　　　　　　　　　　　5
The lasses are lanely, and dowie, and wae;
Nae daffing, nae gabbing, but sighing and sabbing,
Ilk ane lifts her leglin, and hies her away.

In hairst, at the shearing, nae youths now are jeer-
　　　　ing,
The bandsters are lyart, and runkled and gray;　　10
At fair or at preaching, nae wooing, nae fleeching—
The Flowers of the Forest are a' wede away.

At e'en, in the gloaming, nae swankies are roaming
'Bout stacks wi' the lasses at bogle to play;
But ilk ane sits eerie, lamenting her dearie—　　　15
The Flowers of the Forest are a' wede away.

Dool and wae for the order sent our lads to the
    Border!
The English, for ance, by guile wan the day;
The Flowers of the Forest, that fought aye the fore-
    most,
The prime of our land, lie cauld in the clay.   20

We'll hear nae more lilting at our ewe-milking,
Women and bairns are heartless and wae;
Sighing and moaning on ilka green loaning,
The Flowers of the Forest are a' wede away.

                             1756

THOMAS AMORY

[A PEDESTRIAN TOUR IN NORTHERN ENGLAND]

FROM THE LIFE AND OPINIONS OF JOHN BUNCLE

I

With the rising sun then set I out, and was
charmed for several hours with the air and views.
The mountains, the rocky precipices, the woods and
the waters appeared in various striking situations
every mile I travelled on, and formed the most aston-   5
ishing points of view. Sometimes I was above the
clouds, and then crept to enchanting valleys below.
Here glens were seen that looked as if the mountains had been rent asunder to form the amazing
scenes, and there, forests and falling streams cov-   10
ered the sides of the hills. Rivers in many places, in
the most beautiful cascades, were tumbling along;
and cataracts from the tops of mountains came

roaring down. The whole was grand, wonderful, and fine. On the top of one of the mountains I 15 passed over at noon, the air was piercing cold, on account of its great height, and so subtle that we breathed with difficulty, and were a little sick. From hence I saw several black subjacent clouds, big with thunder, and the lightning within them rolled back- 20 wards and forwards, like shining bodies of the brightest luster. One of them went off in the grand- est horrors through the vales below, and had no more to do with the peak I was on, than if it had been a summit in another planet. The scene was 25 prodigiously fine. *Sub pedibus ventos et rauca tonitrua calcat.*

Till the evening, I rode and walked it, and in numberless windings around unpassable hills, and by the sides of rivers it was impossible to cross, 30 journeyed a great many miles. But no human crea- ture, or any kind of house, did I meet with in all the long way. And as I arrived at last at a beautiful lake whose banks the hand of nature had adorned with vast old trees, I sat down by this water in the 35 shade, to dine on a neat's tongue I had got from good Mrs. Price, and was so delighted with the strik- ing beauties and stillness of the place, that I deter- mined to pass the night in this sweet retreat. Nor was it one night only, if I had my will, that I would 40 have rested there. Often did I wish for a convenient little lodge by this sweet water side, and that with the numerous swans and other fowl that lived there, I might have spent my time in peace below, till I was removed to the established seat of happiness 45 above.

II

LEAVING this bottom, we mounted another very high and dangerous hill, and from the top of it de-

scended into twenty acres of as rich and beautiful
ground as my eyes had ever seen. It was covered 50
with flowers and aromatic herbs, and had, in the
center of it, a little grove of beautiful trees, among
which were fruits of several kinds. A flowing spring
of the purest water was in the middle of this sweet
little wood, and ran in pretty windings over the 55
ground. It refreshed and adorned the field, and it
was beautiful to see the deer from the hills, and the
goats come down from the cliffs, to drink at these
streams. The whole was surrounded with precipices
that ascended above the clouds, and through one of 60
these rocky mountains there was an opening that had
a stupendous appearance.

It was a vast, amazing arch that had some resemblance to the gothic isle of a large cathedral church,
and terminated in a view of rocks hanging over 65
rocks in a manner frightful to behold. It measured
an hundred yards in length, forty in breadth, and I
judged it to be fifty yards high. The pending rocks
in view inclosed a space of four acres—as it appeared to me—and the bottom was so very deep that 70
it looked like night below. What line I had could
not reach it, nor could I make anything of the depth
by sound. It seemed to me to be a vast swallow
that went down to the abyss. The whole was a
scene that harrowed the soul with horror. 75

1756

.LAURENCE STERNE

FROM TRISTRAM SHANDY

[THE LESSON OF UNIVERSAL GOOD-WILL]

MY UNCLE TOBY was a man patient of injuries,
—not from want of courage,—I have told you in a

former chapter that he was a man of courage;—and
will add here, that where just occasions presented,
or called it forth, I know no man under whose arm
I would have sooner taken shelter. Nor did this
arise from any insensibility or obtuseness of his intellectual parts, for he felt this insult of my father's
as feelingly as a man could do. But he was of a
peaceful, placid nature,—no jarring element in it,—
all was mixed up so kindly within him. My Uncle
Toby had scarce a heart to retaliate upon a fly.

"Go," says he, one day at dinner, to an over
grown one which had buzzed about his nose, and tormented him cruelly all dinner-time, and which, after
infinite attempts, he had caught at last, as it flew
by him.

"I'll not hurt thee," says my Uncle Toby, rising
from his chair, and going across the room with the
fly in his hand. "I'll not hurt a hair of thy head.
Go," says he, lifting up the sash, and opening his
hand, as he spoke, to let it escape. "Go, poor devil,
get thee gone. Why should I hurt thee? This world
surely is wide enough to hold both thee and me."

I was but ten years old when this happened, but
whether it was that the action itself was more in
unison to my nerves at that age of pity, which instantly set my whole frame into one vibration of
most pleasurable sensation, or how far the manner
and expression of it might go towards it, or in what
degree, or by what secret magic, a tone of voice and
harmony of movement attuned by mercy, might find
a passage to my heart,—I know not. This I know,
that the lesson of universal good-will, then taught
and imprinted by my Uncle Toby, has never since
been worn out of my mind. And though I would not
depreciate what the study of the *Literae humaniores,*
at the university, have done for me in that respect,
or discredit the other helps of an expensive educa-

tion bestowed upon me, both at home and abroad 40
since:—yet I often think that I owe one half of my
philanthropy to that one accidental impression.

1759

[THE DEATH OF LE FEVER]

"In a fortnight or three weeks," added my Uncle
Toby, smiling, "he might march."

"He will never march! an' please your honor, in
this world," said the corporal.

"He will march!" said my Uncle Toby, rising up 5
from the side of the bed, with one shoe off.

"An' please your honor," said the corporal, "he
will never march but to his grave."

"He shall march!" cried my Uncle Toby, march-
ing the foot which had a shoe on, though without 10
advancing an inch. "He shall march to his regi-
ment."

"He cannot stand it," said the corporal.

"He shall be supported," said my Uncle Toby.

"He'll drop at last," said the corporal, "and 15
what will become of his boy?"

"He shall not drop," said my Uncle Toby, firmly.

"A-well-o'day,—do what we can for him," said
Trim, maintaining his point, "the poor soul will die."

"He shall not die! by G—!" cried my Uncle Toby. 20

The Accusing Spirit, which flew up to heaven's
chancery with the oath, blushed as he gave it in, and
the Recording Angel, as he wrote it down, dropped a
tear upon the word, and blotted it out forever.

Chapter IX

—My Uncle Toby went to his bureau, put his 25
purse into his breeches pocket, and having ordered

the corporal to go early in the morning for a physician,—he went to bed, and fell asleep.

Chapter X

The Story of Le Fever Continued.

The sun looked bright the morning after, to every
eye in the village but Le Fever's and his afflicted 30
son's. The hand of death pressed heavy upon his
eye-lids,—and hardly could the wheel at the cistern
turn round its circle, when my Uncle Toby, who
had rose up an hour before his wonted time, entered
the lieutenant's room, and without preface or apol- 35
ogy, sat himself down upon the chair by the bed-side,
and, independently of all modes and customs, opened
the curtain in the manner an old friend and brother
officer would have done it, and asked him how he
did,—how he had rested in the night,—what was his 40
complaint,—where was his pain,—and what he could
do to help him. And without giving him time to
answer any one of the inquiries, went on, and told
him of the little plan which he had been concerting
with the corporal the night before for him. 45
"You shall go home directly, Le Fever," said my
Uncle Toby, "to my house. And we'll send for a
doctor to see what's the matter,—and we'll have
an apothecary,—and the corporal shall be your nurse.
And I'll be your servant, Le Fever." 50
There was a frankness in my Uncle Toby,—not
the effect of familiarity, but the cause of it,—which
let you at once into his soul, and showed you the
goodness of his nature. To this, there was something in his looks, and voice, and manner, super- 55
added, which eternally beckoned to the unfortunate
to come and take shelter under him. So that before
my Uncle Toby had half finished the kind offers

he was making to the father, had the son insensibly
pressed up close to his knees, and had taken hold of 60
the breast of his coat, and was pulling it towards
him. The blood and spirits of Le Fever, which
were waxing cold and slow within him, and were
retreating to their last citadel, the heart—rallied
back. The film forsook his eyes for a moment. He 65
looked up wishfully in my Uncle Toby's face, then
cast a look upon his boy, and that ligament, fine as
it was,—was never broken.—

Nature instantly ebbed again. The film returned
to its place. The pulse fluttered—stopped—went on 70
—throbbed—stopped again—moved—stopped—shall
I go on? No.

1761

[NANNETTE]

A sun-burnt daughter of Labor rose up from
the group to meet me, as I advanced towards them.
Her hair, which was a dark chestnut approaching
rather to a black, was tied up in a knot, all but a
single tress.   5

"We want a cavalier," said she, holding out both
her hands, as if to offer them.

"And a cavalier ye shall have," said I, taking
hold of both of them.

"Hadst thou, Nannette, been arrayed like a duch- 10
ess! But that cursed slit in thy petticoat!"

Nannette cared not for it.

"We could not have done without you," said she,
letting go one hand, with self-taught politeness,
leading me up with the other.   15

A lame youth, whom Apollo had recompensed
with a pipe, and to which he had added a tabourin
of his own accord, ran sweetly over the prelude as
he sat upon the bank.

"Tie me up this tress instantly," said Nannette, 20
putting a piece of string into my hand. It taught
me to forget I was a stranger. The whole knot fell
down—We had been seven years acquainted.

The youth struck the note upon the tabourin,
his pipe followed, and off we bounded.—"The deuce 25
take that slit!"

The sister of the youth, who had stolen her voice
from heaven, sung alternately with her brother.
'Twas a Gascoigne roundelay.

VIVE LA JOIA!   30
FIDON LA TRISTESSA!

The nymphs joined in unison, and their swains an
octave below them.

I would have given a crown to have it sewed up.
Nannette would not have given a sous. Vive la joia! 35
was in her lips.—Vive la joia! was in her eyes. A
transient spark of amity shot across the space betwixt us. She looked amiable! Why could I not
live, and end my days thus?

"Just Disposer of our joys and sorrows," cried I, 40
"why could not a man sit down in the lap of content
here, and dance, and sing, and say his prayers, and
go to heaven with his nut-brown maid?"

1765

FROM A SENTIMENTAL JOURNEY

[MARIA]

WHEN we had got within half a league of Moulines, at a little opening in the road leading to a
thicket, I discovered poor Maria sitting under a poplar. She was sitting with her elbow in her lap, and

her head leaning on one side within her hand. A small brook ran at the foot of the tree.

I bid the postillion go on with the chaise to Moulines, and La Fleur to bespeak my supper, and that I would walk after him.

She was dressed in white, and much as my friend described her, except that her hair hung loose, which before was twisted within a silk net. She had, superadded likewise to her jacket, a pale green ribband, which fell across her shoulder to the waist, at the end of which hung her pipe. Her goat had been as faithless as her lover, and she had got a little dog in lieu of him, which she had kept tied by a string to her girdle. As I looked at her dog, she drew him towards her with the string.

"Thou shalt not leave me, Sylvio," said she. I looked in Maria's eyes, and saw she was thinking more of her father than of her lover or her little goat, for as she uttered them, the tears trickled down her cheeks.

I sat down close by her, and Maria let me wipe them away, as they fell, with my handkerchief. I then steeped it in my own—and then in hers—and then in mine—and then I wiped hers again. And as I did it, I felt such undescribable emotions within me, as I am sure could not be accounted for from any combinations of matter and motion.

I am positive I have a soul. Nor can all the books with which materialists have pestered the world over convince me to the contrary.

1768

A SENTIMENTAL JOURNEY

DEAR sensibility! source inexhausted of all that's precious in our joys, or costly in our sorrows! Thou chainest thy martyr down upon his bed of

straw, and 'tis thou who liftest him up to heaven.
Eternal fountain of our feelings! 'tis here I trace   5
thee, and this is thy "divinity which stirs within me."
Not that in some sad and sickening moments, "my
soul shrinks back upon herself, and startles at destruction." Mere pomp of words! But that I feel
some generous joys and generous cares beyond my-   10
self. All comes from thee, great—great Sensorium
of the world! which vibrates, if a hair of our heads
but falls upon the ground, in the remotest desert of
thy creation. Touched with thee, Eugenius draws
my curtain when I languish, hears my tale of symp-   15
toms, and blames the weather for the disorder of his
nerves. Thou givest a portion of it sometimes to
the roughest peasant who traverses the bleakest
mountains. He finds the lacerated lamb of another's flock. This moment I beheld him leaning   20
with his head against his crook, with piteous inclination, looking down upon it! Oh! had I come
one moment sooner! It bleeds to death. His gentle
heart bleeds with it—

Peace to thee, generous swain! I see thou walkest   25
off with anguish, but thy joys shall balance it, for
happy is thy cottage, and happy is the sharer of it,
and happy are the lambs which sport about you.

1768

JAMES MACPHERSON

from OSSIAN

[FINGAL'S ROMANTIC GENEROSITY
TOWARD HIS CAPTIVE ENEMY]

'King of Lochlin,' said Fingal, 'thy blood flows in
the veins of thy foe. Our fathers met in battle,
because they loved the strife of spears. But often

did they feast in the hall, and send round the joy of
the shell. Let thy face brighten with gladness, and
thine ear delight in the harp. Dreadful as the storm
of thine ocean, thou hast poured thy valor forth;
thy voice has been like the voice of thousands when
they engage in war. Raise, to-morrow, raise thy
white sails to the wind, thou brother of Agandecca!
Bright as the beam of noon, she comes on my mournful soul. I have seen thy tears for the fair one.
I spared thee in the halls of Starno, when my sword
was red with slaughter, when my eye was full of
tears for the maid. Or dost thou choose the fight?
The combat which thy fathers gave to Trenmor is
thine! that thou mayest depart renowned, like the
sun setting in the west!'

'King of the race of Morven!' said the chief of
resounding Lochlin, 'never will Swaran fight with
thee, first of a thousand heroes! I have seen thee
in the halls of Starno: few were thy years beyond my
own. When shall I, I said to my soul, lift the spear
like the noble Fingal? We have fought heretofore,
O warrior, on the side of the shaggy Malmor; after
my waves had carried me to thy halls, and the feast
of a thousand shells was spread. Let the bards send
his name who overcame to future years, for noble
was the strife of Malmor! But many of the ships
of Lochlin have lost their youths on Lena. Take
these, thou king of Morven, and be the friend of
Swaran! When thy sons shall come to Gormal,
the feast of shells shall be spread, and the combat
offered on the vale.'

'Nor ship,' replied the king, 'shall Fingal take, nor
land of many hills. The desert is enough to me,
with all its deer and woods. Rise on thy waves
again, thou noble friend of Agandecca! Spread thy
white sails to the beam of the morning; return to
the echoing hills of Gormal.' 'Blest be thy soul, thou

king of shells,' said Swaran of the dark-brown shield. 'In peace thou art the gale of spring. In war, the mountain-storm. Take now my hand in friendship, king of echoing Selma! Let thy bards mourn those who fell. Let Erin give the sons of Lochlin 45 to earth. Raise high the mossy stones of their fame: that the children of the north hereafter may behold the place where their fathers fought. The hunter may say, when he leans on a mossy tomb, here Fingal and Swaran fought, the heroes of other years. 50 Thus hereafter shall he say, and our fame shall last for ever!'

'Swaran,' said the king of hills, 'to-day our fame is greatest. We shall pass away like a dream. No sound will remain in our fields of war. Our tombs 55 will be lost in the heath. The hunter shall not know the place of our rest. Our names may be heard in song. What avails it when our strength hath ceased? O Ossian, Carril, and Ullin! you know of heroes that are no more. Give us the song of other years. 60 Let the night pass away on the sound, and morning return with joy.'

We gave the song to the kings. A hundred harps mixed their sound with our voice. The face of Swaran brightened, like the full moon of heaven: 65 when the clouds vanish away, and leave her calm and broad in the midst of the sky.

1762

[COLMA'S LAMENT]

It is night; I am alone, forlorn on the hill of storms. The wind is heard in the mountain. The torrent pours down the rock. No hut receives me from the rain, forlorn on the hill of winds.

Rise, moon! from behind thy clouds. Stars of the 5 night, arise! Lead me, some light, to the place where

my love rests from the chase alone! his bow near
him, unstrung; his dogs panting around him.   But
here I must sit alone, by the rock of the mossy
stream.   The stream and the wind roar aloud.   I   10
hear not the voice of my love!   Why delays my
Salgar, why the chief of the hill, his promise?   Here
is the rock, and here the tree! here is the roaring
stream!   Thou didst promise with night to be here.
Ah! whither is my Salgar gone!   With thee I would   15
fly, from my father; with thee, from my brother
of pride.   Our race have long been foes; we are not
foes, O Salgar!

Cease a little while, O wind! stream, be thou silent
a while! let my voice be heard around.   Let my   20
wanderer hear me!   Salgar! it is Colma who calls.
Here is the tree and the rock.   Salgar, my love!   I
am here.   Why delayest thou thy coming? Lo! the
calm moon comes forth.   The flood is bright in the
vale.   The rocks are grey on the steep.   I see him   25
not on the brow.   His dogs come not before him,
with tidings of his near approach.   Here I must sit
alone!

Who lie on the heath beside me?   Are they my
love and my brother?   Speak to me, O my friends!   30
To Colma they give no reply.   Speak to me: I am
alone!   My soul is tormented with fears!   Ah, they
are dead!   Their swords are red from the fight.   O
my brother! my brother! why hast thou slain my
Salgar?   Why, O Salgar! hast thou slain my brother?   35
Dear were ye both to me! what shall I say in your
praise?   Thou wert fair on the hill among thousands!
he was terrible in fight.   Speak to me; hear my
voice; hear me, sons of my love!   They are silent;
silent for ever!   Cold, cold are their breasts of clay.   40
Oh! from the rock on the hill; from the top of the
windy steep, speak, ye ghosts of the dead! speak, I
will not be afraid!   Whither are ye gone to rest?   In

what cave of the hill shall I find the departed? No
feeble voice is on the gale; no answer half-drowned 45
in the storm!

I sit in my grief! I wait for morning in my
tears! Rear the tomb, ye friends of the dead. Close
it not till Colma come. My life flies away like a
dream! why should I stay behind? Here shall I 50
rest with my friends, by the stream of the sounding
rock. When night comes on the hill; when the loud
winds arise; my ghost shall stand in the blast, and
mourn the death of my friends. The hunter shall
hear from his booth. He shall fear, but love my 55
voice! For sweet shall my voice be for my friends:
pleasant were her friends to Colma!

1762

[THE LAST WORDS OF OSSIAN]

SUCH were the words of the bards in the days of
song; when the king heard the music of harps, the
tales of other times! The chiefs gathered from all
their hills and heard the lovely sound. They praised
the voice of Cona [Ossian], the first among a thou- 5
sand bards! But age is now on my tongue; my soul
has failed! I hear at times the ghosts of bards, and
learn their pleasant song. But memory fails on
my mind. I hear the call of years! They say as
they pass along, why does Ossian sing? Soon shall 10
he lie in the narrow house, and no bard shall raise
his fame! Roll on, ye dark-brown years; ye bring
no joy on your course! Let the tomb open to Ossian,
for his strength has failed. The sons of song are
gone to rest. My voice remains, like a blast that 15
roars lonely on a sea-surrounded rock, after the
winds are laid. The dark moss whistles there; the
distant mariner sees the waving trees!

1762

RICHARD HURD

from LETTERS ON CHIVALRY AND ROMANCE

Letter I

THE ages we call barbarous present us with many a subject of curious speculation. What, for instance, is more remarkable than the Gothic chivalry? or than the spirit of romance, which took its rise from that singular institution? 5

Nothing in human nature, my dear friend, is without its reasons. The modes and fashions of different times may appear, at first sight, fantastic and unaccountable. But they who look nearly into them discover some latent cause of their produc- 10 tion.

Nature once known, no prodigies remain,

as sings our philosophical bard; but to come at this knowledge is the difficulty. Sometimes a close atten- tion to the workings of the human mind is sufficient 15 to lead us to it. Sometimes more than that, the diligent observation of what passes without us, is necessary.

This last I take to be the case here. The prodigies we are now contemplating had their origin in the 20 barbarous ages. Why, then, says the fastidious modern, look any farther for the reason? Why not resolve them at once into the usual caprice and absurdity of barbarians?

This, you see, is a short and commodious phi- 25

losophy. Yet barbarians have their *own,* such as it is, if they are not enlightened by our reason. Shall we then condemn them unheard, or will it not be fair to let them have the telling of their own story?

Would we know from what causes the institution of chivalry was derived? The time of its birth, the situation of the barbarians, amongst whom it arose, must be considered. Their wants, designs, and policies must be explored. We must inquire when and where and how it came to pass that the western world became familiarized to this prodigy, which we now start at.

Another thing is full as remarkable, and concerns us more nearly. The spirit of chivalry was a fire which soon spent itself; but that of *romance,* which was kindled at it, burnt long, and continued its light and heat even to the politer ages.

The greatest geniuses of our own and foreign countries, such as Ariosto and Tasso in Italy, and Spenser and Milton in England, were seduced by these barbarities of their forefathers, were even charmed by the Gothic romances. Was this caprice and absurdity in them? Or, may there not be something in the Gothic romance peculiarly suited to the views of a genius, and to the ends of poetry? And may not the philosophic moderns have gone too far, in their perpetual ridicule and contempt of it?

To form a judgment in the case, the rise, progress, and genius of Gothic chivalry must be explained.

The circumstances in the Gothic fictions and manners, which are proper to the ends of poetry (if any such there be) must be pointed out.

Reasons for the decline and rejection of the Gothic taste in later times must be given.

You have in these particulars both the subject and the plan of the following Letters.

Letter VI

Let it be no surprise to you that, in the close of my last Letter, I presumed to bring the *Gierusa-lemme Liberata* into competition with the *Iliad*.

So far as the heroic and Gothic manners are the same, the pictures of each, if well taken, must be 5 equally entertaining. But I go further, and maintain that the circumstances in which they differ are clearly to the advantage of the Gothic designers.

You see, my purpose is to lead you from this forgotten chivalry to a more amusing subject; I 10 mean the *poetry* we still read, and which was founded upon it.

Much has been said, and with great truth, of the felicity of Homer's age, for poetical manners. But as Homer was a citizen of the world, when he had 15 seen in Greece, on the one hand, the manners he has described, could he, on the other hand, have seen in the west the manners of the feudal ages, I make no doubt but he would certainly have preferred the latter. And the grounds of this preference would, 20 I suppose, have been *the improved gallantry of the feudal times and the superior solemnity of their superstitions.*

If any great poet, like Homer, had lived amongst, and sung of, the Gothic knights (for after all, Spen- 25 ser and Tasso came too late, and it was impossible for them to paint truly and perfectly what was no longer seen or believed) this preference, I persuade myself, had been very sensible. But their fortune was not so happy. 30

          —omnes illacrymabiles
     Urgentur, ignotique longâ
      Nocte, carent quia vate sacro.

As it is, we may take a guess of what the subject was capable of affording to real genius from the rude sketches we have of it in the old romancers. And it is but looking into any of them to be convinced that the *gallantry* which inspirited the feudal times was of a nature to furnish the poet with finer scenes and subjects of description in every view, than the simple and uncontrolled barbarity of the Grecian.

The principal entertainment arising from the delineation of these consists in the exercise of the boisterous passions, which are provoked and kept alive from one end of the *Iliad* to the other, by every imaginable scene of rage, revenge, and slaughter. In the other, together with these, the gentler and more humane affections are awakened in us by the most interesting displays of love and friendship; of love, elevated to its noblest heights; and of friendship, operating on the purest motives. The mere variety of these paintings is a relief to the reader, as well as writer. But their beauty, novelty, and pathos give them a vast advantage on the comparison.

Consider, withal, the surprises, accidents, adventures which probably and naturally attend on the life of the wandering knights; the occasion there must be for describing the wonders of different countries, and of presenting to view the manners and policies of distant states: all which make so conspicuous a part of the materials of the greater poetry.

So that, on the whole, though the spirit, passions, rapine, and violence of the two sets of manners were equal, yet there was a dignity, a magnificence, a variety in the feudal, which the other wanted.

As to *religious machinery,* perhaps the popular system of each was equally remote from reason, yet the latter had something in it more amusing, as well as more awakening to the imagination.

The current popular tales of elves and fairies were

even fitter to take the credulous mind, and charm it
into a willing admiration of the *specious miracles*
which wayward fancy delights in, than those of the
old traditionary rabble of pagan divinities. And
then, for the more solemn fancies of witchcraft and   75
incantation, the horrors of the Gothic were above
measure striking and terrible. The mummeries of
the pagan priests were childish, but the Gothic en-
chanters shook and alarmed all nature.

We feel this difference very sensibly in reading   80
the ancient and modern poets. You would not compare the Canidia of Horace with the Witches in
Macbeth. And what are Virgil's myrtles dropping
blood, to Tasso's enchanted forest?

Ovid indeed, who had a fancy turned to romance,   85
makes Medea, in a rant, talk wildly. But was this
the common language of their other writers? The
enchantress in Virgil says coolly of the very chiefest
prodigies of her charms and poisons,

> His ego sæpè lupum fieri, & se condere sylvis   90
> Mœrin; sæpè animas imis excire sepulchris,
> Atque satas alio vidi traducere messes.

The admirable poet has given an air of the marvellous to his subject, by the magic of his expression.
Else, what do we find here, but the ordinary effects   95
of *melancholy,* the vulgar superstition of *evoking
spirits,* and the supposed influence of *fascination* on
the hopes of rural industry.

> Non isthic obliquo oculo mihi commoda quisquam
>   Limat . . .   100

says the poet of his country-seat, as if this security
from a fascinating eye were a singular privilege,
and the mark of a more than common good fortune.

Shakspere, on the other hand, with a terrible sublime (which not so much the energy of his genius,   105

as the nature of his subject drew from him) gives
us another idea of the *rough magic,* as he calls it, of
fairy enchantment.

> . . . I have bedimmed
> The noon-tide sun, called forth the mutinous winds,   110
> And 'twixt the green sea and the azure vault
> Set roaring war; to the dread rattling thunder
> Have I giv'n fire, and rifted Jove's stout oak
> With his own bolt. The strong-based promontory
> Have I made shake, and by the spurs plucked up   115
> The pine and cedar. Graves, at my command,
> Have opened, and let forth their sleepers. . . .

The last circumstance, you will say, is but the
animas imis excire sepulchris of the Latin poet.
But a very significant word marks the difference. 120
The pagan necromancers had a hundred little tricks
by which they pretended to call up the ghosts, or
shadows of the dead; but these, in the ideas of
paganism, were quite another thing from Shakspere's
sleepers.   125

This may serve for a cast of Shakspere's magic.
And I can't but think that, when Milton wanted to
paint the horrors of that night (one of the noblest
parts in his *Paradise Regained*) which the Devil
himself is feigned to conjure up in the wilderness, 130
the Gothic language and ideas helped him to work
up his tempest with such terror. You will judge
from these lines:

> . . . Nor staid the terror there:
> Infernal ghosts and hellish furies round   135
> Environed thee; some howled, some yelled, some shrieked,
> Some bent at thee their fiery darts. . . .

But above all from the following,

> Thus passed the night so foul, till morning fair
> Came forth with pilgrim steps in amice gray,   140
> Who with her *radiant finger* stilled the roar
> Of thunder, chased the clouds, and laid the winds
> And *griesly specters.*

Where the *radiant finger* points at the potent wand
of the Gothic magicians, which could reduce the 145
calm of nature, upon occasion, as well as disturb
it; and the *griesly specters laid* by the approach of
morn, were apparently of their raising, as a sagacious
critic perceived when he took notice "how very in-
judicious it was to retail the *popular superstition* in 150
this place."

After all, the conclusion is not to be drawn so
much from particular passages, as from the *general impression* left on our minds in reading the
ancient and modern poets. And this is so much in 155
favor of the latter that Mr. Addison scruples not to
say, "The ancients have not much of this poetry
among them; for, indeed (continues he) almost the
whole substance of it owes its original to the darkness and superstition of later ages—Our forefathers 160
looked upon nature with more reverence and horror,
before the world was enlightened by learning and
philosophy, and loved to astonish themselves with
the apprehensions of Witchcraft, Prodigies, Charms,
and Inchantments. There was not a village in Eng- 165
land, that had not a Ghost in it; the churchyards
were all haunted; every large common had a circle
of fairies belonging to it; and there was scarce a
Shepherd to be met with who had not seen a
spirit."   170

We are upon enchanted ground, my friend; and
you are to think yourself well used that I detain you
no longer in this fearful circle. The glimpse you
have had of it will help your imagination to conceive
the rest. And without more words you will readily 175
apprehend that the fancies of our modern bards are
not only more gallant, but, on a change of the scene,
more sublime, more terrible, more alarming, than
those of the classic fablers. In a word, you will
find that the *manners* they paint, and the *supersti-* 180

tions they adopt, are the more poetical for being
Gothic.
1762   1762

THOMAS LELAND

FROM LONGSWORD, EARL OF SALISBURY: AN HISTORICAL ROMANCE

Advertisement:

THE outlines of the following story, and some
of the incidents and more minute circumstances are
to be found in the ancient English historians. If too
great liberties have been taken in altering or enlarg-
ing their accounts, the reader who looks only for   5
amusement will probably forgive it; the learned and
critical (if this work should be honored by such
readers) will deem it a matter of too little consequence to call for the severity of their censure. It
is generally expected that pieces of this kind should   10
convey some one useful moral, which moral, not
always perhaps the most valuable or refined is sometimes made to float on the surface of the narrative;
or is plucked up at proper intervals and presented to
the view of the reader with great solemnity. But   15
the author of these sheets hath too high an opinion
of the judgment and penetration of his readers, to
pursue this method. Although he cannot pretend to
be very deep, yet he hopes he is clear. And if anything lies at bottom worth the picking up, it will be   20
discovered without his direction.

                                             1762

[THE BETRAYAL]

THUS had I rashly ventured forth into a wide
and unknown scene of danger under the direction of

a false guide whose treachery was soon discovered.
It was night and the moon cast her mild gleam over
all the prospect that lay before us. D'Aumont repeated his assurances of friendship, spoke with
cheerfulness and confidence, encouraging me to hope
and to fix my reliance on his services. I expected
every instant to be conducted to some place of retirement and friendly reception. Sometimes I expressed my uneasiness, but ever and anon my guide
practised his arts of soothing persuasion and flattering professions to allay my fears; thus we proceeded
for some hours; at length, in our tedious progress
we passed by the skirts of a thick forest from whence
our ears were first pierced with shrill and lamentable shrieks as if from a female voice, and instantly
afterwards, there issued out a small number of
armed men who surrounded us and demanded our
names and quality. My companion, nothing alarmed
at this appearance, made the like inquiries on his
part and learned that they were the soldiers of
Chauvigny, Lord of Poictiers. "I seek that Lord,"
said he, when one of the soldiers surveying him
attentively replied, "D'Aumont!—I know thee now!
what from Count Malleon?" I started at the hideous
name and turning on my companion perceived that
the blood had deserted his cheeks and that he stood
in violent agitation. But ere I could express my
wonder, retiring a few paces from me, he cried out,
"There stands Lord Salisbury, my purpose was to
conduct him to Poictiers, he is now your prisoner
and let him be quickly conveyed to your Lord." I
stood confounded for a moment at this astonishing
treachery, then quickly drawing my sword, I ran
furiously upon D'Aumont; nor was it without the
utmost difficulty that the soldiers restrained my just
vengeance, overpowered and disarmed me.

1762

CHRISTOPHER SMART

FROM A SONG TO DAVID

STRONG is the lion—like a coal
His eyeball, like a bastion's mole
   His chest against the foes;
Strong the gier-eagle on his sail;
Strong against tide th' enormous whale   5
   Emerges as he goes:

But stronger still, in earth and air
And in the sea, the man of prayer,
   And far beneath the tide,
And in the seat to faith assigned,   10
Where ask is have, where seek is find,
   Where knock is open wide.

Beauteous the fleet before the gale;
Beauteous the multitudes in mail,
   Ranked arms and crested heads;   15
Beauteous the garden's umbrage mild,
Walk, water, meditated wild,
   And all the bloomy beds;

Beauteous the moon full on the lawn;
And beauteous when the veil's withdrawn   20
   The virgin to her spouse;
Beauteous the temple, decked and filled,
When to the heaven of heavens they build
   Their heart-directed vows:

Beauteous, yea beauteous more than these,   25
The shepherd King upon his knees,
   For his momentous trust;

With wish of infinite conceit
For man, beast, mute, the small and great,
    And prostrate dust to dust.   30

Precious the bounteous widow's mite;
And precious, for extreme delight,
    The largess from the churl;
Precious the ruby's blushing blaze,
And Alba's blest imperial rays,   45
    And pure cerulean pearl;

Precious the penitential tear;
And precious is the sigh sincere,
    Acceptable to God;
And precious are the winning flowers,   40
In gladsome Israel's feast of bowers,
    Bound on the hallowed sod:

More precious that diviner part
Of David, even the Lord's own heart,
    Great, beautiful, and new;   45
In all things where it was intent,
In all extremes, in each event,
    Proof—answering true to true.

Glorious the sun in mid career;
Glorious th' assembled fires appear;   50
    Glorious the comet's train;
Glorious the trumpet and alarm;
Glorious th' Almighty's stretched-out arm;
    Glorious th' enraptured main;

Glorious the northern lights a-stream;   55
Glorious the song, when God's the theme;
    Glorious the thunder's roar;
Glorious, Hosannah from the den;

Glorious the catholic amen;
   Glorious the martyr's gore: 60

Glorious, more glorious, is the crown
Of Him that brought salvation down,
   By meekness called Thy son;
Thou that stupendous truth believed,
And now the matchless deed's achieved,   65
   Determined, dared, and done.

                                                        1763

EVAN EVANS

[A PANEGYRIC UPON OWAIN GWYNEDD]

I WILL extol the generous hero, descended from
the race of Roderic, the bulwark of his country, a
prince eminent for his good qualities, the glory of
Britain, Owain the brave and expert in arms, a
prince that neither hoardeth nor coveteth riches.—   5
Three fleets arrived, vessels of the main, three powerful fleets of the first rate, furiously to attack him on
a sudden. One from Iwerddon, the other full of
well-armed Lochlynians, making a grand appearance on the floods, the third from the transmarine   10
Normans, which was attended with an immense,
though successless toil.

The Dragon of Mona's sons were so brave in
action, that there was a great tumult on their furious
attack, and before the prince himself, there was vast   15
confusion, havoc, conflict, honorable death, bloody
battle, horrible consternation, and upon Tal Moelvre
a thousand banners. There was an outrageous
carnage, and the rage of spears, and hasty signs of
violent indignation. Blood raised the tide of Menai,   20
and the crimson of human gore stained the brine.

There were glittering cuirasses, and the agony of
gashing wounds, and the mangled warriors prostrate
before the chief, distinguished by his crimson lance.
Lloegria was put into confusion, the contest and con-   25
fusion was great, and the glory of our prince's wide-
wasting sword shall be celebrated in an hundred languages to give him his merited praise.

1764

THOMAS GRAY

[For selections from his earlier work, see p. 151, above.]

[LETTERS ON MACPHERSON'S OSSIAN]

To Horace Walpole

I AM so charmed with the two specimens of Erse
poetry, that I cannot help giving you the trouble to
enquire a little farther about them, and should wish
to see a few lines of the original, that I may form
some slight idea of the language, the measures, and   5
the rhythm.

Is there anything known of the author or authors, and of what antiquity are they supposed to be?
Is there any more to be had of equal beauty, or at
all approaching to it? I have been often told that   10
the poem called *Hardycanute* (which I always admired and still admire) was the work of somebody
that lived a few years ago. This I do not at all believe, though it has evidently been retouched in
places by some modern hand: but however, I am   15
authorized by this report to ask whether the two
poems in question are certainly antique and genuine.
I make this enquiry in quality of an antiquary, and
am not otherwise concerned about it: for, if I were
sure that any one now living in Scotland had writ-   20

ten them to divert himself, and laugh at the credulity of the world, I would undertake a journey into the Highlands only for the pleasure of seeing him.
1760

To Richard Stonhewer

I have received another Scotch packet with a third specimen, inferior in kind (because it is merely description), but yet full of nature and noble wild imagination. Five bards pass the night at the castle of a chief (himself a principal bard); each goes out in his turn to observe the face of things, and returns with an extempore picture of the changes he has seen; it is an October night (the harvest-month of the Highlands). This is the whole plan; yet there is a contrivance, and a preparation of ideas, that you would not expect. The oddest thing is, that every one of them sees ghosts (more or less). The idea that struck and surprised me most, is the following. One of them (describing a storm of wind and rain) says:

> Ghosts ride on the tempest tonight:
> Sweet is their voice between the gusts of wind;
> *Their songs are of other worlds!*

Did you never observe (while rocking winds are piping loud) that pause, as the gust is recollecting itself, and rising upon the ear in a shrill and plaintive note, like the swell of an Æolian harp? I do assure you there is nothing in the world so like the voice of a spirit. Thomson had an ear sometimes: he was not deaf to this; and has described it gloriously, but given it another different turn, and of more horror. I cannot repeat the lines: it is in his "Winter." There is another very fine picture in one of them. It describes the breaking of the clouds after the

storm before it is settled into a calm, and when the 30
moon is seen by short intervals.

> The waves are tumbling on the lake,
> And lash the rocky sides.
> The boat is brim-full in the cove,
> The oars on the rocking tide. 35
> Sad sits a maid beneath a cliff,
> And eyes the rolling stream;
> Her lover promised to come,
> She saw his boat (when it was evening) on the lake;
> *Are these his groans in the gale?* 40
> *Is this his broken boat on the shore?*

June 29, 1760

To Thomas Warton

If you have seen Stonhewer, he has probably told
you of my old Scotch (or rather Irish) poetry. I
am gone mad about them. They are said to be
translations (literal and in prose) from the Erse-
tongue, done by one Macpherson, a young clergy- 5
man in the Highlands. He means to publish a collection he has of these specimens of antiquity; but
what plagues me is, I cannot come at any certainty
on that head. I was so struck, so *extasié* with their
infinite beauty, that I writ into Scotland to make a 10
thousand enquiries. The letters I have in return are
ill wrote, ill reasoned, unsatisfactory, calculated (one
would imagine) to deceive one, and yet not cunning
enough to do it cleverly. In short, the whole external evidence would make one believe these frag- 15
ments (for so he calls them, though nothing can be
more entire) counterfeit; but the internal is so strong
on the other side, that I am resolved to believe them
genuine, spite of the devil and the kirk. It is impossible to convince me that they were invented by 20
the same man that writes me these letters. On the
other hand, it is almost as hard to suppose, if they

are original, that he should be able to translate them so admirably. What can one do? Since Stonhewer went, I have received another of a very different and inferior kind (being merely descriptive), much more modern than the former (he says), yet very old too. This too in its way is extremely fine. In short, this man is the very Demon of poetry, or he has lighted on a treasure hid for ages. The Welch poets are also coming to light. I have seen a discourse in MS. about them (by one Mr. Evans, a clergyman) with specimens of their writings. This is in Latin, and though it don't approach the other, there are fine scraps among it. . . .

June, 1760

To The Reverend William Mason

The Erse fragments have been published five weeks ago in Scotland, though I had them not (by a mistake) till last week. As you tell me new things do not reach you soon at Aston, I inclose what I can; the rest shall follow, when you tell me whether you have not got the pamphlet already. I send the two which I had before, for Mr. Wood, because he has not the affectation of not admiring. I continue to think them genuine, though any reasons for believing the contrary are rather stronger than ever: but I will have them antique, for I never knew a Scotchman of my own time that could read, much less write, poetry; and such poetry too! I have one (from Mr. Macpherson) which he has not printed: it is mere description, but excellent, too, in its kind. If you are good, and will learn to admire, I will transcribe it. . . .

As to their authenticity, having made many enquiries about the authenticity of these fragments,

I have got a letter from Mr. David Hume (the historian), which is more satisfactory than anything I have yet met with on that subject. He says—

"Certain it is that these poems are in everybody's mouth in the Highlands, have been handed down from father to son, and are of an age beyond all memory and tradition. Adam Smith, the celebrated professor in Glasgow, told me that the piper of the Argyleshire Militia repeated to him all of those which Mr. Macpherson had translated, and many more of equal beauty. Major Mackay (Lord Rae's brother) told me that he remembers them perfectly well; as likewise did the Laird of Macfarlane (the greatest antiquarian we have in this country), and who insists strongly on the historical truth as well as the poetical beauty of these productions. I could add the Laird and Lady Macleod, with many more that live in different parts of the Highlands, very remote from each other, and could only be acquainted with what had become (in a manner) national works. There is a country surgeon in Lochaber who has by heart the entire epic poem mentioned by Mr. Macpherson in his preface; and, as he is old, is perhaps the only person living that knows it all. We are in the more haste to recover a monument which will certainly be regarded as a curiosity in the republic of letters. We have, therefore, set about a subscription of a guinea or two guineas apiece, in order to enable Mr. Macpherson to undertake a mission into the Highlands to recover this poem, and other fragments of antiquity."

I forgot to mention to you that the names of Fingal, Ossian, Oscar, etc., are still given in the Highlands to large mastiffs, as we give to ours the names of Cæsar, Pompey, Hector, etc.

Aug. 7, 1760

[ON THE HIGHLANDS]

To the Rev. William Mason:

I am returned from Scotland charmed with my
expedition; it is of the Highlands I speak; the Low-
lands are worth seeing once, but the mountains are
ecstatic, and ought to be visited in pilgrimage once
a year. None but those monstrous creatures of God   5
know how to join so much beauty with so much
horror. A fig for your poets, painters, gardeners,
and clergymen, that have not been among them;
their imagination can be made of nothing but bowl-
ing-greens, flowering shrubs, horse-ponds, Fleet   10
ditches, shell grottoes, and Chinese rails. Then I
had so beautiful an autumn, Italy could hardly produce a nobler scene, and this so sweetly contrasted
with that perfection of nastiness, and total want of
accommodation, that Scotland only can supply. Oh,   15
you would have blessed yourself. I shall certainly
go again; what a pity it is I cannot draw, nor
describe, nor ride on horseback.
1765

THE DESCENT OF ODIN

Uprose the King of Men with speed,
And saddled straight his coal-black steed;
Down the yawning steep he rode,
That leads to Hela's drear abode.
Him the Dog of Darkness spied;   5
His shaggy throat he opened wide,
While from his jaws, with carnage filled,
Foam and human gore distilled,
Hoarse he bays with hideous din,
Eyes that glow, and fangs that grin;   10

And long pursues with fruitless yell,
The Father of the powerful spell.
Onward still his way he takes
(The groaning earth beneath him shakes),
Till full before his fearless eyes   15
The portals nine of hell arise.

    Right against the eastern gate,
By the moss-grown pile he sate,
Where long of yore to sleep was laid
The dust of the prophetic maid.   20
Facing to the northern clime,
Thrice he traced the Runic rhyme;
Thrice pronounced, in accents dread,
The thrilling verse that wakes the dead;
Till from out the hollow ground   25
Slowly breathed a sullen sound.

Prophetess. What call unknown, what charms, pre-
            sume
To break the quiet of the tomb?
Who thus afflicts my troubled sprite,
And drags me from the realms of night?   30
Long on these mould'ring bones have beat
The winter's snow, the summer's heat,
The drenching dews, and driving rain!
Let me, let me sleep again!
Who is he, with voice unblest,   35
That calls me from the bed of rest?

Odin.   A traveller, to thee unknown,
Is he that calls, a warrior's son.
Thou the deeds of light shalt know;
Tell me what is done below;   40
For whom yon glitt'ring board is spread,
Dressed for whom yon golden bed?

Prophetess. Mantling in the goblet see
The pure bev'rage of the bee;
O'er it hangs the shield of gold;   45
'Tis the drink of Balder bold:
Balder's head to death is giv'n;
Pain can reach the sons of Heav'n!
Unwilling I my lips unclose:
Leave me, leave me to repose!   50

Odin. Once again my call obey:
Prophetess, arise, and say
What dangers Odin's child await;
Who the author of his fate?

Prophetess. In Hoder's hand the hero's doom;   55
His brother sends him to the tomb.
Now my weary lips I close:
Leave me, leave me to repose!

Odin. Prophetess, my spell obey:
Once again arise, and say   60
Who th' avenger of his guilt;
By whom shall Hoder's blood be spilt?

Prophetess. In the caverns of the west,
By Odin's fierce embrace comprest,
A wond'rous boy shall Rinda bear,   65
Who ne'er shall comb his raven-hair,
Nor wash his visage in the stream,
Nor see the sun's departing beam,
Till he on Hoder's corse shall smile
Flaming on the funeral pile.   70
Now my weary lips I close:
Leave me, leave me to repose!

Odin. Yet a while my call obey:
Prophetess, awake, and say

What virgins these, in speechless woe,   75
That bend to earth their solemn brow,
That their flaxen tresses tear,
And snowy veils that float in air.
Tell me whence their sorrows rose;
Then I leave thee to repose.   80

Prophetess. Ha! no traveller art thou!
King of Men, I know thee now;
Mightiest of a mighty line—

Odin. No boding maid of skill divine
Art thou, nor prophetess of good;   85
But mother of the giant-brood!

Prophetess. Hie thee hence, and boast at home,
That never shall enquirer come
To break my iron-sleep again,
Till Lok has burst his tenfold chain;   90
Never, till substantial Night
Has reassumed her ancient right;
Till wrapt in flames, in ruin hurled,
Sinks the fabric of the world.
1761   1768

THE TRIUMPHS OF OWEN

A Fragment

Owen's praise demands my song,
Owen swift, and Owen strong;
Fairest flower of Roderic's stem,
Gwyneth's shield, and Britain's gem.
He nor heaps his brooded stores,   5
Nor on all profusely pours;
Lord of every regal art,
Liberal hand, and open heart.

Big with hosts of mighty name,
Squadrons three against him came; 10
This the force of Eirin hiding,
Side by side as proudly riding,
On her shadow long and gay
Lochlin plows the wat'ry way;
There the Norman sails afar 15
Catch the winds and join the war:
Black and huge along they sweep,
Burthens of the angry deep.

    Dauntless on his native sands
The Dragon-Son of Mona stands; 20
In glitt'ring arms and glory drest,
High he rears his ruby crest.
There the thund'ring strokes begin,
There the press, and there the din;
Talymalfra's rocky shore 25
Echoing to the battle's roar.
Where his glowing eye-balls turn,
Thousand banners round him burn:
Where he points his purple spear,
Hasty, hasty rout is there, 30
Marking with indignant eye
Fear to stop, and shame to fly,
There confusion, terror's child,
Conflict fierce, and ruin wild,
Agony, that pants for breath, 35
Despair and honorable death.
1764   1768

CARÀDOC

HAVE ye seen the tusky boar,
Or the bull, with sullen roar,
On surrounding foes advance?
So Caràdoc bore his lance.
1764   1775

CONAN

Conan's name, my lay rehearse,
Build to him the lofty verse,
Sacred tribute of the bard,
Verse, the hero's sole reward.
As the flame's devouring force;   5
As the whirlwind in its course;
As the thunder's fiery stroke,
Glancing on the shivered oak;
Did the sword of Conan mow
The crimson harvest of the foe.   10

1764   1775

THE DEATH OF HOËL

An Ode, Selected from the Gododin

Had I but the torrent's might,
With headlong rage and wild affright
Upon Deïra's squadron's hurled
To rush, and sweep them from the world!

Too, too secure in youthful pride,   5
By them my friend, my Hoël, died,
Great Cian's son: of Madoc old
He asked no heaps of hoarded gold;
Alone in nature's wealth arrayed.
He asked and had the lovely maid.   10

To Cattraeth's vale in glitt'ring row
Thrice two hundred warriors go:
Every warrior's manly neck
Chains of regal honor deck,
Wreathed in many a golden link: 15
From the golden cup they drink

Nectar that the bees produce,
Or the grape's ecstatic juice.
Flushed with mirth and hope they burn:
But none from Cattraeth's vale return,   20
Save Aeron brave, and Conan strong,
(Bursting through the bloody throng)
And I, the meanest of them all,
That live to weep and sing their fall.

1768   1775

THE FATAL SISTERS

An Ode from the Norse Tongue

Now the storm begins to lower,
(Haste, the loom of hell prepare,)
Iron-sleet of arrowy shower
Hurtles in the darkened air.

Glittering lances are the loom,   5
Where the dusky warp we strain,
Weaving many a soldier's doom,
Orkney's woe, and Randver's bane.

See the grisly texture grow,
('Tis of human entrails made,)   10
And the weights, that play below,
Each a gasping warrior's head.

Shafts for shuttles, dipped in gore,
Shoot the trembling cords along.
Sword, that once a monarch bore,   15
Keep the tissue close and strong.

Mista black, terrific maid,
Sangrida, and Hilda see,

Join the wayward work to aid:
'Tis the woof of victory.   20

Ere the ruddy sun be set,
Pikes must shiver, javelins sing,
Blade with clattering buckler meet,
Hauberk crash, and helmet ring.

(Weave the crimson web of war.)   25
Let us go, and let us fly,
Where our friends the conflict share,
Where they triumph, where they die.

As the paths of fate we tread,
Wading through th' ensanguined field: 30
Gondula, and Geira, spread
O'er the youthful king your shield.

We the reins to slaughter give,
Ours to kill, and ours to spare:
Spite of danger he shall live.   35
(Weave the crimson web of war.)

They, whom once the desert-beach
Pent within its bleak domain,
Soon their ample sway shall stretch
O'er the plenty of the plain.   40

Low the dauntless earl is laid,
Gored with many a gaping wound:
Fate demands a nobler head;
Soon a king shall bite the ground.

Long his loss shall Erin weep,   45
Ne'er again his likeness see;
Long her strains in sorrow steep,
Strains of immortality!

Horror covers all the heath,
Clouds of carnage blot the sun.   50
Sisters, weave the web of death;
Sisters, cease, the work is done.

Hail the task, and hail the hands!
Songs of joy and triumph sing!
Joy to the victorious bands;   55
Triumph to the younger king.

Mortal, thou that hear'st the tale,
Learn the tenor of our song.
Scotland, through each winding vale
Far and wide the notes prolong.   60

Sisters, hence with spurs of speed:
Each her thundering falchion wield;
Each bestride her sable steed.
Hurry, hurry to the field.

1768

HORACE WALPOLE

FROM THE CASTLE OF OTRANTO

MANFRED, Prince of Otranto, had one son and
one daughter. The latter, a most beautiful virgin
aged eighteen, was called Matilda. Conrad, the son,
was three years younger, a homely youth, sickly,
and of no promising disposition; yet he was the   5
darling of his father, who never showed any symp-
toms of affection to Matilda. Manfred had contracted a marriage for his son with the Marquis of
Vicenza's daughter, Isabella; and she had already
been delivered by her guardians into the hands of   10
Manfred that he might celebrate the wedding as soon
as Conrad's infirm state of health would permit.

Manfred's impatience for this ceremonial was remarked by his family and neighbors. The former
indeed, apprehending the severity of their Prince's 15
disposition, did not dare to utter their surmises on
this precipitation. Hippolita, his wife, an amiable
lady, did sometimes venture to represent the danger
of marrying their only son so early, considering his
great youth and greater infirmities; but she never 20
received any other answer than reflections on her
own sterility, who had given him but one heir. His
tenants and subjects were less cautious in their discourses. They attributed this hasty wedding to the
Prince's dread of seeing accomplished an ancient 25
prophecy, which was said to have pronounced that
the castle and lordship of Otranto should pass from
the present family whenever the real owner should
be grown too large to inhabit it. It was difficult to
make any sense of this prophecy; and still less easy 30
to conceive what it had to do with the marriage in
question. Yet these mysteries or contradictions did
not make the populace adhere the less to their
opinion.

Young Conrad's birthday was fixed for his es- 35
pousals. The company was assembled in the chapel
of the castle, and everything ready for beginning
the divine office, when Conrad himself was missing.
Manfred, impatient of the least delay, and who had
not observed his son retire, dispatched one of his 40
attendants to summon the young prince. The servant, who had not stayed long enough to have crossed
the court to Conrad's apartment, came running back
breathless, in a frantic manner, his eyes staring, and
foaming at the mouth. He said nothing, but pointed 45
to the court. The company were struck with terror
and amazement. The Princess Hippolita, without
knowing what was the matter, but anxious for her
son. swooned away. Manfred, less apprehensive

than enraged at the proscrastination of the nuptials, 50
and at the folly of his domestic, asked imperiously
what was the matter. The fellow made no answer,
but continued pointing towards the court-yard; and
at last, after repeated questions put to him, cried
out, "Oh! the helmet! the helmet!" In the mean- 55
time, some of the company had run into the court,
from whence was heard a confused noise of shrieks,
horror, and surprise. Manfred, who began to be
alarmed at not seeing his son, went himself to get
information of what occasioned this strange con- 60
fusion. Matilda remained endeavoring to assist her
mother, and Isabella staid for the same purpose and
to avoid showing any impatience for the bridegroom,
for whom, in truth, she had conceived little affection.

The first thing that struck Manfred's eyes was a 65
group of his servants endeavoring to raise something
that appeared to him a mountain of sable plumes.
He gazed without believing his sight. "What are
ye doing?" cried Manfred, wrathfully. "Where is
my son?" A volley of voices replied, "Oh! my 70
lord! the prince! the prince! the helmet! the helmet!"
Shocked with these lamentable sounds, and dreading
he knew not what, he advanced hastily, but what a
sight for a father's eyes! He beheld his child dashed
to pieces and almost buried under an enormous hel- 75
met, an hundred times more large than any casque
ever made for human being, and shaded with a pro-
portionable quantity of black feathers.

The horror of the spectacle, the ignorance of all
around how this misfortune had happened, and above 80
all, the tremendous phenomenon before him, took
away the Prince's speech. Yet his silence lasted
longer than even grief could occasion. He fixed his
eyes on what he wished in vain to believe a vision;
and seemed less attentive to his loss than buried in 85
meditation on the stupendous object that had occa-

sioned it. He touched, he examined the fatal casque;
nor could even the bleeding mangled remains of the
young Prince divert the eyes of Manfred from the
portent before him. All who had known his partial 90
fondness for young Conrad were as much surprised
at their Prince's insensibility, as thunder-struck
themselves at the miracle of the helmet. They conveyed the disfigured corpse into the hall, without re-
ceiving the least direction from Manfred. As little 95
was he attentive to the ladies who remained in the
chapel. On the contrary, without mentioning the
unhappy princesses, his wife and daughter, the first
sounds that dropped from Manfred's lips were,
"Take care of the Lady Isabella." . . . 100

. . . .

As it was now evening, the servant who conducted Isabella bore a torch before her. When they
came to Manfred, who was walking impatiently
about the gallery, he started and said hastily: "Take
away that light, and begone!" Then shutting the 105
door impetuously, he flung himself upon a bench
against the wall, and bade Isabella sit by him. She
obeyed trembling. "I sent for you, lady," said he
and then stopped under great appearance of confusion. "My lord!" "Yes, I sent for you on a mat- 110
ter of great moment," resumed he. "Dry your tears,
young lady. You have lost your bridegroom. Yes,
cruel fate! and I have lost the hopes of my race!
But Conrad was not worthy of your beauty."
"How! my lord," said Isabella. "Sure you do not 115
suspect me of not feeling the concern I ought! My
duty and affection would have always"—"Think no
more of him," interrupted Manfred; "he was a sickly
puny child; and heaven has perhaps taken him away
that I might not trust the honors of my house on 120
so frail a foundation. The line of Manfred calls

for numerous supports. My foolish fondness for
that boy blinded the eyes of my prudence; but it is
better as it is. I hope in a few years to have reason
to rejoice at the death of Conrad."   125

Words cannot paint the astonishment of Isabella.
At first, she apprehended that grief had disordered
Manfred's understanding. Her next thought suggested that this strange discourse was designed to
ensnare her. She feared that Manfred had per-   130
ceived her indifference for his son; and in consequence of that idea she replied: "Good my lord, do
not doubt my tenderness. My heart would have
accompanied my hand. Conrad would have engrossed
all my care; and wherever fate shall dispose of me, 135
I shall always cherish his memory, and regard your
highness and the virtuous Hippolita as my parents."
"Curse on Hippolita!" cried Manfred. "Forget her
from this moment, as I do. In short, lady, you have
missed a husband undeserving of your charms. They 140
shall now be better disposed of. Instead of a sickly
boy, you shall have a husband in the prime of his
age, who will know how to value your beauties, and
who may expect a numerous offspring." "Alas! my
lord," said Isabella; "my mind is too sadly engrossed 145
by the recent catastrophe in your family to think of
another marriage. If ever my father returns, and it
shall be his pleasure, I shall obey, as I did when I
consented to give my hand to your son. But until
his return, permit me to remain under your hos- 150
pitable roof, and employ the melancholy hours in
assuaging yours, Hippolita's and the fair Matilda's
affliction."

"I desired you once before," said Manfred,
angrily, "not to name that woman. From this hour 155
she must be a stranger to you as she must be to me.
In short, Isabella, since I cannot give you my son,
I offer you myself." "Heavens!" cried Isabella,

waking from her delusion; "what do I hear? You! my lord! you! my father-in-law! the father of Con-160 rad! the husband of the virtuous Hippolita!" "I tell you," said Manfred, imperiously, "Hippolita is no longer my wife; I divorce her from this hour. Too long has she cursed me by her unfruitfulness. My fate depends on having sons; and this night I trust 165 will give a new date to my hopes." At those words he seized the cold hand of Isabella, who was half dead with fright and horror. She shrieked and started from him. Manfred rose to pursue her, when the moon, which was now up and gleamed in 170 at the opposite casement, presented to his sight the plumes of the fatal helmet, which rose to the height of the windows, waving backwards and forwards, in a tempestuous manner, and accompanied with a hollow and rustling sound. Isabella, who gathered 175 courage from her situation, and who dreaded nothing so much as Manfred's pursuit of his declaration, cried: "Look! my lord. See! heaven itself declares against your impious intentions." "Heaven nor hell shall impede my designs," said Manfred, advancing 180 again to seize the Princess. At that instant the portrait of his grandfather, which hung over the bench where they had been sitting, uttered a deep sigh and heaved its breast. Isabella, whose back was turned to the picture, saw not the motion, nor knew whence the 185 sound came, but started, and said: "Hark! my lord! What sound was that?" and at the same time made towards the door. Manfred, distracted between the flight of Isabella, who had now reached the stairs, and yet unable to keep his eyes from the picture, 190 which began to move, had, however, advanced some steps after her, still looking backwards on the portrait, when he saw it quit its panel and descend on the floor with a grave and melancholy air. "Do I dream?" cried Manfred, returning; "or are the devils 195

themselves in league against me? Speak, infernal
spectre! Or, if thou art my grandsire, why dost
thou too conspire against thy wretched descendant,
who too dearly pays for—" Ere he could finish
the sentence, the vision sighed again, and made a 200
sign to Manfred to follow him. "Lead on!" cried
Manfred; "I will follow thee to the gulf of perdi-
tion." The spectre marched sedately, but dejected,
to the end of the gallery and turned into a chamber
on the right-hand. Manfred accompanied him at a 205
little distance, full of anxiety and horror, but resolved. As he would have entered the chamber, the
door was clapped to with violence by an invisible
hand. The Prince, collecting courage from this delay, would have forcibly burst open the door with his 210
foot, but found that it resisted his utmost efforts.
"Since hell will not satisfy my curiosity," said Manfred, "I will use the human means in my power for
preserving my race; Isabella shall not escape me."

1764

THOMAS PERCY
(EDITOR)

FROM RELIQUES OF ANCIENT ENGLISH POETRY

THE ANCIENT BALLAD OF CHEVY-CHASE

THE FIRST FIT

THE Persè owt of Northombarlande,
   And a vowe to God mayd he,
That he wolde hunte in the mountayns
   Off Chyviat within dayes thre,
In the mauger of doughtè Dogles,   5
   And all that ever with him be.

The fattiste hartes in all Cheviat
   He sayd he wold kill, and cary them away:
"Be my feth," sayd the dougheti Doglas agayn,
   "I wyll let that hontyng yf that I may."   10

Then the Persè owt of Banborowe cam,
   With him a myghtye meany,
With fifteen hondrith archares bold;
   The wear chosen out of shyars thre.

This begane on a monday at morn   15
   In Cheviat the hillys so he;
The chyld may rue that ys un-born,
   It was the mor pittè.

The dryvars thorowe the woodes went
   For to reas the dear;   20
Bomen bickarte uppone the bent
   With ther browd aras cleare.

Then the wyld thorowe the woodes went
   On every syde shear;
Grea-hondes thorowe the greves glent   25
   For to kyll thear dear.

The begane in Chyviat the hyls abone
   Yerly on a monnyn day;
Be that it drewe to the oware off none
   A hondrith fat hartes ded ther lay.   30

The blewe a mort uppone the bent,
   The semblyd on sydis shear;
To the quyrry then the Persè went
   To se the bryttlyng off the deare.

He sayd, "It was the Duglas promys   35
   This day to meet me hear;

But I wyste he wold faylle verament:"
  A great oth the Persè swear.

At the laste a squyar of Northombelonde
  Lokyde at his hand full ny,   40
He was war ath the doughetie Doglas comynge:
  With him a mightè meany,

Both with spear, byll, and brande:
  Yt was a myghti sight to se.
Hardyar men both off hart nar hande   45
  Wear not in Christiantè.

The wear twenty hondrith spear-men good
  Withouten any fayle;
The wear borne a-long be the watter a Twyde
  Yth bowndes of Tividale.   50

"Leave off the brytlyng of the dear," he sayde,
  "And to your bowys look ye tayk good heed,
For never sithe ye wear on your mothars borne
  Had ye never so mickle need."

The dougheti Dogglas on a stede   55
  He rode all his men beforne;
His armor glytteryde as dyd a glede;
  A bolder barne was never born.

"Tell me what men ye ar," he says,
  "Or whos men that ye be: 60
Who gave youe leave to hunte in this
  Chyviat chays in the spyt of me?"

The first mane that ever him an answear mayd,
  Yt was the good lord Persè:
"We wyll not tell the what men we ar," he says,   65
  "Nor whos men that we be;

But we wyll hount hear in this chays
    In the spyte of thyne, and of the.

"The fattiste hartes in all Chyviat
    We have kyld, and cast to carry them a-way."   70
"Be my troth, sayd the doughtè Dogglas agayn,
    "Ther-for the ton of us shall de this day."

Then sayd the doughtè Doglas
    Unto the lord Persè:
"To kyll all thes giltless men,   75
    A-las! it wear great pittè.

"But, Persè, thowe art a lord of lande,
    I am a yerle callyd within my contre;
Let all our men uppone a parti stande;
    And do the battell off the and of me."   80

"Nowe Cristes cors on his crowne," sayd the lord
        Persè,
    "Who-soever ther-to says nay.
Be my troth, doughtè Doglas," he says,
    "Thow shalt never se that day;

"Nethar in Ynglonde, Skottlonde, nar France,   85
    Nor for no man of a woman born,
But and fortune be my chance,
    I dar met him on man for on."

Then bespayke a squyar off Northombarlonde,
    Ric. Wytharynton was his nam;   90
"It shall never be told in Sothe-Ynglonde," he says,
    "To kyng Herry the fourth for sham.

"I wat youe byn great lordes twaw,
    I am a poor squyar of lande;

I wyll never se my captayne fight on a fylde,   95
 And stande my-selffe, and looke on,
But whyll I may my weppone welde,
 I wyll not fayl both harte and hande."

That day, that day, that dredfull day:
 The first Fit here I fynde,   100
And you wyll here any mor a the hountyng athe
   Chyviat,
 Yet ys ther mor behynde.

THE SECOND FIT

The Yngglishe men hade ther bowys yebent,
 Ther hartes were good yenoughe;
The first of arros that the shote off,   105
 Seven skore spear-men the sloughe.

Yet bydys the yerle Doglas uppon the bent,
 A captayne good yenoughe,
And that was sene verament,
 For he wrought hom both woo and wouche.   110

The Dogglas pertyd his ost in thre,
 Lyk a cheffe cheften off pryde,
With suar speares off myghttè tre
 The cum in on every syde.

Thrughe our Yngglishe archery   115
 Gave many a wounde full wyde;
Many a doughetè the garde to dy,
 Which ganyde them no pryde.

The Yngglyshe men let thear bowys be,
 And pulde owt brandes that wer bright;   120
It was a hevy syght to se
 Bryght swordes on basnites lyght.

Thorowe ryche male, and myne-ye-ple,
  Many sterne the stroke downe streght:
Many a freyke, that was full free,   125
  Ther undar foot dyd lyght.

At last the Duglas and the Persè met,
  Lyk to captayns of myght and mayne;
The swapte togethar tyll the both swat
  With swordes, that wear of fyn myllàn.   130

Thes worthè freckys for to fyght
  Ther-to the wear full fayne,
Tyll the bloode owte off thear basnetes sprente,
  As ever dyd heal or rayne.

"Holde the, Persè," sayd the Doglas,   135
  "And i' feth I shall the brynge
Wher thowe shalte have a yerls wagis
  Of Jamy our Scottish kynge."

"Thoue shalte have thy ransom fre,
  I hight the hear this thinge,   140
For the manfullyste man yet art thowe,
  That ever I conqueryd in filde fightyng."

"Nay, then," sayd the lord Persè,
  "I tolde it the beforne,
That I wolde never yeldyde be   145
  To no man of a woman born."

With that ther cam an arrowe hastely
  Forthe off a mightie wane,
Hit hathe strekene the yerle Duglas
  In at the brest bane.   150

Thoroue lyvar and longs bathe
  The sharp arrowe ys gane,

That never after in all his lyffe days,
  He spake mo wordes but ane,

That was, "Fyghte ye, my merry men, whyllys ye
      may, 155
  For my lyff days ben gan."

The Persè leanyde on his brande,
  And sawe the Duglas de;
He tooke the dede man be the hande,
  And sayd, "Wo ys me for the! 160

"To have savyde thy lyffe, I wold have pertyd with
  My landes for years thre,
For a better man of hart, nare of hande
  Was not in all the north countrè."

Off all that se a Skottishe knyght, 165
  Was callyd Sir Hewe the Mongon-byrry,
He sawe the Duglas to the deth was dyght;
  He spendyd a spear a trusti tre:

He rod uppon a corsiare
  Throughe a hondrith archery; 170
He never styntyde, nar never blane,
  Tyll he cam to the good lord Persè.

He set uppone the lord Persè
  A dynte, that was full soare;
With a suar spear of a myghtè tre 175
  Clean thorow the body he the Persè bore,

Athe tothar syde, that a man myght se,
  A large cloth yard and mare:
Towe bettar captayns wear nat in Christiantè,
  Then that day slain wear thare. 180

An archer off Northomberlonde
 Say slean was the lord Persè,
He bar a bende-bow in his hande,
 Was made off trusti tre:

An arow, that a cloth yarde was lang,   185
 To th' hard stele halyde he;
A dynt, that was both sad and soar,
 He sat on Sir Hewe the Mongon-byrry.

The dynt yt was both sad and sar,
 That he of Mongon-byrry sete;   190
The swane-fethars, that his arrowe bar,
 With his hart blood the wear wete.

Ther was never a freake wone foot wold fle,
 But still in stour dyd stand,
Heawyng on yche othar, whyll the myght dre, 195
 With many a bal-ful brande.

This battell begane in Chyviat
 An owar befor the none,
And when even-song bell was rang
 The battell was nat half done.   200

The tooke "on" on ethar hand
 Be the lyght off the mone;
Many hade no strength for to stande,
 In Chyviat the hyllys aboun.

Of fifteen hondrith archars of Ynglonde 205
 Went away but fifti and thre;
Of twenty hondrith spear-men of Skotlonde,
 But even five and fifti:

But all wear slayne Cheviat within:
 The hade no strengthe to sand on hie; 210

The chylde may rue that ys un-borne,
  It was the mor pittè.

Thear was slayne with the lord Persè
  Sir John of Agerstone,
Sir Roge the hinde Hartly,   215
  Sir Wyllyam the bolde Hearone.

Sir Jorg the worthè Lovele
  A knyght of great renowen,
Sir Raff the ryche Rugbè
  With dyntes wear beaten dowene.   220

For Wetharryngton my harte was wo,
  That ever he slayne shulde be;
For when both his leggis wear hewyne in to,
  He knyled and fought on hys kne.

Ther was slayne with the dougheti Douglas   225
  Sir Hewe the Mongon-byrry,
Sir Davye Lwdale, that worthè was,
  His sistars son was he:

Sir Charles a Murrè, in that place,
  That never a foot wolde fle;   230
Sir Hewe Maxwell, a lorde he was,
  With the Duglas dyd he dey.

So on the morrowe the mayde them byears
  Off byrch, and hasell so gray;
Many wedous with wepyng tears   235
  Cam to fach ther makys a-way.

Tivydale may carpe off care,
  Northombarlond may mayk grat mone,
For towe such captayns, as slayne wear thear,
  On the March-perti shall never be none.   240

Word ys commen to Edden-burrowe,
　　To Jamy the Skottishe kyng,
That dougheti Duglas, lyff-tenant of the Merches,
　　He lay slean Chyviot with-in.

His handdes dyd he weal and wryng,　　　　　245
　　He sayd, "Alas, and woe ys me!
Such another captayn Skotland within,"
　　He sayd, "y-feth shuld never be."

Worde ys commyn to lovly Londone
　　Till the fourth Harry our kyng,　　　　　250
That lord Persè, leyff-tennante of the Merchis,
　　He lay slayne Chyviat within.

"God have merci on his soll," sayd kyng Harry,
　　"Good lord, yf thy will it be!
I have a hondrith captayns in Ynglonde," he sayd, 255
　　"As good as ever was hee:
But Persè, and I brook my lyffe,
　　Thy deth well quyte shall be."

As our noble kyng made his a-vowe,
　　Lyke a noble prince of renowen,　　　　　260
For the deth of the lord Persè,
　　He dyd the battel of Hombyll-down:

Wher syx and thritte Skottish knyghtes
　　On a day wear beaten down:
Glendale glytteryde on ther armor bryght,　　265
　　Over castill, towar, and town.

This was the hontynge off the Cheviat;
　　That tear begane this spurn:
Old men that knowen the grownde well yenoughe,
　　Call it the Battell of Otterburn.　　　　　270

At Otterburn began this spurne
    Uppon a monnyn day:
Ther was the dougghtè Doglas slean,
    The Persè never went away.

Ther was never a tym on the march-partes   275
    Sen the Doglas and the Persè met,
But yt was marvele, and the redde blude ronne not,
    As the reane doys in the stret.

Jhesue Christ our balys bete,
    And to the blys us brynge!   280
Thus was the hountynge of the Chevyat:
    God send us all good ending!

1765

SIR PATRICK SPENCE

THE king sits in Dumferling toune,
    Drinking the blude-reid wine:
"O quhar will I get guid sailor,
    To sail this schip of mine?"

Up and spak an eldern knicht,   5
    Sat at the kings richt kne:
"Sir Patrick Spence is the best sailor,
    That sails upon the se."

The king has written a braid letter,
    And signd it wi' his hand;   10
And sent it to Sir Patrick Spence,
    Was walking on the sand.

The first line that Sir Patrick red,
    A loud lauch lauched he:
The next line that Sir Patrick red,   15
    The teir blinded his ee.

"O quha is this has don this deid,
  This ill deid don to me;
To send me out this time o' the yeir,
  To sail upon the se?   20

"Mak hast, mak haste, my mirry men all,
  Our guid schip sails the morne;"
"O say na sae, my master deir,
  For I feir a deadlie storme.

"Late, late yestreen I saw the new moone,   25
  Wi' the auld moone in hir arme;
And I feir, I feir, my deir mastèr,
  That we will come to harme."

O our Scots nobles wer richt laith
  To weet their cork-heild schoone;   30
Bot lang owre a' the play wer playd,
  Thair hats they swam aboone.

O lang, lang, may thair ladies sit
  Wi' thair fans into their hand,
Or eir they se Sir Patrick Spence   35
  Cum sailing to the land.

O lang, lang, may the ladies stand
  Wi' thair gold kems in their hair,
Waiting for thair ain deir lords,
  For they'll se thame na mair.   40

Have owre, have owre to Aberdour,
  It's fiftie fadom deip:
And thair lies guid Sir Patrick Spence,
  Wi' the Scots lords at his feit.

1765

ROBIN HOOD AND GUY OF GISBORNE

When shaws beene sheene, and shradds full fayre,
    And leaves both large and longe,
Itt is merrye walking in the fayre forrèst
    To heare the small birdes songe.

The woodweele sang, and wold not cease,   5
    Sitting upon the spraye,
Soe lowde, he wakened Robin Hood,
    In the greenwood where he lay.

"Now by my faye," sayd jollye Robin.
    "A sweaven I had this night;   10
I dreamt me of tow wighty yemen,
    That fast with me can fight.

"Methought they did mee beate and binde,
    And tooke my bow mee froe;
If I be Robin alive in this lande,   15
    Ile be wroken on them towe."

"Sweavens are swift, master," quoth John,
    "As the wind blowes ore a hill;
For if itt be never so loude this night,
    Tomorrow it may be still."   20

"Buske yee, bowne yee, my merry men all,
    And John shall goe with mee,
For Ile goe seeke yond wight yeomen,
    In greenwood where thé bee."

Thé cast on their gownes of grene,   25
    And tooke theyr bowes each one;
And they away to the greene forrèst
    A-shooting forth are gone;

Untill they came to the merry greenwood,
  Where they had gladdest bee,   30
There were thé ware of a wight yeomàn,
  His body leaned to a tree.

A sword and a dagger he wore by his side,
  Of manye a man the bane;
And he was clad in his capullhyde,   35
  Topp and tayll and mayne.

"Stand you still, master," quoth Little John,
  "Under this tree so grene,
And I will go to yond wight yeoman
  To know what he doth meane."   40

"Ah John, by me thou settest noe store,
  And that I farley finde:
How offt send I my men beffore
  And tarry my selfe behinde?

"It is no cunning a knave to ken,   45
  And a man but heare him speake;
And itt were not for bursting of my bowe,
  John, I thy head wold breake."

As often wordes they breeden bale,
  So they parted Robin and John;   50
And John is gone to Barnesdale;
  The gates he knoweth eche one.

But when he came to Barnesdale,
  Great heavinesse there hee hadd,
For he found tow of his owne fellowes   55
  Were slaine both in a slade.

And Scarlette he was flying a-foote
  Fast over stocke and stone,

For the sheriffe with seven score men
    Fast after him is gone.   60

"One shoote now I will shoote," quoth John,
    "With Christ his might and mayne:
Ile make yond fellow that flyes soe fast,
    To stopp he shall be fayne."

Then John bent up his long bende-bowe,   65
    And fetteled him to shoote:
The bow was made of tender boughe,
    And fell down to his foote.

"Woe worth, woe worth thee, wicked wood,
    That ere thou grew on a tree;   70
For now this day thou art my bale,
    My boote when thou shold bee."

His shoote it was but loosely shott,
    Yet flewe not the arrowe in vaine,
For itt mett one of the sheriffes men,   75
    Good William a Trent was slaine.

It had bene better of William a Trent
    To have bene abed with sorrowe,
Than to be that day in the green wood slade
    To meet with Little Johns arrowe.   80

But as it is said, when men be mett
    Fyve can doe more than three,
The sheriffe hath taken Little John,
    And bound him fast to a tree.

"Thou shalt be drawen by dale and downe,   85
    And hanged hye on a hill."
"But thou mayst fayle of thy purpose," quoth John,
    "If itt be Christ his will."

Let us leave talking of Little John,
  And thinke of Robin Hood,   90
How he is gone to the wight yeomàn,
  Where under the leaves he stood.

"Good morrowe, good fellowe," sayd Robin so fayre,
  "Good morrowe, good fellow," quoth he:
"Methinkes by this bowe thou beares in thy hande   95
  A good archere thou sholdst bee."

"I am wilfulle of my waye," quo' the yeman,
  "And of my morning tyde."
"Ile lead thee through the wood," sayd Robin;
  "Good fellow, Ile be thy guide."   100

"I seeke an outlàwe," the straunger sayd,
  "Men call him Robin Hood;
Rather Ild meet with that proud outlàwe,
  Than fortye pound soe good."

"Now come with me, thou wighty yeman,   105
  And Robin thou soone shalt see:
But first let us some pastime find
  Under the greenwood tree.

"First let us some masterye make
  Among the woods so even,   110
We may chance to meet with Robin Hood
  Here att some unsett steven."

They cutt them downe two summer shroggs,
  That grew both under a breere,
And sett them threescore rood in twaine   115
  To shoot the prickes y-fere:

"Leade on, good fellowe," quoth Robin Hood,
  "Leade on, I doe bidd thee."

"Nay by my faith, good fellowe," he sayd,
  "My leader thou shalt be."   120

The first time Robin shot at the pricke,
  He mist but an inch it froe:
The yeoman he was an archer good,
  But he cold never shoote soe.

The second shoote had the wightye yeman,   125
  He shote within the garlànde:
But Robin he shott far better than hee,
  For he clave the good pricke wande.

"A blessing upon thy heart," he sayd;
  "Good fellowe, thy shooting is goode;   130
For an thy hart be as good as thy hand,
  Thou wert better then Robin Hoode.

"Now tell me thy name, good fellowe," sayd he,
  "Under the leaves of lyne."
"Nay by my faith," quoth bolde Robin,   135
  "Till thou have told me thine."

"I dwell by dale and downe," quoth hee,
  "And Robin to take Ime sworne;
And when I am called by my right name
  I am Guye of good Gisborne."   140

"My dwelling is in this wood," sayes Robin,
  "By thee I set right nought:
I am Robin Hood of Barnèsdale,
  Whom thou so long hast sought."

He that had neither beene kithe nor kin,   145
  Might have seene a full fayre sight,
To see how together these yeomen went
  With blades both browne and bright.

To see how these yeomen together they fought
    Two howres of a summers day: 150
Yett neither Robin Hood nor Sir Guy
    Them fettled to flye away.

Robin was reachles on a roote,
    And stumbled at that tyde;
And Guy was quick and nimble with-all,   155
    And hitt him ore the left side.

"Ah, deere Lady," sayd Robin Hood, "thou
    That art both mother and may,
I think it was never mans destinye
    To dye before his day."   160

Robin thought on our ladye deere,
    And soone leapt up againe,
And strait he came with a backward stroke,
    And he Sir Guy hath slayne.

He took Sir Guys head by the hayre,   165
    And stuck itt upon his bowes end:
"Thou hast beene a traytor all thy liffe,
    Which thing must have an ende."

Robin pulled forth an Irish kniffe,
    And nicked Sir Guy in the face,   170
That he was never on woman born,
    Cold tell whose head it was.

Saies, "Lye there, lye there, now Sir Guye,
    And with me be not wrothe;
If thou have had the worst strokes at my hand,   175
    Thou shalt have the better clothe."

Robin did off his gowne of greene,
    And on Sir Guy did throwe,

And hee put on that capull-hyde,
    That cladd him topp to toe.   180

"The bowe, the arrowes, and little horne,
    Now with me I will beare;
For I will away to Barnèsdale,
    To see how my men doe fare."

Robin Hood sett Guyes horne to his mouth,   185
    And a loud blast in it did blow.
That beheard the sheriffe of Nottingham,
    As he leaned under a lowe.

"Hearken, hearken," sayd the sheriffe,
    "I heare now tydings good,   190
For yonder I heare Sir Guyes horne blowe,
    And he hath slaine Robin Hoode.

"Yonder I heare Sir Guyes horne blowe,
    Itt blowes soe well in tyde,
And yonder comes that wightye yeoman,   195
    Cladd in his capull-hyde.

"Come hyther, come hyther, thou good Sir Guy,
    Aske what thou wilt of mee."
"O I will none of thy gold," sayd Robin,
    "Nor I will none of thy fee: 200

"But now I have slaine the master," he sayes,
    "Let me goe strike the knave;
For this is all the rewarde I aske;
    Nor noe other will I have."

"Thou art a madman," said the sheriffe,   205
    "Thou sholdst have had a knightes fee:
But seeing thy asking hath beene soe bad,
    Well granted it shale be."

When Little John heard his master speake,
   Well knewe he it was his steven: 210
"Now shall I be looset," quoth Little John,
   "With Christ his might in heaven."

Fast Robin hee hyed him to Little John,
   He thought to loose him belive;
The sheriffe and all his companye   215
   Fast after him can drive.

"Stand abacke, stand abacke," sayd Robin;
   "Why draw you mee soe neere?
Itt was never the use in our countryè,
   Ones shrift another shold heere."   220

But Robin pulled forth an Irysh knife,
   And losed John hand and foote,
And gave him Sir Guyes bow into his hand,
   And bade it be his boote.

Then John he took Guyes bow in his hand,   225
   His boltes and arrowes eche one:
When the sheriffe saw Little John bend his bow,
   He fettled him to be gone.

Towards his house in Nottingham towne
   He fled full fast away;   230
And soe did all his companye:
   Not one behind wold stay.

But he cold neither runne soe fast,
   Nor away soe fast cold ryde,
But Litle John with an arrowe soe broad   235
   He shott him into the 'backe'-syde.

                                          1765

OLIVER GOLDSMITH

[THE VICAR OF WAKEFIELD DESCRIBES HIS FAMILY]

I WAS ever of the opinion that the honest man who married and brought up a large family did more service than he who continued single and only talked of population. From this motive, I had scarce taken orders a year before I began to think seriously of matrimony, and chose my wife as she did her wedding-gown, not for a fine, glossy surface, but such qualities as would wear well. To do her justice, she was a good-natured, notable woman, and as for breeding there were few country ladies who could show more. She could read any English book without much spelling, but for pickling, preserving, and cookery, none could excel her. She prided herself also upon being an excellent contriver in housekeeping, though I could never find that we grew richer with all her contrivances.

However, we loved each other tenderly, and our fondness increased as we grew old. There was, in fact, nothing that could make us angry with the world or each other. We had an elegant house, situated in a fine country and a good neighborhood. The year was spent in moral or rural amusements, in visiting our rich neighbors, and relieving such as were poor. We had no revolutions to fear, nor fatigues to undergo. All our adventures were by the fire-side, and all our migrations from the blue bed to the brown.

As we lived near the road, we often had the traveller or stranger visit us to taste our gooseberry wine, for which we had great reputation, and I profess with the veracity of an historian, that I never knew one of them find fault with it. Our cousins, too, even to the fortieth remove, all remembered their affinity without any help from the herald's office, and came very frequently to see us. 35 Some of them did us no great honor by these claims of kindred, as we had the blind, the maimed, and the halt amongst the number. However, my wife always insisted that as they were the same *flesh and blood,* they should sit with us at the same table. So 40 that if we had not very rich, we generally had very happy friends about us, for this remark will hold good through life that the poorer the guest, the better pleased he ever is with being treated; and as some men gaze with admiration at the colors of a 45 tulip or the wing of a butterfly, so I was by nature an admirer of happy human faces. However, when any one of our relations was found to be a person of very bad character, a troublesome guest, or one we desired to get rid of, upon his leaving my house, I 50 ever took care to lend him a riding coat, or a pair of boots, or sometimes a horse of small value, and I always had the satisfaction of finding he never came back to return them. By this the house was cleared of such as we did not like, but never was the family 55 of Wakefield known to turn the traveller or the poor dependant out of doors.

Thus we lived several years in a state of much happiness, not but that we sometimes had those little rubs which Providence sends to enhance the 60 value of its favors. My orchard was often robbed by schoolboys, and my wife's custards plundered by the cats or the children. The squire would sometimes fall asleep in the most pathetic parts of my sermon, or his lady return my wife's civilities at 65 church with a mutilated courtesy. But we soon got over the uneasiness caused by such accidents, and usually in three or four days began to wonder how they vexed us.

My children, the offspring of temperance, as they were educated without softness, so they were at once well-formed and healthy; my sons hardy and active, my daughters beautiful and blooming. When I stood in the midst of the little circle which promised to be the supports of my declining age, I could not avoid repeating the famous story of Count Abensberg who, in Henry II's progress through Germany, while other courtiers came with their treasures, brought his thirty-two children, and presented them to his sovereign as the most valuable offering he had to bestow. In this manner, though I had but six, I considered them as a very valuable present made to my country, and consequently looked upon it as my debtor.

1766

THE DESERTED VILLAGE

FROM *The Dedication to Sir Joshua Reynolds*

Dear Sir:
   . . . Permit me to inscribe this poem to you.
   How far you may be pleased with the versification and mere mechanical parts of this attempt, I do not pretend to inquire; but I know you will object (and indeed several of our best and wisest friends concur in the opinion) that the depopulation it deplores is nowhere to be seen, and the disorders it laments are only to be found in the poet's own imagination. To this I can scarcely make any other answer than that I sincerely believe what I have written; that I have taken all possible pains, in my country excursions, for these four or five years past, to be certain of what I allege, and that all my views and inquiries have led me to believe those miseries real which I here attempt to display. But this is not the place to enter into an inquiry, whether the country be depopulating or not; the discussion would take up much room, and I should prove myself, at best, an indifferent

politician, to tire the reader with a long preface, when I
want his unfatigued attention to a long poem.

In regretting the depopulation of the country, I inveigh 20
against the increase of our luxuries; and here also I expect
the shout of modern politicians against me. For twenty or
thirty years past it has been the fashion to consider luxury
as one of the greatest national advantages, and all the wisdom of antiquity in that particular as erroneous. Still, 25
however, I must remain a professed ancient on that head,
and continue to think those luxuries prejudicial to states
by which so many vices are introduced, and so many kingdoms have been undone. Indeed, so much has been poured
out of late on the other side of the question that, merely for 30
the sake of novelty and variety, one would sometimes wish
to be in the right.

I am, dear sir, your sincere friend and ardent admirer,
Oliver Goldsmith

THE DESERTED VILLAGE

Sweet Auburn! loveliest village of the plain;
Where health and plenty cheered the laboring swain,   35
Where smiling Spring its earliest visit paid,
And parting summer's lingering blooms delayed:
Dear lovely bowers of innocence and ease,
Seats of my youth, when every sport could please,
How often have I loitered o'er thy green,   40
Where humble happiness endeared each scene!
How often have I paused on every charm,
The sheltered cot, the cultivated farm,
The never-failing brook, the busy mill,
The decent church that topped the neighboring hill,   45
The hawthorn bush, with seats beneath the shade
For talking age and whispering lovers made!
How often have I blest the coming day,
When toil remitting lent its turn to play,
And all the village train, from labor free,   50
Led up their sports beneath the spreading tree,
While many a pastime circled in the shade,
The young contending as the old surveyed;

And many a gambol frolicked o'er the ground,
And sleights of art and feats of strength went round. 55
And still, as each repeated pleasure tired,
Succeeding sports the mirthful band inspired;
The dancing pair that simply sought renown
By holding out to tire each other down;
The swain mistrustless of his smutted face, 60
While secret laughter tittered round the place;
The bashful virgin's side-long looks of love,
The matron's glance that would those looks reprove:
These were thy charms, sweet village! sports like
        these,
With sweet succession, taught even toil to please: 65
These round thy bowers their cheerful influence
        shed:
These were thy charms—but all these charms are
        fled.
   Sweet smiling village, loveliest of the lawn,
Thy sports are fled, and all thy charms withdrawn;
Amidst thy bowers the tyrant's hand is seen, 70
And desolation saddens all thy green:
One only master grasps the whole domain,
And half a tillage stints thy smiling plain.
No more thy glassy brook reflects the day,
But, choked with sedges, works its weedy way; 75
Along the glades, a solitary guest,
The hollow sounding bittern guards its nest;
Amidst thy desert walks the lapwing flies,
And tires their echoes with unvaried cries;
Sunk are thy bowers in shapeless ruin all, 80
And the long grass o'ertops the moldering wall;
And trembling, shrinking from the spoiler's hand,
Far, far away thy children leave the land.
   Ill fares the land, to hastening ills a prey,
Where wealth accumulates, and men decay: 85
Princes and lords may flourish, or may fade;
A breath can make them, as a breath has made:

But a bold peasantry, their country's pride,
When once destroyed, can never be supplied.
    A time there was, ere England's griefs began,   90
When every rood of ground maintained its man;
For him light labor spread her wholesome store,
Just gave what life required, but gave no more:
His best companions, innocence and health;
And his best riches, ignorance of wealth.   95
    But times are altered; trade's unfeeling train
Usurp the land and dispossess the swain;
Along the lawn, where scattered hamlets rose,
Unwieldy wealth and cumbrous pomp repose,
And every want to opulence allied,   100
And every pang that folly pays to pride.
These gentle hours that plenty bade to bloom,
Those calm desires that asked but little room,
Those healthful sports that graced the peaceful
        scene,
Lived in each look, and brightened all the green;   105
These, far departing, seek a kinder shore,
And rural mirth and manners are no more.
    Sweet Auburn! parent of the blissful hour,
Thy glades forlorn confess the tyrant's power.
Here, as I take my solitary rounds   110
Amidst thy tangling walks and ruined grounds,
And, many a year elapsed, return to view
Where once the cottage stood, the hawthorn grew,
Remembrance wakes with all her busy train,
Swells at my breast, and turns the past to pain.   115
    In all my wanderings round this world of care,
In all my griefs—and God has given my share—
I still had hopes, my latest hours to crown,
Amidst these humble bowers to lay me down;
To husband out life's taper at the close,   120
And keep the flame from wasting by repose:
I still had hopes, for pride attends us still,
Amidst the swains to show my book-learned skill,

Around my fire an evening group to draw,
And tell of all I felt, and all I saw;   125
And, as an hare whom hounds and horns pursue
Pants to the place from whence at first she flew,
I still had hopes, my long vexations past,
Here to return—and die at home at last.

O blest retirement, friend to life's decline,   130
Retreats from care, that never must be mine,
How happy he who crowns in shades like these
A youth of labor with an age of ease;
Who quits a world where strong temptations try,
And, since 'tis hard to combat, learns to fly!   135
For him no wretches, born to work and weep,
Explore the mine, or tempt the dangerous deep;
No surly porter stands in guilty state,
To spurn imploring famine from the gate;
But on he moves to meet his latter end,   140
Angels around befriending Virtue's friend;
Bends to the grave with unperceived decay,
While resignation gently slopes the way;
And, all his prospects brightening to the last,
His Heaven commences ere the world be past!   145
    Sweet was the sound, when oft at evening's close
Up yonder hill the village murmur rose.
There, as I passed with careless steps and slow,
The mingling notes came softened from below;
The swain responsive as the milk-maid sung,   150
The sober herd that lowed to meet their young,
The noisy geese that gabbled o'er the pool,
The playful children just let loose from school,
The watch-dog's voice that bayed the whispering
        wind,
And the loud laugh that spoke the vacant mind;—   155
These all in sweet confusion sought the shade,
And filled each pause the nightingale had made.
But now the sounds of population fail,
No cheerful murmurs fluctuate in the gale,

No busy steps the grass-grown foot-way tread,   160
For all the bloomy flush of life is fled.
All but yon widowed, solitary thing,
That feebly bends beside the plashy spring:
She, wretched matron, forced in age, for bread,
To strip the brook with mantling cresses spread,   165
To pick her wintry faggot from the thorn,
To seek her nightly shed, and weep till morn;
She only left of all the harmless train,
The sad historian of the pensive plain.

    Near yonder copse, where once the garden smiled,   170
And still where many a garden flower grows wild;
There, where a few torn shrubs the place disclose,
The village preacher's modest mansion rose.
A man he was to all the country dear,
And passing rich with forty pounds a year;   175
Remote from towns he ran his godly race,
Nor e'er had changed, nor wished to change his
       place;
Unpractised he to fawn, or seek for power,
By doctrines fashioned to the varying hour;
Far other aims his heart had learned to prize,   180
More skilled to raise the wretched than to rise.
His house was known to all the vagrant train;
He chid their wanderings, but relieved their pain:
The long-remembered beggar was his guest,
Whose beard descending swept his aged breast;   185
The ruined spendthrift, now no longer proud,
Claimed kindred there, and had his claims allowed;
The broken soldier, kindly bade to stay,
Sate by his fire, and talked the night away,
Wept o'er his wounds, or, tales of sorrow done,   190
Shouldered his crutch and showed how fields were
       won.
Pleased with his guests, the good man learned to
       glow,
And quite forgot their vices in their woe;

Careless their merits or their faults to scan,
His pity gave ere charity began.   195
   Thus to relieve the wretched was his pride,
And e'en his failings leaned to Virtue's side;
But in his duty prompt at every call,
He watched and wept, he prayed and felt, for all;
And, as a bird each fond endearment tries   200
To tempt its new-fledged offspring to the skies,
He tried each art, reproved each dull delay,
Allured to brighter worlds, and led the way.
   Beside the bed where parting life was laid,
And sorrow, guilt, and pain by turns dismayed,   205
The reverend champion stood. At his control
Despair and anguish fled the struggling soul;
Comfort came down the trembling wretch to raise,
And his last faltering accents whispered praise.
   At church, with meek and unaffected grace,   210
His looks adorned the venerable place;
Truth from his lips prevailed with double sway,
And fools, who came to scoff, remained to pray.
The service past, around the pious man,
With steady zeal, each honest rustic ran;   215
Even children followed with endearing wile,
And plucked his gown to share the good man's smile.
His ready smile a parent's warmth expressed;
Their welfare pleased him, and their cares dis-
      tressed:
To them his heart, his love, his griefs were given,   220
But all his serious thoughts had rest in Heaven.
As some tall cliff that lifts its awful form,
Swells from the vale, and midway leaves the storm,
Though round its breast the rolling clouds are
      spread,
Eternal sunshine settles on its head.   225
   Beside yon straggling fence that skirts the way,
With blossomed furze unprofitably gay,
There, in his noisy mansion, skilled to rule,

The village master taught his little school.
A man severe he was, and stern to view;   230
I knew him well, and every truant knew;
Well had the boding tremblers learned to trace
The days' disasters in his morning face;
Full well they laughed with counterfeited glee
At all his jokes, for many a joke had he;   235
Full well the busy whisper circling round
Conveyed the dismal tidings when he frowned.
Yet he was kind, or, if severe in aught,
The love he bore to learning was in fault:
The village all declared how much he knew;   240
'Twas certain he could write, and cipher too;
Lands he could measure, terms and tides presage,
And even the story ran that he could gauge;
In arguing, too, the parson owned his skill,
For, even though vanquished, he could argue still;   245
While words of learned length and thundering sound
Amazed the gazing rustics ranged around;
And still they gazed, and still the wonder grew,
That one small head could carry all he knew.

But past is all his fame. The very spot   250
Where many a time he triumphed is forgot.
Near yonder thorn, that lifts its head on high,
Where once the sign-post caught the passing eye,
Low lies that house where nut-brown draughts in-
        spired,
Where graybeard mirth and smiling toil retired,   255
Where village statesmen talked with looks profound,
And news much older than their ale went round.
Imagination fondly stoops to trace
The parlor splendors of that festive place:
The whitewashed well, the nicely sanded floor,   260
The varnished clock that clicked behind the door:
The chest contrived a double debt to pay,
A bed by night, a chest of drawers by day;
The pictures placed for ornament and use,

The twelve good rules, the royal game of goose;   265
The hearth, except when winter chilled the day,
With aspen boughs and flowers and fennel gay;
While broken tea-cups, wisely kept for show,
Ranged o'er the chimney, glistened in a row.

Vain transitory splendors could not all   270
Reprieve the tottering mansion from its fall?
Obscure it sinks, nor shall it more impart
An hour's importance to the poor man's heart.
Thither no more the peasant shall repair
To sweet oblivion of his daily care;   275
No more the farmer's news, the barber's tale,
No more the woodman's ballad shall prevail;
No more the smith his dusky brow shall clear,
Relax his ponderous strength, and lean to hear;
The host himself no longer shall be found   280
Careful to see the mantling bliss go round;
Nor the coy maid, half willing to be pressed,
Shall kiss the cup to pass it to the rest.

Yes! let the rich deride, the proud disdain,
These simple blessings of the lowly train;   285
To me more dear, congenial to my heart,
One native charm, than all the gloss of art.
Spontaneous joys, where Nature has its play,
The soul adopts, and owns their first-born sway;
Lightly they frolic o'er the vacant mind,   290
Unenvied, unmolested, unconfined.
But the long pomp, the midnight masquerade,
With all the freaks of wanton wealth arrayed—
In these, ere triflers half their wish obtain,
The toiling pleasure sickens into pain;   295
And, e'en while fashion's brightest arts decoy,
The heart distrusting asks if this be joy.

Ye friends to truth, ye statesmen who survey
The rich man's joys increase, the poor's decay,
'Tis yours to judge, how wide the limits stand   300
Between a splendid and an happy land.

Proud swells the tide with loads of freighted ore,
And shouting Folly hails them from her shore;
Hoards e'en beyond the miser's wish abound,
And rich men flock from all the world around.   305
Yet count our gains! This wealth is but a name
That leaves our useful products still the same.
Not so the loss. The man of wealth and pride
Takes up a space that many poor supplied;
Space for his lake, his park's extended bounds, 310
Space for his horses, equipage, and hounds:
The robe that wraps his limbs in silken sloth
Has robbed the neighboring fields of half their
        growth;
His seat, where solitary sports are seen,
Indignant spurs the cottage from the green: 315
Around the world each needful product flies,
For all the luxuries the world supplies;
While thus the land adorned for pleasure all
In barren splendor feebly waits the fall.
    As some fair female unadorned and plain,   320
Secure to please while youth confirms her reign,
Slights every borrowed charm that dress supplies,
Nor shares with art the triumph of her eyes;
But when those charms are passed, for charms are
        frail,
When time advances, and when lovers fail,   325
She then shines forth, solicitous to bless,
In all the glaring impotence of dress.
Thus fares the land by luxury betrayed:
In nature's simplest charms at first arrayed,
But verging to decline, its splendors rise,   330
Its vistas strike, its palaces surprise;
While, scourged by famine from the smiling land
The mournful peasant leads his humble band,
And while he sinks, without one arm to save,
The country blooms—a garden and a grave.   335
    Where then, ah! where, shall poverty reside,

To 'scape the pressure of contiguous pride?
If to some common's fenceless limits strayed,
He drives his flock to pick the scanty blade,
Those fenceless fields the sons of wealth divide,   340
And even the bare-worn common is denied.
     If to the city sped—what waits him there?
To see profusion that he must not share;
To see ten thousand baneful arts combined
To pamper luxury, and thin mankind;   345
To see those joys the sons of pleasure know
Extorted from his fellow-creature's woe.
Here while the courtier glitters in brocade,
There the pale artist plies the sickly trade;
Here while the proud their long-drawn pomps
          display,   350
There the black gibbet glooms beside the way.
The dome where pleasure holds her midnight reign
Here, richly decked, admits the gorgeous train:
Tumultuous grandeur crowds the blazing square,
The rattling chariots clash, the torches glare.   355
Sure scenes like these no troubles e'er annoy!
Sure these denote one universal joy!
Are these thy serious thoughts?—Ah, turn thine eyes
Where the poor houseless shivering female lies.
She once, perhaps, in village plenty blessed,   360
Has wept at tales of innocence distressed;
Her modest looks the cottage might adorn,
Sweet as the primrose peeps beneath the thorn:
Now lost to all; her friends, her virtue fled,
Near her betrayer's door she lays her head,   365
And, pinched with cold, and shrinking from the
          shower,
With heavy heart deplores that luckless hour,
When idly first, ambitious of the town,
She left her wheel and robes of country brown.
     Do thine, sweet Auburn,—thine, the loveliest
          train,—   370

Do thy fair tribes participate her pain?
Even now, perhaps, by cold and hunger led,
At proud men's doors they ask a little bread!
   Ah, no! To distant climes, a dreary scene,
Where half the convex world intrudes between,   375
Through torrid tracts with fainting steps they go,
Where wild Altama murmurs to their woe.
Far different there from all that charmed before
The various terrors of that horrid shore;
Those blazing suns that dart a downward ray,   380
And fiercely shed intolerable day;
Those matted woods, where birds forget to sing,
But silent bats in drowsy clusters cling;
Those poisonous fields with rank luxuriance
         crowned,
Where the dark scorpion gathers death around;   385
Where at each step the stranger fears to wake
The rattling terrors of the vengeful snake;
Where crouching tigers wait their hapless prey,
And savage men more murderous still than they;
While oft in whirls the mad tornado flies,   390
Mingling the ravaged landscape with the skies.
Far different these from every former scene,
The cooling brook, the grassy vested green,
The breezy covert of the warbling grove,
That only sheltered thefts of harmless love.   395
   Good Heaven! what sorrows gloomed that parting
         day,
That called them from their native walks away;
When the poor exiles, every pleasure passed,
Hung round the bowers, and fondly looked their last,
And took a long farewell, and wished in vain   400
For seats like these beyond the western main,
And shuddering still to face the distant deep,
Returned and wept, and still returned to weep.
The good old sire the first prepared to go
To new-found worlds, and wept for others' woe;   405

But for himself, in conscious virtue brave,
He only wished for worlds beyond the grave.
His lovely daughter, lovelier in her tears,
The fond companion of his helpless years,
Silent went next, neglectful of her charms,   410
And left a lover's for a father's arms.
With louder plaints the mother spoke her woes,
And blest the cot where every pleasure rose,
And kissed her thoughtless babes with many a tear,
And clasped them close, in sorrow doubly dear,   415
Whilst her fond husband strove to lend relief
In all the silent manliness of grief.

   O luxury! thou cursed by Heaven's decree,
How ill exchanged are things like these for thee!
How do thy potions, with insidious joy,   420
Diffuse their pleasure only to destroy!
Kingdoms by thee, to sickly greatness grown,
Boast of a florid vigor not their own.
At every draught more large and large they grow,
A bloated mass of rank unwieldy woe;   425
Till sapped their strength, and every part unsound,
Down, down, they sink, and spread a ruin round.

   Even now the devastation is begun,
And half the business of destruction done;
Even now, methinks, as pondering here I stand,   430
I see the rural Virtues leave the land.
Down where yon anchoring vessel spreads the sail,
That idly waiting flaps with every gale,
Downward they move, a melancholy band,
Pass from the shore, and darken all the strand.   435
Contented Toil, and hospitable Care.
And kind connubial Tenderness, are there;
And Piety with wishes placed above,
And steady Loyalty, and faithful Love.
And thou, sweet Poetry, thou loveliest maid,   440
Still first to fly where sensual joys invade;
Unfit in these degenerate times of shame

To catch the heart, or strike for honest fame;
Dear charming nymph, neglected and decried,
My shame in crowds, my solitary pride;   445
Thou source of all my bliss, and all my woe,
That found'st me poor at first, and keep'st me so;
Thou guide by which the nobler arts excel,
Thou nurse of every virtue, fare thee well!
Farewell, and oh! where'er thy voice be tried,   450
On Torno's cliffs, or Pambamarca's side,
Whether where equinoctial fervors glow,
Or winter wraps the polar world in snow,
Still let thy voice, prevailing over time,
Redress the rigors of th' inclement clime;   455
Aid slighted truth with thy persuasive strain;
Teach erring man to spurn the rage of gain;
Teach him, that states of native strength possessed,
Though very poor, may still be very blessed;
That trade's proud empire hastes to swift decay,   460
As ocean sweeps the labored mole away;
While self-dependent power can time defy,
As rocks resist the billows and the sky.

                              1770

HENRY BROOKE

[For selections from his earlier work see p. 88, above]

[THE CONVENTIONAL CHILD AND THE NATURAL]

FROM THE FOOL OF QUALITY

[Richard is the elder brother; Henry, the younger]

RICHARD speedily became the sole center of all his
mother's solicitude and affections. And though within the space of two succeeding years she was de-

livered of a second boy, yet, as his infant aspect was
less promising and more unformed than his brother's,   5
she sent him forth to be nursed by the robust wife
of a neighboring farmer, where, for the space of
upwards of four years, he was honored with no
token from father or mother, save some casual mes-
sages to know from time to time if the child was   10
in health. . . .

.   .   .   .

Meanwhile the education of the two children was
extremely contrasted. Richard, who was already entitled 'my little lord,' was not permitted to breathe
the rudeness of the wind. On his lightest indisposi-   15
tion the whole house was in alarms; his passions had
full scope in all their infant irregularities; his genius
was put into a hot bed, by the warmth of applauses
given to every flight of his opening fancy; and
the whole family conspired, from the highest to the   20
lowest, to the ruin of promising talents and a benevolent heart.

Young Harry, on the other hand, had every
member as well as feature exposed to all weathers,
would run about, mother-naked, for near an hour in   25
a frosty morning; was neither physicked into delicacy nor flattered into pride; scarce felt the convenience and much less understood the vanity of
clothing; and was daily occupied in playing and
wrestling with the pigs and two mongrel spaniels   30
on the dunghill; or in kissing, scratching or boxing
with the children of the village.

When Harry had passed his fifth year, his father,
on a festival day, humbly proposed to send for him
to his nurse's, in order to observe how the boy   35
might turn out; and my lady in a fit of good humor
assented. Nurse, accordingly, decked him out in

his holiday petticoats and walked with our hero to
the great house, as they called it.

A brilliant concourse of the neighboring gentry 40
were met in a vast parlor, that appeared to be exe-
cuted after the model of Westminster Hall.

There was Sir Christopher Cloudy, who knew
much but said nothing, with his very conversable
lady who scarce knew by halves but spoke by 45
wholesale. . . .

The cloth had been lately removed and a host of
glasses and decanters glowed on the table, when in
comes young Harry escorted by his nurse.

All the eyes of the company were instantly drawn 50
upon him; but he advanced with a vacant and unob-
serving physiognomy, and thought no higher of the
assembly than as of so many peasants at a country
wake.

"Dicky, my dear," says my lady, "go and welcome 55
your brother," whereat Dick went up, took Harry
by the hand and kissed him with much affection.
Harry thereupon having eyed his brother, "I don't
know you," said he bluntly, but at the same time
held up his little mouth to kiss him again. 60

"Dick," says my lady, "put your laced-hat upon
Harry, till we see how it becomes him," which he
immediately did; but Harry, feeling an unusual in-
cumbrance on his head, took off the hat and having
for some time looked contemptuously at it, he cast 65
it from him with a sudden and agile jerk, as he used
to cast flat stones in order to make ducks and
drakes in the mill-pond. The hat took the glasses
and decanters in full career; smash go the glasses,
abroad pours the wine on circling laces, Dresden 70
aprons, silvered silks and rich brocades; female
screams fill the parlor, the rout is equal to the uproar
and it was long ere most of them could be composed
to their places.

In the meanwhile Harry took no kind of interest 75
in their outcries or distresses but, spying a large
Spanish pointer that just then came from under
the table, he sprung at him like lightning, seized him
by the collar and vaulted on his back with incon-
ceivable agility. The dog, wholly disconcerted by so 80
unaccustomed a burden, capered and plunged about
in a violent manner; but Harry was a better horse-
man than to be so easily dismounted: whereon the
dog grew outrageous and rushing into a group of
little misses and masters, the children of the visi- 85
tants, he overthrew them like ninepins, thence proceeding with equal rapidity between the legs of Mrs.
Dowdy, a very fat and elderly lady; she instantly
fell backward with a violent shriek, and in her fall
unfortunately overthrew Frank the foxhunter, who 90
overthrew Andrew the angler, who overthrew Bob
the beau, who closed the catastrophe.

Our hero, meantime, was happily dismounted by
the intercepting petticoats and fairly laid, without
damage, in the fallen lady's lap. From thence he 95
arose at his leisure and strolled about the room, with
as unconcerned an aspect as if nothing had happened amiss and as though he had neither act or part
in this frightful discomfiture.

When matters were once more in some measure 100
set to rights, "My Heavens!" exclaimed my lady, "I
shall faint, the boy is positively an idiot, he has no
apprehension or conception of persons or things.
Come hither, sirrah," she cried with an angry tone;
but instead of complying Harry cast on her a look 105
of resentment and sidled over toward his nurse.
"Dicky, my dear," said my lady, "go and pretend
to beat his foster mother, that we may try if the
child has any kind of ideas." Here, her ladyship,
by ill fortune, was as much unadvised as her favorite 110
was unhappy in the execution of her orders; for

while Dick struck at the nurse with a counterfeited passion, Harry instantly reddened and gave his brother such a sudden push in the face, that his nose and mouth gushed out with blood. Dick set up the roar, my lady screamed out, and rising and running at Harry with all imaginable fury, she caught him up, as a falcon would truss a robin; turned over his petticoats, and chastised him with all the violence of which her delicacy was capable. Our hero, however, neither uttered cry or tear, but being set down, he turned round on the company an eye of indignation, then cried, "Come away, mammy," and issued from the assembly.

Harry had scarce made his exit when his mother exclaimed after him, "Aye, aye, take him away, nurse, take him away, the little devil, and never let me see his face more."

I shall not detain my readers with a tedious detail of the many and differing opinions that the remaining company expressed with regard to our hero; let it suffice to observe that they generally agreed that though the boy did not appear to be endowed by nature with a single faculty of the "animal rationale," he might nevertheless be rendered capable in time of many places of very honorable and lucrative employment.

Mr. Meekly, alone, though so gentle and complying at other times, now presumed to dissent from the sense of the company. "I rather hold," said he, "that this infant is the promise of the greatest philosopher and hero that our age is likely to produce. By refusing his respect to those superficial distinctions, which fashion has inadequately substituted as expressions of human greatness, he approves himself the philosopher; and by the quickness of his feelings for injured innocence and his boldness in defending those to whom his heart is attached he approves himself at once the hero and the man."

Harry had now remained six months more with 150 his nurse engaged in his customary exercises and occupations. He was already, by his courage, his strength, and action, become tremendous to all the little boys of the village; they had all things to fear from his sudden resentment, but nothing from his 155 memory or recollection of a wrong, and this also was imputed to his native stupidity. The two mongrel dogs were his inseparable playfellows, they were all tied together in the strictest bonds of friendship and caressed each other with the most warm and un- 160 feigned affection.

On a summer's day as he strolled forth with these his faithful attendants and rambled into a park whose gate he saw open, he perceived in a little copse that bordered on a fish pond a stranger seated 165 on a bench of turf. Harry drew near with his usual intrepidity, till he observed that the man had a reverend beard that spread over his breast, that he held something in his hand on which he gazed with a fixed attention, and that the tears rolled down 170 his cheeks without ceasing and in silence except the half suppressed sobs that often broke from his bosom. Harry stood awhile immovable, his little heart was affected, he approached the old man with a gentle reverence and looking up in his face and 175 seating himself by his side, the muscles of his infant aspect began to relax and he wept and sobbed as fast as his companion.

1766

FROM CONRADE, A FRAGMENT

WHAT do I love—what is it that mine eyes
Turn round in search of—that my soul longs after,

But cannot quench her thirst?—'Tis Beauty, Phelin!
I see it wide beneath the arch of heaven,
When the stars peep upon their evening hour,   5
And the moon rises on the eastern wave,
Housed in a cloud of gold! I see it wide
In earth's autumnal taints of various landscape
When the first ray of morning tips the trees,
And fires the distant rock! I hear its voice   10
When thy hand sends the sound along the gale,
Swept from the silver strings or on mine ear
Drops the sweet sadness! At my heart I feel
Its potent grasp, I melt beneath the touch,
When the tale pours upon my sense humane   15
The woes of other times! What art thou, Beauty?
Thou art not color, fancy, sound, nor form—
These but the conduits are, whence the soul quaffs
The liquor of its heaven. Whate'er thou art,
Nature, or Nature's spirit, thou art all   20
I long for! Oh, descend upon my thoughts!
To thine own music tune, thou power of grace,
The cordage of my heart! Fill every shape
That rises to my dream or wakes to vision;
And touch the threads of every mental nerve,   25
With all thy sacred feelings!

                                        1778

HENRY MACKENZIE

[HARLEY'S FAREWELL TO HIS BELOVED]

FROM THE MAN OF FEELING

"THERE are some remembrances," said Harley,
"which rise involuntarily on my heart, and make me
almost wish to live. I have been blessed with a few
friends, who redeem my opinion of mankind. I
recollect, with the tenderest emotion, the scenes of   5

pleasure I have passed among them; but we shall
meet again, my friend, never to be separated. There
are some feelings which perhaps are too tender to
be suffered by the world. The world is in general
selfish, interested, and unthinking, and throws the
imputation of romance or melancholy on every temper more susceptible than its own. I cannot think
but in those regions which I contemplate, if there
is anything of mortality left about us, that these feelings will subsist;—they are called—perhaps they are
—weaknesses here;—but there may be some better
modifications of them in heaven, which may deserve
the name of virtues." He sighed as he spoke these
last words. He had scarcely finished them, when
the door opened, and his aunt appeared leading in
Miss Walton. "My dear," says she, "here is Miss
Walton, who has been so kind as to come and enquire
for you herself." I could observe a transient glow
upon his face. He rose from his seat. "If to know
Miss Walton's goodness," said he, "be a title to
deserve it, I have some claim." She begged him
to resume his seat and placed herself on the sofa
beside him. I took my leave. Mrs. Margery accompanied me to the door. He was left with Miss
Walton alone. She inquired anxiously about his
health. "I believe," said he, "from the accounts
which my physicians unwillingly give me, that they
have no great hopes of my recovery." She started
as he spoke; but recollecting herself immediately, endeavored to flatter him into a belief that his apprehensions were groundless. "I know," said he, "that
it is usual with persons at my time of life to have
these hopes which your kindness suggests, but I
would not wish to be deceived. To meet death as
becomes a man is a privilege bestowed on few.—I
would endeavor to make it mine;—nor do I think
that I can ever be better prepared for it than now:—

It is that chiefly which determines the fitness of its
approach." "Those sentiments," answered Miss Walton, "are just; but your good sense, Mr. Harley, will   45
own that life has its proper value. As the province
of virtue, life is ennobled; as such, it is to be desired.
To virtue has the Supreme Director of all things assigned rewards enough even here to fix its attachment."   50

The subject began to overpower her. Harley
lifted his eyes from the ground. "There are," said
he, in a very low voice, "there are attachments, Miss
Walton ——" His glance met hers; they both betrayed a confusion, and were both instantly with-   55
drawn. He paused some moments. "I am in such
a state as calls for sincerity, let that also excuse it—
It is perhaps the last time we shall ever meet. I
feel something particularly solemn in the acknowl-
edgment, yet my heart swells to make it, awed as it   60
is by a sense of my presumption, by a sense of your
perfections." He paused again. "Let it not offend
you to know their power over one so unworthy—It
will, I believe, soon cease to beat, even with that
feeling which it shall lose the latest.—To love Miss   65
Walton could not be a crime—if to declare it is
one—the expiation will be made." Her tears were
now flowing without control. "Let me intreat you,"
said she, "to have better hopes—Let not life be so
indifferent to you; if my wishes can put any value on   70
it—I will not pretend to misunderstand you—I know
your worth—I have known it long—I have esteemed
it—What would you have me say!—I have loved it
as it deserved." He seized her hand—a languid
color reddened her cheek—a smile brightened faintly   75
in his eye. As he gazed on her, it grew dim, it
fixed, it closed—He sighed, and fell back on his seat
—Miss Walton screamed at the sight—His aunt and
the servants rushed into the room—They found them

lying motionless together. His physician happened 80
to call at that instant. Every art was tried to recover them—With Miss Walton they succeeded—
But Harley was gone for ever!

[ANTI-SLAVERY]

FROM JULIA DE ROUBIGNÉ

I HAVE often been tempted to doubt whether there
is not an error in the whole plan of negro servitude;
and whether whites or creoles born in the West
Indies, or perhaps cattle, after the manner of European husbandry, would not do the business better and 5
cheaper than the slaves do. The money which the
latter cost at first, the sickness—often owing to despondency of mind—to which they are liable after
their arrival, and the proportion that die in consequence of it, make the machine, if it may be so called, 10
of a plantation extremely expensive in its operations.
In the list of slaves belonging to a wealthy planter,
it would astonish you to see the number unfit for
service, pining under disease, a burden on their
master. I am only talking as a merchant; but as a 15
man—good Heavens! when I think of the many
thousands of my fellow-creatures groaning under
servitude and misery!—great God! hast thou peopled
those regions of thy world for the purpose of casting
out their inhabitants to chains and torture? No; 20
thou gavest them a land teeming with good things,
and lightedst up thy sun to bring forth spontaneous
plenty; but the refinements of man, ever at war with
thy works, have changed this scene of profusion
and luxuriance into a theatre of rapine, of slavery, 25
and of murder!

Forgive the warmth of this apostrophe! Here it

would not be understood; even my uncle, whose
heart is far from a hard one, would smile at my
romance, and tell me that things must be so. Habit, 30
the tyrant of nature and of reason, is deaf to the
voice of either; here she stifles humanity and de-
bases the species—for the master of slaves has seldom the soul of a man.

                                                                    1777

[ON ROBERT BURNS]

I KNOW not if I shall be accused of such enthusiasm and partiality, when I introduce to the notice
of my readers a poet of our own country with whose
writings I have lately become acquainted; but if I
am not greatly deceived, I think I may safely pro-   5
nounce him a genius of no ordinary rank. The
person to whom I allude is Robert Burns, an Ayr-
shire plowman, whose poems were some time ago
published in a county town in the west of Scotland
with no other ambition, it would seem, than to circu- 10
late among the inhabitants of the county where he
was born, to obtain a little fame from those who had
heard of his talents. I hope I shall not be thought
to assume too much if I endeavor to place him in a
higher point of view, to call for a verdict of his coun- 15
try on the merit of his works, and to claim for him
those honors which their excellence appears to deserve.

In mentioning the circumstance of his humble station, I mean not to rest his pretensions solely on that 20
title, or to urge the merits of his poetry when considered in relation to the lowness of his birth, and
the little opportunity of improvement which his education could afford. These particulars, indeed, might
excite our wonder at his productions; but his poetry, 25
considered abstractedly, and without the apologies

arising from his situation, seems to me fully entitled
to command our feelings, and to obtain our applause.
One bar, indeed, his birth and education have opposed to his fame,—the language in which most of 30
his poems are written.   Even in Scotland, the pro-
vincial dialect which Ramsay and he have used is now
read with a difficulty which greatly damps the pleasure of the reader: in England it cannot be read at
all without such a constant reference to a glossary 35
as nearly to destroy that pleasure. . . .

The power of genius is not less admirable in trac-
ing the manners than in painting the passions or in
drawing the scenery of nature.   That intuitive
glance with which a writer like Shakspere discerns 40
the characters of men, with which he catches the
many changing hues of life, forms a sort of problem
in the science of mind, of which it is easier to see
the truth than to assign the cause.   Though I am
very far from meaning to compare our rustic bard 45
to Shakspere, yet whoever will read his lighter and
more humorous poems, his *Dialogue of the Dogs,*
his *Dedication to G—— H——, Esq.,* his *Epistles
to a Young Friend,* and to *W. S——n,* will perceive
with what uncommon penetration and sagacity this 50
heaven-taught plowman, from his humble and unlettered station, has looked upon men and manners.

Dec. 9, 1786

JEAN ADAMS

THERE'S NAE LUCK ABOUT THE HOUSE

AND are ye sure the news is true,
    And are ye sure he's weel?
Is this a time to think of wark?
    Ye jauds, fling by your wheel.

Is this the time to think of wark, 5
    When Colin's at the door?
Gi'e me my cloak! I'll to the quay
    And see him come ashore.

For there's nae luck about the house,
    There's nae luck ava; 10
There's little pleasure in the house,
    When our gudeman's awa'.

Rise up and mak' a clean fireside;
    Put on the muckle pot;
Gi'e little Kate her cotton gown, 15
    And Jock his Sunday coat:
And mak' their shoon as black as slaes,
    Their hose as white as snaw;
It's a' to please my ain gudeman,
    For he's been long awa'. 20

There's twa fat hens upon the bauk,
    Been fed this month and mair;
Mak' haste and thraw their necks about,
    That Colin weel may fare;
And mak' the table neat and clean, 25
    Gar ilka thing look braw;
It's a' for love of my gudeman,
    For he's been long awa'.

O gi'e me down my bigonet,
    My bishop satin gown,
For I maun tell the bailie's wife 30
    That Colin's come to town.
My Sunday's shoon they maun gae on,
    My hose o' pearl blue;
'Tis a' to please my ain gudeman,
    For he's baith leal and true. 35

Sae true his words, sae smooth his speech,
　　His breath's like caller air!
His very foot has music in't,
　　As he comes up the stair.   40
And will I see his face again?
　　And will I hear him speak?
I'm downright dizzy with the thought,—
　　In troth, I'm like to greet.

The cauld blasts o' the winter wind,   45
　　That thrilled through my heart,
They're a' blawn by; I ha'e him safe,
　　Till death we'll never part:
But what puts parting in my head?
　　It may be far awa';   50
The present moment is our ain,
　　The neist we never saw.

Since Colin's weel, I'm weel content,
　　I ha'e nae more to crave;
Could I but live to mak' him blest,   55
　　I'm blest above the lave:
And will I see his face again?
　　And will I hear him speak?
I'm downright dizzy wi' the thought,—
　　In troth, I'm like to greet.   60

c.1771

LADY ANNE LINDSAY

AULD ROBIN GRAY

WHEN the sheep are in the fauld, and the kye at
　　hame,
And a' the warld to rest are gane,
The waes o' my heart fa' in showers frae my e'e,
While my gudeman lies sound by me.

Young Jamie lo'ed me weel, and sought me for his
     bride;   5
But saving a croun he had naething else beside;
To make the croun a pund, young Jamie gaid to sea;
And the croun and the pund were baith for me.

He hadna been awa' a week but only twa,
When my father brak his arm, and the cow was
     stown awa';   10
My mother she fell sick,—and my Jamie at the sea—
And auld Robin Gray came a-courtin' me.

My father couldna work, and my mother couldna
     spin;
I toiled day and night, but their bread I couldna win;
Auld Rob maintained them baith, and wi' tears in his
     e'e   15
Said, 'Jennie, for their sakes, O, marry me!'

My heart it said nay; I looked for Jamie back;
But the wind it blew high, and the ship it was a
     wrack;
His ship it was a wrack—Why didna Jamie dee?
Or why do I live to cry, Wae's me!   20

My father urged me sair: my mother didna speak;
But she looked in my face till my heart was like to
     break:
They gi'ed him my hand, though my heart was in the
     sea;
Sae auld Robin Gray he was gudeman to me.

I hadna been a wife a week but only four,   25
When mournfu' as I sat on the stane at the door,
I saw my Jamie's wraith,—for I couldna think it he,
Till he said, 'I'm come hame to marry thee.'

O sair, sair did we greet, and muckle did we say;
We took but ae kiss, and we tore ourselves away: 30
I wish that I were dead, but I'm no like to dee;
And why was I born to say, Wae's me!

I gang like a ghaist, and I carena to spin;
I daurna think on Jamie, for that wad be a sin;
But I'll do my best a gude wife aye to be,   35
For auld Robin Gray he is kind unto me.

1771

JAMES BEATTIE

FROM THE MINSTREL; OR, THE PROGRESS OF GENIUS

FRET not thyself, thou glittering child of pride,
That a poor villager inspires my strain;
With thee let pageantry and power abide:
The gentle Muses haunt the sylvan reign;
Where through wild groves at eve the lonely
    swain   5
Enraptured roams, to gaze on Nature's charms.
They hate the sensual, and scorn the vain,
The parasite their influence never warms,
Nor him whose sordid soul the love of gold alarms.

Though richest hues the peacock's plumes adorn,   10
Yet horror screams from his discordant throat.
Rise, sons of harmony, and hail the morn,
While warbling larks on russet pinions float;
Or seek at noon the woodland scene remote,
Where the gray linnets carol from the hill: 15
O let them ne'er, with artificial note,
To please a tyrant, strain the little bill,
But sing what Heaven inspires, and wander where
    they will!

And yet poor Edwin was no vulgar boy.
Deep thought oft seemed to fix his infant eye.   20
Dainties he heeded not, nor gaud, nor toy,
Save one short pipe of rudest minstrelsy;
Silent when glad; affectionate, though shy;
And now his look was most demurely sad;
And now he laughed aloud, yet none knew why.   25
The neighbors stared and sighed, yet blessed the
          lad;
Some deemed him wondrous wise, and some believed
          him mad.

.   .   .   .

In truth, he was a strange and wayward wight,
Fond of each gentle and each dreadful scene.
In darkness and in storm he found delight,   30
Nor less than when on ocean-wave serene
The southern sun diffused his dazzling sheen.
Even sad vicissitude amused his soul;
And if a sigh would sometimes intervene,
And down his cheek a tear of pity roll,   35
A sigh, a tear, so sweet, he wished not to control.

.   .   .   .

When the long-sounding curfew from afar
Loaded with loud lament the lonely gale,
Young Edwin, lighted by the evening star,
Lingering and listening, wandered down the vale.   40
There would he dream of graves, and corses pale,
And ghosts that to the charnel-dungeon throng,
And drag a length of clanking chain, and wail,
Till silenced by the owl's terrific song,
Or blast that shrieks by fits the shuddering isles
          along.   45

Or when the setting moon, in crimson dyed,
Hung o'er the dark and melancholy deep,
To haunted stream, remote from man, he hied,
Where fays of yore their revels wont to keep;
And there let fancy rove at large, till sleep   50
A vision brought to his entrancèd sight.
And first, a wildly murmuring wind 'gan creep
Shrill to his ringing ear; then tapers bright,
With instantaneous gleam, illumed the vault of night.

.   .   .   .

Nor was this ancient dame a foe to mirth.   55
Her ballad, jest, and riddle's quaint device
Oft cheered the shepherds round their social
    hearth;
Whom levity or spleen could ne'er entice
To purchase chat or laughter at the price
Of decency.   Nor let it faith exceed   60
That Nature forms a rustic taste so nice.
Ah! had they been of court or city breed,
Such delicacy were right marvellous indeed.

Oft when the winter storm had ceased to rave,
He roamed the snowy waste at even, to view   65
The cloud stupendous, from th' Atlantic wave
High-towering, sail along th' horizon blue;
Where, midst the changeful scenery, ever new,
Fancy a thousand wondrous forms descries,
More wildly great than ever pencil drew—   70
Rocks, torrents, gulfs, and shapes of giant size,
And glittering cliffs on cliffs, and fiery ramparts rise.

Thence musing onward to the sounding shore,
The lone enthusiast oft would take his way,
Listening, with pleasing dread, to the deep roar   75
Of the wide-weltering waves.   In black array

When sulphurous clouds rolled on th' autumnal
    day,
Even then he hastened from the haunts of man,
Along the trembling wilderness to stray,
What time the lightning's fierce career began,   80
And o'er heaven's rending arch the rattling thunder
    ran.

Responsive to the sprightly pipe when all
In sprightly dance the village youth were joined,
Edwin, of melody aye held in thrall,
From the rude gambol far remote reclined,   85
Soothed with the soft notes warbling in the wind.
Ah then all jollity seemed noise and folly
To the pure soul by fancy's fire refined!
Ah, what is mirth but turbulence unholy
When with the charm compared of heavenly melan-
    choly!   90

1771

ROBERT FERGUSON

FROM LEITH RACES

In JULY month, ae bonny morn,
    Whan Nature's rokelay green
Was spread o'er ilka rigg o' corn,
    To charm our roving een,
Glouring about I saw a quean,   5
    The fairest 'neath the lift;
Her een ware o' the siller sheen,
    Her skin like snawy drift,
        Sae white that day.

Quod she, "I ferly unco sair   10
    That ye sud musand gae,

Ye what hae sun o' Hallow-fair,
   Her winter's pranks and play,
Whan on Leith-Sands the racers rare,
   Wi' jocky louns, are met,   15
Their orrow pennies there to ware
   And drown themsel's in debt
      Fu' deep that day."

"And wha are ye, my winsome dear,
   That takes the gate sae early?   20
Whare do ye win, gin ane may spier,
   For I right meikle ferly
That sic braw buskit laughing lass
   Thir bonny blinks shou'd gi'e,
An' loup like Hebe o'er the grass,   25
   As wanton and as free,
      Frae dule this day."

"I dwall amang the caller springs
   That weet the Land o' Cakes,
And aften tune my canty strings   30
   At bridals and late-wakes.
They ca' me Mirth; I ne'er was kend
   To grumble or look sour,
But blyth wad be a lift to lend,
   Gif ye wad sey my pow'r   35
      An' pith this day."

"A bargain be 't; and, by my feggs,
   Gif ye will be my mate,
Wi' you I'll screw the cheery pegs—
   Ye shanna find me blate.
We'll reel and ramble thro' the sands,   40
   And jeer wi' all me meet;
Nor hip the daft and gleesome bands

That fill Edina's street
            Sae thrang this day."   45
                                    July 22, 1773

JOHN LANGHORNE

FROM THE COUNTRY JUSTICE

[GENERAL MOTIVES FOR LENITY]

BE THIS, ye rural Magistrates, your plan:
Firm be your justice, but be friends to man.
He whom the mighty master of this ball
We fondly deem, or farcically call,
To own the patriarch's truth however loth,   5
Holds but a mansion crushed before the moth.
Frail in his genius, in his heart, too, frail,
Born but to err, and erring to bewail;
Shalt thou his faults with eye severe explore,
And give to life one human weakness more?   10
Still mark if vice or nature prompts the deed;
Still mark the strong temptation and the need;
On pressing want, on famine's powerful call,
At least more lenient let thy justice fall.

[APOLOGY FOR VAGRANTS]

FOR him who, lost to every hope of life,
Has long with fortune held unequal strife,
Known to no human love, no human care,
The friendless, homeless object of despair;
For the poor vagrant, feel while he complains,   5
Nor from sad freedom send to sadder chains.
Alike, if folly or misfortune brought
Those last of woes his evil days have wrought;
Believe with social mercy and with me,

Folly's misfortune in the first degree.   10
   Perhaps on some inhospitable shore
The houseless wretch a widowed parent bore,
Who, then no more by golden prospects led,
Of the poor Indian begged a leafy bed;
Cold on Canadian hills, or Minden's plain,   15
Perhaps that parent mourned her soldier slain,
Bent o'er her babe, her eye dissolved in dew,
The big drops mingling with the milk he drew,
Gave the sad presage of his future years,
The child of misery, baptized in tears!   20

1774

THOMAS DAY

FROM THE DESOLATION OF AMERICA

I SEE, I see, swift bursting through the shade,
The cruel soldier, and the reeking blade.
And there the bloody cross of Britain waves,
Pointing to deeds of death an host of slaves.
To them unheard the wretched tell their pain,   5
And every human sorrow sues in vain:
Their hardened bosoms never knew to melt;
Each woe unpitied, and each pang unfelt.—
See! where they rush, and with a savage joy,
Unsheathe the sword, impatient to destroy.   10
Fierce as the tiger, bursting from the wood,
With famished jaws, insatiable of blood!
   Yet, yet a moment, the fell steel restrain;
Must Nature's sacred ties all plead in vain?
Ah! while your kindred blood remains unspilt,   15
And Heaven allows an awful pause from guilt,
Suspend the war, and recognize the bands,
Against whose lives you arm your impious hands!—
Not these, the boast of Gallia's proud domains,
Nor the scorched squadrons of Iberian plains;   20

Unhappy men! no foreign war you wage,
In your own blood you glut your frantic rage;
And while you follow where oppression leads,
At every step, a friend, or brother, bleeds.

.　　.　　.　　.　　.　　.　　.

Devoted realm! what now avails thy claim,　　25
To milder virtue, or sublimer flame?
Or what avails, unhappy land! to trace
The generous labors of thy patriot race?
Who, urged by fate, and fortitude their guide,
On the wild surge their desperate fortune tried;　　30
Undaunted every toil and danger bore,
And fixed their standards on a savage shore;
What time they fled, with an averted eye,
The baneful influence of their native sky,
Where slowly rising through the dusky air,　　35
The northern meteors shot their lurid glare.
In vain their country's genius sought to move,
With tender images of former love,
Sad rising to their view, in all her charms,
And weeping wooed them to her well-known arms.　　40
The favored clime, the soft domestic air,
And wealth and ease were all below their care,
Since there an hated tyrant met their eyes
And blasted every blessing of the skies.

.　　.　　.　　.　　.　　.　　.

And now, no more by nature's bounds confined　　45
He * spreads his dragon pinions to the wind.
The genius of the West beholds him near,
And freedom trembles at her last barrier.
In vain she deemed in this sequestered seat
To fix a refuge for her wandering feet;　　50

* The monster, tyranny.

To mark one altar sacred to her fame,
And save the ruins of the human name.

.   .   .   .   .   .

Lo! Britain bended to the servile yoke,
Her fire extinguished, and her spirit broke,
Beneath the pressure of [a tyrant's] sway,   55
Herself at once the spoiler and the prey,
Detest[s] the virtues she can boast no more
And envies every right to every shore!
At once to nature and to pity blind,
Wages abhorrèd war with humankind;   60
And wheresoe'er her ocean rolls his wave,
Provokes an enemy, or meets a slave.
   But free-born minds inspired with noble flame,
Attest their origin, and scorn the claim.
Beyond the sweets of pleasure and of rest,   65
The joys which captivate the vulgar breast;
Beyond the dearer ties of kindred blood;
Or brittle life's too transitory good;
The sacred charge of liberty they prize,
That last, and noblest, present of the skies.   70

.   .   .   .   .   .

Yet, gracious Heaven! though clouds may intervene,
And transitory horrors shade the scene;
Though for an instant virtue sink depressed,
While vice exulting rears her bloody crest;
Thy sacred truth shall still inspire my mind,   75
To cast the terrors of my fate behind!
Thy power which nature's utmost bound pervades,
Beams through the void, and cheers destruction's
            shades,
Can blast the laurel on the victor's head,
And smooth the good man's agonizing bed,   80

To songs of triumph change the captive's groans,
And hurl the powers of darkness from their thrones!

1777

THOMAS CHATTERTON

[SONGS FROM "ÆLLA, A TRAGYCAL EN-TERLUDE WROTENN BIE THOMAS ROWLEIE"]

[THE BODDYNGE FLOURETTES BLOSHES ATTE THE LYGHTE]

FYRSTE MYNSTRELLE

The boddynge flourettes bloshes atte the lyghte;
The mees be sprenged wyth the yellowe hue;
Ynn daiseyd mantels ys the mountayne dyghte;
The nesh yonge coweslepe blendethe wyth the
   dewe;
The trees enlefèd, yntoe Heavenne straughte,   5
Whenn gentle wyndes doe blowe to whestlyng dynne
   ys brought.

The evenynge commes, and brynges the dewe
   alonge;
The roddie welkynne sheeneth to the eyne;
Arounde the alestake Mynstrells synge the songe;
Yonge ivie rounde the doore poste do entwyne;   10
I laie mee onn the grasse; yette, to mie wylle,
Albeytte alle ys fayre, there lackethe somethynge
   stylle.

SECONDE MYNSTRELLE

So Adam thoughtenne, whann, ynn Paradyse,
All Heavenn and Erthe dyd hommage to hys
   mynde;

Ynn Womman alleyne mannès pleasaunce lyes;   15
As Instrumentes of joie were made the kynde.
Go, take a wyfe untoe thie armes, and see
Wynter and brownie hylles wyll have a charm for
      thee.

THYRDE MYNSTRELLE

Whanne Autumpne blake and sonne-brente doe
      appere,
With hys goulde honde guylteynge the falleynge
      lefe,   20
Bryngeynge oppe Wynterr to folfylle the yere,
Beerynge uponne hys backe the ripèd shefe;
Whan al the hyls wythe woddie sede ys whyte;
Whanne levynne-fyres and lemes do mete from far
      the syghte;

Whann the fayre apple, rudde as even skie,   25
Do bende the tree unto the fructyle grounde;
When joicie peres, and berries of blacke die,
Doe daunce yn ayre, and call the eyne arounde;
Thann, bee the even foule or even fayre,
Meethynckes mie hartys joie ys steyncèd wyth
      somme care.   30

SECONDE MYNSTRELLE

Angelles bee wrogte to bee of neidher kynde;
Angelles alleyne fromme chafe desyre bee free:
Dheere ys a somwhatte evere yn the mynde,
Yatte, wythout wommanne, cannot styllèd bee;
Ne seyncte yn celles, botte, havynge blodde and
      tere,   35
Do fynde the spryte to joie on syghte of womanne
      fayre;

Wommen bee made, notte for hemselves, botte
    manne,
Bone of hys bone, and chyld of hys desire;
Fromme an ynutyle membere fyrste beganne,
Ywroghte with moche of water, lyttele fyre;   40
Therefore theie seke the fyre of love, to hete
The milkyness of kynde, and make hemselfes com-
    plete.

Albeytte wythout wommen menne were pheeres
To salvage kynde, and wulde botte lyve to slea,
Botte wommenne efte the spryghte of peace so
    cheres,   45
Tochelod yn Angel joie heie Angeles bee:
Go, take thee swythyn to thie bedde a wyfe;
Bee bante or blessed hie yn proovynge marryage lyfe.
                     1777

AN EXCELENTE BALADE OF CHARITIE

As Wroten Bie the Gode Prieste Thomas Rowley, 1464

In Virgynè the sweltrie sun gan sheene,
    And hotte upon the mees did caste his raie;
    The apple rodded from its palie greene,
    And the mole peare did bende the leafy spraie;
    The peede chelandri sunge the livelong daie;   5
'Twas nowe the pride, the manhode, of the yeare,
And eke the grounde was dighte in its most defte
    aumere.

The sun was glemeing in the midde of daie,
    Deadde still the aire, and eke the welken blue;
    When from the sea arist in drear arraie   10
    A hepe of cloudes of sable sullen hue,

The which full fast unto the woodlande drewe,
Hiltring attenes the sunnis fetive face,
And the blacke tempeste swolne and gathered up
    apace.

Beneathe an holme, faste by a pathwaie side   15
Which dide unto Seyncte Godwine's covent lede,
A hapless pilgrim moneynge dyd abide,
Pore in his viewe, ungentle in his weede,
Longe bretful of the miseries of neede;
Where from the hailstone coulde the almer flie?   20
He had no housen theere, ne anie covent nie.

Look in his glommèd face, his spright there
    scanne:
Howe woe-be-gone, how withered, forwynd,
    deade!
Haste to thie church-glebe-house, ashrewed
    manne;
Haste to thie kiste, thie onlie dorture bedde: 25
Cale as the claie whiche will gre on thie hedde
Is Charitie and Love aminge highe elves;
Knightis and Barons live for pleasure and them-
    selves.

The gathered storme is rype; the bigge drops
    falle;
The forswat meadowes smethe, and drenche the
    raine;   30
The comyng ghastness do the cattle pall,
And the full flockes are drivynge ore the plaine;
Dashde from the cloudes, the waters flott againe;
The welkin opes, the yellow levynne flies,
And the hot fierie smothe in the wide lowings dies.   35

Liste! now the thunder's rattling clymmynge
    sound

Cheves slowie on, and then embollen clangs,
Shakes the hie spyre, and, losst, dispended,
    drowned,
Still on the gallard eare of terroure hanges;
The windes are up, the lofty elmen swanges;   40
Again the levynne and the thunder poures,
And the full cloudes are braste attenes in stonen
    showers.

Spurreynge his palfrie oere the watrie plaine,
The Abbote of Seyncte Godwyne's convente
    came:
His chapournette was drented with the reine,   45
And his pencte gyrdle met with mickle shame;
He aynewards tolde his bederoll at the same.
The storme encreasen, and he drew aside
With the mist almes-craver neere to the holme to
    bide.

His cope was all of Lyncolne clothe so fyne,   50
With a gold button fastened neere his chynne;
His autremete was edged with golden twynne,
And his shoone pyke a loverds mighte have
    binne—
Full well it shewn he thoughten coste no sinne;
The trammels of the palfrye pleasde his sighte,   55
For the horse-millanare his head with roses dighte.

'An almes, sir prieste!' the droppynge pilgrim
    saide;
'O let me waite within your covente dore,
Till the sunne sheneth hie above our heade,
And the loude tempeste of the aire is oer.   60
Helpless and ould am I, alas! and poor;
No house, ne friend, ne moneie in my pouche;
All yatte I calle my owne is this my silver crouche.'

'Varlet,' replyd the Abbatte, 'cease your dinne!
This is no season almes and prayers to give.   65
Mie porter never lets a faitour in;
None touch mie rynge who not in honor live.'
And now the sonne with the blacke cloudes did
    stryve,
And shettynge on the ground his glairie raie:
The Abbatte spurrde his steede, and eftsoones roadde
    awaie.   70

Once moe the skie was blacke, the thounder rolde:
Faste reyneynge oer the plaine a prieste was seen,
Ne dighte full proude, ne buttoned up in golde;
His cope and jape were graie, and eke were clene;
A Limitoure he was of order seene.   75
And from the pathwaie side then turnèd hee,
Where the pore almer laie binethe the holmen tree.

'An almes, sir priest!' the droppynge pilgrim
    sayde,
'For sweete Seyncte Marie and your order sake!'
The Limitoure then loosened his pouche threade,   80
And did thereoute a groate of silver take:
The mister pilgrim dyd for halline shake.
'Here, take this silver; it maie eathe thie care:
We are Goddes stewards all, nete of our owne we
    bare.

'But ah, unhailie pilgrim, lerne of me   85
Scathe anie give a rentrolle to their Lorde.
Here, take my semecope—thou arte bare, I see;
'Tis thyne; the Seynctes will give me mie re-
    warde.'
He left the pilgrim, and his waie aborde.
Virgynne and hallie Seyncte, who sitte yn gloure,   90
Or give the mittee will, or give the gode man power!
    1777

MAURICE MORGANN

[ON SHAKSPERE]

I DISTINGUISH between *mental Impressions,* and
the *Understanding.* I wish to avoid everything that
looks like subtlety and refinement; but this is a distinction, which we all comprehend. There are none
of us unconscious of certain feelings or sensations   5
of mind, which do not seem to have passed through
the Understanding; the effects, I suppose, of some
secret influences from without, acting upon a certain mental sense, and producing feelings and passions in just correspondence to the force and variety   10
of those influences on the one hand, and to the
quickness of our sensibility on the other. Be the
cause, however, what it may, the fact is undoubtedly
so; which is all I am concerned in. And it is equally
a fact, which every man's experience may avouch,   15
that the Understanding and those feelings are frequently at variance. The latter often arise from the
most minute circumstances, and frequently from
such as the Understanding cannot estimate, or even
recognize; whereas the Understanding delights in ab-   20
straction, and in general propositions; which, however true considered as such, are very seldom, I
had like to have said *never,* perfectly applicable to
any particular case. And hence, among other causes,
it is, that we often condemn or applaud characters   25
and actions on the credit of some logical process,
while our hearts revolt, and would fain lead us to a
very different conclusion.

The Understanding seems for the most part to
take cognizance of *actions* only, and from these to   30
infer *motives* and *character;* but the sense we have

been speaking of proceeds in a contrary course; and determines of *actions* from certain *first principles of character,* which seem wholly out of the reach of the Understanding. We cannot, indeed, do otherwise 35 than admit that there must be distinct principles of character in every distinct individual: the manifest variety even in the minds of infants will oblige us to this. But what *are* these first principles of character? Not the objects, I am persuaded, of the Un- 40 derstanding; and yet we take as strong Impressions of them as if we could compare and assort them in a syllogism. We often love or hate at first sight; and indeed, in general, dislike or approve by some secret reference to these *principles;* and we judge even of 45 conduct, not from any idea of abstract good or evil in the nature of actions, but by referring those actions to a supposed original character in the man himself. I do not mean that we *talk* thus; we could not indeed, if we would explain ourselves in detail 50 on this head; we can neither account for Impressions and passions, nor communicate them to others by *words.* Tones and looks will sometimes convey the *passion* strangely, but the *Impression* is incommunicable. . . . 55

But if there was *one man* in the world, who could make a more perfect draught of real nature, and steal such Impressions on his audience, without their special notice, as should keep their hold in spite of any error of their Understanding, and should there- 60 upon venture to introduce an apparent incongruity of character and action, for ends which I shall presently endeavor to explain; such an imitation would be worth our nicest curiosity and attention.

. . . .

Whatever may be the neglect of some, or the cen- 65 sure of others, there are those who firmly believe

that this wild, this uncultivated Barbarian, has not
yet obtained one-half of his fame; and who trust
that some new Stagyrite will arise, who instead of
pecking at the surface of things will enter into the 70
inward soul of his compositions, and expel by the
force of congenial feelings, those foreign impurities
which have stained and disgraced his page. And as
to those *spots* which will still remain, they may perhaps become invisible to those who shall seek them 75
through the medium of his beauties, instead of looking for those beauties, as is too frequently done,
through the smoke of some real or imputed obscurity.
When the hand of time shall have brushed off his
present Editors and Commentators, and when the 80
very name of *Voltaire,* and even the memory of the
language in which he has written, shall be no more,
the *Apalachian* mountains, the banks of the *Ohio,*
and the plains of *Sciota* shall resound with the accents of this barbarian. In his native tongue he shall 85
roll the genuine passions of nature; nor shall the
griefs of *Lear* be alleviated, or the charms and wit
of *Rosalind* be abated by time. There is indeed nothing perishable about him, except that very learning
which he is said so much to want. He had not, it 90
is true, enough for the demands of the age in which
he lived, but he had perhaps too much for the reach
of his genius and the interest of his fame. *Milton*
and he will carry the decayed remnants and fripperies
of ancient mythology into more distant ages than 95
they are by their own force entitled to extend; and
the *Metamorphoses* of *Ovid,* upheld by them, lay in a
new claim to unmerited immortality.

Shakspere is a name so interesting, that it is ex-
cusable to stop a moment, nay it would be indecent 100
to pass him without the tribute of some admiration.
He differs essentially from all other writers. Him
we may profess rather to feel than to understand;

and it is safer to say, on many occasions, that we are possessed by him, than that we possess him. And no wonder.—He scatters the seeds of things, the principles of character and action, with so cunning a hand yet with so careless an air, and master of our feelings, submits himself so little to our judgment, that everything seems superior. We discern not his course, we see no connection of cause and effect, we are rapt in ignorant admiration, and claim no kindred with his abilities. All the incidents, all the parts, look like chance, whilst we feel and are sensible that the whole is design. His Characters not only act and speak in strict conformity to nature, but in strict relation to us; just so much is shown as is requisite, just so much is impressed; he commands every passage to our heads and to our hearts, and molds us as he pleases, and that with so much ease, that he never betrays his own exertions. We see these Characters act from the mingled motives of passion, reason, interest, habit, and complexion, in all their proportions, when they are supposed to know it not themselves; and we are made to acknowledge that their actions and sentiments are, from those motives, the necessary result. He at once blends and distinguishes everything;—everything is complicated, everything is plain. I restrain the further expressions of my admiration lest they should not seem applicable to man; but it is really astonishing that a mere human being, a part of humanity only, should so perfectly comprehend the whole; and that he should possess such exquisite art, that whilst every woman and every child shall feel the whole effect, his learned Editors and Commentators should yet so very frequently mistake or seem ignorant of the cause. A sceptre or a straw are in his hands of equal efficacy; he needs no selection; he converts everything into excellence; nothing is too great,

nothing is too base. Is a character efficient like
Richard, it is everything we can wish. Is it otherwise, like *Hamlet,* it is productive of equal admiration. Action produces one mode of excellence and
inaction another. The Chronicle, the Novel, or the 145
Ballad; the king, or the beggar, the hero, the madman, the sot or the fool; it is all one;—nothing is
worse, nothing is better. The same genius pervades
and is equally admirable in all. Or, is a character to
be shown in progressive change, and the events of 150
years comprised within the hour;—with what a
Magic hand does he prepare and scatter his spells!
The Understanding must, in the first place, be subdued; and lo! how the rooted prejudices of the child
spring up to confound the man! The Weird Sisters 155
rise, and order is extinguished. The laws of nature
give way, and leave nothing in our minds but wildness and horror. No pause is allowed us for reflection. Horrid sentiment, furious guilt and com-
punction, air-drawn daggers, murders, ghosts, and 160
enchantment, shake and *possess us wholly.* In the
meantime the *process* is completed. *Macbeth* changes
under our eye, *the milk of human kindness is con-
verted to gall; he has supped full of horrors,* and his
May of life is fallen into the sear, the *yellow leaf;* 165
whilst we the fools of amazement, are insensible to
the shifting of place and the lapse of time, and till
the curtain drops, never once wake to the truth of
things, or recognize the laws of existence.—On such
an occasion, a fellow like *Rymer,* waking from his 170
trance, shall lift up his Constable's staff and charge
this great Magician, this daring *practicer of arts in-
hibited,* in the name of *Aristotle,* to surrender; whilst
Aristotle himself, disowning his wretched Officer,
would fall prostrate at his feet and acknowledge his 175
supremacy.—O supreme of Dramatic excellence!
(*might he say*) not to me be imputed the insolence

of fools. The bards of *Greece* were confined within
the narrow circle of the Chorus, and hence they
found themselves constrained to practise, for the 180
most part, the precision, and copy the details of nature. I followed them, and knew not that a larger
circle might be drawn, and the Drama extended to
the whole reach of human genius. Convinced, I
see that a more compendius *nature* may be obtained; 185
a nature of *effects* only, to which neither the relations of place, or continuity of time are always essential. Nature condescending to the faculties and
apprehensions of man, has drawn through human
life a regular chain of visible causes and effects. 190
But Poetry delights in surprise, conceals her steps,
seizes at once upon the heart, and obtains the Sublime of things without betraying the rounds of her
ascent. True Poesy is *magic,* not *nature;* an effect
from causes hidden or unknown. To the Magician 195
I prescribed no laws; his law and his power are
one; his power is his law. Him, who neither imi-
tates, nor is within the reach of imitation, no prece-
dent can or ought to bind, no limits to contain. If
his end is obtained, who shall question his course? 200
Means, whether apparent or hidden, are justified in
poesy by success; but then most perfect and most
admirable when most concealed.

1774   1777

JOHN MAYNE

LOGAN BRAES

By Logan's streams that rin sae deep,
Fu' aft wi' glee I've herded sheep,
Herded sheep and gathered slaes,
Wi' my dear lad on Logan braes.

But wae's my heart, thae days are gane,   5
And I wi' grief may herd alane,
While my dear lad maun face his faes,
Far, far frae me and Logan braes.

Nae mair at Logan kirk will he
Atween the preachings meet wi' me: 10
Meet wi' me, or when it's mirk,
Convoy me hame frae Logan kirk.
I weel may sing thae days are gane:
Frae kirk and fair I come alane,
While my dear lad maun face his faes,   15
Far, far frae me and Logan braes.

At e'en, when hope amaist is gane,
I dauner out and sit alane;
Sit alane beneath the tree
Where aft he kept his tryst wi' me.   20
Oh! could I see thae days again,
My lover skaithless, and my ain!
Beloved by friends, revered by faes,
We'd live in bliss on Logan braes!

1781

THOMAS JAMES MATHIAS

from DIALOGUE AT THE TOMB OF ARGANTYR

Hervor

THY daughter calls; Argantyr, break
The bonds of death; she calls, awake.
Reach me forth the tempered blade,
Beneath thy dusty pillow laid,
Which once a sceptered warrior bore,   5
Forged by dwarfs in years of yore.

Where are the sons of Angrim fled?
Mingled with the valiant dead.
From under twisted roots of oak
Blasted by the thunder's stroke,   10
Arise, arise, ye men of blood,
Ye who prepared the vulture's food;
Give me the sword and studded belt;
Armies whole their force have felt:
Or grant my prayer or moldering rot,   15
Your name, your deeds alike forgot.
Argantyr, rouse thee from thy rest;
'Tis an only child's request.

                                        1781

FROM THE TWILIGHT OF THE GODS

FROM the chambers of the east
In robes of terror grimly dressed,
Ymir hath his course begun,
Rival of the unwearied sun.
Now in many a glistering wreath,   5
Above, around, and underneath,
The serpent dread, of dateless birth,
Girds the devoted globe of earth;
And, as charmed by powerful spell,
Ocean heaves with furious swell.   10

                                        1781

FROM AN INCANTATION, FOUNDED ON THE NORTHERN MYTHOLOGY

HEAR, ye rulers of the north,
Spirits of exalted worth;
By the silence of the night,
By subtle magic's secret rite;
By Peolphan, mirky king,   5
Master of the enchanted ring;

By all and each of hell's grim host,
Howling demon, tortured ghost;
By each spell and potent word,
Burst from lips of Glauron's lord;   10
By Coronzon's awful power;
By the dread and solemn hour
When Gual fierce and Damael strong
Stride the blast that roars along;
Or in fell descending swoop,   15
Bid the furious spirit stoop
O'er desolation's gloomy plain,
Haunt of warriors battle-slain,
Now the world in sleep is laid,
Thorbiorga calls your aid.   20

1781

FROM THE RENOVATION OF THE WORLD, AND FUTURE RETRIBUTION

Now the spirit's plastic might,
Brooding o'er the formless deep,
O'er the dusk abysm of night,
Bids creation cease to sleep!

Instant from the river main   5
Starts the renovated earth;
Pine-clad mountain, shaded plain,
See, 'tis Nature's second birth.

.   .   .   .

Gods on Inda spread the board;
Such was the supreme decree: 10
Swell the strains in full accord,
Strains of holiest harmony!

"Pour the sparkling beverage high;
Be the song with horror fraught;

Laboring earth and ruined sky,   15
Fill the soul and fix the thought.

"Odin next inspire the verse,
Gored by the relentless fang;
Ether felt the conflict fierce,
Dying groan and parting pang.   20

"Where is now his vaunted might?
Where the terror of his eye?
Fled from aye from scenes of light:
Pour the sparkling beverage high."
                                          1781

TUDOR

FILL the horn of glossy blue,
Ocean's bright cerulean hue;
Briskly quaff the flavorous mead,
'Tis a day to joy decreed.
Strike the harp's symphonic string,   5
Tudor none refuse to sing;
Ne'er shall he belie his birth,
Valor his, and conscious worth.

Have you seen the virgin snow
That tops old Aran's peering brow,   10
Or lucid web by insect spun,
Purpureal gleam in summer sun?
With such, yet far diviner light,
Malvina hits the dazzled sight:
The guerdon such, can Tudor's breast   15
Dare to court ignoble rest?

From the cliff sublime and hoary
See descending martial glory;
Armèd bands aloft uprear

Crimson banner, crimson spear; 20
Venodotia's ancient boast
Meets the pride of London's host;
On they move with step serene,
And form a dreadly pleasing scene.

Heard you that terrific clang? 25
Through the pathless void it rang:
The expecting raven screams afar,
And snuffs the reeking spoils of war.
Have you e'er on barren strand
Ta'en your solitary stand, 30
And seen the whirlwind's spirit sped
O'er the dark green billowy bed?
Glowing in the thickest fight,
Such resistless Tudor's might.

1781

HUGH DOWNMAN

FROM DEATH SONG OF RAGNAR LODBRACH

WITH our sword's resistless might
We have thinned the ranks of fight.
In early life, his volumed train
The crested serpent rolled in vain.
Thora's charms, the matchless prize; 5
Gothland saw my fame arise.
Thronging crowds the monster scan,
Shouts applausive hail me Man.
All his fierceness prompt to try,
The shaggy vestment clothed my thigh; 10
Soon transpierced, in death he lay,
My falchion smote for splendid pay.

Still a youth, we steer our course,
Toward the morning's distant source;
Through the vast Oreonic flood   15
Torrents run of crimson blood.
The yellow-footed bird we feast,
Plenty fills the ravenous beast.
Our steel-struck helms sublime resound,
The sea is all one bleeding wound.   20
Our foes lie weltering on the shore,
Deep the raven wades in gore.

                                        1781

JAMES JOHNSTONE

FROM LODBROKAR-QUITHA

Chorus

We hewed with our swords!

Lodbroc

1. When first we landed on the Gothic shore, vengeance soon o'ertook the wily dragon miner of the
ground—'twas then I won my Thora. Men called
me Lod-broc from what time I slew the snaky   5
dweller of the heath. At that assault my point, in-
laid with burnished gold, transfixed the circling
monster of the earth.

We hewed with our swords!

2. Blooming was my youth when east at Eyra's   10
straits opposing bands we gashed for the insulting
wolves and golden-footed king of birds—there, while
our tempered steel sung on the high-seamed helm,

they found a rich repast. Gore distained the deep.
The raven waded through the blood of the slain.   15

1782

WILLIAM COWPER

TO A YOUNG LADY

SWEET stream, that winds through yonder glade,
Apt emblem of a virtuous maid—
Silent and chaste she steals along,
Far from the world's gay busy throng:
With gentle yet prevailing force,   5
Intent upon her destined course;
Graceful and useful all she does.
Blessing and blest where'er she goes;
Pure-bosomed as that watery glass
And Heaven reflected in her face.   10

1782

FROM THE TASK

THE INHUMANITY OF MAN

OH FOR a lodge in some vast wilderness,
Some boundless contiguity of shade,
Where rumor of oppression and deceit,
Of unsuccessful or successful war,
Might never reach me more! My ear is pained,   5
My soul is sick, with every day's report
Of wrong and outrage with which earth is filled.
There is no flesh in man's obdurate heart,
It does not feel for man; the natural bond
Of brotherhood is severed as the flax   10
That falls asunder at the touch of fire.

He finds his fellow guilty of a skin
Not colored like his own, and, having power
T' enforce the wrong, for such a worthy cause
Dooms and devotes him as his lawful prey.   15
Lands intersected by a narrow frith
Abhor each other. Mountains interposed
Make enemies of nations who had else
Like kindred drops been mingled into one.
Thus man devotes his brother, and destroys;   20
And worse than all, and most to be deplored,
As human nature's broadest, foulest blot,
Chains him, and tasks him, and exacts his sweat
With stripes that Mercy, with a bleeding heart,
Weeps when she sees inflicted on a beast.   25
Then what is man? And what man seeing this,
And having human feelings, does not blush
And hang his head, to think himself a man?
I would not have a slave to till my ground,
To carry me, to fan me while I sleep,   30
And tremble when I wake, for all the wealth
That sinews bought and sold have ever earned.
No: dear as freedom is, and in my heart's
Just estimation prized above all price,
I had much rather be myself the slave   35
And wear the bonds than fasten them on him.
We have no slaves at home: then why abroad?
And they themselves, once ferried o'er the wave
That parts us, are emancipate and loosed.
Slaves cannot breathe in England; if their lungs   40
Receive our air, that moment they are free;
They touch our country, and their shackles fall.
That's noble, and bespeaks a nation proud
And jealous of the blessing. Spread it, then,
And let it circulate through every vein   45
Of all your empire; that where Britain's power
Is felt, mankind may feel her mercy, too.

[LOVE OF ENGLAND]

ENGLAND, with all thy faults, I love thee still,
My country! and, while yet a nook is left
Where English minds and manners may be found,
Shall be constrained to love thee. Though thy clime
Be fickle, and thy year, most part, deformed   5
With dripping rains, or withered by a frost,
I would not yet exchange thy sullen skies
And fields without a flower, for warmer France
With all her vines; nor for Ausonia's groves
Of golden fruitage, and her myrtle bowers.   10
To shake thy senate, and from heights sublime
Of patriot eloquence to flash down fire
Upon thy foes, was never meant my task;
But I can feel thy fortunes, and partake
Thy joys and sorrows with as true a heart   15
As any thunderer there. And I can feel
Thy follies too, and with a just disdain
Frown at effeminates, whose very looks
Reflect dishonor on the land I love.
How, in the name of soldiership and sense,   20
Should England prosper, when such things, as smooth
And tender as a girl, all-essenced o'er
With odors, and as profligate as sweet,
Who sell their laurel for a myrtle wreath,
And love when they should fight,—when such as these   25
Presume to lay their hand upon the ark
Of her magnificent and awful cause?
Time was when it was praise and boast enough
In every clime, and travel where we might,
That we were born her children; praise enough   30
To fill the ambition of a private man,
That Chatham's language was his mother tongue,

And Wolfe's great name compatriot with his own.
Farewell those honors, and farewell with them
The hope of such hereafter! They have fallen 35
Each in his field of glory: one in arms,
And one in council—Wolfe upon the lap
Of smiling Victory that moment won,
And Chatham, heart-sick of his country's shame!
They made us many soldiers. Chatham still 40
Consulting England's happiness at home,
Secured it by an unforgiving frown
If any wronged her. Wolfe, where'er he fought,
Put so much of his heart into his act,
That his example had a magnet's force, 45
And all were swift to follow whom all loved.
Those suns are set. Oh, rise some other such!
Or all that we have left is empty talk
Of old achievements, and despair of new.

[COWPER, THE RELIGIOUS RECLUSE]

I WAS a stricken deer that left the herd
Long since; with many an arrow deep infixed
My panting side was charged, when I withdrew
To seek a tranquil death in distant shades.
There was I found by One who had Himself 5
Been hurt by th' archers. In His side He bore,
And in His hands and feet, the cruel scars.
With gentle force soliciting the darts,
He drew them forth, and healed, and bade me live.
Since then, with few associates, in remote 10
And silent woods I wander, far from those
My former partners of the peopled scene,
With few associates, and not wishing more.
Here much I ruminate, as much I may,
With other views of men and manners now 15
Than once, and others of a life to come.

I see that all are wanderers, gone astray
Each in his own delusions; they are lost
In chase of fancied happiness, still wooed
And never won; dream after dream ensues,   20
And still they dream that they shall still succeed,
And still are disappointed: rings the world
With the vain stir. I sum up half mankind,
And add two-thirds of the remaining half,
And find the total of their hopes and fears   25
Dreams, empty dreams.

[THE BASTILLE]

THEN shame to manhood, and opprobrious more
To France than all her losses and defeats
Old or of later date, by sea or land,
Her house of bondage worse than that of old
Which God avenged on Pharaoh—the Bastille!   5
Ye horrid towers, th' abode of broken hearts,
Ye dungeons and ye cages of despair,
That monarchs have supplied from age to age
With music such as suits their sovereign ears—
The sighs and groans of miserable men,   10
There's not an English heart that would not leap
To hear that ye were fallen at last, to know
That even our enemies, so oft employed
In forging chains for us, themselves were free:
For he that values liberty, confines   15
His zeal for her predominance within
No narrow bounds; her cause engages him
Wherever pleaded; 'tis the cause of man.
There dwell the most forlorn of human kind,
Immured though unaccused, condemned untried,   20
Cruelly spared, and hopeless of escape.
There, like the visionary emblem seen
By him of Babylon, life stands a stump,

And filleted about with hoops of brass,
Still lives, though all its pleasant boughs are gone. 25
To count the hour-bell and expect no change;
And ever as the sullen sound is heard,
Still to reflect that though a joyless note
To him whose moments all have one dull pace,
Ten thousand rovers in the world at large   30
Account it music—that it summons some
To theatre, or jocund feast, or ball;
The wearied hireling finds it a release
From labor; and the lover, who has chid
Its long delay, feels every welcome stroke   35
Upon his heart-strings trembling with delight:
To fly for refuge from distracting thought
To such amusements as ingenious woe
Contrives, hard-shifting and without her tools—
To read engraven on the muddy walls,   40
In staggering types, his predecessor's tale,
A sad memorial, and subjoin his own;
To turn purveyor to an overgorged
And bloated spider, till the pampered pest
Is made familiar, watches his approach,   45
Comes at his call, and serves him for a friend;
To wear out time in numbering to and fro
The studs that thick emboss his iron door,
Then downward and then upward, then aslant
And then alternate, with a sickly hope   50
By dint of change to give his tasteless task
Some relish, till, the sum exactly found
In all directions, he begins again:—
Oh comfortless existence! hemmed around
With woes, which who that suffers would not kneel 55
And beg for exile or the pangs of death?
That man should thus encroach on fellow-man,
Abridge him of his just and native rights,
Eradicate him, tear him from his hold

Upon th' endearments of domestic life   60
And social, nip his fruitfulness and use,
And doom him for perhaps an heedless word
To barrenness and solitude and tears,
Moves indignation; makes the name of king
(Of king whom such prerogative can please)   65
As dreadful as the Manichean god,
Adored through fear, strong only to destroy.

[MEDITATION IN WINTER]

THE night was winter in his roughest mood,
The morning sharp and clear. But now at noon,
Upon the southern side of the slant hills,
And where the woods fence off the northern blast,
The season smiles, resigning all its rage,   5
And has the warmth of May. The vault is blue
Without a cloud, and white without a speck
The dazzling splendor of the scene below.
Again the harmony comes o'er the vale,
And through the trees I view the embattled tower   10
Whence all the music. I again perceive
The soothing influence of the wafted strains,
And settle in soft musings as I tread
The walk, still verdant, under oaks and elms,
Whose outspread branches overarch the glade.   15
The roof, though moveable through all its length
As the wind sways it, has yet well sufficed,
And intercepting in their silent fall
The frequent flakes, has kept a path for me.
No noise is here, or none that hinders thought.   20
The redbreast warbles still, but is content
With slender notes, and more than half suppressed:
Pleased with his solitude, and flitting light
From spray to spray, where'er he rests he shakes
From many a twig the pendent drops of ice,   25

That tinkle in the withered leaves below.
Stillness, accompanied with sounds so soft,
Charms more than silence. Meditation here
May think down hours to moments. Here the heart
May give a useful lesson to the head,   30
And learning wiser grow without his books.
Knowledge and wisdom, far from being one,
Have ofttimes no connection. Knowledge dwells
In heads replete with thoughts of other men,
Wisdom in minds attentive to their own.   35
Knowledge, a rude unprofitable mass,
The mere materials with which wisdom builds,
Till smoothed and squared and fitted to its place,
Does but encumber whom it seems to enrich.
Knowledge is proud that he has learned so much;   40
Wisdom is humble that he knows no more.
Books are not seldom talismans and spells,
By which the magic art of shrewder wits
Holds an unthinking multitude enthralled.
Some to the fascination of a name   45
Surrender judgment hoodwinked. Some the style
Infatuates, and through labyrinths and wilds
Of error leads them, by a tune entranced.
While sloth seduces more, too weak to bear
The insupportable fatigue of thought,   50
And swallowing therefore, without pause or choice,
The total grist unsifted, husks and all.
But trees, and rivulets whose rapid course
Defies the check of winter, haunts of deer,
And sheepwalks populous with bleating lambs,   55
And lanes in which the primrose ere her time
Peeps through the moss that clothes the hawthorn
          root,
Deceive no student. Wisdom there, and Truth,
Not shy as in the world, and to be won
By slow solicitation, seize at once   60
The roving thought, and fix it on themselves.

[KINDNESS TO ANIMALS]

I WOULD not enter on my list of friends,
Though graced with polished manners and fine sense,
Yet wanting sensibility, the man
Who needlessly sets foot upon a worm.
An inadvertent step may crush the snail   5
That crawls at evening in the public path;
But he that has humanity, forewarned,
Will tread aside and let the reptile live.
The creeping vermin, loathsome to the sight,
And charged perhaps with venom, that intrudes,   10
A visitor unwelcome, into scenes
Sacred to neatness and repose—th' alcove,
The chamber, or refectory,—may die:
A necessary act incurs no blame.
Not so when, held within their proper bounds   15
And guiltless of offence, they range the air,
Or take their pastime in the spacious field:
There they are privileged; and he that hunts
Or harms them there is guilty of a wrong,
Disturbs th' economy of Nature's realm,   20
Who, when she formed, designed them an abode.

                                                   1785

ON THE RECEIPT OF MY MOTHER'S
PICTURE

O THAT those lips had language! Life has passed
With me but roughly since I heard thee last.
Those lips are thine—thy own sweet smile I see,
The same that oft in childhood solaced me;
Voice only fails, else how distinct they say,   5
'Grieve not, my child, chase all thy fears away!'
The meek intelligence of those dear eyes
(Blest be the art that can immortalize,

The art that baffles Time's tyrannic claim
To quench it) here shines on me still the same.   10
  Faithful remembrancer of one so dear,
O welcome guest, though unexpected here!
Who bidd'st me honor with an artless song,
Affectionate, a mother lost so long,
I will obey, not willingly alone,   15
But gladly, as the precept were her own:
And, while that face renews my filial grief,
Fancy shall weave a charm for my relief,
Shall steep me in Elysian revery,
A momentary dream that thou art she.   20
  My mother! when I learned that thou wast dead,
Say, wast thou conscious of the tears I shed?
Hovered thy spirit o'er thy sorrowing son,
Wretch even then, life's journey just begun?
Perhaps thou gav'st me, though unfelt, a kiss;   25
Perhaps a tear, if souls can weep in bliss—
Ah, that maternal smile! it answers 'Yes.'
I heard the bell tolled on thy burial day,
I saw the hearse that bore thee slow away,
And, turning from my nursery window, drew   30
A long, long sigh, and wept a last adieu!
But was it such? It was: where thou art gone
Adieus and farewells are a sound unknown.
May I but meet thee on that peaceful shore,
The parting word shall pass my lips no more!   35
Thy maidens, grieved themselves at my concern,
Oft gave me promise of thy quick return.
What ardently I wished I long believed,
And, disappointed still, was still deceived,
By expectation every day beguiled,   40
Dupe of to-morrow even from a child.
Thus many a sad to-morrow came and went,
Till, all my stock of infant sorrow spent,
I learnt at last submission to my lot,
But, though I less deplored thee, ne'er forgot.   45

Where once we dwelt our name is heard no more:
Children not thine have trod my nursery floor;
And where the gardener Robin, day by day,
Drew me to school along the public way,
Delighted with my bauble coach, and wrapped   50
In scarlet mantle warm, and velvet-capped,
'Tis now become a history little known
That once we called the pastoral house our own.
Short-lived possession! But the record fair
That memory keeps, of all thy kindness there,   55
Still outlives many a storm that has effaced
A thousand other themes less deeply traced.
Thy nightly visits to my chamber made,
That thou mightst know me safe and warmly laid;
Thy morning bounties ere I left my home,   60
The biscuit or confectionary plum;
The fragrant waters on my cheeks bestowed
By thy own hand, till fresh they shone and glowed;
All this, and, more endearing still than all,
Thy constant flow of love, that knew no fall,   65
Ne'er roughened by those cataracts and breaks
That humor interposed too often makes;
All this, still legible on memory's page,
And still to be so to my latest age,
Adds joy to duty, makes me glad to pay   70
Such honors to thee as my numbers may,
Perhaps a frail memorial, but sincere,
Not scorned in heaven though little noticed here.
Could Time, his flight reversed, restore the hours
When, playing with thy vesture's tissued flowers,   75
The violet, the pink, the jessamine,
I pricked them into paper with a pin
(And thou wast happier than myself the while,
Wouldst softly speak, and stroke my head and
          smile),
Could those few pleasant days again appear,   80
Might one wish bring them, would I wish them here?

I would not trust my heart—the dear delight
Seems so to be desired, perhaps I might.
But no—what here we call our life is such,
So little to be loved, and thou so much, 85
That I should ill requite thee to constrain
Thy unbound spirit into bonds again.

Thou, as a gallant bark from Albion's coast,
The storms all weathered and the ocean crossed,
Shoots into port at some well-havened isle, 90
Where spices breathe and brighter seasons smile,
There sits quiescent on the floods, that show
Her beauteous form reflected clear below,
While airs impregnated with incense play
Around her, fanning light her streamers gay, 95
So thou, with sails how swift, hast reached the shore
'Where tempests never beat nor billows roar,'
And thy loved consort on the dangerous tide
Of life long since has anchored by thy side.
But me, scarce hoping to attain that rest, 100
Always from port withheld, always distressed,
Me howling blasts drive devious, tempest-tossed,
Sails ripped, seams opening wide, and compass lost,
And day by day some current's thwarting force
Sets me more distant from a prosperous course. 105
Yet, oh, the thought that thou art safe, and he,
That thought is joy, arrive what may to me.
My boast is not that I deduce my birth
From loins enthroned and rulers of the earth;
But higher far my proud pretensions rise— 110
The son of parents passed into the skies!

And now, farewell. Time unrevoked has run
His wonted course, yet what I wished is done:
By contemplation's help, not sought in vain,
I seem t' have lived my childhood o'er again, 115
To have renewed the joys that once were mine,
Without the sin of violating thine;
And while the wings of Fancy still are free,

And I can view this mimic show of thee,
Time has but half succeeded in his theft—   120
Thyself removed, thy power to soothe me left.

1798

TO MARY

THE twentieth year is well-nigh past,
Since first our sky was overcast;
Ah, would that this might be the last!
                    My Mary!

Thy spirits have a fainter flow,   5
I see thee daily weaker grow;
'Twas my distress that brought thee low,
                    My Mary!

Thy needles, once a shining store,
For my sake restless heretofore,   10
Now rust disused, and shine no more,
                    My Mary!

For though thou gladly wouldst fulfil
The same kind office for me still,
Thy sight now seconds not thy will,   15
                    My Mary!

But well thou playedst the housewife's part,
And all thy threads with magic art
Have wound themselves about this heart,
                    My Mary!   20

Thy indistinct expressions seem
Like language uttered in a dream;
Yet me they charm, what'er the theme,
                    My Mary!

Thy silver locks, once auburn bright,   25
Are still more lovely in my sight
Than golden beams of orient light,
         My Mary!

For, could I view nor them nor thee,
What sight worth seeing could I see?   30
The sun would rise in vain for me,
         My Mary!

Partakers of thy sad decline,
Thy hands their little force resign,
Yet, gently pressed, press gently mine,   35
         My Mary!

Such feebleness of limbs thou provest,
That now at every step thou movest
Upheld by two, yet still thou lovest,
         My Mary!   40

And still to love, though pressed with ill,
In wintry age to feel no chill,
With me is to be lovely still,
         My Mary!

But ah! by constant heed I know,   45
How oft the sadness that I show
Transforms thy smiles to looks of woe,
         My Mary!

And should my future lot be cast
With much resemblance of the past,   50
Thy worn-out heart will break at last,
         My Mary!

c.1795   1803

THE CASTAWAY

OBSCUREST night involved the sky,
   The Atlantic billows roared,
When such a destined wretch as I,
   Washed headlong from on board,
Of friends, of hope, of all bereft,   5
His floating home forever left.

No braver chief could Albion boast
   Than he with whom he went,
Nor ever ship left Albion's coast
   With warmer wishes sent.   10
He loved them both, but both in vain,
Nor him beheld, nor her again.

Not long beneath the whelming brine,
   Expert to swim, he lay;
Nor soon he felt his strength decline,   15
   Or courage die away;
But waged with death a lasting strife,
Supported by despair of life.

He shouted: nor his friends had failed
   To check the vessel's course,
But so the furious blast prevailed,   20
   That, pitiless perforce,
They left their outcast mate behind,
And scudded still before the wind.

Some succor yet they could afford;   25
   And such as storms allow,
The cask, the coop, the floated cord,
   Delayed not to bestow.
But he (they knew) nor ship nor shore,
Whate'er they gave, should visit more.   30

Nor, cruel as it seemed, could he
   Their haste himself condemn,
Aware that flight, in such a sea,
   Alone could rescue them;
Yet bitter felt it still to die   35
Deserted, and his friends so nigh.

He long survives, who lives an hour
   In ocean, self-upheld;
And so long he, with unspent power,
   His destiny repelled;   40
And ever, as the minutes flew,
Entreated help, or cried 'Adieu!'

At length, his transient respite past,
   His comrades, who before
Had heard his vioce in every blast,   45
   Could catch the sound no more:
For them, by toil subdued, he drank
The stifling wave, and then he sank.

No poet wept him; but the page
   Of narrative sincere,   50
That tells his name, his worth, his age,
   Is wet with Anson's tear:
And tears by bards or heroes shed
Alike immortalize the dead.

I therefore purpose not, or dream,   55
   Descanting on his fate,
To give the melancholy theme
   A more enduring date:
But misery still delights to trace
Its semblance in another's case.   60

No voice divine the storm allayed,
   No light propitious shone,

When, snatched from all effectual aid,
    We perished, each alone:
But I beneath a rougher sea,   65
And whelmed in deeper gulfs than he.

c.1790   1803

HUGH BLAIR

[ON PASTORAL POETRY]

I MUCH question, however, whether, this insipidity be not owing to the fault of the poets, and to
their barren and slavish imitation of the ancient pastoral topics, rather than to the confined nature of
the subject. For why may not pastoral poetry take 5
a wider range? Human nature, human passions,
are much the same in every rank of life; and
wherever these passions operate on objects that are
within the rural sphere, there may be a proper subject for pastoral. One would indeed choose to   10
remove from this sort of composition the operations
of violent and direful passions, and to present such
only as are consistent with innocence, simplicity, and
virtue. But under this limitation, there will still be
abundant scope for a careful observer of nature to 15
exert his genius. The various adventures which
give occasion to those engaged in country life to
display their disposition and temper; the scenes of
domestic felicity or disquiet; the attachment of
friends and of brothers; the rivalship and compe-   20
titions of lovers; the unexpected successes or misfortunes of families, might give occasion to many a
pleasing and tender incident; and were more of the
narrative and sentimental intermixed with the descriptive in this kind of poetry, it would become   25

much more interesting than it now generally is, to
the bulk of readers.

1783?

EDWARD JERNINGHAM

[THE WEAVING OF THE RAVEN BANNER]

SEE on the horrid battle's bleeding plain
The raven-brood rejoicing o'er the slain!
Yet then in vain they gorge the grateful food;
Death smites them at the dire repast of blood.
When lo! their pinions to the wondering view   5
Combining, into one vast texture grew;
The gory heads conjoined in one dread fold,
Around the frame a grisly margin rolled.
Now self-upborne the sable banner flings
Bold to the wind its wide-expanding wings.   10
"Exalt," the genius cries, "thy plumes on high,
Wave thy dark signal to the warrior's eye;
The intrepid youth beneath thy magic shade
Through slaughtered heaps to victory shall wade."

1784

[A NEW POETIC WORLD]

WHEN urged by destiny the eventful year
Sailed through the portal of the northern sphere,
Of Scandinavia the rude genius rose,
His breast deep-laboring with creation's throes.
Thrice o'er his head a powerful wand he whirled,   5
Then called to life a new poetic world.

First through the yawning waves that roared around,
Uprising slow from out the gulph profound
Amidst the fury of the beating storm,
The giant Ymir heaved his horrid form.   10

Now on the stormy cloud the rainbow glows,
Where gay diversity her coloring throws.
Beyond the sun the power now cast his eyes
And bade the splendid city Asgard rise;
Obedient to the loud creative call   15
She rises, circled with a crystal wall,
Her sapphire mansions crowned with opal towers,
O'er which the power a flood of radiance showers.

1784

ROBERT BURNS

MARY MORISON

O MARY, at thy window be;
　It is the wished, the trysted hour!
Those smiles and glances let me see
　That make the miser's treasure poor!
How blythely wad I bide the stoure,   5
　A weary slave frae sun to sun,
Could I the rich reward secure,
　The lovely Mary Morison.

Yestreen, when to the trembling string
　The dance gaed thro' the lighted ha',   10
To thee my fancy took its wing;
　I sat, but neither heard nor saw:
Tho' this was fair, and that was braw,
　And yon the toast of a' the town,
I sighed, and said amang them a',   15
　'Ye are na Mary Morison.'

O Mary, canst thou wreck his peace
　Wha for thy sake wad gladly die?

Or canst thou break that heart of his
    Whase only faut is loving thee?   **20**
If love for love thou wilt na gie,
    At least be pity to me shown!
A thought ungentle canna be
    The thought o' Mary Morison.

1784?   1800

THE HOLY FAIR

Upon a simmer Sunday morn,
    When Nature's face is fair,
I walkèd forth to view the corn,
    An' snuff the caller air.
The rising sun, owre Galston muirs,   **5**
    Wi' glorious light was glintin;
The hares were hirplin down the furs,
    The lav'rocks they were chantin
                    Fu' sweet that day.

As lightsomely I glowered abroad,   **10**
    To see a scene sae gay,
Three hizzies, early at the road,
    Cam skelpin up the way.
Twa had manteeles o' dolefu' black,
    But ane wi' lyart lining;   **15**
The third, that gaed a wee a-back,
    Was in the fashion shining
                    Fu' gay that day.

The twa appeared like sisters twin,
    In feature, form, an' claes;   **20**
Their visage withered, lang an' thin,
    An' sour as onie slaes:
The third cam up, hap-step-an'-lowp,
    As light as onie lambie,

An' wi' a curchie low did stoop,   25
   As soon as e'er she saw me,
       Fu' kind that day.

Wi' bonnet aff, quoth I, 'Sweet lass,
   I think ye seem to ken me;
I'm sure I've seen that bonie face,   30
   But yet I canna name ye.'
Quo' she, an' laughin as she spak,
   An' taks me by the han's,
'Ye, for my sake, hae gi'en the feck
   Of a' the Ten Comman's   35
       A screed some day.

'My name is Fun—your cronie dear,
   The nearest friend ye hae;
An' this is Superstition here,
   An' that's Hypocrisy.   40

I'm gaun to Mauchline Holy Fair,
   To spend an hour in daffin:
Gin ye'd go there, yon runkled pair,
   We will get famous laughin
       At them this day.   45

.   .   .   .

Here sits a raw of tittlin' jads,
   Wi' heavin breasts an' bare neck;
An' there a batch o' wabster lads,
   Blackguarding frae Kilmarnock,
       For fun this day.   50

Here some are thinkin on their sins,
   An' some upo' their claes;
Ane curses feet that fyled his shins,
   Anither sighs and prays;

On this hand sits a chosen swatch,   55
   Wi' screwed-up grace-proud faces;
On that a set o' chaps, at watch,
   Thrang winkin on the lasses
               To chairs that day.

O happy is that man an' blest   60
   (Nae wonder that it pride him!)
Whase ain dear lass, that he likes best,
   Comes clinkin down beside him!
Wi' arm reposed on the chair-back,
   He sweetly does compose him;   65
Which, by degrees, slips round her neck,
   An's loof upon her bosom,
               Unkend that day.

Now a' the congregation o'er
   Is silent expectation;   70
For Moodie speels the holy door
   Wi' tidings o' damnation.
Should Hornie, as in ancient days,
   'Mang sons o' God present him,
The vera sight o' Moodie's face   75
   To 's ain het hame had sent him
               Wi' fright that day.

Hear how he clears the points o' faith
   Wi' rattlin an wi' thumpin!
Now meekly calm, now wild in wrath,   80
   He's stampin an' he's jumpin!
His lengthened chin, his turned-up snout,
   His eldritch squeel an' gestures,
O how they fire the heart devout—
   Like cantharidian plaisters,   85
               On sic a day!

But hark! the tent has changed its voice;
  There's peace an' rest nae langer;
For a' the real judges rise,
  They canna sit for anger: 90
Smith opens out his cauld harangues
  On practice and on morals;
An' aff the godly pour in thrangs,
  To gie the jars an' barrels
              A lift that day.   95

What signifies his barren shine
  Of moral pow'rs an' reason?
His English style an' gesture fine
  Are a' clean out o' season.
Like Socrates or Antonine,   100
  Or some auld pagan heathen,
The moral man he does define,
  But ne'er a word o' faith in
              That's right that day.

In guid time comes an antidote   105
  Against sic poisoned nostrum;
For Peebles, frae the water-fit,
  Ascends the holy rostrum:
See, up he's got the word o' God,
  An' meek an' mim has viewed it,   110
While Common Sense has taen the road,
  An' aff, an' up the Cowgate
              Fast, fast that day.

Wee Miller niest the guard relieves,
  An' orthodoxy raibles,   115
Tho' in his heart he weel believes
  An' thinks it auld wives' fables;
But faith! the birkie wants a manse,
  So cannilie he hums them,

Altho's his carnal wit an' sense   120
  Like hafflins-wise o'ercomes him
                    At times that day.

Now butt an' ben the change-house fills
  Wi' yill-caup commentators;
Here's crying out for bakes an' gills,   125
  An' there the pint-stowp clatters;
While thick an' thrang, an' loud an' lang,
  Wi' logic an' wi' Scripture,
They raise a din that in the end
  Is like to breed a rupture   130
                    O' wrath that day.

Leeze me on drink! it gies us mair
  Than either school or college;
It kindles wit, it waukens lear,
  It pangs us fou o' knowledge.   135
Be 't whisky-gill or penny-wheep,
  Or onie stronger potion,
It never fails, on drinkin deep,
  To kittle up our notion,
                    By night or day.   140

The lads an' lasses, blythely bent
  To mind baith saul an' body,
Sit round the table weel content,
  An' steer about the toddy.
On this ane's dress an' that ane's leuk   145
  They're makin observations;
While some are cozie i' the neuk,
  An' formin assignations
                    To meet some day.

But now the Lord's ain trumpet touts,   150
  Till a' the hills are rairin,

And echoes back return the shouts;
   Black Russell is na spairin:
His piercin words, like Highlan' swords,
   Divide the joints an' marrow;   155
His talk o' hell, whare devils dwell,
   Our verra 'sauls does harrow'
              Wi' fright that day!

A vast, unbottomed, boundless pit,
   Filled fou o' lowin brunstane,   160
Whase ragin flame an' scorchin heat
   Wad melt the hardest whun-stane!
The half-asleep start up wi' fear,
   An' think they hear it roarin,
When presently it does appear   165
   'Twas but some neebor snorin,
              Asleep that day.

'Twad be owre lang a tale to tell
   How monie stories passed,
An' how they crouded to the yill,   170
   When they were a' dismissed;
How drink gaed round, in cogs an' caups,
   Amang the furms an' benches,
An' cheese an' bread, frae women's laps,
   Was dealt about in lunches   175
              An' dawds that day.

In comes a gawsie, gash guidwife,
   An' sits down by the fire,
Syne draws her kebbuck an' her knife;
   The lasses they are shyer;   180
The auld guidmen about the grace
   Frae side to side they bother,
Till some ane by his bonnet lays
   And gi'es them 't, like a tether,
              Fu' lang that day.   185

Waesucks for him that gets nae lass,
　Or lasses that hae naething!
Sma' need has he to say a grace,
　Or melvie his braw claithing!
O wives, be mindfu', ance yoursel   190
　How bonie lads ye wanted,
An' dinna for a kebbuck-heel
　Let lasses be affronted
　　　　　　On sic a day!

Now Clinkumbell, wi' rattlin tow,   195
　Begins to jow an' croon;
Some swagger hame the best they dow,
　Some wait the afternoon.
At slaps the billies halt a blink,
　Till lasses strip their shoon;   200
Wi' faith an' hope, an' love an' drink,
　They're a' in famous tune
　　　　　　For crack that day.

How monie hearts this day converts
　O' sinners and o' lasses!   205
Their hearts o' stane, gin night, are gaen
　As saft as onie flesh is.
There's some are fou o' love divine,
　There's some are fou o' brandy;
An' monie jobs that day begin,   210
　May end in houghmagandie
　　　　　　Some ither day.

1785   1786

FROM EPISTLE TO J. LAPRAIK

I AM nae poet, in a sense,
But just a rhymer like by chance,
An' hae to learning nae pretence;
　Yet what the matter?

Whene'er my Muse does on me glance,   5
    I jingle at her.

Your critic-folk may cock their nose,
And say, 'How can you e'er propose,
You wha ken hardly verse frae prose,
    To mak a sang?'   10
But, by your leaves, my learnèd foes,
    Ye're maybe wrang.

What's a' your jargon o' your schools,
Your Latin names for horns an' stools?
If honest Nature made you fools,   15
    What sairs your grammers?
Ye'd better taen up spades and shools
    Or knappin-hammers.

A set o' dull, conceited hashes
Confuse their brains in college classes;   20
They gang in stirks, and come out asses,
    Plain truth to speak;
An' syne they think to climb Parnassus
    By dint o' Greek!

Gie me ae spark o' Nature's fire,   25
That's a' the learning I desire;
Then, tho' I drudge thro' dub an' mire
    At pleugh or cart,
My Muse, tho' hamely in attire,
    May touch the heart.   30

1785   1786

THE COTTER'S SATURDAY NIGHT

My LOVED, my honored, much respected friend!
    No mercenary bard his homage pays;

With honest pride, I scorn each selfish end,
  My dearest meed a friend's esteem and praise:
To you I sing, in simple Scottish lays,   5
The lowly train in life's sequestered scene;
  The native feelings strong, the guileless ways,
What Aiken in a cottage would have been;
Ah, though his worth unknown, far happier there,
        I ween!

November chill blaws loud wi' angry sugh;   10
  The shortening winter-day is near a close;
The miry beasts retreating frae the pleugh;
  The blackening trains o' craws to their repose:
  The toil-worn cotter frae his labor goes—
This night his weekly moil is at an end,—   15
  Collects his spades, his mattocks, and his hoes,
Hoping the morn in ease and rest to spend,
And weary, o'er the moor, his course does hame-
        ward bend.

At length his lonely cot appears in view,
  Beneath the shelter of an aged tree;   20
Th' expectant wee-things, toddlin, stacher through
  To meet their dad, wi' flichterin' noise and glee.
  His wee bit ingle, blinkin bonilie,
His clean hearth-stane, his thrifty wifie's smile,
  The lisping infant, prattling on his knee,   25
Does a' his weary kiaugh and care beguile,
And makes him quite forget his labor and his toil.

Belyve the elder bairns come drapping in,
  At service out amang the farmers roun';
Some ca' the pleugh, some herd, some tentie rin   30
  A cannie errand to a neebor town.
  Their eldest hope, their Jenny, woman-grown,
In youthfu' bloom, love sparkling in her e'e,

Comes hame, perhaps to shew a braw new
gown,
Or deposite her sair-won penny-fee,   35
To help her parents dear if they in hardship be.

With joy unfeigned, brothers and sisters meet,
And each for other's weelfare kindly spiers;
The social hours, swift-winged, unnoticed fleet;
Each tells the uncos that he sees or hears.   40
The parents, partial, eye their hopeful years;
Anticipation forward points the view.
The mother, wi' her needle and her sheers,
Gars auld claes look amaist as weel's the new;
The father mixes a' wi' admonition due: 45

Their master's and their mistress's command
The younkers a' are warnèd to obey,
And mind their labors wi' an eydent hand,
And ne'er, tho' out o' sight, to jauk or play:
'And O be sure to fear the Lord alway,   50
And mind your duty duly, morn and night;
Lest in temptation's path ye gang astray,
Implore His counsel and assisting might:
They never sought in vain that sought the Lord
aright!'

But hark! a rap comes gently to the door.   55
Jenny, wha kens the meaning o' the same,
Tells how a neebor lad came o'er the moor,
To do some errands and convoy her hame.
The wily mother sees the conscious flame
Sparkle in Jenny's e'e, and flush her cheek;   60
With heart-struck anxious care enquires his
name,
While Jenny hafflins is afraid to speak;
Weel-pleased the mother hears it's nae wild, worth-
less rake.

With kindly welcome Jenny brings him ben:
    A strappin' youth, he takes the mother's eye;   65
Blythe Jenny sees the visit's no ill-taen;
    The father cracks of horses, pleughs, and kye.
    The youngster's artless heart o'erflows wi' joy,
But blate and laithfu', scarce can weel behave;
    The mother, wi' a woman's wiles, can spy   70
What makes the youth sae bashfu' and sae grave,
Weel-pleased to think her bairn's respected like the
        lave.

Oh happy love, where love like this is found!
    Oh heart-felt raptures! bliss beyond compare!
I've pacèd much this weary, mortal round,   75
    And sage experience bids me this declare:
    'If Heaven a draught of heavenly pleasure
        spare,
One cordial in this melancholy vale,
    'Tis when a youthful, loving, modest pair
In other's arms breathe out the tender tale,   80
Beneath the milk-white thorn that scents the evening
        gale.'

Is there, in human form, that bears a heart,
    A wretch! a villain! lost to love and truth!
That can, with studied, sly, ensnaring art,
    Betray sweet Jenny's unsuspecting youth?   85
    Curse on his perjured arts! dissembling
        smooth!
Are honor, virtue, conscience, all exiled?
    Is there no pity, no relenting ruth,
Points to the parents fondling o'er their child?
Then paints the ruined maid, and their distraction
        wild?   90

But now the supper crowns their simple board:
    The healsome parritch, chief o' Scotia's food:

The soupe their only hawkie does afford,
    That 'yont the hallan snugly chows her cood.
    The dame brings forth, in complimental mood,   95
To grace the lad, her weel-hained kebbuck, fell;
    And aft he's prest, and aft he ca's it guid;
    The frugal wifie, garrulous, will tell
How 't was a towmond auld sin' lint was i' the bell.

The cheerfu' supper done, wi' serious face   100
    They round the ingle form a circle wide;
The sire turns o'er, wi' patriarchal grace,
    The big ha'-Bible, ance his father's pride;
    His bonnet reverently is laid aside,
His lyart haffets wearing thin and bare;   105
    Those strains that once did sweet in Zion glide,
He wales a portion with judicious care,
And 'Let us worship God!' he says, with solemn air.

They chant their artless notes in simple guise;
    They tune their hearts, by far the noblest aim: 110
Perhaps 'Dundee's' wild-warbling measures rise,
    Or plaintive 'Martyrs,' worthy of the name;
    Or noble, 'Elgin' beets the heavenward flame,
The sweetest far of Scotia's holy lays.
    Compared with these, Italian trills are tame;   115
The tickled ears no heart-felt raptures raise;
Nae unison hae they with our Creator's praise.

The priest-like father reads the sacred page;
    How Abram was the friend of God on high,
Or Moses bade eternal warfare wage   120
    With Amalek's ungracious progeny;
    Or how the royal bard did groaning lie
Beneath the stroke of Heaven's avenging ire;
    Or Job's pathetic plaint and wailing cry,
Or rapt Isaiah's wild, seraphic fire;   125
Or other holy seers that tune the sacred lyre.

Perhaps the Christian volume is the theme:
　　How guiltless blood for guilty man was shed;
How He Who bore in Heaven the second name
　　Had not on earth whereon to lay His head;　130
　　How His first followers and servants sped;
The precepts sage they wrote to many a land;
　　How he who lone in Patmos banished,
Saw in the sun a mighty angel stand,
And heard great Bab'lon's doom pronounced by
　　Heaven's command.　135

Then kneeling down to Heaven's Eternal King,
　　The saint, the father, and the husband prays;
Hope 'springs exulting on triumphant wing,'
　　That thus they all shall meet in future days,
　　There ever bask in uncreated rays,　140
No more to sigh or shed the bitter tear,
　　Together hymning their Creator's praise,
In such society, yet still more dear,
While circling Time moves round in an eternal
　　sphere.

Compared with this, how poor Religion's pride,　145
　　In all the pomp of method and of art,
When men display to congregations wide
　　Devotion's ev'ry grace except the heart!
　　The Power, incensed, the pageant will desert,
The pompous strain, the sacerdotal stole;　150
　　But haply, in some cottage far apart,
May hear, well pleased, the language of the soul,
And in His Book of Life the inmates poor enroll.

Then homeward all take off their several way;
　　The youngling cottagers retire to rest;　155
The parent-pair their secret homage pay,
　　And proffer up to Heaven the warm request
　　And He who stills the raven's clamorous nest,

And decks the lily fair in flowery pride,
    Would, in the way His wisdom sees the best, 160
For them and for their little ones provide,
But chiefly in their hearts with grace divine preside.

From scenes like these old Scotia's grandeur
        springs,
    That makes her loved at home, revered abroad:
Princes and lords are but the breath of kings, 165
    'An honest man's the noblest work of God.'
    And certes in fair virtue's heavenly road,
The cottage leaves the palace far behind:
    What is a lordling's pomp? a cumbrous load,
Disguising oft the wretch of human kind, 170
Studied in arts of hell, in wickedness refined!

O Scotia! my dear, my native soil!
    For whom my warmest wish to Heaven is sent!
Long may thy hardy sons of rustic toil
    Be blest with health and peace and sweet con-
        tent! 175
    And O may Heaven their simple lives prevent
From luxury's contagion, weak and vile!
    Then, howe'er crowns and coronets be rent,
A virtuous populace may rise the while,
And stand a wall of fire around their much-loved
        isle. 180

O Thou, Who poured the patriotic tide
    That streamed thro' Wallace's undaunted heart,
Who dared to nobly stem tyrannic pride,
    Or nobly die, the second glorious part!
    (The patriot's God peculiarly Thou art, 185
His friend, inspirer, guardian, and reward!)
    Oh never, never Scotia's realm desert,

But still the patriot and the patriot-bard
In bright succession raise, her ornament and guard!
1785-86   1786

TO A MOUSE

ON TURNING HER UP IN HER NEST WITH THE PLOUGH, NOVEMBER, 1785

WEE, sleekit, cowrin, tim'rous beastie,
O what a panic's in thy breastie!
Thou need na start awa sae hasty,
        Wi' bickering brattle!
I wad be laith to rin an' chase thee,   5
        Wi' murdering pattle!

I'm truly sorry man's dominion
Has broken Nature's social union,
An' justifies that ill opinion
        Which makes thee startle   10
At me, thy poor, earth-born companion,
        An' fellow-mortal!

I doubt na, whyles, but thou may thieve;
What then? poor beastie, thou maun live!
A daimen icker in a thrave   15
        'S a sma' request;
I'll get a blessin' wi' the lave,
        An' never miss 't!

Thy wee-bit housie, too, in ruin!
Its silly wa's the win's are strewin!   20
An' naething now to big a new ane,
        O' foggage green!
An' bleak December's win's ensuin,
        Baith snell an' keen!

Thou saw the fields laid bare an' waste,   25
An' weary winter comin fast,
An' cozie here, beneath the blast,
    Thou thought to dwell—
Till, crash! the cruel coulter passed
    Out thro' thy cell.   30

That wee bit heap o' leaves an' stibble
Has cost thee monie a weary nibble!
Now thou's turned out, for a' thy trouble,
    But house or hald,
To thole the winter's sleety dribble,   35
    An' cranreuch cauld!

But mousie, thou art no thy lane
In proving foresight may be vain:
The best-laid schemes o' mice an' men
    Gang aft agley,   40
An' lea'e us naught but grief an' pain
    For promised joy!

Still, thou art blest compared wi' me!
The present only toucheth thee:
But och! I backward cast my e'e,   45
    On prospects drear!
An' forward, tho' I canna see,
    I guess an' fear!

1785   1786

TO A MOUNTAIN DAISY

On Turning One Down with the Plough in
April, 1786

Wee, modest, crimson-tippèd flow'r,
Thou's met me in an evil hour,

For I maun crush among the stoure
    Thy slender stem;
To spare thee now is past my pow'r,   *5
    Thou bonie gem.

Alas! it's no thy neebor sweet,
The bonie lark, companion meet,
Bending thee 'mang the dewy weet,
    Wi' spreckled breast,   10
When upward springing, blythe, to greet
    The purpling east.

Cauld blew the bitter-biting north
Upon thy early, humble birth;
Yet cheerfully thou glinted forth   15
    Amid the storm,
Scarce reared above the parent-earth
    Thy tender form.

The flaunting flow'rs our gardens yield,
High shelt'ring woods and wa's maun shield;   20
But thou, beneath the random bield
    O' clod or stane,
Adorns the histie stibble-field,
    Unseen, alane.

There, in thy scanty mantle clad,   25
Thy snawie bosom sunward spread,
Thou lifts thy unassuming head
    In humble guise;
But now the share uptears thy bed,
    And low thou lies!   30

Such is the fate of artless maid,
Sweet flow'ret of the rural shade!
By love's simplicity betrayed,
    And guileless trust,

Till she, like thee, all soiled is laid,　　35
　　Low i' the dust.

Such is the fate of simple bard,
On life's rough ocean luckless starred!
Unskilful he to note the card
　　Of prudent lore,　　40
Till billows rage, and gales blow hard,
　　And whelm him o'er!

Such fate to suffering worth is giv'n,
Who long with wants and woes has striv'n,
By human pride or cunning driv'n　　45
　　To mis'ry's brink;
Till, wrench'd of ev'ry stay but Heav'n,
　　He, ruined, sink!

Ev'n thou who mourn'st the daisy's fate,
That fate is thine—no distant date;　　50
Stern Ruin's plough-share drives, elate,
　　Full on thy bloom,
Till crush'd beneath the furrow's weight
　　Shall be thy doom!

1786

EPISTLE TO A YOUNG FRIEND

I LANG hae thought, my youthfu' friend
　　A something to have sent you,
Tho' it should serve nae ither end
　　Than just a kind memento.
But how the subject-theme may gang,　　5
　　Let time and chance determine;
Perhaps it may turn out a sang,
　　Perhaps turn out a sermon.

Ye'll try the world soon, my lad;
　　And, Andrew dear, believe me,　　　　　10
Ye'll find mankind an unco squad,
　　And muckle they may grieve ye:
For care and trouble set your thought,
　　Ev'n when your end's attainèd;
And a' your views may come to nought,　　15
　　Where ev'ry nerve is strainèd.

I'll no say men are villains a';
　　The real, harden'd wicked,
Wha hae nae check but human law,
　　Are to a few restricket;　　　　　　20
But, och! mankind are unco weak,
　　An' little to be trusted;
If self the wavering balance shake,
　　It's rarely right adjusted!

Yet they wha fa' in fortune's strife,　　25
　　Their fate we shouldna censure,
For still th' important end of life
　　They equally may answer;
A man may hae an honest heart,
　　Tho' poortith hourly stare him;　　30
A man may tak a neebor's part,
　　Yet hae nae cash to spare him.

Aye free, aff-han', your story tell,
　　When wi' a bosom crony;
But still keep something to yoursel　　35
　　Ye scarcely tell to ony.
Conceal yoursel as weel's ye can
　　Frae critical dissection;
But keek thro' ev'ry other man,
　　Wi' sharpen'd, sly inspection.　　　40

The sacred lowe o' weel-placed love,
   Luxuriantly indulge it;
But never tempt th' illicit rove,
   Tho' naething should divulge it;
I wave the quantum o' the sin,   45
   The hazard of concealing;
But, och! it hardens a' within,
   And petrifies the feeling!

To catch dame Fortune's golden smile,
   Assiduous wait upon her;   50
And gather gear by ev'ry wile
   That's justified by honor;
Not for to hide it in a hedge,
   Nor for a train attendant;
But for the glorious privilege   55
   Of being independent.

The fear o' hell's a hangman's whip,
   To haud the wretch in order;
But where ye feel your honor grip,
   Let that aye be your border;   60
Its slightest touches, instant pause—
   Debar a' side-pretences;
And resolutely keep its laws,
   Uncaring consequences.

The great Creator to revere,   65
   Must sure become the creature;
But still the preaching cant forbear,
   And ev'n the rigid feature;
Yet ne'er with wits profane to range,
   Be complaisance extended;   70
An atheist-laugh's a poor exchange
   For Deity offended!

When ranting round in pleasure's ring,
   Religion may be blinded;
Or, if she gie a random sting,   75
   It may be little minded;
But when on life we're tempest-driv'n—
   A conscience but a canker,
A correspondence fixed wi' Heav'n
   Is sure a noble anchor!   80

Adieu, dear amiable Youth!
   Your heart can ne'er be wanting!
May prudence, fortitude, and truth,
   Erect your brow undaunting!
In ploughman phrase, 'God send you speed,'   85
   Still daily to grow wiser;
And may you better reck the rede,
   Than ever did th' adviser!

1786

A BARD'S EPITAPH

Is THERE a whim-inspirèd fool,
Owre fast for thought, owre hot for rule,
Owre blate to seek, owre proud to snool?
     Let him draw near;
And owre this grassy heap sing dool,   5
     And drap a tear.

Is there a bard of rustic song,
Who, noteless, steals the crowds among,
That weekly this area throng?—
     Oh, pass not by!   10
But with a frater-feeling strong
     Here heave a sigh.

Is there a man whose judgment clear
Can others teach the course to steer,

Yet runs himself life's mad career   15
      Wild as the wave?—
Here pause—and thro' the starting tear
      Survey this grave.

The poor inhabitant below
Was quick to learn and wise to know,   20
And keenly felt the friendly glow
      And softer flame;
But thoughtless follies laid him low,
      And stained his name!

Reader, attend! whether thy soul   25
Soars fancy's flights beyond the pole,
Or darkling grubs this earthly hole
      In low pursuit;
Know, prudent, cautious self-control
      Is wisdom's root.   30

                          1786

ADDRESS TO THE UNCO GUID
OR THE RIGIDLY RIGHTEOUS

O ye wha are sae guid yoursel,
    Sae pious and sae holy,
Ye've nought to do but mark and tell
    Your neebor's fauts and folly!
Whase life is like a weel-gaun mill,   5
    Supplied wi' store o' water,
The heapet happer's ebbing still,
    And still the clap plays clatter,—

Hear me, ye venerable core,
    As counsel for poor mortals   10
That frequent pass douce Wisdom's door
    For glaikit Folly's portals;

I for their thoughtless, careless sakes
    Would here propone defences—
Their donsie tricks, their black mistakes,   15
    Their failings and mischances.

Ye see your state wi' theirs compared,
    And shudder at the niffer;
But cast a moment's fair regard,
    What maks the mighty differ?   20
Discount what scant occasion gave,
    That purity ye pride in,
And (what's aft mair than a' the lave)
    Your better art o' hidin.

Think, when your castigated pulse   25
    Gies now and then a wallop,
What ragings must his veins convulse
    That still eternal gallop:
Wi' wind and tide fair i' your tail,
    Right on ye scud your sea-way;   30
But in the teeth o' baith to sail,
    It maks an unco leeway.

See Social Life and Glee sit down,
    All joyous and unthinking,
Till, quite transmugrify'd, they're grown   35
    Debauchery and Drinking:
O would they stay to calculate
    Th' eternal consequences,
Or—your more dreaded hell to state—
    Damnation of expenses!   40

Ye high, exalted, virtuous dames,
    Tied up in godly laces,
Before ye gie poor Frailty names,
    Suppose a change o' cases:

A dear-lov'd lad, convenience snug,   45
   A treach'rous inclination—
But, let me whisper i' your lug,
   Ye're aiblins nae temptation.

Then gently scan your brother man,
   Still gentler sister woman;   50
Tho' they may gang a kennin wrang,
   To step aside is human:
One point must still be greatly dark,
   The moving *why* they do it;
And just as lamely can ye mark   55
   How far perhaps they rue it.

Who made the heart, 'tis He alone
   Decidedly can try us;
He knows each chord, its various tone,
   Each spring, its various bias: 60
Then at the balance, let's be mute,
   We never can adjust it;
What's done we partly may compute,
   But know not what's resisted.

1787

JOHN ANDERSON, MY JO

John Anderson, my jo, John,
   When we were first acquent,
Your locks were like the raven,
   Your bonie brow was brent:
But now your brow is beld, John,   5
   Your locks are like the snaw;
But blessings on your frosty pow,
   John Anderson, my jo!

John Anderson, my jo, John,
   We clamb the hill thegither;   10

And monie a cantie day, John,
    We've had wi' ane anither:
Now we maun totter down, John,
    And hand in hand we'll go,
And sleep thegither at the foot,   15
    John Anderson, my jo!

c.1788   1796

THE LOVELY LASS OF INVERNESS

THE lovely lass of Inverness,
Nae joy nor pleasure can she see;
For e'en to morn she cries, 'Alas!'
And aye the saut tear blin's her e'e:

'Drumossie moor—Drumossie day—   5
A waefu' day it was to me!
For there I lost my father dear,
My father dear, and brethren three.

'Their winding-sheet the bluidy clay,
Their graves are growing green to see: 10
And by them lies the dearest lad
That ever blest a woman's e'e!

'Now wae to thee, thou cruel lord,
A bluidy man I trow thou be;
For mony a heart thou hast made sair   15
That ne'er did wrang to thine or thee!'

c.1788   1796

A RED, RED ROSE

O, MY luv is like a red, red rose,
    That's newly sprung in June:
O, my luv is like the melodie
    That's sweetly played in tune.

As fair art thou, my bonie lass,   5
    So deep in luve am I;
And I will luve thee still, my dear,
    Till a' the seas gang dry:

Till a' the seas gang dry, my dear,
    And the rocks melt wi' the sun;   10
And I will luve thee still, my dear,
    While the sands o' life shall run.

And fare thee weel, my only luve!
    And fare thee weel awhile!
And I will come again, my luve,   15
    Tho' it were ten thousand mile!

c.1788   1796

AULD LANG SYNE

Should auld acquaintance be forgot,
    And never brought to mind?
Should auld acquaintance be forgot,
    And auld lang syne?

Chorus:

For auld lang syne, my dear,   5
    For auld lang syne,
We'll tak a cup o' kindness yet,
    For auld lang syne!

And surely ye'll be your pint-stowp,
    And surely I'll be mine;   10
And we'll take a cup o' kindness yet
    For auld lang syne!

We twa hae run about the braes,
    And pou'd the gowans fine;

But we've wandered monie a weary fit   15
　　Sin' auld lang syne.

We twa hae paidled in the burn,
　　Frae morning sun till dine;
But seas between us braid hae roared
　　Sin' auld lang syne.   20

And there's a hand, my trusty fiere,
　　And gie's a hand o' thine;
And we'll tak a right guid-willie waught,
　　For auld lang syne!

c.1788   1796

SWEET AFTON

Flow gently, sweet Afton, among thy green braes!
Flow gently, I'll sing thee a song in thy praise!
My Mary's asleep by thy murmuring stream,
Flow gently, sweet Afton, disturb not her dream!

Thou stock-dove, whose echo resounds through the
　　glen,   5
Ye wild whistling blackbirds in yon thorny den,
Thou green-crested lapwing, thy screaming forbear,
I charge you disturb not my slumbering fair!

How lofty, sweet Afton, thy neighboring hills,
Far marked with the courses of clear winding rills!   10
There daily I wander as noon rises high,
My flocks and my Mary's sweet cot in my eye.

How pleasant thy banks and green valleys below,
Where wild in the woodlands the primroses blow!
There oft, as mild evening weeps over the lea,   15
The sweet-scented birk shades my Mary and me.

Thy crystal stream, Afton, how lovely it glides,
And winds by the cot where my Mary resides!
How wanton thy waters her snowy feet lave,
As gathering sweet flowerets she stems thy clear
        wave!   20

Flow gently, sweet Afton, among thy green braes!
Flow gently, sweet river, the theme of my lays!
My Mary's asleep by thy murmuring stream,
Flow gently, sweet Afton, disturb not her dream!
c.1789   1796

TO MARY IN HEAVEN

THOU lingering star, with lessening ray,
    That lov'st to greet the early morn,
Again thou usher'st in the day
    My Mary from my soul was torn.
O Mary! dear departed shade!   5
    Where is thy place of blissful rest?
See'st thou thy lover lowly laid?
    Hear'st thou the groans that rend his breast?

That sacred hour can I forget,
    Can I forget the hallowed grove,   10
Where by the winding Ayr we met
    To live one day of parting love?
Eternity cannot efface
    Those records dear of transports past,
Thy image at our last embrace—   15
    Ah! little thought we 'twas our last!

Ayr, gurgling, kissed his pebbled shore,
    O'erhung with wild woods, thickening green;
The fragrant birch and hawthorn hoar
    Twined amorous round the raptured scene: 20

The flowers sprang wanton to be pressed,
  The birds sang love on every spray,
Till too, too soon the glowing west
  Proclaimed the speed of wingèd day.

Still o'er these scenes my memory wakes,   25
  And fondly broods with miser care!
Time but th' impression stronger makes,
  As streams their channels deeper wear.
My Mary, dear departed shade!
  Where is thy place of blissful rest?   30
See'st thou thy lover lowly laid?
  Hear'st thou the groans that rend his breast?

1789   1796

WILLIAM BECKFORD

FROM THE HISTORY OF THE CALIPH VATHEK

VATHEK, ninth Caliph of the race of the Abas-
sides, was the son of Motassem, and the grandson
of Haroun Al Raschid. From an early accession
to the throne, and the talents he possessed to adorn
it, his subjects were induced to expect that his reign   5
would be long and happy. His figure was pleasing
and majestic; but when he was angry one of his eyes
became so terrible, that no person could bear to behold it, and the wretch upon whom it was fixed instantly fell backward, and sometimes expired. For   10
fear, however, of depopulating his dominions and
making his palace desolate, he but rarely gave way
to his anger.

Being much addicted to women and the pleasures
of the table, he sought by his affability to procure   15
agreeable companions; and he succeeded the better

as his generosity was unbounded, and his indulgences unrestrained, for he was by no means scrupulous, nor did he think with the Caliph Omar Ben Abdalaziz, that it was necessary to make a hell of this world to enjoy Paradise in the next.

He surpassed in magnificence all his predecessors. The palace of Alkoremmi, which his father Motassem had erected on the hill of Pied Horses, and which commanded the whole city of Samarah, was in his idea far too scanty; he added, therefore, five wings, or rather other palaces, which he destined for the particular gratification of each of his senses.

In the first of these were tables continually covered with the most exquisite dainties, which were supplied both by night and by day according to their constant consumption, whilst the most delicious wines and the choicest cordials flowed forth from a hundred fountains that were never exhausted. This palace was called "The Eternal or Unsatiating Banquet."

The second was styled "The Temple of Melody, or the Nectar of the Soul." It was inhabited by the most skilful musicians and admired poets of the time, who not only displayed their talents within, but, dispersing in bands without, caused every surrounding scene to reverberate their songs, which were continually varied in the most delightful succession.

The palace named "The Delight of the Eyes, or the Support of Memory," was one entire enchantment. Rarities collected from every corner of the earth were there found in such profusion as to dazzle and confound, but for the order in which they were arranged. One gallery exhibited the pictures of the celebrated Mani, and statues that seemed to be alive. Here a well-managed perspective attracted the sight, there the magic of optics agreeably deceived it; whilst the naturalist on his part exhibited, in their several classes, the various gifts that Heaven had bestowed on our globe. In a word, Vathek omitted 55 nothing in this palace that might gratify the curiosity of those who resorted to it, although he was not able to satisfy his own, for he was of all men the most curious.

"The Palace of Perfumes," which was termed 60 likewise "The Incentive to Pleasure," consisted of various halls where the different perfumes which the earth produces were kept perpetually burning in censers of gold. Flambeaus and aromatic lamps were here lighted in open day. But the too powerful 65 effects of this agreeable delirium might be avoided by descending into an immense garden, where an assemblage of every fragrant flower diffused through the air the purest odors.

The fifth palace, denominated "The Retreat of 70 Joy, or the Dangerous," was frequented by troops of young females beautiful as the houris and not less seducing, who never failed to receive with caresses all whom the Caliph allowed to approach them; for he was by no means disposed to be jealous, 75 as his own women were secluded within the palace he inhabited himself.

Notwithstanding the sensuality in which Vathek indulged, he experienced no abatement in the love of his people, who thought that a sovereign immersed 80 in pleasure was not less tolerable to his subjects than one that employed himself in creating them foes. But the unquiet and impetuous disposition of the Caliph would not allow him to rest there; he had studied so much for his amusement in the lifetime of his father, 85 as to acquire a great deal of knowledge, though not a sufficiency to satisfy himself; for he wished to know everything, even sciences that did not exist. He was fond of engaging in disputes with the learned, but liked them not to push their opposition 90 with warmth; he stopped the mouths of those with presents whose mouths could be stopped, whilst others, whom his liberality was unable to subdue, he sent to prison to cool their blood, a remedy that often succeeded.   95

[THE HALL OF EBLIS]

AFTER some time Vathek and Nouronihar perceived a gleam brightening through the drapery, and entered a vast tabernacle carpeted with the skins of leopards; an infinity of elders with streaming beards, and Afrits in complete armor, had prostrated them-   5
selves before the ascent of a lofty eminence, on the top of which, upon a globe of fire, sat the formidable Eblis. His person was that of a young man, whose noble and regular features seemed to have been tarnished by malignant vapors; in his large eyes ap-   10
peared both pride and despair; his flowing hair retained some resemblance to that of an angel of light; in his hand, which thunder had blasted, he swayed the iron sceptre that causes the monster Ouranabad, the Afrits, and all the powers of the   15
abyss to tremble; at his presence the heart of the Caliph sank within him, and for the first time, he fell prostrate on his face. Nouronihar, however, though greatly dismayed, could not help admiring the person of Eblis; for she expected to have seen some stu-   20
pendous Giant. Eblis, with a voice more mild than might be imagined, but such as transfused through the soul the deepest melancholy, said:

"Creatures of clay, I receive you into mine empire; ye are numbered amongst my adorers; enjoy   25
whatever this palace affords; the treasures of the pre-adamite Sultans, their bickering sabres, and those talismans that compel the Dives to open the subterranean expanses of the mountain of Kaf,

which communicate with these; there, insatiable as 30
your curiosity may be, shall you find sufficient to
gratify it; you shall possess the exclusive privilege
of entering the fortress of Aherman, and the halls
of Argenk, where are portrayed all creatures endowed with intelligence, and the various animals that 35
inhabited that earth prior to the creation of that
contemptible being, whom ye denominate the Father
of Mankind."

Vathek and Nouronihar, feeling themselves re-
vived and encouraged by this harangue, eagerly 40
said to the Giaour:

"Bring us instantly to the place which contains
these precious talismans."

"Come!" answered this wicked Dive, with his malignant grin, "come! and possess all that my Sov- 45
ereign hath promised, and more."

He then conducted them into a long aisle adjoining the tabernacle, preceding them with hasty steps,
and followed by his disciples with the utmost alacrity.
They reached, at length, a hall of great extent, and 50
covered with a lofty dome, around which appeared
fifty portals of bronze, secured with as many fasten-
ings of iron; a funereal gloom prevailed over the
whole scene; here, upon two beds of incorruptible
cedar, lay recumbent the fleshless forms of the Pre- 55
adamite Kings, who had been monarchs of the
whole earth; they still possessed enough of life to be
conscious of their deplorable condition; their eyes
retained a melancholy motion; they regarded each
other with looks of the deepest dejection, each hold- 60
ing his right hand motionless on his heart; at their
feet were inscribed the events of their several
reigns, their power, their pride, and their crimes;
Soliman Raad, Soliman Daki, and Soliman Di Gian
Ben Gian, who, after having chained up the Dives 65
in the dark caverns of Kaf, became so presumptuous

as to doubt of the Supreme Power; all these maintained great state, though not to be compared with the eminence of Soliman Ben Daoud.

This king, so renowned for his wisdom, was on the loftiest elevation, and placed immediately under the dome; he appeared to possess more animation than the rest; though from time to time he labored with profound sighs, and, like his companions, kept his right hand on his heart; yet his countenance was more composed, and he seemed to be listening to the sullen roar of a vast cataract, visible in part through the grated portals; this was the only sound that intruded on the silence of these doleful mansions. A range of brazen vases surrounded the elevation.

"Remove the covers from these cabalistic depositaries," said the Giaour to Vathek, "and avail thyself of the talismans, which will break asunder all these gates of bronze; and not only render thee master of the treasures contained within them, but also of the spirits by which they are guarded."

The Caliph, whom this ominous preliminary had entirely disconcerted, approached the vases with faltering footsteps, and was ready to sink with terror when he heard the groans of Soliman. As he proceeded, a voice from the livid lips of the Prophet articulated these words:

"In my life-time I filled a magnificent throne, having on my right hand twelve thousand seats of gold, where the patriarchs and the prophets heard my doctrines; on my left the sages and doctors, upon as many thrones of silver, were present at all my decisions. Whilst I thus administered justice to innumerable multitude, the birds of the air librating over me served as a canopy from the rays of the sun; my people flourished, and my palace rose to the clouds; I erected a temple to the Most High, which was the wonder of the universe; but I basely suffered myself to be seduced by the love of women, 105 and a curiosity that could not be restrained by sublunary things; I listened to the counsels of Aherman and the daughter of Pharaoh, and adored fire and the hosts of heaven; I forsook the holy city, and commanded the Genii to rear the stupendous palace 110 of Istakhar, and the terrace of the watch-towers, each of which was consecrated to a star; there for a while I enjoyed myself in the zenith of glory and pleasure; not only men, but supernatural existences were subject also to my will. I began to think, as 115 these unhappy monarchs around had already thought, that the vengeance of Heaven was asleep; when at once the thunder burst my structures asunder and precipitated me hither; where, however, I do not remain, like the other inhabitants, totally destitute 120 of hope, for an angel of light hath revealed that, in consideration of the piety of my early youth, my woes shall come to an end when this cataract shall forever cease to flow; till then I am in torments, ineffable torments! an unrelenting fire preys on my 125 heart."

Having uttered this exclamation Soliman raised his hands towards Heaven, in token of supplication, and the Caliph discerned through his bosom, which was transparent as crystal, his heart enveloped in 130 flames. At a sight so full of horror Nouronihar fell back, like one petrified, into the arms of Vathek, who cried out with a convulsive sob:

"O Giaour! whither hast thou brought us? Allow us to depart, and I will relinquish all thou hast 135 promised. O Mahomet! remains there no more mercy?"

"None! none!" replied the malicious Dive. "Know, miserable prince! thou art now in the abode of vengeance and despair; thy heart also will be 140

kindled, like those of the other votaries of Eblis.
A few days are allotted thee previous to this fatal
period; employ them as thou wilt; recline on these
heaps of gold; command the Infernal Potentates;
range at thy pleasure through these immense sub- 145
terranean domains; no barrier shall be shut against
thee; as for me, I have fulfilled my mission; I now
leave thee to thyself." At these words he vanished.
1783   1786

ANONYMOUS

[REVIEW OF THE POETIC EDDA, 1787]

THE poems of the Edda are either genealogic,
dramatic, or historic, and sometimes composed of
all three. To settle a theogony seems to have been
a greater object with the Skalds than even with the
Ionian poets, nor is it a new remark that tenacity   5
of pedigree and dotage on descent are legitimate
children of the north. Such poems, involved in
darkness and turbid with conjecture, can only be
interesting to the antiquarian: but the specimens we
have selected are dramatic and historic, and, though 10
often entangled by hopeless ambiguity, teem with
such primitive simplicity, such grandeur of imagery,
such boldness of manners, such energy of expression, as cannot fail to impress the reader with the
genuine emotions of poetry.   15

[SKIRNER ENCHANTS GERDA]

See'st thou, virgin, this sharp
Clear-sounding blade
That arms my hand?
Under its edge

The hoary giant falls!   20
Death tramples on thy fire!

With this taming wand I charm thee!
With thy wand I tame thee thus,
Virgin, to my will!
Waft thee far,   25
Where human eye
Never see thee more!

With the dawn shalt thou be fixed
In the eagle's nook;
Turned from earth thy eye shall gaze   30
On the gates of hell.
Far more shalt thou loath thy food
Than the race of man
Loaths the scaly worm.

Shuddering in the giant's hall,   35
Anguish shall embrace thee:
Naked, age-bent, shalt thou haunt
The fell prison-house;
Weep and scorn shall mock the tear
On thy channelled cheek.   40

Amid the three-skulled race
Drag thou a weary life!
Drag thou thy hermit-day!
With mind forever torn!
A sapless thorn   45
Stuck in the elder's head!

To the wood I came,
To the greenwood forest:
The wand of charms to win,
The wand of charms I won!   50

Odin hates thee!
Braga hates thee!
Freyr loaths thee!
Yet e'er the wrath of gods
Seize thee   55
Devoted maid.

1787

[THE SOURCE OF GRAY'S "DESCENT OF ODIN"]

WE SHALL conclude our extracts with the *Veg-*
tains Quitha, or as it is called by Mr. Gray, who imitated it in rhyme, the *Descent of Odin:* its own
sublimity and the celebrity of the imitation must
render its communication highly acceptable to every   5
reader of taste, who is thus enabled to compare the
rugged materials of the Skald with the polished
stanzas and arrangements of the poet. . . .

Up rose Odin
The fire of men,   10
O'er Sleipner straight
His saddle threw:
The road he took
Of Niflheim dark,
And met the whelp   15
Of murky Hell.

Gore him distained
Athwart the breast,
Wide flashed his jaw
Rent to devour: 20
Aloud he barked,
Amain he yawned,
And long howled round
The fire of spells.

On rode Odin   25
His thunder-shaken path,
On to the roof
Of Hela high:
What spot, before
The orient-door,   30
He knew full well
Volva was laid.

Turned to the north
The fire of exorcism
Began to tune   35
The song of death:
The eddying wand
The mighty spell,
Unlocked to moans
The hell-bound voice.   40

Dec., 1788

WILLIAM LISLE BOWLES

EVENING

EVENING! as slow thy placid shades descend,
   Veiling with gentlest hush the landscape still,
   The lonely battlement, the farthest hill
And wood, I think of those who have no friend;
Who now, perhaps, by melancholy led,   5
   From the broad blaze of day, where pleasure
      flaunts,
   Retiring, wander to the ringdove's haunts
Unseen; and watch the tints that o'er thy bed
Hang lovely; oft to musing Fancy's eye
   Presenting fairy vales, where the tired mind   10
   Might rest beyond the murmurs of mankind,
Nor hear the hourly moans of misery!

Alas for man! that Hope's fair views the while
Should smile like you, and perish as they smile!

1789

DOVER CLIFFS

ON THESE white cliffs, that calm above the flood
　Uprear their shadowing heads, and at their feet
　Hear not the surge that has for ages beat,
How many a lonely wanderer has stood!
And, whilst the lifted murmur met his ear,　　　5
　And o'er the distant billows the still eve
　Sailed slow, has thought of all his heart must
　　leave
To-morrow; of the friends he loved most dear;
Of social scenes, from which he wept to part!
　Oh! if, like me, he knew how fruitless all　　10
　The thoughts that would full fain the past recall,
Soon would he quell the risings of his heart,
And brave the wild winds and unhearing tide—
The world his country, and his God his guide.

1789

GILBERT WHITE

[THE TORTOISE]

(FROM THE NATURAL HISTORY AND ANTIQUITIES OF SELBORNE)

WHILE I was in Sussex last autumn, my residence
was at the village near Lewes, from whence I had
formerly the pleasure of writing to you. On the
1st of November I remarked that the old tortoise,
formerly mentioned, began first to dig the ground,　5
in order to the forming its hibernaculum, which it

had fixed on just beside a great tuft of hepaticas.
It scrapes out the ground with its fore-feet, and
throws it up over its back with its hind; but the
motion of its legs is ridiculously slow, little exceeding 10
the hour-hand of a clock, and suitable to the composure of an animal said to be a whole month in
performing one feat of copulation. Nothing can be
more assiduous than this creature, night and day,
in scooping the earth and forcing its great body into 15
the cavity; but, as the noons of that season proved
unusually warm and sunny, it was continually interrupted and called forth by the heat in the middle
of the day; and though I continued there till the 13th
of November, yet the work remained unfinished. 20
Harsher weather and frosty mornings would have
quickened its operations.

No part of its behavior ever struck me more than
the extreme timidity it always expresses with regard
to rain; for though it has a shell that would secure 25
it against the wheel of a loaded cart, yet does it
discover as much solicitude about rain as a lady
dressed in all her best attire, shuffling away on the
first sprinklings, and running its head up in a corner.
If attended to, it becomes an excellent weather-glass; 30
for as sure as it walks elate, and, as it were, on
tiptoe, feeding with great earnestness in a morning,
so sure will it rain before night. It is totally a
diurnal animal, and never pretends to stir after it
becomes dark. 35

The tortoise, like other reptiles, has an arbitrary
stomach, as well as lungs; and can refrain from eating as well as breathing for a great part of the year.
When first awakened, it eats nothing; nor again in
the autumn, before it retires: through the height of 40
the summer it feeds voraciously, devouring all the
food that comes in its way. I was much taken with
its sagacity in discerning those that do it kind offices;

for as soon as the good old lady comes in sight who
has waited on it for more than thirty years, it hobbles 45
towards its benefactress with awkward alacrity, but
remains inattentive to strangers. Thus not only "the
ox knoweth his owner, and the ass his master's
crib," but the most abject reptile and torpid of beings distinguishes the hand that feeds it, and is 50
touched with the feelings of gratitude!

In about three days after I left Sussex the tortoise retired into the ground under the hepatica. . . .

When one reflects on the state of this strange
being, it is a matter of wonder to find that Provi- 55
dence should bestow such a profusion of days, such
a seeming waste of longevity, on a reptile that appears to relish it so little as to squander more than
two-thirds of its existence in a joyless stupor, and
be lost to all sensation for months together in the 60
profoundest of slumbers.

1789

ERASMUS DARWIN

FROM THE BOTANIC GARDEN

[PROCUL ESTE, PROFANI]

STAY your rude steps! whose throbbing breasts in-
    fold
The legion-fiends of glory or of gold!
Stay! whose false lips seductive simpers part,
While cunning nestles in the harlot-heart!—
For you no Dryads dress the roseate bower, 5
For you no Nymphs their sparkling vases pour;
Unmarked by you, light Graces swim the green,
And hovering Cupids aim their shafts, unseen.

But thou! whose mind the well-attempered ray
Of taste and virtue lights with purer day;   10
Whose finer sense each soft vibration owns
With sweet responsive sympathy of tones;
(So the fair flower expands its lucid form
To meet the sun, and shuts it to the storm);
For thee my borders nurse the fragrant wreath,   15
My fountains murmur, and my zephyrs breathe;
Slow slides the painted snail, the gilded fly
Smooths his fine down, to charm thy curious eye;
On twinkling fins my pearly nations play,
Or win with sinuous train their trackless way;   20
My plumy pairs, in gay embroidery dressed,
Form with ingenious bill the pensile nest,
To love's sweet notes attune the listening dell,
And Echo sounds her soft symphonious shell.

And if with thee some hapless maid should stray,   25
Disastrous love companion of her way,
Oh, lead her timid steps to yonder glade,
Whose arching cliffs depending alders shade;
There, as meek evening wakes her temperate breeze,
And moonbeams glimmer through the trembling
          trees,   30
The rills that gurgle round shall soothe her ear,
The weeping rocks shall number tear for tear;
There as sad Philomel, alike forlorn,
Sings to the night from her accustomed thorn;
While at sweet intervals each falling note   35
Sighs in the gale, and whispers round the grot;
The sister-woe shall calm her aching breast,
And softer slumbers steal her cares to rest.

[THE SENSITIVE PLANT]

WEAK with nice sense, the chaste Mimosa stands,
From each rude touch withdraws her timid hands;   40

Oft as light clouds o'erpass the summer-glade,
Alarmed she trembles at the moving shade;
And feels, alive through all her tender form,
The whispered murmurs of the gathering storm;
Shuts her sweet eyelids to approaching night,   45
And hails with freshened charms the rising light.
Veiled, with gay decency and modest pride,
Slow to the mosque she moves, an eastern bride,
There her soft vows unceasing love record,
Queen of the bright seraglio of her lord.   50

                                                1789-1792

JOSEPH STERLING

SCALDER: AN ODE

I

ILLUSTRIOUS chiefs whose deathless fame
    The Scalder's song shall blazon wide,
In any prospect see! they stream,
    Kings and heroes swell the tide:
A shining train (their tribute to receive)   5
From bright Valhalla pours (the mansion of the
        brave)
    In long array the godlike forms appear,
(Their harness brightening in the western beam)
    They shake the glittering sword and pointed spear,
Their polished helms with dreadful splendor gleam; 10
On airy steeds the warriors rush along,
Swift as the lightnings flash, as wintry tempests
        strong.

II

Now the rage of combat burns;
Haughty chiefs on chiefs lie slain.

The battle glows and sinks by turns, 15
Death and carnage load the plain.
Pale fear, grim horror stalk around,
The blood of heroes dyes the verdant ground.
  But at the brazen trumpet's shrilling call
Quick into life the eager champions spring; 20
  With headlong speed they crowd the bannered hall
Where sits enthroned in gold the sceptered king,
Immortal Odin, sovereign of the gods,
Who rays with glory's beams Valhalla's bright
    abodes.

1789

(FROM THE TWILIGHT OF THE GODS)

THE dusky moon is streaked with blood,
The demons of the tempest roar,
  A deluge swells the mountain flood,
The clouds descend in streams of gore:
From the dark mansions of the north 5
Now the great winter rushes headlong forth.
  His sacred beam the golden sun shall hide,
Nor spring nor summer shall enrich the plain;
  No vales shall flourish in autumnal pride
But winter drear shall hold unceasing reign 10
Till the great dragon, terrible and strong,
Unwinds his sweepy folds and shoots the seas along.

1789

RICHARD HOLE

FROM ARTHUR, OR THE NORTHERN ENCHANTMENT

[DESCRIPTION OF VALHALLA]

AWAKE, arise, and in your might confide!
Rush on, and let destruction be your guide!

Think on your fathers' fame, your own renown,
My favor, who with joys perpetual crown
The chiefs who boldly in the combat fall   5
And guide their spirits to my lofty hall,
O'er-arched with golden shields, whose dazzling
    blaze
Exceeds the mid-day sun's unclouded rays.
There shall each hero share, a welcome guest,
The foaming goblet and perpetual feast.   10
Again their souls with martial fire shall burn,
And host conflicting adverse host o'erturn.
While bright Valkeries, blue-eyed nymphs, shall
    crown
With plausive smiles their actions of renown.
Be conquest yours and fame's unfading wreath,   15
Or, more than victory, a glorious death!

                                        1789

[HENGIST'S CURSE OF THE PARCAE]

THE combat's o'er—the shrieks of death resound;
The tempest rolls away, and on the ground
Brave Valdemar lies breathless; by his side
Stern Hengist sinking, thus in fury cried:
"Such agonizing pangs as these I feel,   5
Keen as the searchings of this deadly steel,
Ye hags of darkness, be it yours to know
In Nifleim's gloomy depth, the abode of woe!—
Ha! it is thou, whose erring hand destroys
My life and blasts my hope of promised joys?"   10
(For now the moon her splendid course resumed,
And her bright train the ethereal arch illumed)
"But 'tis enough! thy death's thy folly's meed:
Not meanly foiled, nor unrevenged, I bleed.
High be my seat in Odin's lofty hall!   15
No warrior lives to boast of Hengist's fall."

On Valdemar's deep wounds he bends his eyes
With joy malignant—grimly smiles and dies.

1789

(FROM THE TOMB OF GUNNAR)

"WHAT mean those awful sounds that rise
From the tomb where Gunnar lies?"
Exclaims the shepherd in affright,
As by the moon's uncertain light
Athwart the solitary plain,   5
He homeward drives his fleecy train.

Sarpedine, Hogner, mark the tale;
Then fearless cross the dreary vale
And stand the stately tomb beside,
While darkly-rolling vapors hide   10
In their dun veil night's glittering pride.

A moonbeam on the cave of death
Sudden glanced athwart the heath.
Its line of splendor, full opposed,
The deep recess to view disclosed.   15

Fronting the beam, in arms arrayed
Majestic sat the hero's shade.
The cell four blazing tapers crowned
And poured a flood of light around.

With conscious joy his visage glows,   20
And smiles invest his awful brows.
He wakes the loud-resounding song
And echoing rocks the strain prolong.

1789

FRAGMENT

"SEE, brother, see, athwart the strand,
Twelve youths advance, a hostile band.
Ere evening spreads her vapors gray
Must we the voice of Fate obey.

For us prepared is Odin's hall,   5
But they shall live and boast our fall!"
   "Mistaken youth!" Hialmur cries,
"Ere eve's gray shadows dim the skies,
Pierced with many a grievous wound
Shall yonder warriors press the ground.   10
Inmates they of Odin's hall,
But we shall live and boast their fall."

                                                           1789

FRANK SAYERS

[FREA'S PLEA TO HELA]

   DEEP in thy misty caverns Balder lies,
Alas! how withered by the touch of woe!
   Dim is the lustre of his fading eyes
And sullen sadness dwells upon his brow.

   Quick through his frame divine chill languors
         shoot,   5
The boasted roses of his cheek are pale,
   The soothing tongue of eloquence is mute;
O let his tears, his ceaseless groans avail!

   Come, gentle pity, come, unwonted guest,
And speed thy hasty flight to Hela's cave;   10
   Soul-softening spirit, hover o'er her breast
And teach her yielding heart to feel and save.

   And canst thou, Hela, see with ruthless look
The fairest form that wails along thy shore?—
   Tear the black leaf from Fate's unerring book,   15
The grief-worn Balder to my arms restore.

                                                           1790

[THE DYING RHAPSODY OF OSWALD]

YES, friendly steel, thy searching point is moist
With Oswald's blood.
              [After a pause.
            —What glorious visions rise!
I see the festive gods at Odin's board!
I hear the splendid warrior's gladsome din.   5
Yon golden seat is vacant—'tis for me—
I come, I come, the gloom of death has wrapt
My eyes in mist.—Hark, hark!—the notes of joy
Die on my ear—and now a louder peal
Bursts on my fluttering soul—   10
              [He dies.

1790

WILLIAM GILPIN

[PICTURESQUE BEAUTY]

ALL forms that are unnatural, displease. A tree
lopped into a maypole, as you generally see in the
hedge-rows of Surry and some other countries, is
disgusting. Clipped yews, lime hedges, and pol-
lards are, for the same reason disagreeable; and yet 5
I have sometimes seen a pollard produce a good
effect, when nature has been suffered for some years,
to bring it again into form: but I never saw a good
effect produced by a pollard on which some single
item was left to grow into a tree. The item is of a 10
different growth; it is disproportioned; and always
unites awkwardly with the trunk.

Not only all forms that are unnatural, displease;
but even natural forms when they bear a resemblance
to art, unless indeed these forms are characteristic of 15

the species. A cypress pleases in a conic form; but an oak or an elm trimmed into that appearance, would disgust. In the cypress, nature adapts the spray and branches to the form of the tree. In the oak and elm, the spray and branches form a dif-   20
ferent character.

Lightness also is a characteristic of beauty in a tree; for though there are beautiful trees of a heavy as well as of a light form, yet their extremities must in some parts be separated, and hang with a degree   25
of looseness from the fulness of the foliage, which occupies the middle of the tree, or the whole will only be a large bush. From position, indeed, and contrast, heaviness, though in itself a deformity, may be of singular use in the composition both of natural   30
and of artificial landscape.

A tree also must be *well-balanced* to be beautiful. It may have form and it may have lightness; and yet lose all its effect, by wanting a proper poise. The bole must appear to support the branches. We do   35
not desire to see it supporting its burden with the perpendicular firmness of a column. An easy sweep is always agreeable; but at the same time it should not be such a sweep as discovers one side plainly overbalanced.   40

On bleak sea-coasts, trees generally take an un-balanced form; and indeed in general, some foreign cause must operate to occasion it; for nature work-ing freely, is as much inclined to balance a tree upon its trunk, as an animal upon its legs.   45

And yet in some circumstances, I have seen beauty arise even from an unbalanced tree; but it must arise from some peculiar situation, which gives it a local propriety. A tree, for instance, hanging from a rock, though totally unpoised, may be beautiful; or   50
it may have a good effect, when we see it bending over a road; because it corresponds with its peculiar

situation. We do not, in these cases, admire it as a tree, but as the adjunct of an effect; the beauty of which does not give the eye leisure to attend to the 55 deformity of the instrument, through which the effect is produced.

Without these requisites, therefore, *form, lightness,* and *a proper balance,* no tree can have that *species of beauty,* which we call *picturesque.* 60

1791

JAMES BRUCE

FROM TRAVELS TO DISCOVER THE SOURCE OF THE NILE

[THE DISCOVERY OF THE SOURCE OF THE NILE]

"Come, come," said I, "we understand each other; no more words; it is now late, lose no more time, but carry me to Geesh and the head of the Nile directly, without preamble, and show me the hill that separates me from it." 5

He then carried me round to the south side of the church out of the grove of trees that surrounded it. "This is the hill," says he, looking archly, "that, when you was on the other side of it, was between you and the fountains of the Nile; there is no 10 other. Look at that hillock of green sod in the middle of that watery spot—it is in that the two fountains of the Nile are to be found: Geesh is on the face of the rock where yon green trees are. If you go the length of the fountains pull off your shoes 15 as you did the other day, for these people are all Pagans, worse than those that were at the ford, and they believe in nothing that you believe, but only in this river, to which they pray every day as if it were God; but this perhaps you may do likewise." 20

Half undressed as I was by loss of my sash, and throwing my shoes off, I ran down the hill towards the little island of green sods which was about two hundred yards distant; the whole side of the hill was thick grown over with flowers, the large bulbous 25 roots of which appearing above the surface of the ground, and their skins coming off on treading upon them, occasioned two very severe falls before I reached the brink of the marsh; I after this came to the island of green turf, which was in form of an 30 altar, apparently the work of art, and I stood in rapture over the principal fountain which rises in the middle of it.

It is easier to guess than to describe the situation of my mind at that moment—standing in that spot 35 which had baffled the genius, industry, and inquiry of both ancients and moderns for the course of near three thousand years. Kings had attempted this discovery at the head of armies, and each expedition was distinguished from the last only by the difference 40 of the numbers which had perished, and agreed alone in the disappointment which had uniformly, and without exception, followed them all. Fame, riches, and honor had been held out for a series of ages to every individual of those myriads these princes com- 45 manded, without having produced one man capable of gratifying the curiosity of his sovereign, or wiping off this stain upon the enterprise and abilities of mankind, or adding this desideratum for the encouragement of geography. Though a mere private 50 Briton I triumphed here, in my own mind, over kings and their armies; and every comparison was leading nearer and nearer to presumption when the place itself where I stood, the object of my vain-glory, suggested what depressed my short-lived triumphs. 55

I was but a few minutes arrived at the sources of
the Nile through numberless dangers and sufferings,
the least of which would have overwhelmed me but
for the continual goodness and protection of Providence; I was, however, but then half through my   60
journey and all those dangers which I had already
passed awaited me again on my return. I found a
despondency gaining ground fast upon me, and blast-
ing the crown of laurels I had too rashly woven for
myself.   65

1790

[KIRCHER'S ACCOUNT OF PAEZ'S DE-
SCRIPTION OF THE SOURCE]

ON THE twenty-first of April, in the year 1618,
being here together with the king and his army, I
ascended the place and observed everything with
great attention. I discovered first two round fountains, each about four palms in diameter, and saw   5
with the greatest delight what neither Cyrus, king
of the Persians, nor Cambyses, nor Alexander the
Great, nor the famous Julius Caesar could ever discover. The two openings of these fountains have no
issue in the plain on the top of the mountain but   10
flow from the root of it. The second fountain lies
about a stone-cast west from the first. The inhabitants say that this whole mountain is full of water
and add that the whole plain about the fountain is
floating and unsteady, a certain mark that there is   15
water concealed under it; for which reason the water
does not overflow at the fountain, but forces itself
with great violence out at the foot of the mountain.
The inhabitants, together with the emperor, who was
then present with his army, maintain that that year   20
it trembled little on account of the drought, but other
years, that it trembled and overflowed so as that it

could scarce be approached without danger. The
breadth of the circumference may be about the cast
of a sling. Below the top of this mountain the people 25
live about a league distant from the fountain to the
west; and this place is called Geesh, and the fountain
seems to be a cannon-shot distant from Geesh; more-
over, the field where the fountain is, is upon all sides
difficult of access, except on the north side, where it 30
may be ascended with ease.

                                                    1790

[A ROYAL SAVAGE]

As FOR me, the king's behavior showed me plainly
all was not right, and an accident in the way con-
firmed it. He had desired me to ride before him and
show him the horse I had got from Fasil, which was
then in great beauty and order, and which I had 5
kept purposely for him. It happened that, crossing
the deep bed of a brook, a plant of the kantuffa hung
across it. I had upon my shoulders a white goat
skin, of which it did not take hold; but the king, who
was dressed in the habit of peace, his long hair float- 10
ing all around his face, wrapped up in his mantle or
thin cotton cloak so that nothing but his eyes could
be seen, was paying more attention to the horse
than to the branch of kantuffa beside him; it took
first hold of his hair and the fold of the cloak that 15
covered his head, then spread itself over his whole
shoulder in such a manner that, notwithstanding all
the help that could be given him and that I had, at
first seeing it, cut the principal bough asunder with
my knife, no remedy remained but he must throw 20
off the upper garment and appear in the under one
or waistcoat, with his head and face bare before all
the spectators.

This is accounted great disgrace to a king, who

always appears covered in public. However, he did 25
not seem to be ruffled, nor was there anything particular in his countenance more than before, but with
great composure and in rather a low voice, he called
twice, "Who is the Shum of this district?" Un-
happily he was not far off. A thin old man of sixty 30
and his son about thirty came trotting, as their custom is naked to their girdle, and stood before the
king, who was, by this time, quite clothed again.
What had struck the old man's fancy, I know not,
but he passed my horse laughing and seemingly won- 35
derfully content with himself. I could not help considering him as a type of mankind in general, never
more confident and careless than when on the brink
of destruction. The king asked if he was Shum of
that place. He answered in the affirmative and added, 40
which was not asked of him, that the other was his
son.

There is always near the king, when he marches,
an officer called Kanitz Kitzera, the executioner of
the camp; he has upon the tore of his saddle a quan- 45
tity of thongs made of bull hide, rolled up very arti-
ficially. This is called the tarade. The king made
a sign with his head and another with his hand without speaking, and two loops of the tarade were instantly thrown round the Shum and his son's neck, 50
and they were both hoisted upon the same tree, the
tarade cut, and the end made fast to a branch. They
were both left hanging, but I thought so awkwardly
that they should not die for some minutes and might
surely have been saved had anyone dared to cut 55
them down; but fear had fallen upon every person
who had not attended the king to Tigré.

This cruel beginning seemed to me an omen that
violent resolutions had been taken, the execution of
which was immediately to follow; for though the 60
king had certainly a delight in the shedding of human

blood in the field, yet till that time I never saw him
order an execution by the hands of the hangman;
on the contrary, I have often seen him shudder and
express disgust, lowly and in half words, at such 65
executions ordered every day by Ras Michael. In
this instance he seemed to have lost that feeling;
and rode on, sometimes conversing about Fasil's
horse or other indifferent subjects to those who
were around him without once reflecting upon the 70
horrid execution he had then so recently occasioned.

1790

WILLIAM BARTRAM

[INCIDENTS AND SCENES IN FLORIDA]

THE evening was temperately cool and calm. The
crocodiles began to roar and appear in uncommon
numbers along the shores and in the river. I fixed
my camp in an open plain, near the utmost projection
of the promontory, under the shelter of a large live 5
oak which stood on the highest part of the ground,
and but a few yards from my boat. From this open
high situation I had a free prospect of the river,
which was a matter of no trivial consideration to
me, having good reason to dread the subtle attacks 10
of the alligators who were crowding about my harbor. Having collected a good quantity of wood for
the purpose of keeping up a light and smoke during
the night, I began to think of preparing my supper,
when, upon examining my stores, I found but a 15
scanty provision. I thereupon determined, as the
most expeditious way of supplying my necessities,
to take my bob and try for some trout. About one
hundred yards above my harbor began a cove or bay
of the river, out of which opened a large lagoon. The 20

mouth or entrance from the river to it was narrow, but the waters soon after spread and formed a little lake extending into the marshes: its entrance and shores within I observed to be verged with floating lawns of the pistia and nymphea and other aquatic 25 plants; these I knew were excellent haunts for trout.

The verges and islets of the lagoon were elegantly embellished with flowering plants and shrubs; the laughing coots with wings half spread were tripping over the little coves and hiding themselves in the 30 tufts of grass; young broods of the painted summer teal, skimming the still surface of the waters and following the watchful parent unconscious of danger, were frequently surprised by the voracious trout; and he, in turn, as often by the subtle greedy alliga- 35 tor. Behold him rushing forth from the flags and reeds. His enormous body swells. His plaited tail, brandished high, floats upon the lake. The waters like a cataract descend from his opening jaws. Clouds of smoke issue from his dilated nostrils. The 40 earth trembles with his thunder. When immediately from the opposite coast of the lagoon, emerges from the deep his rival champion. They suddenly dart upon each other. The boiling surface of the lake marks their rapid course, and a terrific combat com- 45 mences. They now sink to the bottom folded together in horrid wreaths. The water becomes thick and discolored. Again they rise, their jaws clap together, re-echoing through the deep surrounding forests. Again they sink, when the contest ends at 50 the muddy bottom of the lake, and the vanquished makes a hazardous escape, hiding himself in the muddy turbulent waters and sedge on a distant shore. The proud victor exulting returns to the place of action. The shores and forests resound his 55 dreadful roar, together with the triumphing shouts of the plaited tribes around, witnesses of the horrid combat.

.   .   .   .

About noon the weather became extremely sultry, not a breath of wind stirring, hazy or cloudy, with 60 very heavy distant thunder which was answered by the crocodiles, sure presage of a storm!

Soon after ascending this branch of the river, on the right hand presents itself to view a delightful little bluff, consisting chiefly of shells, and covered 65 with a dark grove of red cedar, zanthoxylon, and myrtle. I could not resist the temptation to stop here, although the tremendous thunder all around the hemisphere alarmed me greatly, having a large lake to cross. From this grove appears to view an 70 expansive and pleasing prospect. The beauteous long lake in front, about northeast from me, its most distant east shores adorned with dark high forests of stately trees; north and south almost endless green plains and meadows, embellished with 75 islets and projecting promontories of high dark forests where the pyramidal magnolia grandiflora, palma elata, and shady oak conspicuously tower.

Being heretofore so closely invested by high forests and deep swamps of the great river, I was pre- 80 vented from seeing the progress and increase of the approaching tempest, the terrific appearance of which now at once confounded me. How purple and fiery appeared the tumultuous clouds swiftly ascending or darting from the horizon upwards! they seemed 85 to oppose and dash against each other; the skies appeared streaked with blood or purple flame overhead, the flaming lightning streaming and darting about in every direction around seemed to fill the

world with fire; whilst the heavy thunder kept the 90
earth in a constant tremor.

.   .   .   .

What a beautiful display of vegetation is here
before me! seemingly unlimited in extent and variety: how the dew-drops twinkle and play upon
the sight, trembling on the tips of the lucid, green 95
savanna, sparkling as the gem that flames on the
turban of the eastern prince. . . .

I was, however, induced to deviate a little from
my intended course, and touch at the enchanting
little Isle of Palms. This delightful spot, planted 100
by nature, is almost an entire grove of palms with a
few pyramidal magnolias, live oaks, golden orange,
and the animating zanthoxylon. What a beautiful
retreat is here! blessed unviolated spot of earth, rising from the limpid waters of the lake; its fragrant 105
groves and blooming lawns invested and protected
by encircling ranks of the yucca gloriosa. A fascinating atmosphere surrounds this blissful garden;
the balmy lantana, ambrosial citra, perfumed crinum,
perspiring their mingled odors, wafted through zan- 110
thoxylon groves. I at last broke away from the enchanting spot and stepped on board my boat, hoisted
sail, and soon approached the coast of the main at
the cool eve of day: then traversing a capacious semi-
circular cove of the lake, verged by low extensive 115
grassy meadows, I at length by dusk made a safe
harbor in a little lagoon on the sea shore or strand
of a bold sandy point which descended from the surf
of the lake.

.   .   .   .

I seated myself upon a swelling green knoll at 120
the head of the crystal basin. Near me on the left

was a point or projection of an entire grove of the
aromatic *illicium floridanum;* on my right and all
around behind me was a fruitful orange grove, with
palms and magnolias interspersed; in front, just 125
under my feet, was the enchanting and amazing
crystal fountain which incessantly threw up from
dark rocky caverns below, tons of water every minute, forming a basin, capacious enough for large
shallops to ride in, and a creek of four or five feet 130
depth of water and near twenty yards over, which
meanders six miles through green meadows, pouring
its limpid waters into the great Lake George where
they seem to remain pure and unmixed. About
twenty yards from the upper edge of the basin and 135
directly opposite to the mouth or outlet of the creek,
is a continual and amazing ebullition where the
waters are thrown up in such abundance and amazing
force, as to jet and swell up two or three feet above
the common surface: white sand and small particles 140
of shells are thrown up with the waters near to the
top, when they diverge from the center, subside with
the expanding flood, and gently sink again, forming
a large rim or funnel round about the aperture or
mouth of the fountain which is a vast perforation 145
through a bed of rocks, the ragged points of which
are projected out on every side.

.   .   .   .

The ebullition is astonishing and continual, though
its greatest force of fury intermits, regularly, for the
space of thirty seconds of time: the waters appear 150
of a lucid sea green color, in some measure owing to
the reflection of the leaves above: the ebullition is
perpendicular upwards, from a vast ragged orifice
through a bed of rocks, a great depth below the
common surface of the basin, throwing up small par- 155

ticles or pieces of white shells, which subside with the waters at the moment of intermission, gently settling down round about the orifice, forming a vast funnel. At those moments when the waters rush upwards, the surface of the basin immediately over 160 the orifice is greatly swollen or raised a considerable height; and then it is impossible to keep the boat or any other floating vessel over the fountain; but the ebullition quickly subsides; yet, before the surface becomes quite even, the fountain vomits up the 165 waters again, and so on perpetually. The basin is generally circular, about fifty yards over; and the perpetual stream from it into the river is twelve or fifteen yards wide, and ten or twelve feet in depth; the basin and stream continually peopled with prodi- 170 gious numbers and variety of fish and other animals; as the alligator, and the manate or sea cow, in the winter season.

.   .   .   .

This trader being near the place (before it had any visible existence in its present appearance), 175 about three years ago, as he was looking for some horses which he expected to find in these parts, on a sudden was astonished by an inexpressible rushing noise like a mighty hurricane or thunder storm; and looking around, he saw the earth overflowed 180 by torrents of water which came, wave after wave, rushing down a vale or plain very near him, which it filled with water, and soon began to overwhelm the higher grounds, attended with a terrific noise and tremor of the earth. Recovering from his first 185 surprise, he immediately resolved to proceed for the place from whence the noise seemed to come; and soon came in sight of the incomparable fountain, and saw, with amazement, the floods rushing upwards many feet high, and the expanding waters, 190 which prevailed every way, spreading themselves far and near. He at length concluded (he said) that the fountains of the deep were again broken up and that an universal deluge had commenced; and instantly turned about and fled to alarm the town about nine 195 miles distance: but before he could reach it, he met several of the inhabitants, who, already alarmed by the unusual noise, were hurrying on towards the place; upon which he returned with the Indians, taking their stand on an eminence to watch its progress 200 and the event. It continued to jet and flow in this manner for several days forming a large rapid creek or river, descending and following the various courses and windings of the valley for the distance of seven or eight miles, emptying into a vast savanna 205 where was a lake and sink which received and gave vent to its waters.

The fountain, however, gradually ceased to overflow and finally withdrew itself beneath the common surface of the earth, leaving this capacious basin of 210 waters, which, though continually near full, hath never since overflowed. There yet remains, and will I suppose remain for ages, the dry bed of the river or canal, generally four, five, and six feet below the natural surface of the land; the perpendicular rag- 215 ged banks of which, on each side, show the different strata of the earth; and at places where ridges or a swelling bank crossed and opposed its course and fury, are vast heaps of fragments of rocks, white chalk, stones, and pebbles, which were collected and 220 thrown into the lateral valleys.

1792

MARY WOLLSTONECRAFT

FROM THE RIGHTS OF WOMAN

IT IS vain to expect virtue from women till they
are, in some degree, independent of men; nay, it is
vain to expect that strength of natural affection
which would make them good wives and mothers.
Whilst they are absolutely dependent on their hus-   5
bands they will be cunning, mean, and selfish; and
the men who can be gratified by the fawning fondness of spaniel-like affection have not much delicacy,
for love is not to be bought, in any sense of the
words, its silken wings are instantly shrivelled up   10
when any thing beside a return in kind is sought.
Yet whilst wealth enervates men, and women live,
as it were, by their personal charms, how can we
expect them to discharge those ennobling duties
which equally require exertion and self-denial.   15

.   .   .   .

The private or public virtue of woman is very
problematical; for Rousseau and a numerous list of
male writers insist that she should all her life be
subjected to a severe restraint, that of propriety.
Why subject her to propriety—blind propriety—if   20
she be capable of acting from a nobler spring, if she
be an heir of immortality? Is sugar always to be
produced by vital blood? Is one half of the human
species, like the poor African slaves, to be subject to
prejudices that brutalize them, when principles would   25
be a surer guard, only to sweeten the cup of man?
Is not this indirectly to deny woman reason? for a
gift is a mockery if it be unfit for use.

.   .   .   .

To render her really virtuous and useful, she must not, if she discharge her civil duties, want, individually, the protection of civil laws; she must not be dependent on her husband's bounty for her subsistence during his life or support after his death—for how can a being be generous who has nothing of its own? or virtuous who is not free? The wife, in the present state of things, who is faithful to her husband and neither suckles nor educates her children, scarcely deserves the name of a wife and has no right to that of a citizen. But take away natural rights and duties become null.

Women, then, must be considered as only the wanton solace of men when they become so weak in mind and body that they cannot exert themselves unless to pursue some frothy pleasure or to invent some frivolous fashion. What can be a more melancholy sight to a thinking mind than to look into the numerous carriages that drive helter-skelter about this metropolis in a morning, full of pale-faced creatures who are flying from themselves! I have often wished, with Dr. Johnson, to place some of them in a little shop with half a dozen children looking up to their languid countenances for support. I am much mistaken, if some latent vigor would not soon give health and spirit to their eyes, and some lines drawn by the exercise of reason on the blank cheeks, which before were only undulated by dimples, might restore lost dignity to the character, or rather enable it to attain the true dignity of its nature. Virtue is not to be acquired even by speculation, much less by the negative supineness that wealth naturally generates.

Besides, when poverty is more disgraceful than even vice, is not morality cut to the quick? Still to avoid misconstruction, though I consider that women in the common walks of life are called to

fulfill the duties of wives and mothers by religion
and reason, I cannot help lamenting that women of
a superior cast have not a road open by which they
can pursue more extensive plans of usefulness and
independence. I may excite laughter by dropping   70
a hint which I mean to pursue some future time,
for I really think that women ought to have rep-
resentatives, instead of being arbitrarily governed
without having any direct share allowed them in
the deliberations of government.   75

.   .   .   .

It is a melancholy truth; yet such is the blessed
effect of civilization! The most respectable women
are the most oppressed; and, unless they have understandings far superior to the common run of understandings, taking in both sexes, they must, from   80
being treated like contemptible beings, become contemptible. How many women thus waste life away,
the prey of discontent, who might have practised as
physicians, regulated a farm, managed a shop, and
stood erect supported by their own industry, instead   85
of hanging their heads surcharged with the dew of
sensibility that consumes the beauty to which it at
first gave lustre; nay, I doubt whether pity and love
are so near akin as poets feign, for I have seldom
seen much compassion excited by the helplessness   90
of females unless they were fair; then, perhaps, pity
was the soft handmaid of love, or the harbinger
of lust.

How much more respectable is the woman who
earns her own bread, by fulfilling any duty, than the   95
most accomplished beauty!—beauty did I say?—so
sensible am I of the beauty of moral loveliness or
the harmonious propriety that attunes the passions

of a well-regulated mind, that I blush at making
the comparison; yet I sigh to think how few women 100
aim at attaining this respectability by withdrawing
from the giddy whirl of pleasure or the indolent
calm that stupefies the good sort of women it sucks
in.

1792

WILLIAM GODWIN

FROM POLITICAL JUSTICE

[THE SUPERIORITY OF REASONING OVER PUNISHMENT]

PUNISHMENT is not the appropriate mode of cor-
recting the errors of mankind. It will probably be
admitted that the only true end of punishment is cor-
rection. That question will be discussed in another
part of the present inquiry. "I have done something 5
which, though wrong in itself, I believe to be right;
or I have done something which I usually admit to
be wrong, but my conviction upon the subject is not
so clear and forcible as to prevent my yielding to a
powerful temptation." There can be no doubt, that 10
the proper way of conveying to my understanding a
truth of which I am ignorant, or of impressing upon
me a firmer persuasion of a truth with which I am
acquainted, is by an appeal to my reason. Even an
angry expostulation with me upon my conduct will 15
but excite similar passions in me and cloud instead
of illuminate my understanding. There is certainly
a way of expressing truth with such benevolence
as to command attention and such evidence as to
enforce conviction in all cases whatever. 20

Punishment inevitably excites in the sufferer, and ought to excite, a sense of injustice. Let its purpose be to convince me of the truth of a proposition which I at present believe to be false. It is not abstractedly considered of the nature of an argument, and therefore it cannot begin with producing conviction. Punishment is a specious name, but is in reality nothing more than force put upon one being by another who happens to be stronger. Now strength apparently does not constitute justice, nor ought "might," according to a trite proverb, to "overcome right." The case of punishment, which we are now considering, is the case of you and I differing in opinion, and your telling me that you must be right, since you have a more brawny arm, or have applied your mind more to the acquiring skill in your weapons than I have.

But let us suppose "that I am convinced of my error, but that my conviction is superficial and fluctuating, and the object you propose is to render it durable and profound." Ought it to be thus durable and profound? There are no doubt arguments and reasons calculated to render it so. Is it in reality problematical, and do you wish by the weight of your blows to make up for the deficiency of your logic? This can never be defended. An appeal to force must appear to both parties, in proportion to the soundness of their understanding, to be a confession of imbecility. He that has recourse to it, would have no occasion for this expedient, if he were sufficiently acquainted with the powers of that truth it is his office to communicate. If there be any man, who, in suffering punishment, is not conscious of injustice, he must have had his mind previously debased to slavery and his sense of moral right and wrong blunted by a series of oppression.

[REASON THE ONLY SANCTION OF LAW AND GOVERNMENT]

LEGISLATION, as it has been usually understood, is not an affair of human competence. Reason is the only legislator, and her decrees are irrevocable and uniform. The functions of society extend, not to the making, but the interpreting of law; it cannot decree, it can only declare that which the nature of things has already decreed, and the propriety of which irresistibly flows from the circumstances of the case. Montesquieu says that "in a free state every man will be his own legislator." This is not true, setting apart the functions of the community, unless in the limited sense already explained. It is the office of conscience to determine, "not like an Asiatic cadi, according to the ebbs and flows of his own passions, but like a British judge, who makes no new law but faithfully declares that law which he finds already written."

The same distinction is to be made upon the subject of authority. All political power is strictly speaking executive. It has appeared to be necessary, with respect to men as we at present find them, that force should sometimes be employed in repressing injustice; and for the same reasons it appears that this force should as far as possible be vested in the community. To the public support of justice, therefore, the authority of the community extends. But no sooner does it wander in the smallest degree from the great line of justice than its authority is at an end, it stands upon a level with the obscurest individual, and every man is bound to resist its decisions.

.   .   .   .

No truth can be more simple, at the same time
that no truth has been more darkened by the glosses
of interested individuals, than that one man can in no
case be bound to yield obedience to any other man   35
or set of men upon earth.

There is one rule to which we are universally
bound to conform ourselves: justice, the treating
every man precisely as his usefulness and worth
demand, the acting under every circumstance in the   40
manner that shall procure the greatest quantity of
general good. When we have done thus, what province is there left to the disposal of obedience?

.   .   .   .

[THE INDIVIDUAL REASON TO BE SUPREME]

DEPRAVITY would have gained little ground in the
world if every man had been in the exercise of his
independent judgment. The instrument by which
extensive mischiefs have in all ages been perpetrated
has been the principle of many men being reduced   5
to mere machines in the hands of the few. Man
while he consults his own understanding is the ornament of the universe. Man when he surrenders
his reason and becomes the partisan of implicit faith
and passing obedience, is the most mischievous of   10
all animals. Ceasing to examine every proposition
that comes before him for the direction of his conduct, he is no longer the capable subject of moral
instruction. He is, in the instant of submission,
the blind instrument of every nefarious purpose of   15
his principal; and, when left to himself, is open to
the seduction of injustice, cruelty, and profligacy.

These reasonings lead to a proper explanation of
the word subject. If by the subject of any govern-

ment we mean a person whose duty it is to obey, 20
the true inference from the preceding principles is,
that no government has any subjects. If, on the
contrary, we mean a person whom the government
is bound to protect or may justly restrain, the word
is sufficiently admissible.   25

[VIRTUE TO FLOURISH IN FREEDOM]

ALL moral science may be reduced to this one
head, calculation of the future. We cannot reason-
ably expect virtue from the multitude of mankind if
they be induced by the perverseness of the con-
ductors of human affairs to believe that it is not their 5
interest to be virtuous. But this is not the point
upon which the question turns. Virtue is nothing
else but the pursuit of general good. Justice is the
standard which discriminates the advantage of the
many and of the few, of the whole and a part. If   10
this first and most important of all subjects be
involved in obscurity, how shall the well being of
mankind be substantially promoted? The most
benevolent of our species will be engaged in crusades
of error; while the cooler and more phlegmatic   15
spectators, discerning no evident clue that should
guide them amidst the labyrinth, sit down in selfish
neutrality and leave the complicated scene to produce
its own dénouement.

. . . .

Of all the principles of justice there is none so   20
material to the moral rectitude of mankind as this—
that no man can be distinguished but by his personal
merit. Why not endeavor to reduce to practice so
simple and sublime a lesson? When a man has
proved himself a benefactor to the public, when he   25

has already by laudable perseverance cultivated in
himself talents which need only encouragement and
public favor to bring them to maturity, let that man
be honored. In a state of society where fictitious
distinctions are unknown, it is impossible he should 30
not be honored. But that a man should be looked
up to with servility and awe because the king has
bestowed on him a spurious name or decorated him
with a ribband; that another should wallow in luxury because his ancestor three centuries ago bled in 35
the quarrel of Lancaster or York; do we imagine
that these iniquities can be practised without injury?

.   .   .   .

Let us for a moment give the reins to reflection
and endeavor accurately to conceive the state of mankind where justice should form the public and gen- 40
eral principle. In that case our moral feelings would
assume a firm and wholesome tone, for they would
not be perpetually counteracted by examples that
weakened their energy and confounded their clear-
ness. Men would be fearless, because they would 45
know that there were no legal snares lying in wait
for their lives. They would be courageous, because
no man would be pressed to the earth that another
might enjoy immoderate luxury, because every one
would be secure of the just reward of his industry 50
and prize of his exertions. Jealousy and hatred
would cease, for they are the offspring of injustice.
Every man would speak truth with his neighbor, for
there would be no temptation to falsehood and deceit. Mind would find its level, for there would be 55
every thing to encourage and to animate. Science
would be unspeakably improved, for understanding
would convert into a real power, no longer an *ignis
fatuus,* shining and expiring by turns, and leading us

into sloughs of sophistry, false science, and specious 60
mistake. All men would be disposed to avow their
dispositions and actions: none would endeavor to
suppress the just eulogium of his neighbor, for, so
long as there were tongues to record, the suppres-
sion would be possible; none would fear to detect the 65
misconduct of his neighbor, for there would be no
laws converting the sincere expression of our con-
victions into a libel.

[THE EVIL OF MARRIAGE]

ALL attachments to individuals, except in proportion to their merits, are plainly unjust. It is, therefore, desirable that we should be the friends of man
rather than of particular men and that we should
pursue the chain of our own reflections with no other 5
interruption than information or philanthropy requires.

This subject of cohabitation is particularly interesting as it includes in it the subject of marriage. It
will, therefore, be proper to extend our inquiries 10
somewhat further upon this head. Cohabitation is
not only an evil as it checks the independent progress
of mind—it is also inconsistent with the imperfec-
tions and propensities of man. It is absurd to expect
that the inclinations and wishes of two human beings 15
should coincide through any long period of time.
To oblige them to act and to live together is to subject them to some inevitable portion of thwarting,
bickering, and unhappiness. This cannot be otherwise so long as man has failed to reach the standard 20
of absolute perfection. The supposition that I must
have a companion for life is the result of a compli-
cation of vices. It is the dictate of cowardice and
not of fortitude. It flows from the desire of being
loved and esteemed for something that is not desert. 25

But the evil of marriage as it is practised in European countries lies deeper than this. The habit is, for a thoughtless and romantic youth of each sex to come together, to see each other for a few times and under circumstances full of delusion, and then to vow to each other eternal attachment. What is the consequence of this? In almost every instance they find themselves deceived. They are reduced to make the best of an irretrievable mistake. They are presented with the strongest imaginable temptation to become the dupes of falsehood. They are led to conceive it their wisest policy to shut their eyes upon realities, happy if by any perversion of intellect they can persuade themselves that they were right in their first crude opinion of their companion. The institution of marriage is a system of fraud; and men who carefully mislead their judgments in the daily affair of their life, must always have a crippled judgment in every other concern. We ought to dismiss our mistake as soon as it is detected; but we are taught to cherish it. We ought to be incessant in our search after virtue and worth; but we are taught to check our inquiry, and shut our eyes upon the most attractive and admirable objects. Marriage is law, and the worst of all laws. Whatever our understandings may tell us of the person from whose connection we should derive the greatest improvement, of the worth of one woman and the demerits of another, we are obliged to consider what is law, and not what is justice.

Add to this that marriage is an affair of property, and the worst of all properties. So long as two human beings are forbidden by positive institution to follow the dictates of their own mind, prejudice is alive and vigorous. So long as I seek to engross one woman to myself and to prohibit my neighbor from proving his superior desert and reaping the

fruits of it, I am guilty of the most odious of all
monopolies. Over this imaginary prize men watch
with perpetual jealousy, and one man will find his 65
desires and his capacity to circumvent as much excited as the other is excited to traverse his projects
and frustrate his hopes. As long as this state of
society continues, philanthropy will be crossed and
checked in a thousand ways, and the still augmenting 70
stream of abuse will continue to flow.

The abolition of marriage will be attended with
no evils. We are apt to represent it to ourselves
as the harbinger of brutal lust and depravity. But
it really happens in this, as in other cases, that the 75
positive laws which are made to restrain our vices
irritate and multiply them. Not to say, that the
same sentiments of justice and happiness which in a
state of equal property would destroy the relish for
luxury, would decrease our inordinate appetites of 80
every kind, and lead us universally to prefer the
pleasures of intellect to the pleasures of sense.

1793

RICHARD POLWHELE

[REGNER LODBROG]

WHAT'S surer to the warrior brave,
    Than to meet death's grisly form—
Though he seem to mock the grave,
    Firm amidst the battle's storm?

He alone in sorrow dies,   5
    Who hath never felt a pang!
Lo, where pale the dastard flies,
    Eagles stretch the bloody fang.

Life its lingering light in vain
    To the coward soul affords,   10
While he dreads the carnaged plain,
    Trembling at the sport of swords.

Fairly matched to battle go:
    This is glorious—this is great!
Striplings, deal the mutual blow,   15
    Nor let man from man retreat.

.   .   .   .

Now my bright career is run!
    Quivers yet my vital fire!
Gasping—panting—lo! 'tis done!
    With a smile I shall expire!   20

1792

FROM GRAM AND GRO

When Gram in youthful ardor bold
By busy rumor had been told,
A giant, with imperious pride,
Claimed Sictrug's daughter for his bride,
With Bessus eager for the fight   5
He moved toward Gothland in his might;
His troops in savage spoils arrayed
To strike his foes with greater dread.
Himself a rugged goat skin wore,
His hand a mace terrific bore;   10
Or, seeming furious to engage,
Wielded as with giant rage.
Thus armed, where through a wood she strayed,
They met by chance the royal maid.
Trembling with fear her reins she shook,   15
And thus in faltering accents spoke:

GRO.

Methinks the giant I espy;
His darkening footsteps thwart my eye.
Or roves my sight in error wide?
For oft beneath some shaggy hide 20
The valiant warrior stalks unseen,
Veiling his form and comely mein.

1792

FROM HOTHER

HOTHER left the sounding shore,
Through the woods he sought the boar.
O'er his head a tempest passed;
His companions shunned the blast.
Him a glittering cloud led on, 5
(Hother, valor's chosen son!)
'Till before his wondering eyes
He a lofty portal spies;
There the fatal sisters stand,
He accosts the virgin band: 10

"Who are ye, whose floor I tread?
Wherefore am I hither led?"

"We o'er war and death preside,
We direct the battle's tide;
Closely hid from mortal view, 15
We protect the favored few;
Whom we please success shall crown,
Dreadful is our angry frown.
We the warrior kill or save,
We to conquest urge the brave. 20
Take these arms, for thee decreed,
Thou in battle shalt not bleed.

Thine the helm and shield of proof
Forged beneath our magic roof.
But with Balder shun the fight,   25
He shall ne'er confess thy might:
(Balder, secret seed of heaven!)
Take the armor we have given."

Forth they rush on wings of wind,
Not a trace is left behind.   30

FROM THE INCANTATION OF HERVA

HERVA

AWAKE, Angantyr!—wandering wild,
Thine and Sufa's only child,
Herva, bids uplift thy head
From the slumbers of the dead.
From the tomb thy aid afford;   5
Give, Oh! give the hardened sword
Which to Sufurlama brave
The spirits of the mountain gave.

Hervardyr! Hior! Rani! hear!
Where with shield and bloody spear,   10
With helmet, mail, and falchion keen
You lie by human eyes unseen.
Where the trees o'er shade the ground,
Where they spread their roots around,
With Angantyr heed my call,   15
From sleep, from sleep, I rouse you all.

                                      1792

ANN RADCLIFFE

FROM THE MYSTERIES OF UDOLPHO

[THE CASTLE OF UDOLPHO]

FROM this sublime scene the travellers continued to ascend among the pines, till they entered a narrow pass of the mountains which shut out every feature of the distant country and in its stead exhibited only tremendous crags impending over the road, where no vestige of humanity or even of vegetation appeared, except here and there the trunk and scathed branches of an oak that hung nearly headlong from the rock into which its strong roots had fastened. This pass, which led into the heart of the Apennines, at length opened to day and a scene of mountains stretched in long perspective as wild as any the travellers had yet passed. Still vast pine forests hung upon their base and crowned the ridgy precipice that rose perpendicularly from the vale, while, above, the rolling mists caught the sunbeams and touched their cliffs with all the magical coloring of light and shade. The scene seemed perpetually changing, and its features to assume new forms as the winding road brought them to the eye in different attitudes; while the shifting vapors, now partially concealing their minuter beauties and now illuminating them with splendid tints, assisted the illusions of the sight.

Though the deep valleys between these mountains were for the most part clothed with pines, sometimes an abrupt opening presented a perspective of only barren rocks with a cataract flashing from their summit among broken cliffs till its waters, reaching the bottom, foamed along with louder fury; and

sometimes pastoral scenes exhibited their "green de- 30
lights" in the narrow vales, smiling amid surrounding horror. There herds and flocks of goats and
sheep browsing under the shade of hanging woods
and the shepherd's little cabin reared on the margin
of a clear stream, presented a sweet picture of re- 35
pose.

Wild and romantic as were these scenes, their
character had far less of the sublime than had those
of the Alps which guard the entrance of Italy. Emily
was often elevated, but seldom felt those emotions 40
of indescribable awe which she had so continually
experienced in her passage over the Alps.

Towards the close of day the road wound into a
deep valley. Mountains, whose shaggy steeps appeared to be inaccessible, almost surrounded it. To 45
the east a vista opened and exhibited the Apennines
in their darkest horrors; and the long perspective of
retiring summits rising over each other, their ridges
clothed with pines, exhibited a stronger image of
grandeur than any that Emily had yet seen. The 50
sun had just sunk below the top of the mountains
she was descending, whose long shadow stretched
athwart the valley; but his sloping rays, shooting
through an opening of the cliffs, touched with a yellow gleam the summits of the forest that hung upon 55
the opposite steeps and streamed in full splendor
upon the towers and battlements of a castle that
spread its extensive ramparts along the brow of a
precipice above. The splendor of these illuminated
objects was heightened by the contrasted shade 60
which involved the valley below.

"There," said Montoni, speaking for the first
time in several hours, "is Udolpho."

Emily gazed with melancholy awe upon the castle,
which she understood to be Montoni's, for, though it 65
was now lighted up by the setting sun, the gothic

greatness of its features and its mouldering walls of
dark gray stone rendered it a gloomy and sublime
object. As she gazed, the light died away on its walls
leaving a melancholy purple tint which spread deeper 70
and deeper as the thin vapor crept up the mountain,
while the battlements above were still tipped with
splendor. From those, too, the rays soon faded and
the whole edifice was invested with the solemn duski-
ness of evening. Silent, lonely, and sublime, it seemed 75
to stand the sovereign of the scene and to frown defi-
ance on all who dared to invade its solitary reign. As
the twilight deepened, its features became more
awful in obscurity; and Emily continued to gaze
till its clustering towers were alone seen rising over 80
the tops of the woods beneath whose thick shade
the carriages soon after began to ascend.

1794

[THE PICTURE BEHIND THE VEIL]

To WITHDRAW her thoughts, however, from the
subject of her misfortunes, she attempted to read;
but her attention wandered from the page and, at
length, she threw aside the book and determined to
explore the adjoining chambers of the castle. Her 5
imagination was pleased with the view of ancient
grandeur, and an emotion of melancholy awe awakened all its powers as she walked through rooms,
obscure and desolate, where no footsteps had passed
probably for many years, and remembered the 10
strange history of the former possessor of the edifice.
This brought to her recollection the veiled picture
which had attracted her curiosity on the preceding
night, and she resolved to examine it. As she passed
through the chambers that led to this, she found her- 15
self somewhat agitated; its connection with the
late lady of the castle and the conversation of An-

nette, together with the circumstance of the veil,
throwing a mystery over the object that excited a
faint degree of terror. But a terror of this nature, 20
as it occupies and expands the mind and elevates it
to high expectation, is purely sublime and leads us,
by a kind of fascination, to seek even the object from
which we appear to shrink.

Emily passed on with faltering steps; and, having 25
paused a moment at the door before she attempted
to open it, she then hastily entered the chamber and
went towards the picture, which appeared to be inclosed in a frame of uncommon size, that hung in
a dark part of the room. She paused again and 30
then with a timid hand lifted the veil; but instantly
let it fall, perceiving that what it had concealed was
no picture, and before she could leave the chamber
she dropped senseless on the floor.

When she recovered her recollection, the remem- 35
brance of what she had seen had nearly deprived her
of it a second time. She had scarcely strength to
remove from the room and regain her own, and,
when arrived there, wanted courage to remain alone.
Horror occupied her mind and excluded for a time 40
all sense of past and dread of future misfortune; she
seated herself near the casement because from thence
she heard voices, though distant, on the terrace and
might see people pass; and these, trifling as they
were, were reviving circumstances. When her spirits 45
had recovered their tone, she considered whether she
should mention what she had seen to Madame Montoni, and various and important motives urged her
to do so, among which the least was the hope of the
relief which an overburdened mind finds in speaking 50
of the subjects of its interest. But she was aware
of the terrible consequences which such a communication might lead to; and, dreading the indis-
cretion of her aunt, at length endeavored to arm her-

self with resolution to observe a profound silence on 55
the subject.

1794

[THE EXPLANATION OF THE VEILED PORTRAIT]

It may be remembered that in a chamber of Udolpho hung a black veil whose singular situation had excited Emily's curiosity and which afterwards disclosed an object that had overwhelmed her with horror; for on lifting it, there appeared, instead of 5 the picture she had expected, within a recess of the wall a human figure, of ghastly paleness, stretched at its length, and dressed in the habiliments of the grave. What added to the horror of the spectacle was that the face appeared partly decayed and dis- 10 figured by worms which were visible on the features and hands. On such an object it will be readily believed that no person could endure to look twice. Emily, it may be recollected had after the first glance let the veil drop, and her terror had prevented her 15 from ever after provoking a renewal of such suffering as she had then experienced. Had she dared to look again her delusion and her fears would have vanished together, and she would have perceived that the figure before her was not human but formed 20 of wax.

The history of it is somewhat extraordinary, though not without example in the records of that fierce severity which monkist superstition has sometimes inflicted on mankind. A member of the house 25 of Udolpho, having committed some offence against the prerogative of the church, had been condemned to the penance of contemplating, during certain hours of the day, a waxen image made to resemble a human body in the state to which it is reduced after 30

death. This penance, serving as a memento of the
condition at which he must himself arrive, had been
designed to reprove the pride of the Marquis of
Udolpho. . . .

1794

MATTHEW GREGORY LEWIS

[THE CONJURATION OF THE WANDERING JEW]

FROM THE MONK

HE WAS a man of majestic presence; his countenance was strongly marked and his eyes were large,
black, and sparkling, yet there was a something in
his look which, the moment that I saw him, inspired
me with a secret awe, not to say horror. He was 5
dressed plainly, his hair hung wildly upon his brow,
and a band of black velvet which encircled his forehead spread over his features an additional gloom.
His countenance wore the marks of profound melancholy, his step was slow, and his manner grave, 10
stately, and solemn.

He saluted me with politeness; and having replied to the usual compliments of introduction, he
motioned to Theodore to quit the chamber. The
page instantly withdrew. 15

"I know your business," said he without giving
me time to speak. "I have the power of releasing
you from your nightly visitor, but this cannot be
done before Sunday. On the hour when the Sabbath
morning breaks, spirits of darkness have least influ- 20
ence over mortals. After Saturday the nun shall
visit you no more."

"May I not inquire," said I, "by what means you

are in possession of a secret which I have carefully concealed from the knowledge of every one?"   25

"How can I be ignorant of your distresses when their cause at this moment stands beside you?"

I started. The stranger continued ——

"Though to you only visible for one hour in the twenty-four, neither day or night does she ever quit   30 you; nor will she ever quit you till you have granted her request."

"And what is that request?"

"That she must herself explain; it lies not in my knowledge. Wait with patience for the night of Sat-   35 urday; all shall be then cleared up." . . .

The wished-for night arrived. To avoid creating suspicion I retired to bed at my usual hour, but as soon as my attendants had left me I dressed myself again and prepared for the stranger's reception. He   40 entered my room upon the turn of midnight. A small chest was in his hand, which he placed near the stove. He saluted me without speaking; I returned the compliment, observing an equal silence.

The first thing which he produced was a small   45 wooden crucifix. He sunk upon his knees, gazed upon it mournfully, and cast his eyes towards heaven. He seemed to be praying devoutly. At length he bowed his head respectfully, kissed the crucifix thrice, and quitted his kneeling posture. He   50 next drew from the chest a covered goblet. With the liquor which it contained and which appeared to be blood, he sprinkled the floor, and then dipping in it one end of the crucifix, he described a circle in the middle of the room. Round about this he placed   55 various relics, skulls, thigh bones, and so forth. I observed that he disposed them all in the forms of crosses. Lastly, he took out a large Bible and beckoned me to follow him into the circle. I obeyed.

"Be cautious not to utter a syllable," whispered 60
the stranger, "Step not out of the circle, and, as you
love yourself, dare not to look upon my face!"

Holding the crucifix in one hand, the Bible in the
other, he seemed to read with profound attention.
The clock struck one! As usual, I heard the spectre's 65
steps upon the staircase, but I was not seized with
the accustomed shivering. I waited her approach
with confidence. She entered the room, drew near
the circle, and stopped. The stranger muttered some
words, to me unintelligible. Then raising his head 70
from the book and extending the crucifix towards
the ghost, he pronounced, in a voice distinct and solemn ——

"Beatrice! Beatrice! Beatrice!"

"What wouldst thou?" replied the apparition in a 75
hollow faltering tone.

"What disturbs thy sleep? Why dost thou afflict and torture this youth? How can rest be restored to thy unquiet spirit?"

"I dare not tell! I must not tell! Fain would I 80
repose in my grave, but stern commands force me to
prolong my punishment."

"Knowest thou this blood? Knowest thou in
whose veins it flowed? Beatrice! Beatrice! in his
name I charge thee to answer me!" 85

"I dare not disobey my taskers."

"Darest thou disobey me?"

He spoke in a commanding tone and drew the
sable band from his forehead. In spite of his in-
junctions to the contrary, curiosity would not suffer 90
me to keep my eyes off his face: I raised them and
beheld a burning cross impressed upon his brow.
For the horror with which this object inspired me
I cannot account, but I never felt its equal. My
senses left me for some moments, a mysterious 95

dread overcame my courage, and had not the exorciser caught my hand I should have fallen out of the circle.

When I recovered myself, I perceived that the burning cross had produced an effect no less violent upon the spectre. Her countenance expressed reverence and horror, and her visionary limbs were shaken by fear.

"Yes," she said at length, "I tremble at that mark! I respect it! I obey you! Know then, that my bones lie still unburied: they rot in the obscurity of Lindenberg Hole. None but this youth has the right of consigning them to the grave. His own lips have made over to me his body and his soul: never will I give back his promise; never shall he know a night devoid of terror, unless he engages to collect my mouldering bones and deposit them in the family vault of his Andalusian castle. Then let thirty masses be said for the repose of my spirit, and I trouble this world no more. Now let me depart. Those flames are scorching!"

He let the hand drop slowly which held the crucifix, and which till then he had pointed towards her. The apparition bowed her head, and her form melted into air. The exorciser led me out of the circle. He replaced the Bible, and so forth in the chest and then addressed himself to me, who stood near him speechless from astonishment.

"Don Raymond, you have heard the conditions on which repose is promised you. Let it be your business to fulfil them to the letter. For me, nothing more remains than to clear up the darkness still spread over the spectre's history and inform you that when living, Beatrice bore the name of las Cisternas. She was the great aunt of your grandfather. In quality of your relation, her ashes demand respect

from you, though the enormity of her crimes must
excite your abhorrence. . . ."

1795

WILLIAM TAYLOR

LENORA

AT break of day, with frightful dreams
  Lenora struggled sore:
"My William, art thou slaine, say'd she
  Or dost thou love no more?"

He went abroade with Richard's host,   5
  The Paynim foes to quell:
But he no word to her had writt,
  An he were sick or well.

With sowne of trump, and beat of drum,
  His fellow soldyers come;   10
Their helmes bydeckt with oaken boughs,
  They seeke their long'd-for-home.

And ev'ry roade and ev'ry lane
  Was full of old and young,
To gaze at the rejoicing band,   15
  To hail with gladsome toung.

"Thank God!" their wives and children saide,
  "Welcome!" the brides did saye:
But greete or kiss Lenora gave
  To none upon that daye.   20

She askte of all the passing traine,
  For him she wisht to see:

But none of all the passing traine
    Could tell if lived hee.

And when the soldyers all were bye,   25
    She tore her raven haire,
And cast herself upon the growne
    In furious despaire.

Her mother ran and lyfte her up,
    And clasped in her arme,   30
"My child, my child, what dost thou ail?
    God shield thy life from harm!"

"O mother, mother! William's gone!
    What's all besyde to me?
There is no mercye, sure, above!   35
    All, all were spar'd but hee!"

"Kneel downe, thy paternoster saye,
    'Twill calm thy troubled spright:
The Lord is wyse, the Lord is good;
    What hee hath done is right."   40

"O mother, mother! say not so;
    Most cruel is my fate:
I prayde, and prayde; but watte avayl'd?
    'Tis now! alas, too late."

"Our Heavenly Father if we praye,   45
    Will help a suff'ring childe:
Go take the holy sacrament;
    So shall thy grief grow milde."

"O mother, what I feel within,
    No sacrament can staye;   50
No sacrament can teche the dead
    To bear the sight of daye."

"May be, among the heathen folk
    Thy William false doth prove,
And puts away his faith and troth,   55
    And takes another love.

"Then wherefore sorrow for his loss?
    Thy moans are all in vain:
And when his soul and body parte,
    His falsehode brings him paine."   60

"O mother, mother! gone is gone:
    My hope is all forlorne:
The grave mie onlye safeguarde is—
    O, had I ne'er been borne!

"Go out, go out, my lampe of life;   65
    In grislie darkness die:
There is no mercye, sure, above!
    For ever let me lie!"

"Almighty God! O do not judge
    My poor unhappy childe;   70
She knows not what her lips pronounce,
    Her anguish makes her wilde.

"My girl, forget thine earthly woe,
    And think on God and bliss;
For so, at least, shall not thy soule   75
    Its heavenly bridegroom miss."

"O mother, mother! what is blisse,
    And what the fiendis celle?
With him 'tis heaven anywhere,
    Without my William, helle.   80

"Go out, go out, my lamp of life;
    In endless darkness die:

Without him I must loathe the earth,
 Without him scorne the skye."

And so despaire did rave and rage   85
 Athwarte her boiling veins;
Against the Providence of God
 She hurlde her impious strains.

She bet her breaste, and wrung her hands,
 And rollde her tearlesse eye,   90
From rise of morne, till the pale stars
 Again did freeke the skye.

When harke! abroade she hearde the trampe
 Of nimble-hoofed steed;
She hearde a knighte with clank alight,   95
 And climb the staire in speede.

And soon she hearde a tinkling hande,
 That twirled at the pin;
And thro' her door, that open'd not,
 These words were breathed in.   100

"What ho! what ho! thy dore undoe;
 Art watching or asleepe?
My love, dost yet remember mee,
 And dost thou laugh or weep?"

"Ah, William here so late at night!   105
 Oh! I have wachte and wak'd:
Whence dost thou come? For thy return
 My herte has sorely ak'd."

"At midnight only we may ride;
 I come o'er land and sea: 110
I mounted late, but soone I go;
 Aryse, and come with me."

"O William, enter first my bowre,
  And give me one embrace:
The blasts athwarte the hawthorne hiss; 115
  Awayte a little space."

"Tho' blasts athwarte the hawthorne hiss,
  I may not harboure here;
My spurre is sharpe, my courser pawes,
  My houre of flighte is nere. 120

"All as thou lyest upon thy couch,
  Aryse, and mounte behinde;
To-night we'le ride a thousand miles,
  The bridal bed to finde."

"How, ride to-night a thousand miles? 125
  Thy love thou dost bemocke:
Eleven is the stroke that still
  Rings on within the clocke."

"Look up; the moone is bright, and we
  Outstride the earthlie men: 130
I'll take thee to the bridal bed,
  And night shall end but then."

"And where is, then, thy house and home;
  And where thy bridal bed?"
"'Tis narrow, silent, chilly, dark, 135
  Far hence I rest my head."

"And is there any room for mee,
  Wherein that I may creepe?"
"There's room enough for thee and mee,
  Wherein that wee may sleepe. 140

"All as thou ly'st upon thy couch,
  Aryse, no longer stop;

The wedding guests thy coming waite,
    The chamber dore is ope."

All in her sarke, as there she lay,   145
    Upon his horse she sprung:
And with her lily hands so pale
    About her William clung.

And hurry-skurry forth they goe,
    Unheeding wet or drye;   150
And horse and rider snort and blowe,
    And sparkling pebbles flye.

How swift the flood, the mead, the wood,
    Aright, aleft, are gone.
The bridges thunder as they pass,   155
    But earthlie sowne is none.

Tramp, tramp, across the land they speede;
    Splash, splash, across the see;
"Hurrah! the dead can ride apace;
    Dost feare to ride with mee?   160

"The moone is bryghte, and blue the nyghte;
    Dost quake the blast to stem?
Dost shudder, mayde, to seeke the dead?"
    "No, no, but what of them?

"How glumlie sownes yon dirgye song!   165
    Night-ravens flappe the wing,
What knell doth slowlie toll ding dong?
    The psalmes of death who sing?

"It creeps, the swarthie funeral traine,
    The corse is onn the beere;   170
Like croke of todes from lonely moores,
    The chaunte doth meet the eere."

"Go, bear her corse when midnight's past,
　With song, and tear, and wayle;
I've gott my wife, I take her home,　　175
　My howre of wedlocke hayl.

"Lead forth, O clarke, the chaunting quire,
　To swell our nuptial song:
Come, preaste, and reade the blessing soone;
　For bed, for bed we long."　　180

They heede his calle, and husht the sowne;
　The biere was seene no more;
And followde him ore feeld and flood
　Yet faster than before.

Hallo! hallo! away they goe,　　185
　Unheeding wet or drye;
And horse and rider snort and blowe,
　And sparkling pebbles flye.

How swifte the hill, how swifte the dale,
　Aright, aleft, are gone!　　190
By hedge and tree, by thorpe and towne,
　They gallop, gallop on.

Tramp, tramp, across the land they speede;
　Splash, splash, across the see;
"Hurrah! the dead can ride apace;　　195
　Dost fear to ride with mee?

"Look up, look up, an airy crewe
　In roundel daunces reele:
The moone is bryghte, and blue the nyghte,
　Mayst dimlie see them wheele.　　200

"Come to, come to, ye gostlie crew,
　Come to, and follow mee,

And daunce for us the wedding daunce,
   When we in bed shall be."

And brush, brush, brush, the gostlie crew,   205
   Come wheeling ore their heads,
All rustling like the wither'd leaves,
   That wyde the whirlwind spreads.

Halloo! halloo! away they goe,
   Unheeding wet or drye;   210
And horse and rider snort and blowe,
   And sparkling pebbles flye.

And all that in the moonshyne lay,
   Behynde them fled afar;
And backwarde scudded overhead   215
   The skye and every star.

Tramp, tramp, across the lande they speede;
   Splash, splash, across the sea:
"Hurrah! the dead can ride apace;
   Dost fear to ride with mee?   220

"I weene the cock prepares to crowe;
   The sand will soon be runne:
I snuff the earlye morning aire;
   Downe, downe! our work is done.

"The dead, the dead can ryde apace;   225
   Oure wed-bed here is fit:
Our race is ridde, our journey ore,
   Our endlesse union knit."

And lo! an yren-grated gate
   Soon biggens to their viewe: 230
He crackte his whyppe; the clangynge boltes,
   The doores asunder flewe.

They pass, and 'twas on graves they trode;
" 'Tis hither we are bounde;"
And many a tombstone gostlie white 235
    Lay in the moonshyne round.

And when hee from his steed alytte,
    His armour, black as cinder,
Did moulder, moulder all awaye,
    As were it made of tinder. 240

His head became a naked scull;
    Nor haire nor eyne had hee.
His body grew a skeleton,
    Whilome so blythe of blee.

And att his dry and boney heele 245
    No spur was left to be;
And inn his witherde hand you might
    The scythe and hour-glasse see.

And lo! his steede did thin to smoke,
    And charnel fires outbreathe; 250
And pal'd, and bleach'd, then vanish'd quite
    The mayde from undernethe.

And hollow howlings hung in aire,
    And shrekes from vaults arose.
Then knew the mayde she mighte no more 255
    Her living eyes unclose.

But onwarde to the judgment-seat,
    Thro' myste and moonlighte dreare,
The gostlie crewe their flyghte persewe,
    And hollowe inn her eare:— 260

"Be patient; tho' thyne herte should breke,
    Arrayne not Heven's decree;

Thou nowe art of thie bodie refte,
Thie soule forgiven bee!"

March, 1796

FROM WORTIGERNE, A PLAYE

Hengist. Mie brodherre seemeth you thisse Brydyan
    kinge
  Not a vilde trecherre to wythhalde the londe
  Wyche   whyle   hisse   Pykishe   foen   wesen
    menacynge
  Hisse promyse made the meede of oure bystonde?
  Itte reweth me to have yrearde a honde   5
  To save hisse cowarde liegemen fro mishappe.
  Falle theie hynceforthe byfore the steelie bronde
  Ov the bolde Pykkes: I joye gyf theie awhappe
Ne long mie vengeaunce sleepes in dulle unactions
    lappe.

Horsa. Inn trothe 'twere betterre gyf yleng the
    coste   10
  Oure speedie shyppes yette croisedde merrilie;
  Daunger and toyle hadde lesse forworne our hoste
  And richerre bootie inne the sacke shuld lie.
  Aletubbes and corne and hammes yheped hie
  Ere thisse hadde storde our winter-hame, I weene, 15
  And Romayne gaudes devysedde daintilie
  Ygladde oure wyves and daughterres wyth theire
    sheene,
The modherres honest pryde our darynge hadde
    bewreene.

    These too had pleasaunce of tenerre ymet
  Oure lustie younglynges on thun wittynge shore. 20
  Hynse the coie mayde is fledde on warie fet.
  Where the grimme nighbourhode of warre doth
    lowre,
  The modherre pyghtes her in the hylsterde bowre,

Ne standes she to the warryerres wishe confeste.
Who clasps her hasatie inne the daungerous howre 25
Fyndes in withstonden love a twyfolde zeste,—
Of rosier hewe the cheeke, of wermer throbbe the
    breste.

Hengist. From Wortigerne hisse unryghte I ne
    brooke.
Watte saie ye, shuln we falle uponne these men
Nowe theie ygallde with fyghte doen lowlie looke, 30
For leech and frere bie tornes do wend theire ken,
And kneede theire fetherie beddes lyche nestlynge
    hen,
As gyf an achynge lymbe misseemde the grounde?

Horsa. Thie well are worthe itte; but the foen are
    ten to one ayenst usse.

Hengist. Dearer evrie wounde 35
Whan is ywon the daie yatte in oure syde is
    founde.

                      1801

FROM WORTIGERNE

RERVE the cuppes ov skulles ameyne,
    Freer draughtes ov carnage spylle,
The bowles wyth bloodde of Brydyanes steyne,
    Father Woden, drynke dhie fylle.

Walkyres ope dhie pallase-dore, 5
    Sowghles ov strevers thider tronge.
Skaldes belowe their prayses yore;
    Bragger, yond their prayse prolonge.

Lette the Chrystayne goddes avaunce
   Seylynge inne embattelde hostes,   10
Seynktes maie couche the airie launce,
   Theires the feeble arme of gostes.

Woden, snatche the charmed roode,
   Woden, Chrystyane banneres, Woden!
Father Woden, Chrystyane bloode,   15
   Woden, Chrystyane vyctymmes, Woden!

Lette theire aungelles hove in are
   Sweepe the skyen with swerdes ov flame,
Sone theie pale the ydel glare
Some theie shrynke atte Woden's name.   20

1801

AMOS SIMON COTTLE

FROM THE DESCENT OF ODIN

THEN, uprising from his place,
Odin—friend of human race,—
Straight caparisoned his steed—
Sleipner of etherial breed.
As down to Hela's realms he drew   5
Thick the shades of darkness grew:
The dog of hell, with ceaseless bay,
Pursued the traveller on his way.

Roused from his feast of death, with gore
His shaggy limbs were crimsoned o'er;   10
Still round his fangs the fibers hung,
Quivering on his frothy tongue.
He barked! and through the void profound,
Hell re-echoed to the sound.

With dauntless soul the hero rode;   15
Safe he reached the dire abode;
Now the sacred portals prest;
Trembling earth the God confessed!
Towards the east then bent his way,
Where low beneath the sorceress lay.   20

With magic rites the concave rung,
Necromantic airs he sung,
Hyperborean climates viewed,
Runic rhymes around he strewed,

Deep the incantation wrought;   25
Then the maid sepulchral sought.
From the hollow tomb beneath,
Volva's voice was heard to breathe!

Volva:

What mortal he who dares invade
The dwelling where my bones are laid?   30
The snows of ages long I've worn,
Long the driving tempest borne,
Long the rains have drenched my head,
Long I've mouldered with the dead.

Odin:

Vegtam is the invader's name,   35
Sprung from sires of warlike fame.
Mortal truths will he reveal;
Thou no work of fate conceal.
Tell me for what hero's shade,
Yon seat with costliest care arrayed.   40
Destined for whom, that radiant bed
Rich with golden trappings spread.

1797

JOSEPH COTTLE

FROM ALFRED

ALFRED victorious o'er the Danes, I sing.

Prepared to seek again the British shore,
Within his father's hall Ivar now sat
Musing on future spoils. Around him thronged
His wrathful sisters, rousing up his heart   5
To vengeance against the race who slew their sire.
At Regner's name, Ivar uprose, his eye
Beamed fearful indignation when he cried,

"Death to our foes! my spirit thirsts to see
The blood of Saxons flowing ocean-like,   10
Before my greedy eyes, whilst ever round
Some mangled corse, writhing in agony,
Shall add new transport to my bounding heart.
Odin, immortal chief! I hear thy call,
And like thee forth I go to scorn the looks   15
And scatter wide the bones and heap the skulls
Of vanquished enemies. Death! view in me
Thy proudest champion, soon ordained to swell
Slaughter's rank pile and for the ravenous wolves
Provide new banquets! By the rapturous hope   20
Of one day joining the celestial throng
Amid Valhalla, hearing as I stalk,
From each brave warrior, gratulations loud:—
By that proud confidence, here do I swear
To scorn all mercy!"   25

[IVAR AND THE SORCERESS]

Around I gazed in dread perplexity,
Then, sudden, looked aghast! A coffin, black,

Slow rising from the yawning sepulchre,
My sight arrested. As I earnest viewed
I saw the sorceress! In her narrow bed   5
Senseless she lay, oppressed with death-like sleep!
All sounds were hushed. A stillness reigned as
          though
Nature herself had paused. I toward her moved
With spell to break her slumber, when, I saw—
Her winding sheet was snow, her coffin stone.   10
I would have spoken, but, when I beheld
Her still and livid visage and her eye
That through the thin, thin eye-lid half appeared,
Back I recoiled, unconscious, yet again,
Drew nigh her coffin, and in tremulous tones   15
Chanted the runic song.

                              Slowly the witch
Her form upraised, stiff with the cavern's damp
Half red, half blue, whilst venomed drops distilled
Upon her bare head, from the craggy roof,
Where countless reptiles hung and things unknown   20
Forming one mass of life, which, as it moved,
Rapid or slow, gave back the cauldron's light
In ghastly radiance. The sorceress spake,
Rolling her troubled eyes. "I hear the call.
What mortal dares disturb my long repose   25
And tread these mansions?" Then she cast her eye,
Her black and shining eye stern in my face,
And cried, "Who *art* thou?"

                                           1800

JAMES LAWRENCE

FROM THE EMPIRE OF THE NAIRS

THE Nairs are the nobility of the Malabar Coast,
and affirm that they are the oldest in the world.

They are mentioned in the most ancient writers of
Indostan. It is the privilege of the Nair lady to
choose and change her lover. When he visits her,
he walks round the house and strikes with his sabre
on his buckler as a signal of his approach. To an-
nounce his presence to any rival, he, if admitted,
leaves a domestic with his arms in a kind of porch.
The mother only has the charge of the children; and
even the Samorin and the other princes have no other
heirs than the children of their sisters, that, having
no family, they may be always ready to march
against an enemy. When the nephews are of an age
to bear arms, they follow their uncle. The name of
a father is unknown to a Nair child; he speaks of
the lovers of his mother and of his uncles, but never
of his father.

Such are the Nairs. At present they are to be
found chiefly on the Malabar coast. The mighty
empire, which is ceded to them in this novel, like
Brobdingnag and Lilliput, will be found in no book
of geography. Indostan is, in fact, governed by
Sultans, Subahs, Rajahs, and Nabobs, and not
divided into principalities and baronies. A feudal
government has been given to this Utopia because
if the Nair system be compatible with a government where all the distinctions, privileges, and im-
munities of birth are in force, there can be less
doubt of its possibility under a more simple constitution. The Paradise of the Mothersons is merely
ideal; but for the customs and opinions of Persia
and other eastern nations, the most creditable authors have been consulted; and many of the European anecdotes are founded on facts. This work
was designed to show the possibility of a nation's
reaching the highest civilization without marriage.
This may seem a paradox, *"Car on est convenu,"*

says Mercier, *"d'appeler de ce nom toute vérité nou-*
velle, qui n'a pas encore eu son passeport."   40

However singular this system may at first appear,
the Nairs maintain that it is the system of nature.
"All the other animals are free in love, and to the
mothers alone falls the care of the offspring. Why
has mankind deviated from a system which, from   45
analogy, we may pronounce the original system of
our species?   Marriage, whenever it was introduced, was an innovation. Let not our system be
deemed unnatural, because confined to so small a portion of mankind; if numbers were the test of truth,   50
Christianity must give way to Mohammedanism,
monogamy to polygamy. It not only has always ex-
isted among ourselves, who have preceded other
nations in civilization, but is practised by some of
the tribes in America, whose savage state approaches   55
the nearest to the state of nature."

Such are the arguments with which the Nairs
vindicate their system. But, without discussing its
origin, let us consider its advantages.

Marriage is a domestic yoke; the Nair system,   60
the freedom of nature.

1793 (in German)
1811 (in English)

NOTES AND COMMENTS
HOW THIS VOLUME MAY BEST
BE STUDIED

When you come to study Volumes III, IV, and V (the selections from the great Romantics), you will find that they contain scarcely anything that is not of the highest literary value. But of Volume II this cannot be said, except for the selections from Collins, Gray, Goldsmith, Sterne, Cowper, and Burns. In this volume there is much material that has little intrinsic beauty but is remarkable for its historical value. Its study should therefore be approached with a different attitude of mind from that which will be proper in the study of the last three volumes. Here your aim is, not to understand and appreciate romantic literature in its perfection, but to trace its causes and to observe the often crude experiments in thought, feeling, and expression which preceded the successful achievements of the later period.

For an outline of the pre-romantic movement, and of each author's relation thereto, see the *Guide*.

As you read these specimens, necessarily brief, you will be rapidly passing from one subject to another, and often to a seemingly quite unrelated one. At first you may feel that the movement is distressingly incoherent, contradictory, and chaotic. No collection which presented it otherwise,— neatly systematized in clear-cut phases,—would be a true reflection of the actual drift of Pre-romanticism.

After reading each passage, ask yourself what particular kind of Pre-romanticism it seems to illustrate. In trying to answer that question, you may find it helpful to recall that among the many diverse currents which coalesce into the pre-romantic stream, the following are perhaps the most vigorous:

1) the School of Sensibility (in drama, short story, novel, philosophy, and verse), expressing faith in the instinctive goodness of human beings, and exalting sympathy and benevolence

2) the nature-poetry and nature-prose that tends to interpret nature mystically or pantheistically

3) the poetry of mourning, of death, of the graveyard

4) the editing or imitating of older forms of verse, such as ballads, sonnets, and Spenserian stanzas

5) the Scotch dialect verse

6) the translation or imitation of Oriental tales

7) the translation or imitation of ancient Scandinavian literature

8) the translation or imitation of ancient Celtic literature

9) the development of literary theories and literary criticism opposed to the neo-classical

10) the Gothic School, or School of Terror

11) radical attacks upon the established order and conventions, political, economic, educational, or social.

Mark each selection in the book with that figure from the above list which seems best to classify it. Thus you would mark the first selection with a 1, and the last with an 11. Some selections, belonging to more than one category, you would attach more than one figure to; e. g., a Scotch ballad would be both 4 and 5. When you have marked each selection is this way, you will be able in reviewing to trace each of the main tributaries by itself.

LORD SHAFTESBURY

13.—THE MORAL SENSE. S. asserts that all men naturally and without education feel the difference between good and evil. This instinctive feeling he calls the moral sense,— a term not invented by him but brought into vogue through his work.—Acceptance of this doctrine encouraged faith in the instinctive goodness of man.

13.—6. *affections.* all kinds of feelings.

13.—10. *sensible.* perceptible by the senses.

14.—27. *still.* always.

14.—34. *honest.* good, just, honorable.—Observe the tacit assumption that the good is the natural, and evil a corruption thereof.

14.—51. *a sense of right and wrong before, etc.* Our moral sense is not a consequence of our spiritual nature. It precedes our religious development. Morality is accordingly not dependent upon religion.

15.—66. *be taken with any show.* be attracted by any manifestation.

15.—67. *social passion.* sympathy for humanity,—in modern jargon, "social-mindedness."

15.—THE MORALISTS. Chiefly a dialogue between Theocles, an enthusiast, and his friend Philocles, who begins as a sceptic but is finally persuaded to accept Theocles' new religion,—a worship of the Genius of Nature. Nature is absolutely good and harmonious and evil is only an appearance caused by our imperfect vision.—The style conforms to the sub-title, "A Rhapsody."

15.—1. *balance of Europe.* The political balance,—the equilibrium of strength between the rival powers.

15.—8. *order . . . would then equal.* The constitution of the moral world would then manifestly be as harmonious as the constitution of physical nature.

15.—17. *known seats.* famous estates of noblemen.

15.—18. *prospects.* views, landscapes.

16.—40. *in loose numbers.* not in regular verse (actually in a kind of prose-poetry).

16.—42. *resolve.* unite.

17.—60. *if it be possible to exclude ill, it will exclude it.* Can you see any ambiguity or other weakness in this argument?

17.—78. *imaginary wealth.* gold and precious stones, which S. regarded as corrupting mankind.

17.—83. *artificial labyrinths.* The mazes, grottoes, etc., of over-elaborate landscape gardening.

17.—87. *beauteous in themselves.* Somewhat anticipates William Blake's sentiment in *The Tiger;* see iii, 35.

18.—92. *economy.* general system.

18.—98. *Atlas.* The wildly romantic mountain-region, here beheld in a vision, in which Shelley a century later laid the scene of his *Witch of Atlas.*

18.—106. *horror.* An agitation of the senses not always, in the eighteenth century, signifying fear and dread only, but sometimes also the astonishment and fascination with which we behold strange and mighty objects, hence the commonplace "a pleasing horror." The "horrid" might mean not merely the revolting but also anything rugged or gloomy,—e.g., "a horrid wood."

19.—145. *that mysterious Being.* the Genius of Nature, the Spirit of the Universe, God.—Observe that the "horrid" scenes just described have ultimately a sublime effect upon the beholder, in whom they awaken the consciousness of the divine.

19.—148. *have at last prevailed.* i.e., the sceptical Philocles is convinced that the Universe is spiritual, and that the natural is the good.

19.—150. *conceit.* vain ingenuity.

19.—157. *formal gardens.*—Note the attack upon them.

19.—162. *vulgar.* ordinary (without the modern sense of "coarse," "low").

20.—167. *lovers of the Muses or . . . Graces.* lovers of the beautiful or the civilized.

20.—169. *romantic.* Like "enthusiasm" (171), a word then used contemptuously.

20.—178. *shadow.* the vanities pursued by the worldly, in contrast to the really substantial values enjoyed by the devotee of Nature.

COLLEY CIBBER

20.—LOVE'S LAST SHIFT. This selection and the following exemplify those scenes in sentimental comedy in which men are reformed by beholding the pitiable distress of their virtuous victims. Compare *Jenny Distaff,* below, p. 26,— the same sort of thing in the form of a short story.

20.—*Shift.* Device.

22.—6. *vizor.* mask. **23.**—27. *steenkirk.* neckcloth.

RICHARD STEELE

23.—THE POETS AND VIRTUE. The first three selections from Steele, and the fifth, state the literary theories on which the drama of sensibility (i.e., sentimental comedy and domestic tragedy) are based.

24.—18. *mistake · fortune for nature.*—They think a tragedy-king is not of the same nature as themselves, whereas really he differs only in the fortune of his station.

25.—THE CONSCIOUS LOVERS. **25.**—7. *evades the quarrel.* Steele here attacked the custom of duelling, to which the fashionable young men ("Goths and Vandals") were addicted.

25.—11. *father and daughter.* This incident was pathetic, and therefore objected to by the neo-classic formalists who insisted that a comedy should be comic throughout.

25.—20. *tears which were shed.* Sentimental comedy was (especially in France) derisively called "lachrymose comedy."

25.—25. *of Mr. Wilks.* by the actor Wilks.

25.—26. *a General.* Brigadier-General Charles Churchill, whose mistress acted the part of the heroine, Indiana.— Steele, had he lived in the days of Nelson, would have found justification for Wilks's remark in that valiant fighter's emotionalism (see, below, iv, Southey's *Life of Nelson*).

25.—26. *Indiana.*—The heroine of *The Conscious Lovers.*

26.—JENNY DISTAFF. See the note above, p. 20, on *Love's Last Shift.* This sketch points forward to the story of Amanda, p. 31. Jenny's speech is ludicrously stilted and out of keeping with her humble station in life.

27.—THE CALAMITIES OF THE VIRTUOUS. Traditionally the downfall of a hero was tragic only when he himself by a flaw in his character contributed to it. But the School of Sensibility, preferring perfect heroes, attempted in domestic tragedies (like Lillo's *Fatal Curiosity,* 1736) to evoke sympathy for those who suffered through no fault of their own. In the German pre-romantic school this experiment was repeatedly made in the so-called "Schicksalstragödien," or Tragedies of Fate. Steele's discussion and examples anticipate this development by many years.

JOHN HUGHES

31.—VIRTUE IN DISTRESS. See the note on *Jenny Distaff,* p. 26, above. This story, almost certainly known to Richardson, foreshadows his novel *Pamela.*

31.—19. *decency.* decorum, right conduct.

32.—42. *loose education.* Observe that the vice is attributed not to his nature but his false education.

32.—54. *execution.* e.g. foreclosure of a mortgage.

33.—70. *nice.* fastidious.

35.—REMARKS ON THE FAIRIE QUEEN. The first step towards the recognition by the pre-Romantics of Spenser's merits,—a very cautious step. Important is the perception that poems of one age are not to be judged by the conventions of another.

36.—THE ARABIAN NIGHTS. It is owing to the kindness of the learned Professor Duncan B. Macdonald of Hartford, Connecticut, owner of a collection of rare versions of *The Arabian Nights,* that I am enabled to reprint, for the first time, this passage from the first English translation,—a translation whose effect upon eighteenth century literature was enormous. The style of this version is, to be sure, disgustingly unworthy of the original, in its colloquial vulgarity; but such was the splendor of the substance that it shone through the coarseness of the medium. The ineptness of the style is characteristic of pre-romanticism in general,—which is new wine poured into old bottles.

37.—51. *therefore I must kill thee.* This is the passage which Coleridge quoted as an example of the logic of poetry in distinction to the logic of common sense.

38.—87. *doubt.* suspect.

LADY WINCHILSEA

42.—A NOCTURNAL REVERIE. Wordsworth (*Essay, Supplementary to the Preface,* 1815) stated that this was one of the very few exceptional cases between Milton and Thomson (c. 1676-1726) in which "poetry contains a single new image of external nature." The other poetry, according to him, "scarcely presents a familiar one from which it can be inferred that the eye of the poet had been steadily fixed upon his object." It is to be noted, however, that Lady W's verses are not so different from the classical as Wordsworth's statement suggests. There is in them nothing mystical in the relationship between Man and Nature. The latter is "the inferior world" and not, except in mistaken fancy, "like her (the soul's) own" (46).

42.—4. *Philomel*. the nightingale. 6. *she*. the owl.

SAMUEL CROXALL

44.—THE VISION. Here, again, is interest in Nature, and direct observation; but is it romantic in interpreting man's relation thereto?

GEORGE HICKES

44.—INCANTATION OF HERVOR. From *Linguarum Veterum Septentrionalium Thesaurus* (Oxford, 1703), I, 193. The oldest translation of a complete Norse poem. It appeared in a learned work, but presently became known to the general reading public, and was repeatedly versified in the latter part of the eighteenth century. See pp. 298 and 399.

LADY ELIZABETH WARDLAW

45.—HARDYKNUTE. She published this as if it were medieval, but it is an imitation. It is based upon a Scotch repulsion of a Scandinavian invasion c. 1263, but the Lord High Steward of Scotland is absurdly given the Scandinavian name Hardyknute. The use of "Britons" for Englishmen is likewise an anachronism. Despite these blunders, it helped the movement onward, and was long admired. Thomas Warton (*Observations on the Fairie Queene*, i, 212-216) regretfully supposed that it was lost. Sir Walter Scott said "Hardyknute was the first poem I ever learnt—the last that I shall forget." He called it "a most spirited and beautiful imitation of the ancient ballads."

45.—1. *the wa'*. upon the wall or rampart of his castle.
46.—10. *ha's*. halls. **13.** *sae*. so. *ance*. once.
46.—15. *marrow*. equal. 16. *Eleanor*. Queen of England, and mother of "Hardyknute."

46.—20. *bot.* without. 27. *gimp.* slender.
46.—28. *gowden.* golden. 28. *glist.* shone.
47.—62. *shill.* shrill.

WILLIAM HAMILTON OF BANGOUR

48.—The Braes of Yarrow. The banks of the beautiful
Scotch river.—Three of Wordsworth's poems are on the
Yarrow.—"A" is the rival who has slain the maiden's beloved, "B" is a bystander, and "C" is the maiden herself
who at the end, in the frenzy of her grief, thinks she beholds
the bloody spectre of the dead youth.

48.—1. *Busk.* Make ready. 2. *marrow.* mate.
48.—7. *dare na weil be seen.* He does not well dare to
be seen there, because of the slaying.
48.—8. *puing the birks.* pulling (cutting down) the
birches.
48.—11. *leive.* leave, stop. 19. *lang maun.* long must.
48.—22. *dule.* dole. 49.—21. *tint.* lost.
49.—25. *reid.* red. 27. *weids.* garments.
49.—47. *bauld.* bold. 50.—52. *flowan.* flowing.
50.—53. *Tweed.* His home is near this river.
50.—54. *gowan.* daisy. 72. *as he.* as if he.
51.—79. *to-fall.* close.
51.—85. *barbarous father.* Her father is furious because
she loved the other youth, her sisters taunt her with her loss.
Observe that, in imitation of the manner of the old ballads,
such things are not clearly explained but swiftly hinted at.—
On the other hand, "barbarous" is rather in the style of the
eighteenth century than in that of the ballads.

ALLAN RAMSAY

52.—The Evergreen. "A collection," Ramsay called it,
"of Scots poems, wrote by the ingenious before 1600." Besides
genuinely old materials, it included some (like *Hardyknute,*
above, p. 45) mistakenly believed old.

53.—33. *spleened.* soured, irritated.
53.—46. *beautiful irregularity.* mark the phrase.
54.—56. *amusing.* pleasantly entertaining and divert-
ing.—In that century the word did not usually suggest the
colloquial modern meaning, "funny."
54.—82. *the vulgar.* the common people.
55.—Sweet William's Ghost. From Ramsay's second
collection, *The Tea-Table Miscellany,* 9th. ed., 1740. A
genuine old ballad, not apparently much damaged by "im-

provements" in its editing. Perhaps a derivative of a very ancient Danish ballad, *The Betrothed.* It had a new and important career in the pre-romantic movement,—being used by the German poet Bürger in his *Lenore* (1774), which was translated into English by William Taylor (given above, p. 409), and which in its turn inspired Sir Walter Scott's translation *William and Helen* (see iv, 11, and note).

Compare the three English versions with one another.

55.—3. *tirled at the pin.* rattled at the doorlatch.

55.—18. *Of me shalt nevir win.* In later ed., "Nor yet will I thee lend."

56.—35. *sprite.* spirit, as in later ed. 52. *meet.* close, scant.

DAVID MALLET

57.—WILLIAM AND MARGARET. Professor George Saintsbury (*Cambr. Hist. Eng. Lit.*, ix, 185) opines that no one other poem of this period deserves "so much credit for setting the eighteenth century back on the road of the true romantic poetry by an easy path, suited to its own tastes and powers." The extent of Mallet's originality is in dispute. In 1893 Professor W. L. Phelps (*Beginnings of the Engl. Rom. Movement,* Appendix II) asserted that Mallet stole the ballad,—"one of the prettiest cases of literary forgery on record,"—his assumption being that what Mallet offered as his own was an ancient ballad. Mallet did largely take the poem from a broadside edition of c. 1711, but by that time the ancient ballad had been, as Professor Child's *English and Scottish Popular Ballads* (ed. Sargent and Kittredge, 1904) puts it, "rewritten in what used to be called an elegant style." Mallet introduced a few changes of his own. The most "antique" stanza is the first. Ramsay published Mallet's version (privately printed in 1723) in his *Miscellany* (1724) as an "old ballad."

To appreciate the difference between a genuine ancient ballad and a modification thereof acceptable to eighteenth-century taste, compare with Mallet's version the following authentic text:

FAIR MARGARET AND SWEET WILLIAM

As it fell out on a long summer's day,
  Two lovers they sat on a hill;
They sat together that long summer's day,
  And could not talk their fill.

'I see no harm by you, Margaret,
 Nor you see none by me;
Before tomorrow eight a clock
 A rich wedding shall you see.'

Fair Margaret sat in her bower-window,
 A combing of her hair,
And there she spy'd Sweet William and his bride,
 As they were riding near.

Down she layd her ivory comb,
 And up she bound her hair;
She went her way forth of her bower,
 But never more did come there.

When day was gone, and night was come,
 And all men fast asleep,
Then came the spirit of Fair Margaret,
 And stood at William's feet.

'God give you joy, you two true lovers,
 In bride-bed fast asleep;
Loe I am going to my green grass grave,
 And am in my winding-sheet.'

When day was come, and night was gone,
 And all men wak'd from sleep,
Sweet William to his lady said,
 'My dear, I have cause to weep.

'I dreamed a dream, my dear lady;
 Such dreams are never good;
I dreamed my bower was full of red swine,
 And my bride-bed full of blood.'

'Such dreams, such dreams, my honoured lord,
 They never do prove good,
To dream thy bower was full of swine,
 And [thy] bride-bed full of blood.'

He called up his merry men all,
 By one, by two, and by three,
Saying, I'll away to Fair Margaret's bower,
 By the leave of my lady.

And when he came to Fair Margaret's bower,
 He knocked at the ring;

So ready was her seven brethren
  To let Sweet William in.

He turned up the covering-sheet:
  'Pray let me see the dead;
Methinks she does look pale and wan,
  She has lost her cherry red.

'I'll do more for thee, Margaret,
  Than any of thy kin;
For I will kiss thy pale wan lips,
  Tho a smile I cannot win.'

With that bespeak her seven brethren,
  Making most pitious moan:
'You may go kiss your jolly brown bride,
  And let our sister alone.'

'If I do kiss my jolly brown bride,
  I do but what is right;
For I made no vow to your sister dear,
  By day or yet by night.

'Pray tell me then how much you'll deal
  Of your white bread and your wine;
So much as is dealt at her funeral today
  Tomorrow shall be dealt at mine.'

Fair Margaret dy'd today, today,
  Sweet William he dy'd the morrow;
Fair Margaret dy'd for pure true love,
  Sweet William he dy'd for sorrow.

Margaret was buried in the lower chancel,
  Sweet William in the higher;
Out of her breast there sprung a rose,
  And out of his a brier.

They grew as high as the church-top,
  Till they could grow no higher,
And then they grew in a true lover's knot,
  Which made all people admire.

There came the clerk of the parish,
  As you this truth shall hear,
And by misfortune cut them down,
  Or they had now been there.

JAMES THOMSON

59.—PREFACE OF THE SEASONS. 3. *amuse*. See note upon p. 54, l. 56, above.

60.—10. *pendant gardens*. flowering plants in hanging baskets, window-boxes, etc., on the houses.

60.—10. *Cheapside*. A business street in the heart of London. The shopkeepers (some of whom were Aldermen) often lived above their shops.

60.—THE SEASONS. Try to distinguish between passages in the new style,—i.e., comparatively simple and objective (such as, generally speaking, ll. 7-10 and 28-34 in the first selection) and passages in the older manner (such as "the bleating kind," l. 39, and the last seven lines).

60.—1. *fuming dun*. arising dark.

61.—39. *bleating kind*. sheep. **62.**—45. *at will*. freely.

62.—45. *below the storm*. e.g., in such a sheltered hollow as is described below, l. 50.

62.—56. *loose-revolving fields*. In the whirling snow-storm the boundaries of the fields seem to move around.

62.—59. *shag*. roughen.

62.—76. *covered pits, etc*. He fears to walk onward, since the snow may conceal fatal pits and precipices.

63.—89. *officious*. duteous.

63.—89-93. Gray remembered these lines; see, below, the *Elegy* ll. 21-24, "For them no more the blazing hearth shall burn," etc.

63.—109. *variance*. discord.

63.—110. *dungeon glooms*. Thomson was sympathetically interested in the humanitarian efforts of the prison-reformers of his time.

64.—123. *honest passions*. feelings that are honorable,—such as grief and pity.

64.—130. *vice . . . impulse, etc*. Observe his reverting to personification.

64.—SUMMER. 3. *formful brain*. mind full of images or fancies.

65.—12. *still*. constantly. 13. *gives*. causes.

65.—SPRING. 5. *Hertford*. "*Spring*," writes Dr. Johnson (*Lives of the Poets,* ed. G. B. Hill, iii, 287) "was published next year, with a dedication to the Countess of Hertford, whose practice it was to invite every summer some poet into the country to hear her verses and assist her studies. This honor was one summer conferred on Thomson, who took more delight in carousing with Lord Hertford and his friends than assisting her ladyship's poetical operations, and therefore never received another summons."

65.—22. *bittern.* a wading bird. It makes a noise which Goldsmith calls "booming."

66.—26. *Aries . . . Bull.* The signs of the Zodiac, Aries and Taurus. When the sun enters the first, on March 21, Spring begins.

66.—41. *share.* plough. **43.** *winds.* controls, guides.

66.—55. *Maro.* Virgil. **68.—98.** *liberal.* free.

68.—108. *Augusta.* London.

68.—118. *God . . . pervades, etc.* Observe how such a passage prepares the way for a more mystical interpretation of the relation of Nature to God.

69.—AUTUMN. 5. *These.* The woods, which draw the Muse into their walks.

70.—31. *dull, despondent flock, etc.* Are birds thus in Autumn, or is this a pathetic fallacy?

71.—53. *woods . . . all around.* The prospect all around the woods, etc., thrills the soul.

71.—HYMN TO THE SEASONS. Mark (a) the passages in which God and Nature seem to melt into one another, and (b) those in which Nature remains, as in the *Psalms,* one of the wonderful works of God.

72.—47. *from whom you rage.* who it is (God) that gives you the power to storm.

72.—48. *His praise, ye brooks attune, etc.* Compare the majestic Canticle in the *Book of Common Prayer,* "Benedicite, omnia Opera," "O all ye works of the Lord, bless ye the Lord."

73.—72. *Bleat . . . hills, etc.,* are thought of as the flock of the Great Shepherd.

73.—81. *Ye chief.* You human beings.

74.—114. *seeming evil.* Cf., above, p. 16-17, Shaftesbury's doctrine that evil is only apparent not real.

74.—THE CASTLE OF INDOLENCE. "This poem being writ in the manner of Spenser," says Thomson in his preface, "the obsolete words, and a simplicity of diction in some of the lines which borders on the ludicrous, were necessary to make the imitation more perfect."

74.—3. *emmet.* ant. **75.—8.** *bale.* sorrow.

75.—10. *fast.* close. **21.** *kest.* cast.

75.—33. *plain.* complain. **35.** *coil.* noise.

75.—36. *yblent.* blended together.

76.—46. *drowsyhed.* drowsiness.

77.—70. *Ymolten.* Melted. **87.** *ne.* nor.

77.—97. *Astræa.* Justice. **78.—113.** *soote.* sweetly.

JOHN DYER

79.—Grongar Hill. In southern Wales.
79.—1. *Silent Nymph.* The muse of painting, a sister of the muse of poetry (l. 9).
80.—23. *Towy.* a river.
80.—31. *spreads.* i.e., to his sight, as he ascends the hill.
82.—100. *To instruct.* Here and below, l. 121., "So we mistake the future's face," observe what kind of effect Nature has upon Dyer.

GEORGE BERKELEY

84.—Planting Arts and Learning in America. This celebrated idealistic philosopher dreamed of founding a university in America. He was in New England from 1730-1731. The significant traits of the poem are the assumption that Europe is in decay, and that in America, seat of natural innocence, human nature as well as literature would be the noblest ever known.

GEORGE LILLO

85.—George Barnwell. With the principles stated in the preface, compare those stated by Steele (above, p. 24).

SOAME JENYNS

86.—An Essay on Virtue. 12. *or itch.* or would itch.

HENRY BROOKE

88.—Nature Superior. 11. *here unite.* stand here on one side, with the other manifestations of Nature; while kings and courts, mean products of human artificial invention, stand on the other.
89.—24. *pernicion.* perniciousness.
90.—10. *Decii.* Members of the public-spirited Roman family Decius.
90.—2. *annual.* annually migrating.
90.—15. *rhomb display, etc.* the flock of birds grouping themselves either as a parallelogram or as a wedge.
91.—Gustavus Vasa. A drama which, like Brooke's poem, was conservative in style but liberal in sentiment. Its performance was, for political reasons, forbidden. It

celebrated the Swedish hero, Gustavus Vasa (1496-1560), who freed Sweden from the dominion of the Danes and who favored the Protestant Reformation. The prologue gives a partisan interpretation of the political situation.

91.—13. *hardy northern sons.* The mountaineers of the Swedish province Dalecarlia.

91.—14. *untainted, and unread, etc.* Observe the implication: the less learned, the more noble.—It should perhaps be added that Gustavus himself was highly educated.

92.—24. *mightier freedom against Caesar fought, etc.* The same contrast between a virtuous nature-people and a venal civilized nation (with the Celts substituted for the Saxons) was presently to be made in Macpherson's *Ossian.*

For the later development of Henry Brooke, see selections below, p. 262.

WILLIAM SHENSTONE

92.—The Schoolmistress. An imitation of Spenser which, like Thomson's later *Castle of Indolence,* introduced a humorous note foreign to the "sage and serious" original.

93.—20. *eftsoons.* at once.

93.—22. *pellucid horn.*—A piece of transparent horn was framed over the page; hence a "horn-book."

93.—30. *Mulla.* The stream near which Spenser wrote part of the *Fairie Queene.*

93.—34. *brogues.* trousers. 36. *ermilin.* ermine.

EDWARD YOUNG

94.—Night Thoughts. In blank verse instead of the heroic couplet, but notice the retention in several passages of balance and antithesis.

96.—Welcome Death. Much the same theme is treated in Shelley's *Adonais,* stanzas 39-40,

> he is not dead, he doth not sleep:
> He hath awakened from the dream of life

(below, v. 224). Contrast the difference between the two treatments or styles.

97.—Original Composition. 1. *there are who.* there are those who.

97.—5. *Elysium.* Paradise.

97.—5. *Tempe.* A fertile valley in Greece.

98.—23. *Armida.* An enchantress in Tasso's *Jerusalem Delivered.* Scarcely an apt simile, since her wizardry was chiefly exerted on the side of evil.

99.—61. *Pope.* An historically important attack upon Pope's celebrated translation of Homer on the grounds that the tone should have been a virile one, and the meter blank verse.

99.—76. *extreme parts.* jocose for the endings of the lines.

99.—77. *Achilles heel* was not hardened by immersion in the river Styx,—and Pope's translation was not inspired by the waters of the Muse's spring.

100.—105. *Augustan age.* A supreme age of literature; in Latin literature, the age of Augustus.

ROBERT BLAIR

100.—The Grave. Try to distinguish between the passages of merit and such phrases as "untasted cheek" (stilted) and "dear man" (flat). This poem is one of the influences upon William Cullen Bryant's *Thanatopsis.*

WILLIAM WHITEHEAD

103.—On Ridicule. Some of the most brilliant works of the ages of Dryden and Pope were satirical comedies and satires in verse.

103.—4. *Momus.* God of Mockery. 4. *Astræa.* Justice.

103.—10. *a Bacon's avarice, etc.* They pass over the great virtues of a Bacon or Cicero, to dwell upon their faults. Compare the modern fashion in biography.

103.—18. *expletives.* words not necessary to the sense, but put in to fill a vacancy.

104.—57. *Clio's numbered prose.* Addison's balanced prose.

MARK AKENSIDE

108.—Pleasures of Imagination. 6. *imp.* strengthen.

109.—29. *nor culture.* i.e., good taste is innate,—like Shaftesbury's moral sense.

109.—37. *he loiters.* Does he?

JOSEPH WARTON

111.—The Enthusiast. 8. *Stow.* A typically formal park.

111.—9. *Attic fanes.* Greek temples.

112.—21. *Versailles.* Typical of French classical taste.

112.—26. *Anio.* A romantic stream in Italy, with a high waterfall.

113.—71. *Boreas.* The North Wind.

113.—76. *Hecat.* Goddess of witchcraft.

115.—118. *Iberean.* Spanish. **124.** *deserts.* any untilled region.

115.—126. *cates.* delicacies.

115.—THE GENIUS AND WRITINGS OF POPE. **9.** *Donne,* etc. Modern criticism would agree as to Swift's verse; but not as to Donne's, the seventeenth-century poet.

115.—14. *Fontenelle . . . La Motte.* French authors, the latter almost forgotten, the former remembered only for his prose.

116.—27. *acer spiritus ac vis.* vehement spirit and power.

116.—50. *Non satis est, etc.* It does not suffice to set down correct words in the line.

117.—57. *Neque enim, etc.* You would not assert that it is enough merely to fill out the line of verse.

117.—71. *Yes, you despise, etc.* Paraphrased from Pope's verse.

117.—86. *qui fit Mæcenas.* Horace's first satire.

118.—98. *nihil inane, etc.* nothing meaningless, nothing dragged in; but he is a pure spring rather than a great river.

118.—100. *Lysias.* A famous Greek orator (c. 400 B.C.)

118.—104. *Boileau.* The greatest critic of the French classical school (c. 1660-1700).

118.—105. *Incapable peut-être.* incapable perhaps of that sublimity which elevates the soul, and of those sentiments which move it, but created to enlighten those whom nature had given those two gifts; laborious, severe, exact, harmonious, he became, in short, the poet of the Reason.

118.—117. *Dryden, etc.* Few in this list would be placed so high today, except Dryden and perhaps Cowley.

118.—122. *Butler, etc.* We should place Donne in a different class, and omit all the others except Butler and Swift.

119.—126. *Pitt, etc.* All of these have failed to survive.

120.—168. *Palamon and Arcite.* Dryden's version of Chaucer's *Knight's Tale.*

120.—174. *lies more level to.* is more nearly on the same level as.

120.—177. *Churchill.* Charles Churchill (1731-1764) a satirical poet who wrote on topics momentarily interesting, and alluded to contemporary celebrities like Lord Chesterfield and Walpole, the Prime Minister.

121.—200. *Music Ode.* Either the *Song for St. Cecilia's Day* (1687) or *Alexander's Feast* (1697).

WILLIAM COLLINS

121.—CYMBELINE. See Act IV, ii, the obsequies of Imogen (Fidele). Guiderus and Arviragus are huntsmen,—hence *chace,* l. 19.

122.—ODE: 1746. In 1745 and 1746 British troops had suffered heavy losses in battles of Fontenoy, Prestonpans, and Falkirk.

123.—ODE TO EVENING. The absence of rhyme is noteworthy. In the older manner are the personifications; in the newer, the prevalent tone and the exquisitely chosen details which sustain it.

The dependent clause which begins with l.1 and ends with l. 14, describes phenomena created by Evening herself, which may please her better than the poet's song.

123.—11. *winds . . . his horn.* hums.

123.—21. *folding-star.* evening star. "The star that bids the shepherd fold" (Milton).

124.—49. The closing stanza is a reversion to the flat and vague.

125.—POETICAL CHARACTER. "That part of it," says Coleridge (Letter to Thelwall, December, 1796), "beginning with 'The band, as fairy legends say,
        Was wove on that creating day.'
has inspired and whirled *me* along with greater agitations of enthusiasm than any the most *impassioned* scene in Schiller or Shakspere."

125.—1-22. Even as only one lady was permitted to wear the magic girdle, so Fancy permits few to enjoy the gift of poetry.

125.—2. *bard.* Spenser. 19. *cest.* girdle.

125.—23. *band.* girdle (emblem of poetical genius).

125.—24. *wove on that creating day, etc.* Poetic genius was created by God at the same time with the Universe.

126.—29. *enthusiast.* Fancy. 46. *tarsel.* falcon.

126.—54. *work.* the girdle.

126.—55. *cliff, etc.* symbolically, Milton.

127.—69. *Waller.* A seventeenth century poet, here typifying the neo-classic style.

127.—72. *one alone.* Milton.

127.—THE PASSIONS. In the days of Greece, Collins says, the passions successfully expressed themselves; now they fail to. Some decades later (see below, iii, 12) William Blake still complains, in *To The Muses:*

        The languid strings do scarcely move,
        The sound is forced, the notes are few!

127.—3. *shell.* lyre.

129.—65. *haunted stream . . . holy calm.* A passage in Coleridge's mind when he wrote Kubla Khan (J. L. Lowes, *Xanadu,* 399).

131.—POPULAR SUPERSTITIONS OF THE HIGHLANDS. The long interval between the date of composition (c. 1749) and that of publication (1788) is noteworthy. The bracketed passages, filling out gaps in an imperfect copy are probably not by Collins, but illustrate the ordinary stylistic standards of the time. For the best discussion of the complicated problem of the true text, see *Poems of Collins,* ed. W. C. Bronson, 1898, pp. 121-132.

Collins' knowledge of Scotch superstitions was derived partly from M. Martin's *Description of the Western Islands of Scotland* (1716),—the book which helped to arouse in Dr. Johnson's mind (c. 1763) a desire to visit those islands, —a desire which Boswell thought "a very romantick fancy" (ed. G. B. Hill, I, 521). Collins also learned Scotch lore from the lips of John Home, the Scotch dramatist to whom his poem is addressed, and who was returning to the Highlands after a sojourn in London.

131.—4. *shall melt, etc.* A prediction fulfilled in 1757, when Home's tragedy *Douglas* began its successful career in London.

131.—5. *cordial youth.* John Barrow, a mutual friend of Home and Collins, who lived in Essex near the river Levant (6).

132.—17. *own.* call it theirs. 18. *Doric.* simple, natural.

132.—23. *swart tribes.* Brownies.

133.—37. *boreal.* northern.

133.—39. *had.* would have. 41. *Runic.* northern and ancient.

133.—42. *uncouth.* strange (probably not in a contemptuous sense).

133.—45. *dirge,* etc. Sir Walter Scott may be said to have taken this advice when he imitated the coronach (see below, iv, 49) and the pibroch (iv, 59) of the Highlands.

133.—48. *shiel.* a rude shelter.

133.—57. *dreary dreams, etc.* Martin (pp. 300, 321) tells of the "second-sight" and of the fatal predictions of witchcraft.

133.—59. *strath.* valley.

134.—65. *them.* those possessed of evil powers.

134.—73. *Charles.* Charles I, beheaded in 1649. The Highlanders were pro-Stuart, sympathized with the rebellion against George I, and consequently rejoiced at the victories

of Prestonpans and Falkirk, and lamented the defeat of
Colloden (where the victor was William, Duke of Cumber-
land). Observe that this stanza is a digression from the
chief theme, out of tune with it, and not a very happy
topic to touch upon in a poem addressed to a Scotch friend.

134.—83. *one William.* William III, King of England,
whose accession in 1689 brought the reign of the Stuarts
to an end.

135.—91. *dank Will.* the will-o'-the-wisp.

135.—100. *wily monster.* The water-demon, or kelpie,—
again mentioned in ll. 108 and 137.

136.—121. *For him in vain.* An echo of Thomson's
passage (above, p. 63, 89 ff.) directly, or through Gray
(below, p. 153, 21ff.).

136.—123. *to-fall.* close.

136.—142. *hoar pile.* An island on which the bones of
pigmies were believed to have been found (Martin, p. 82).

136.—147. *three fair realms.* Scotland, Ireland, and
Norway, many of whose kings were supposed to be buried
on the island of St. Iona (Martin, pp. 260-261).

137.—155. *Kilda.* Martin (pp. 280-295) ascribed a high
moral character to the natives of St. Kilda.

138.—177. *sheen.* bright.

138.—180. *From them he sung, etc.* In those scenes he
laid *Macbeth*.

138.—192. *Tasso, etc.* Alluding to *Jerusalem Delivered*
(translated by Fairfax in 1600), canto xiii, 41-43, 46.

139.—215. *Jonson, etc.* Ben Jonson visited William
Drummond, the poet, at his estate near Edinburgh in 1619.—
Their conversation was upon topics of less primitive char-
acter from those which Collins recommends.

THOMAS WARTON

141.—PLEASURES OF MELANCHOLY. Before reading this,
read Milton's *Il Penseroso*. What do you find in Warton
that is not in Milton?

141.—17. *charnel.* tomb.

142.—38. *Busyrane, etc.* Spenser (*Fairie Queene*, III,
xi-xii) describes the brave female knight Britomart ventur-
ing to the house of the dreaded enchanter Busyrane.

142.—42. *towering, armed, etc.* From *Paradise Lost*,
vi, 110.

142.—50. *fated fair.* Pope's Belinda who was fated to
lose her lock (See *The Rape of the Lock*, ii).—Observe that
this attack on Pope preceded Joseph Warton's prose *Essay
on Pope* (above, p. 115).

143.—OBSERVATIONS ON THE FAIRY QUEEN. 9-11. *Spenser . . . did not live in an age of planning.* But see the plan for the *Fairy Queen* in his prefatory letter,—"to portray in Arthur. . . . the image of a brave knight, perfected in the twelve moral virtues, which is the purpose of these first twelve books."

145.—63. *disgusts.* displeases.

146.—107. *sensible.* i.e., as a rule sensible, though mistaken in the following remark.

148.—GRAVE OF KING ARTHUR. 10. *Camlan.* A river in Cornwall, where Arthur fought against his treacherous nephew Mordred.

148.—20. *Merlin.* The enchanter.

149.—DUGDALE'S MONASTICON. An important antiquarian work, in three volumes (1655-1673) by Sir William Dugdale, describing the ancient English monasteries.

149.—5. *Henry's rage.* They were dissolved by Henry VIII.

150.—STONEHENGE. The prehistoric group of huge stones on Salisbury Plain. Warton muses on four legendary explanations of its unknown origin: (1) that Arthur's father Pendragon conveyed it by Merlin's magic from the Orient, (2) that it was a Druid temple, (3) that it was erected by the Danish invaders, and (4) that it was the burial place of the earliest British kings, descendants of Brutus the Trojan.

150.—LODON. The river Loddon, in central England.

THOMAS GRAY

Observe the differences in substance, sentiments, diction, and metre, between the earlier poems and the later.

152.—ELEGY . . . IN A COUNTRY CHURCHYARD. Mark the three principal themes: (1) churchyard reflections on death, (2) the dignity of humble life, (3) the unknown young poet, a melancholy lover of nature and of man.

152.—2. *lea.* grassy field.

153.—21. *For them no more, etc.* Perhaps a reminiscence of Thomson's Seasons (above, p. 63).

154.—35. *awaits,* not "await." Death waits to snatch away "the pomp of power," etc.

154.—41. *storied urn.* An urn, containing the ashes, with an inscription giving the history of the departed.

154.—41. *animated.* looking alive.

154.—57. *Hampden.* The patriot who resisted Charles I's attempt to impose a tax unconstitutionally. Originally Gray

chose classical personages for this passage,—Cato, Tully, and
Caesar.

155.—78. *still.* always.

155.—85. *who, to dumb forgetfulness.* who, about to
become, etc., or, whoever resigned this life and became a
prey, etc.

155.—105-112. These stanzas are inscribed on the monument to Gray at Stoke Poges.

157.—120. *Science.* Knowledge.

157.—THE PROGRESS OF POESY. The motto (Pindar,
Olympics ii, 153-4) intimated that this Pindaric ode, and
the next, would be clear only to the intelligent.

157.—1. *Awake, etc.* "The various sources of poetry,
which gives life and lustre to all it touches are here described; its quiet majestic progress, enriching every subject
(otherwise dry and barren) with a pomp of diction and
luxuriant harmony of numbers, and its more rapid and
irresistible course, when swoln and hurried away by the conflict of tumultuous passions."—Gray.

157.—9. *Ceres' reign.* grain fields.

158.—13-24. "Power of harmony to calm the turbulent
passions of the soul."—Gray.

158.—21. *feathered king.* eagle.

158.—21-41. "Power of harmony to produce all the graces
of motion in the body."—Gray.

158.—27. *Idalia.* A town famous for its temple of Venus.

158.—36. *Queen.* Venus.

159.—42-53. "To compensate the real and the imaginary
ills of life, the Muse was given to mankind by the same
Providence that sends the Day, by its cheerful presence, to
dispel the gloom and terrors of the Night."—Gray.

159.—46. *fond.* foolish. 53. *Hyperion.* The Sun.

159.—54-65. "Extensive influence of poetic genius over
the remotest and most uncivilized nations, its connection
with liberty, and the virtues that naturally attend on it.
(See the Erse, Norwegian, and Welsh fragments, the Lap-
land and American songs)."—Gray.

159.—66-82. "Progress of Poesy from Greece to Italy
and from Italy to England."—Gray.

160.—78. *Latian.* Roman. 84. *Nature's Darling.* Shakspere.

160.—95. *Nor second he, etc.* Milton.

161.—112. *what daring spirit.* Gray himself.

161.—115. *Theban eagle.* Pindar. 123. *great.* worldly
great.

162.—THE BARD. After Edward I had conquered Wales
(1277-1284), he issued the usual edicts against strolling min-

strels. By the seventeenth century his act had come to be misrepresented as an order to exterminate all the Welsh bards; and in this form the tradition reached Gray, who had recently been aroused to enthusiasm for Welsh poetical remains by his acquaintance Parry and in other ways. In his preface to *The Bard,* Gray said: "The following ode is founded on a tradition current in Wales, that Edward I, when he completed the conquest of the country, ordered all the bards that fell into his hands to be put to death." Gray's own outline of the poem is as follows:

"The army of Edward I as they march through a deep valley, are suddenly stopped by the appearance of a venerable figure seated on the summit of an inaccessible rock, who, with a voice more than human, reproaches the King with all the misery and desolation which he had brought on his country; foretells the misfortunes of the Norman race, and with prophetic spirit declares, that all his cruelty shall never extinguish the noble ardor of poetic genius in this island; and that men shall never be wanting to celebrate true virtue and valor in immortal strains, to expose vice and infamous pleasure, and boldly censure tyranny and oppression. His song ended, he precipitates himself from the mountain, and is swallowed up by the river that rolls at its foot."

162.—8. *Cambria.* Wales. **163.—28.** *Hoel.* a prince and poet.

163.—28. *Llewellyn.* a gentle prince.

163.—29. *Cadwallo.* a poet.

163.—29. *Urien.* a poet. 33. *Modred.* an unknown.

163.—48-100. In these lines, the ghosts of the slain bards join. Gray says: "See the Norwegian Ode,—*The Fatal Sisters;*" below, p. 219.

164.—55. *Berkley's roofs, etc.* Edward II was murdered at Berkley Castle, his queen, Isabel of France, being in rebellion against him. Their son Edward III won victories in France.

164.—64. "Death of that king, abandoned by his children, and even robbed in his last moments by his courtiers and his mistress."—Gray.

164.—67. "The Black Prince, dead some time before his father."—Gray.

164.—70. "Magnificence of Richard II's reign."—Gray.

165.—77-82. "Richard II was starved to death."—Gray.

165.—83-86. "Ruinous civil wars of York and Lancaster."—Gray.

165.—87. "Henry VI, George Duke of Clarence, Edward

V, Richard Duke of York, etc. believed to be murdered secretly in the Tower of London."—Gray.

165.—89. *his consort.* Margaret of Anjou, Henry VI's queen.

165.—89. *his father.* Henry V. **90.** *Usurper.* Henry VI.

165.—91. *rose, etc.* "The white and red roses, devices of York and Lancaster."—Gray.

165.—93. *boar.*—The villainous Richard III.

165.—99. *Half of thy heart.* Edward I's beloved queen Eleanor, who died soon after the conquest of Wales.

165.—102. *me.* the Bard.

166.—110. *ye genuine kings, etc.* When Henry VIII of the house of Tudor (Welsh), ascended the throne, the Welsh were appeased.

166.—115. *a form divine.* Queen Elizabeth.

166.—121. *Taliessin.* "Chief of the Bards."—Gray.

166.—128. *buskin'd measure.* dramatic form, the age of Shakspere.

167.—131. *a voice.* Milton.

167.—133. *distant warblings.*—"The succession of poets after Milton's time."—Gray.

SAMUEL RICHARDSON

167.—THE POWER OF INNOCENCE. The pursuer Lovelace seems to have Clarissa Harlowe securely in his power,—imprisoned in a house occupied only by his villainous hired agents.

168.—12. *Will.* Another one of Lovelace's hirelings.

170.—THE DEATH OF CLARISSA. Long after the above episode, Clarissa has been forcibly seduced; and now she lies dying.

171.—41. *the blame-able kindness.* he is kind in wishing her to live, but blame-able because she would be happier dead.

171.—66. *I remember.* This remark and "words of scripture," two lines below, are intended to characterize Lovelace's friend as a worldling.

174.—THE DEATH OF LOVELACE. Wounded in a duel by an avenger of Clarissa's betrayal.

DAVID HARTLEY

175.—OBSERVATIONS ON MAN. **176.—50.** *sensible ones.* sensations.

178.—100. *catachrestically.* figuratively.

JOHN DALTON

179.—DESCRIPTIVE POEM. Praising scenes which, two generations later, were to be haunts of Wordsworth, Coleridge, Southey, etc.

JANE ELLIOT

181.—THE FLOWERS OF THE FOREST. A dirge for the Scottish youth slain at the battle of Flodden Field, 1513.

181.—1. *lilting.* singing. 3. *loaning.* lane.

181.—4. *wede.* plucked. 5. *at bughts.* in the pens.

181.—6. *dowie.* drooping. 8. *leglin.* milk-pail.

181.—9. *hairst.* harvest-time. 10. *bandsters.* binders of sheaves.

181.—10. *lyart.* gray-haired. 10. *runkled.* wrinkled.

181.—11. *fleeching.* wheedling. 13. *swankies.* youths.

181.—17. *dool.* sorrow.

THOMAS AMORY

182.—JOHN BUNCLE. **183.**—26. *Sub pedibus, etc.* He treads beneath his feet storms and harsh thunders.

LAURENCE STERNE

184.—TRISTRAM SHANDY. **185.**—37. *Literae humaniores.* Polite literature.

186.—42. *philanthropy.* love of mankind.

186.—DEATH OF LE FEVER. Contrast with Clarissa Harlowe's, above, p. 170.

188.—67. *ligament.* tie which bound Uncle Toby to the orphaned boy.

191.—11. *Sensorium.* heart, or nerve center.

JAMES MACPHERSON

191.—FINGAL. Swaran, King of Lochlin (Scandinavia), has been captured in battle by Fingal, King of Morven (Scotland); but Fingal gives him life and liberty, recalling that they have the same ancestor Trenmor (whose deeds have just been sung), and being especially moved by love and gratitude to Swaran's sister Agandecca, who was slain by her father Starno because she warned Fingal of a plot against his life.

192.—36. *desert.* uncultivated land. **193.—45.** *Erin.*
North Britain.

193.—59. *Ossian, Carril, Ullin.* The bards.

193.—COLMA'S LAMENT. Sung before Fingal by the
female bard Minona.

195.—LAST WORDS OF OSSIAN. 7. *ghosts of the bards.*
Five years before Macpherson, Gray had them join in chorus
with his Bard (see above, p. 162).

RICHARD HURD

196.—LETTERS ON CHIVALRY. 13. *our philosophical bard.*
Pope (*Moral Essays,* i, 208; but Pope wrote "Nature *well*
known").

198.—2. *Gierusalemme Liberata.* Tasso's *Jerusalem Delivered* (1581) a romantic epic of Godfrey of Bouillon's
crusade.

198.—15. *But as Homer was, etc.* Inasmuch as Homer
was broadminded, he would have preferred feudal manners
above Greek, could he have known them.

198.—31. *omnes illacrymabiles* [*for inlacrimabiles*], *etc.*
"All are overwhelmed by the long night of death,—beyond
the reach of tears and forgotten, because they had no sacred
bard" (Horace, *Odes,* IV, ix, 26).

199.—35. *rude.* Observe the very gradual appreciation
of the medieval. When it is treated by sixteenth century
poets, such as Tasso and Spenser, Hurd can appreciate it;
but the really medieval (except, possibly, Chaucer) has to
wait for the further progress of taste and knowledge.

199.—45. *Iliad.* Macpherson had the audacity to compare the "barbarity" of Homer's heroes with the kindness
and generosity of Ossian's.

200.—82. *Canidia.* A sorceress.

200.—83. *Virgil's myrtles, etc. Æneid,* iii, 23; *Jerusalem Delivered,* iii, stanza 43ff.

200.—86. *Medea, in a rant.* Metamorphoses, vii, 1.

200.—90. *His ego, etc.* "I have often seen Moeris [a
magician] turn into a wolf and take to the woods; I have
seen him summon spirits from the depths of the tomb, and
remove harvests" (*Eclogues,* viii, 97).

200.—99. *Non isthic, etc.* "Here no one reduces my
possessions with an envious eye." (Horace, *Epistles,* I,
xiv, 27.)

201.—119. *animas, etc.* Quoted above, l. 91.

201.—126. *Shakspere, etc. The Tempest,* V, i, 41.—The
true reading of the last line is: "Have waked their sleepers,
oped, and let them forth."

201.—134. *Nor staid, etc.* Paradise Regained, iv, 421-430.

202.—148. *sagacious critic.* Said ironically.

202.—177. *gallant.* civilized.

THOMAS LELAND

203.—THE BETRAYAL. Salisbury, the chief character, is being guided by D'Aumont, the betrayer.

CHRISTOPHER SMART

205.—SONG TO DAVID. The objects are intended to be contrasted with King David at prayer (ll. 9 and 26).

205.—2. *bastion's mole.* projecting part of a fortification.

205.—4. *gier-eagle.* vulture (Biblical word).

205.—9. *And far beneath the tide.* In sense, follows immediately after "in the sea."

206.—29. *mute.* the inanimate. 33. *largess.* alms.

206.—35. *Alba.* the sun? **207.**—59. *catholic.* general, congregational.

207.—64. *Thou that stupendous truth believed.* See, e.g., Psalm ii.

EVAN EVANS

207.—OWAIN GWYNEDD. From *Some Specimens of the Poetry of the Ancient Welsh Bards, translated into English, with Explanatory Notes on the Historical Passages.*—Owen Gwynedd was a prince of Wales, c. 1157.

207.—8. *Iwerdden.* Ireland. 9. *Lochlynians.* Danes.

207.—20. *Menai.* The bay in which the invaders landed.

THOMAS GRAY

208.—LETTERS ON OSSIAN. The first letter refers, not to the printed edition, but to manuscript copies of the samples which Macpherson had submitted to John Howe.

208.—1. *Erse.* Gaelic.

208.—11. *Hardycanute.* Given above, p. 45; see also the note.—Gray was mistaken in believing it ancient.

209.—20. *recollecting.* gathering itself for a new onslaught.

210.—9. *so extasié.* in such ecstasy.

210.—19. *devil and kirk.* powers of evil and good.

211.—32. *Mr. Evans.* See above, p. 207.

211.—12. *Scotchman of my own time.* i.e., since Thomson.

212.—26. *Adam Smith, etc.* This array of witnesses, who at best were confusing brief oral remains with Macpherson's elaborate fabrications, illustrates the low state of philological learning in this field at the time.

213.—DESCENT OF ODIN. From the Old Norse *Poetic Edda,* through Bartholin's Latin verse translation (1689). See p. 358. Odin, disguised as a traveller, descends to the lower world to learn the future fate of his favorite son Balder. Balder is destined to be killed by a mistletoe shot by his blind brother Hoder; and Hoder, in turn, will be slain by the child of Odin and Rinda.

213.—4. *Hela.* a goddess of the lower world.

214.—22. *Runic.* magical.—Compare this passage with Hickes' *Incantation of Hervor,* above, p. 44.

215.—44. *bev'rage of the bee.* Rather "from the bee," it being mead, fermented from honey.

216.—75. *what virgins.* Odin sees the Fates, whom mortal eyes cannot see; therefore the Prophetess recognizes his divinity. He in turn now knows her to be the ruling goddess of the lower world.

216.—90. *Lok.* The evil god, bound in chains until the crack of doom.

216.—THE TRIUMPHS OF OWEN. Compare this with its original, Evans' prose translation, above, p. 207.—The following three selections are also based on Evans' *Specimens;* but on Latin, not English, versions.

219.—THE FATAL SISTERS. Based upon a Latin version of an Old Norse poem, supposed to be sung by the Valkyrs, or Choosers of the Slain, before they fly to the battle between the Scandinavians and the Irish in which (1014) the Earl of the Orkneys was slain.

219.—17. *Mista, etc.* Valkyrs. **220.—31.** *Gondula, etc.* Valkyrs.

220.—41. *dauntless earl.* of Orkney. **44.** *King.* of Ireland.

THOMAS PERCY

227.—CHEVY CHASE. For the best text, see Childs's *Ballads,* (*The Hunting of the Cheviot*). Bishop Percy's text is fairly good.—*Chevy Chase* is probably founded on the battle fought in 1388 between the Scotch under Douglas and the English under Percy, which is likewise the subject of the ballad, *The Battle of Otterburn.* In *Chevy Chase,*

Percy is represented as starting the conflict by hunting in Douglas' territory. As this is an English ballad, and not a Scottish, everything is put into the best light from the English point of view.

The difficulty of reading these ballads will be much lessened if you will read them aloud, for the unfamiliar appearance of the words is often due only to their spelling; thus if you will speak "owar" (l. 29.) you will recognize it as "hour," and so with "Percè" (for Percy), bomen (for bowmen), the (for they). Such words are therefore not glossed here.

227.—fit. part. 5. *in the mauger.* despite.

228.—10. *let.* hinder. 12. *meany.* company.

228.—16. *he.* high. 20. *reas.* rouse.

228.—21. *bickarte.* coursed. 21. *bent.* field.

228.—22. *aras.* arrows. 25. *greves glent.* groves glanced.

228.—27. *abone.* above. 28. *yerly.* early.

228.—28. *monnyn.* Monday.

228.—31. *mort.* note signifying the death.

228.—32. *sydis shear.* all sides. 33. *guyrry.* dead game.

228.—34. *bryttling.* quartering. **229.—37.** *verament.* truly.

229.—40. *at his hand.* shading his eyes with his hand.

229.—57. *glede.* glowing coal. 58. *barne.* fellow.

230.—70. *cast.* intend. **230.—72.** *ton.* one.

230.—78. *yerle.* earl. 81. *cors.* curse.

231.—101. *And you.* If you. 106. *sloughe.* slew.

231.—107. *bydys.* abides. 107. *bent.* business.

231.—110. *wouche.* harm. 117. *garde.* caused.

231.—122. *basnites.* helmets. **232.—123.** *male.* armor.

232.—123. *myne-ye-ple.* gauntlet. 124. *sterne.* stern warriors.

232.—125. *freyke.* man. 130. *myllàn.* Milan steel.

232.—134. *heal.* hail. **233.—165.** *se.* saw.

235.—214. *Sir John, etc.* The heroes named in this list are mostly identifiable, although the names have in some cases been corrupted.

235.—236. *makys.* husbands. **237.** *carpe.* talk.

236.—268. *that tear, etc.* The meaning of this line is unknown.

237.—279. *balys bete.* remedy our evils.

237.—SIR PATRICK SPENCE. It is possible that this ballad commemorates the loss of a company of Scottish nobles sent to Norway in 1290 to bring back the fiancée of Edward I's eldest son. Its chief purpose was to glorify the mariner who obeyed his king in the face of certain death.

237.—9. *braid.* large or long. 14. *lauch.* laugh.

238.—29. *laith.* loath. 30. *weet.* wet.

239.—ROBIN HOOD AND GUY OF GISBORNE. One of the oldest of the Robin Hood ballads.—Percy's text is a fairly good one, but even the best texts (see Child's) must be defective, since they omit information necessary for an understanding of the story. The two yeomen that Robin dreams about must be Sir Guy and the Sheriff of Nottingham; and somehow Robin must have learned that Little John has been captured by the Sheriff.

239.—1. *shaws.* groves. 1. *shradds.* coppices.

239.—5. *woodweele.* thrush. 10. *sweaven.* dream.

239.—11. *yemen.* yeomen. 21. *buske . . . bowne.* make ready.

240.—35. *capullhyde.* horsehide. 42. *farley.* strange.

240.—46. *And a.* if a. 56. *slade.* glade.

241.—66. *fetteled him.* made ready. 72. *boote.* help.

242.—97. *wilfulle, etc.* lost.

242.—112. *unsett steven.* unexpected moment.

242.—113. *shroggs.* saplings. 116. *y-fere.* together.

243.—126. *garlande.* the ring in which the saplings stood.

244.—153. *reachles.* careless. **245.**—188. *lowe.* hill.

OLIVER GOLDSMITH

250.—THE DESERTED VILLAGE. 45. *decent.* seemly, becoming.

253.—155. *vacant.* untroubled, at ease.

256.—242. *terms and tides presage.* foretell the dates of the terms, or divisions of the year, and the changes of the tides.

256.—243. *gauge.* calculate the capacity of a barrel.

257.—265. *game of goose.* a game played with dice.

257.—282. *pressed.* urged to do so.

260.—377. *Altama.* The river Altamaha in Georgia.

262.—451. *Torno.* The river Tornea, which flows into the Gulf of Bothnia (in the Baltic), "the polar world."

262.—451. *Pambamarca.* a mountain in Ecuador, South America.

JEAN ADAMS

273.—THERE'S NAE LUCK. 4. *jauds.* jades.

274.—10. *ava.* at all. 17. *slaes.* sloes.

274.—21. *bauk.* cross-beam. 23. *thraw.* twist.
274.—29. *bigonet.* linen cap. **275.**—38. *caller.* cool, fresh.
275.—44. *greet.* cry. 52. *neist.* next.
275.—56. *lave.* rest.

LADY ANNE LINDSAY

275.—Auld Robin Gray. 1. *kye.* cattle.
276.—9. *a week but only twa.* only two weeks.

JAMES BEATTIE

277.—The Minstrel. Compare this poet with the one in Gray's *Elegy,* above, p. 152.
278.—33. *amused.* drew his sympathetic interest. See above, note on p. 54, 1. 56.
279.—55. *ancient dame.* she was the conveyer of oral tradition.

ROBERT FERGUSON

280.—Leith Races. The youth meets Mirth, who tempts him to go to the races.
280.—2. *rokelay.* short cloak.
280.—3. *rigg o' corn.* stretch of grain field.
280.—6. *lift.* sky. 10. *ferly.* wonder.
281.—16. *ware.* bet. 20. *gate.* way.
281.—21. *win, gin.* go, if.
281.—21. *spier.* ask. 30. *canty.* cheerful.
281.—37. *feggs.* faith. 39. *screw, etc.* dance.
281.—40. *blate.* shy. 43. *hip.* miss.

JOHN LANGHORNE

282.—The Country Justice. Contrast this stilted effort to praise loving-kindness with Chatterton's attempt, the *Balade of Charitie* (p. 288), and with Burns's *The Unco Guid* (p. 344).
282.—3. *He.* Man. 6. *Holds but a mansion.* dwells in a frail body.
283.—15. *Canadian . . . Minden.* Alluding to scenes of the war (1754-1763) between England and France. They fought a battle at Minden, Germany.

THOMAS DAY

283.—DESOLATION OF AMERICA. 3. *there.* in the American colonies.

283.—4. *slaves.* the Hessian hired troops, or perhaps all the British forces.

284.—25. *Devoted realm, etc.* Alluding to the Pilgrims of the seventeenth century.

THOMAS CHATTERTON

286.—BODDYNGE FLOURETTES. Chatterton gave a wrong sense to some of his archaic words. The following glosses give only the meaning he attributed to them.—Many of the unfamiliar looking words you will recognize when you speak them.

286.—1. *boddynge.* budding. 1. *flourettes.* flowers.

286.—2. *mees.* meadows. 4. *nesh.* tender.

286.—5. *straughte,* stretched. 6. *dynne.* noise.

286.—9. *alestake.* alehouse sign. 12. *albeytte.* albeit.

287.—23. *woddie sede.* willow seed. 24. *levynne.* lightning.

287.—24. *lemes.* gleams. 30. *steyncèd.* stained.

287.—31. *neidher.* neither. 32. *chafe.* warm.

288.—43. *pheeres.* mates. 48. *bante.* accursed.

288.—48. *hie.* highly.

288.—CHARITIE. 1. *Virgnè.* The sign of the Virgin (Zodiac).

288.—4. *mole.* soft. 5. *peede chelandri.* pied goldfinch.

288.—7. *aumere.* mantle. **289.**—13. *hiltring.* hiding.

289.—13. *fetive.* festive. 15. *holme.* oak.

289.—16. *covent.* convent. 19. *bretful.* brimful.

289.—22. *glommed.* gloomy. 22. *spright.* spirit.

289.—23. *frowynd.* withered. 25. *dorture.* sleeping.

289.—26. *gre.* grow. 30. *forswat.* sunburned.

289.—30. *smethe.* smoke. 30. *drenche.* drink.

289.—35. *lowings.* flashings. 36. *clymmynge.* noisy.

290.—37. *Cheves.* moves. 37. *embollen.* swelled.

290.—39. *gallard.* frightened. 45. *chapournette.* round hat.

290.—49. *mist.* poor. 52. *autremette.* white robe.

290.—56. *horse-millanare.* saddler; one who decks out a horse.

290.—63. *crouche.* cross. **291.—66.** *faitour.* vaga-bond.

291.—75. *Limitoure.* begging friar.
291.—82. *halline.* joy. 85. *unhailie.* unhappy.
291.—87. *semecope.* coat. 91. *mittee.* mighty.

MAURICE MORGANN

292.—Shakspere. **293.—56.** *one man.* viz., Shakspere.
294.—69. *Stagyrite.* Aristotle.—This hope was fulfilled in the days of Coleridge and Hazlitt.
294.—84. *Sciota.* correctly, Scioto, a river in Ohio.
294.—97. *lay in.* established. 100. *indecent.* improper.
295.—123. *complexion.* temperament.
296.—145. *The Chronicle, etc.* From whatever source Shakspere draws it is all made equally good.
296.—155. *Weird Sisters.* The Witches in *Macbeth*.
296.—163. *the milk of human kindness, etc.* Quotations from *Macbeth*.
296.—168. *wake to the truth of things, etc.* Somewhat anticipating De Quincey's *On the Knocking at the Gate in Macbeth* (below, v, 307).

JOHN MAYNE

297.—Logan Braes. 4. *braes.* banks. **298.—7.** *faes.* foes.
298.—11. *mirk.* dark. 18. *dauner.* wander.
298.—22. *skaithless.* unharmed.

THOMAS JAMES MATHIAS

298.—Tomb of Argantyr. Compare this with Hickes' prose version, above, p. 44, and note.
299.—Twilight of the Gods. The earth-giant Ymir, once slain by Odin, and the world-embracing Serpent, will one day arise and bring the world to an end.
300.—Renovation. Describing the new epoch of peace and joy after the old world and gods have been destroyed.

HUGH DOWNMAN and JAMES JOHN-STONE

302-303.—Death Song *and* Lodbrokar-Quitha. Versions of passages concerning the Ragnar Lodbrok, the celebrated half-legendary Viking.

WILLIAM COWPER

304.—THE INHUMANITY OF MAN. With this attack on the slave-traffic, compare the selection from Henry Mackenzie, above, p. 271.—Since 1772 slaves were free in England, but not until 1834 did they become so in the British colonies.

306.—LOVE OF ENGLAND. 9. *Ausonia.* Italy.

306.—32. *Chatham.* William Pitt, first Earl of Chatham, who, after a brilliant career as orator and statesman, died in 1778.

307.—33. *Wolfe.* General James Wolfe fell in the victorious battle of Quebec, Sept. 13, 1759.

308.—THE BASTILLE. The prison in Paris in which political prisoners were incarcerated, and which was stormed by the populace July 14, 1789, four years after these lines were published.

308.—22. *visionary emblem.* The tree seen in a dream by Nebuchadnezzar (*Daniel* iv, 10).

310.—66. *Manichean god.* Evil, by the ancient Manicheans regarded as co-eternal with Good, and as creator of man.

311.—53. *But trees, etc.* An anticipation of Wordsworth's *Expostulation and Reply* (below, iii, 110).

312.—KINDNESS TO ANIMALS. Compare Jago, *The Goldfinches* (above, p. 178) and Sterne's Uncle Toby letting the fly escape (p. 185).

312.—MY MOTHER'S PICTURE. Cowper had no picture of his mother until a cousin sent him one, fifty-two years after his mother's death.

316.—TO MARY. Addressed to his "second mother," Mrs. Unwin, then in her second childhood.

318.—THE CASTAWAY. Cowper had read in George Anson's *Voyage Round the World* (1748) the incident here related, and believed it a parallel to his own spiritual experience.

HUGH BLAIR

320.—PASTORAL POETRY. 1. *this insipidity.* i.e., of conventional pastoral poetry.

EDWARD JERNINGHAM

321.—A NEW POETIC WORLD. **322.**—14. *Asgard.* The realm of the Scandinavian gods.

ROBERT BURNS

322.—MARY MORISON. 5. *bide the stoure.* endure the conflict of life.

323.—THE HOLY FAIR. A church gathering, at which the fanatical are seen, as well as those who make it a picnic.—For a prototype of the allegorical figure Fun, see *Leith Races,* above, p. 280.

323.—7. *hirplin.* limping. 7. *furs.* furrows.

323.—8. *lav'rocks.* larks. 12. *hizzies.* jades.

323.—13. *skelpin.* proceding noisily. 16. *lyart.* gray.

324.—25. *curchie.* curtsy. 34. *feck.* most.

324.—36. *screed.* rip. 42. *daffin.* merriment.

324.—43. *gin.* if. 43. *runkl'd.* wrinkled.

324.—46. *tittlin.* whispering. 48. *wabster.* weaver.

324.—53. *fyled.* soiled. 325.—55. *swatch.* sample.

325.—67. *an's loof.* and his hand.

325.—71. *Moodie etc.* The names are those of actual ministers of the district. They differed in doctrine or in method.

325.—71. *speels the holy door.* climbs the pulpit.

325.—73. *Hornie.* the devil. 83. *eldritch.* unearthly.

325.—85. *cantharidian.* blistering.

326.—107. *water-fit.* river's mouth. 110. *mim.* prim.

326.—111. *Common Sense.* Burns's friend, Dr. Mackenzie, leaves the meeting.

326.—115. *raibles.* rattles off. 118. *manse.* parsonage.

327.—121. *hafflins-wise.* halfways. 123. *butt an' ben.* quickly.

327.—123. *change-house.* tavern.—The preaching tent had a convenient back-entrance into it.

327.—124. *yill-caup.* ale cup. 131. *Leeze me on.* Bless.

327.—133. *lear.* learning. 134. *pangs.* crams.

327.—136. *penny-wheep.* weak beer.

327.—144. *toddy.* whiskey and hot water.

328.—162. *whun-stane.* mill-stone. 172. *cogs.* basins.

328.—176. *dawds.* hunks. 177. *gawsie.* buxom.

328.—177. *gash.* shrewd. 179. *kebbuck.* cheese.

189. *gi'es them 't, etc.* gives them a free rein.

329.—186. *waesucks.* alas. 189. *melvie.* soil with meal.

329.—199. *slaps.* fence gaps. 199. *billies.* fellows.

329.—203. *crack.* talking. 211. *houghmagandie.* fornication.

329.—EPISTLE TO J. LAPRAIK. Lapraik was a local wit and poet, admired by Burns.

330.—16. *sairs.* serves. 18. *knappin-hammers.* stone-hammers. 21. *stirks.* young steers.

330.—COTTER'S SATURDAY NIGHT. 1. *friend.* Robert Aiken, a lawyer in Ayr, and a friend and patron of Burns.

331.—21. *stacher.* stagger. 22. *flichterin'.* fluttering.

331.—23. *ingle.* fireside. 26. *kiaugh.* worry.

331.—30. *tentie.* heedful. 332.—40. *uncos.* news.

332.—48. *eydent.* diligent. 49. *jauk.* trifle.

333.—69. *blate.* shy. 69. *laithfu'.* sheepish.

333.—82. *Is there, etc.* Observe the recurrence of the same motif as in the Jenny Distaff story, above, p. 26.

333.—92. *parritch.* porridge. 334.—93. *hawkie.* cow.

334.—94. *hallan.* partition. 96. *weel-hained.* carefully saved.

334.—99. *towmond.* twelve-month. 99. *lint.* flax.

334.—99. *bell.* flower. 105. *lyart haffets.* gray locks.

334.—107. *wales.* selects. 335.—133. *he.* St. John.

336.—166. *An honest man, etc.* Pope, *Essay on Man,* iv, 248.

336.—182. *Wallace.* The thirteenth-century Scotch patriot who resisted the English conquest unto death.

337.—TO A MOUSE.—Burns saved the mouse from being killed by the boy who was leading his ploughhorses.

337.—1. *sleekit.* sleek. 4. *bickering brattle.* hurrying scamper.

337.—6. *pattle.* paddle to clean the plough with.

337.—15. *daimen icker in a thrave.* an ear or two in a whole shock.

338.—29. *coulter.* the part of the plough which cuts the sward first.

338.—35. *thole.* endure. 36. *canreuch.* hoar-frost.

338.—MOUNTAIN DAISY. 339.—3. *stoure.* dust. 23. *histie.* dry.

340.—EPISTLE TO A YOUNG FRIEND. 341.—30. *poortith.* poverty.

341.—30. *stare.* watches. 343.—87. *reck the rede.* take the advice.

344.—THE UNCO GUID. 7. *heapit happer.* full hopper.

344.—11. *douce.* prudent. 12. *glaikit.* foolish.

345.—15. *donsie.* unlucky. 18. *niffer.* difference.

346.—47. *lug.* ear. 48. *aiblins.* maybe.

346.—51. *kennin.* trifle.

346.—JOHN ANDERSON. 4. *brent.* smooth.

346.—5. *beld.* bald. 7. *pow.* pate, head.

348.—AULD LANG SYNE. 9. *be your pint-stowp.* be good for your two quart flagon.

349.—21. *fiere.* chum. 23. *guid-willie waught.* good-will draught.

WILLIAM BECKFORD

351.—VATHEK. The theme: "The Caliph Vathek, who for the sake of empty pomp and forbidden power, had sullied himself with a thousand crimes, became a prey to grief without end, and remorse without mitigation" (Beckford).

THE POETIC EDDA

358.—From *The Analytical Review,* ii, 461, December, 1788.

GILBERT WHITE

362.—THE TORTOISE. 6. *hibernaculum.* winter-quarters.

ERASMUS DARWIN

364.—*Procul este, profani.* Away, ye profane!

WILLIAM GILPIN

371.—PICTURESQUE BEAUTY. For the text of this passage I am obliged to Professor Walter Graham.

JAMES BRUCE AND WILLIAM BARTRAM

373 ff.—The tales of these travellers stimulated the imagination of Coleridge. See the notes on *The Ancient Mariner* and *Kubla Khan* in volume iii.

WILLIAM GODWIN

388.—POLITICAL JUSTICE. **390.**—9. *Montesquieu.* The philosophic and liberal author of *The Spirit of Laws* (1748). This passage is in xi, 6.

390.—13. *"not like,"* etc. From Sterne's sermon, *On a Good Conscience.*

393.—58. *ignis fatuus.* will-o'-the-wisp.

RICHARD POLWHELE

396.—REGNER LODBROG. Compare with the versions of Downman and Johnstone, above, p. 302.

398.—HOTHER. See the notes on Gray's *Descent of Odin.*

399.—INCANTATION OF HERVA. Compare with the versions of Hickes and Mathias, above, pp. 44 and 298.

WILLIAM TAYLOR

409.—LENORA. *From the German,* by Bürger. See the note on *Sweet William's Ghost,* above, p. 55.

409.—5. *Richard.* Richard Coeur-de-Lion. 8. *an.* if.

410.—35. *There is no mercye, etc.*—She begins to utter the despairing "impious strains" which put her into the power of "the ghostlie crewe."

414.—145. *sark.* nightgown.

414.—157 ff. *Tramp, tramp, etc.*—This is the stanza which aroused young Walter Scott's enthusiasm. See note on his *William and Helen,* below, iv, 11.

415.—191. *thorpe.* village.

418.—WORTIGERNE. The archaizing is in the manner of Chatterton; and here, too, many of the apparently strange words are recognizable on being pronounced.

418.—1. *Brydyan.* British, Celtic, King, who has summoned the Anglo-Saxons to help him against the Picts.

418.—3. *wesen.* were. 4. *meede.* reward.

418.—4. *bystonde.* assistance. 10. *gyf.* if.

418.—11. *croisedde.* cruised. 18. *bewreene.* awarded.

418.—23. *pyghtes.* hides. **419.**—25. *hasatie.* hastily.

419.—28. *brooke.* tolerate. 30. *ygallde.* chafed, worn.

419.—31. *leech.* physician. 31. *frere.* friar.

419.—31. *wend their ken.* look. 33. *misseemde.* did not suit.

419.—1. *Rerve.* Raise. 6. *Sowghles.* Souls.

419.—6. *strevers.* warriors. **420.**—13. *roode.* cross.

JAMES LAWRENCE

423.—THE EMPIRE OF THE NAIRS. Compare Godwin's doctrine on marriage, above, p. 394.—On the actual history of such "ideal" practices as are here set forth, see Edward A. Westermarck's *History of Human Marriage.*

424.—20. *Malabar Coast.* The western coast of British India.

424.—22. *Brobdingnag and Lilliput.* The lands respectively of the giants and the pigmies in Swift's *Gulliver's Travels.*

424.—23. *Indostan.* Hindustan, the land of the Hindoos.

424.—38. *Car on est convenu, etc.* "For men have agreed to call by this word (paradox) every new truth which has not yet received its passport."—Louis Sebastian Mercier (1740-1814).

INDEX TO AUTHORS AND TITLES

Names of authors are in **bold type**; titles, in ordinary type

Adams, Jean.. 273
Aella, Songs from... 286
Akenside, Mark.. 108
Alfred.. 422
Amanda... 31
Amory, Thomas.. 182
Arabian Nights, The....................................... 36
Argantyr... 298
Arthur... 367
Auld Lang Syne... 348
Auld Robin Gray.. 275

Balade of Charitie, An Excelente.......................... 288
Bard, The.. 162
Bard's Epitaph, A... 343
Bartram, William...................................... 378
Beattie, James.. 277
Beckford, William..................................... 351
Berkeley, George...................................... 84
Blair, Hugh... 320
Blair, Robert... 100
Boddynge Flourettes Bloshes, The......................... 286
Botanic Garden, The....................................... 364
Bowles, William Lisle................................. 361
Braes of Yarrow, The...................................... 48
Brooke, Henry.................................... 88, 262
Bruce, James.. 373
Buncle, The Life and Opinions of.......................... 182
Burns, Robert... 322
Burns, On Robert... 272

Calamities of the Virtuous, The........................... 27
Caradoc.. 217
Careless Husband, The..................................... 22
Castaway, The.. 318
Castle of Indolence, The.................................. 74
Castle of Otranto, The.................................... 221
Chatterton, Thomas.................................... 286
Chevy Chase.. 227

465

Chivalry and Romance, Letters on...................... 196
Cibber, Colley................................... 20
Clarissa Harlowe....................................... 167
Collins, William................................. 121
Complaint, The... 94
Conan.. 218
Conjectures on Original Composition.................... 97
Conrade.. 267
Cooper, John Gilbert............................ 139
Cotter's Saturday Night, The........................... 330
Cottle, Amos Simon.............................. 420
Cottle, Joseph.................................. 422
Country Justice, The................................... 282
Cowper, William................................. 304
Croxall, Samuel................................. 44

Dalton, John.................................... 179
Darwin, Erasmus................................. 364
Day, Thomas..................................... 283
Death of Hoel, The..................................... 218
Descent of Odin (Cottle).............................. 420
Descent of Odin (Gray)................................ 213
Descriptive Poem, A.................................... 179
Deserted Village, The.................................. 249
Desolation of America, The............................. 283
Dover Cliffs... 362
Downman, Hugh................................... 302
Dugdale's Monasticon.................................. 149
Dyer, John...................................... 79
Dying Rhapsody of Oswald, The......................... 371

Elegy Written in a Country Churchyard................. 152
Elliot, Jane.................................... 181
Empire of the Nairs, The.............................. 423
Enthusiast, The (Warton).............................. 111
Enthusiast, The (Whitehead)........................... 105
Epistle to a Young Friend............................. 340
Epistle to J. Lapraik................................. 329
Essay on Pope... 115
Essay on Virtue, An................................... 86
Evans, Evan..................................... 207
Evening... 361
Evergreen, The.. 52

Fatal Sisters, The.................................... 219
Ferguson, Robert................................ 280
Florida, Incidents and Scenes in..................... 378
Fool of Quality, The.................................. 262

Frea's Plea to Hela.. 370
Flowers of the Forest, The............................ 181

George Barnwell.. 85
Gilpin, William...................................... 371
Godwin, William...................................... 388
Goldfinches, The... 178
Goldsmith, Oliver................................... 247
Gram and Gro... 397
Grave, The... 100
Grave of King Arthur, The............................... 148
Gray, Thomas.................................... 151, 208
Grongar Hill... 79
Gustavus Vasa.. 91

Hamilton, William................................... 48
Hardyknute... 45
Hartley, David....................................... 175
Hickes, George....................................... 44
Hole, Richard.. 367
Holy Fair, The... 323
Hother... 398
Hughes, John... 31
Hurd, Richard.. 196
Hymn to Adversity 151

Iago, Richard.. 178
Incantation, An (Mathias)................................ 299
Incantation of Herva, The (Polwhele).................... 399
Incantation of Hervor, The (Hickes)..................... 44
Inquiry Concerning Virtue and Merit..................... 13

Jenny Distaff.. 26
Jenyns, Soame.. 86
Jerningham, Edward................................... 321
John Anderson, My Jo..................................... 346
Johnstone, James..................................... 303
Julia de Roubigné.. 271

Langhorne, John...................................... 282
Lawrence, James...................................... 423
Leith Races.. 280
Leland, Thomas....................................... 203
Lenora... 409
Lewis, Matthew Gregory............................... 405
Lillo, George.. 85
Lindsay, Lady Anne................................... 275
Lodbrokar-Quitha... 303

Lodon, Sonnet to the River.......................... 150
Logan Braes.. 297
Longsword.. 203
Lovely Lass of Inverness, The....................... 347
Love's Last Shift.................................... 23

Mackenzie, Henry................................... 268
Macpherson, James................................. 191
Mallet, David....................................... 57
Man of Feeling, The................................. 268
Mary Morison....................................... 322
Mathias, Thomas James............................. 298
Mayne, John.. 297
Minstrel, The....................................... 277
Monk, The.. 405
Moralists, The...................................... 15
Morgann, Maurice.................................. 292
Mysteries of Udolpho............................... 400

Natural History of Selborne......................... 362
New Poetic World, A................................ 321
Night Thoughts..................................... 94
Nocturnal Reverie, A............................... 42

Observations on Man................................ 175
Observations on the Fairy Queen.................... 143
Ode on the Poetical Character....................... 125
Ode on the Popular Superstitions of the Highlands.... 131
Ode to Evening..................................... 123
Ode Written in 1746................................ 122
On Ridicule... 103
On Receipt of My Mother's Picture.................. 312
Ossian.. 191
Owain Gwynedd.................................... 207

Passions, The....................................... 127
Pastoral Poetry..................................... 320
Percy, Thomas...................................... 227
Picturesque Beauty.................................. 371
Pleasures of Imagination, The....................... 108
Pleasures of Melancholy, The....................... 141
Poetic Edda, The................................... 358
Political Justice..................................... 388
Polwhele, Richard.................................. 396
Power of Harmony, The............................. 139
Progress of Poesy, The.............................. 157
Prospect of Planting Arts in America................ 84

Radcliffe, Ann.. 400
Ragnar Lodbrach, Death Song of...................... 302
Ramsay, Allan... 52
Red, Red, Rose, A..................................... 347
Regner Lodbrog (Polwhele)............................ 396
Remarks on the Fairie Queen 35
Renovation of the World, The......................... 300
Richardson, Samuel................................... 167
Rights of Woman, The.................................. 385
Robin Hood and Guy of Gisborne....................... 239

Sayers, Frank.. 370
Scalder: An Ode....................................... 366
Schoolmistress, The................................... 92
Seasons, The.. 59
Sentimental Journey................................... 189
Shaftesbury, Lord.................................... 13
Shakspere's Cymbeline, Song from...................... 121
Shakspere, On... 292
Shenstone, William.................................. 92
Sir Patrick Spence.................................... 237
Smart, Christopher.................................. 205
Song to David, A...................................... 205
Steele, Richard..................................... 23
Sterling, Joseph.................................... 366
Sterne, Laurence.................................... 184
Stonehenge, Sonnet At................................. 150
Sweet Afton... 349
Sweet William's Ghost................................. 55

Task, The... 304
Taylor, William..................................... 409
There's Nae Luck About the House...................... 273
Thomson, James...................................... 59
To a Mountain Daisy................................... 338
To a Mouse.. 337
To a Young Lady....................................... 304
To Mary... 316
To Mary in Heaven..................................... 350
Tomb of Gunnar, The................................... 369
Tortoise, The... 362
Travels in America.................................... 378
Travels to the Source of the Nile.................... 373
Triumphs of Owen, The................................. 216
Tristram Shandy....................................... 184
Tudor... 301
Twilight of the Gods, The (Mathias).................. 299
Twilight of the Gods, The (Sterling)................. 367

Unco Guid, Address to the............................. 344
Universal Beauty...................................... 88

Vathek... 351
Vicar of Wakefield.................................... 247
Vision, The... 44

Walpole, Horace.................................... 221
Wardlaw, Lady Elizabeth........................... 45
Warton, Joseph.................................... 111
Warton, Thomas.................................... 141
Weaving of the Raven Banner, The..................... 321
White, Gilbert.................................... 362
Whitehead, William................................ 103
William and Margaret.................................. 57
Winchilsea, Lady.................................. 42
Wollstonecraft, Mary.............................. 385
Wortigerne.. 418

Young, Edward..................................... 94

END OF VOLUME TWO